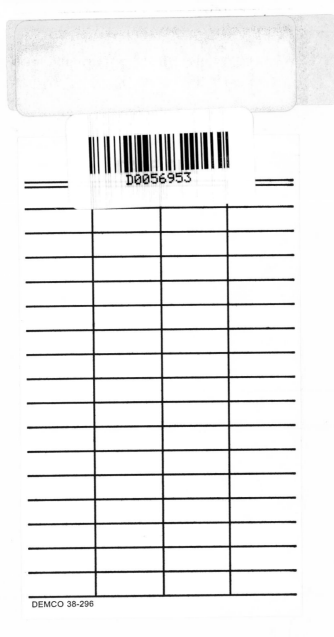

1986
The Supreme Court Review

1986
The

"Judges as persons, or courts as institutions, are entitled to
no greater immunity from criticism than other persons
or institutions . . . [J]udges must be kept mindful of their limitations and
of their ultimate public responsibility by a vigorous
stream of criticism expressed with candor however blunt."
—*Felix Frankfurter*

". . . while it is proper that people should find fault when
their judges fail, it is only reasonable that they should recognize the
difficulties. . . . Let them be severely brought to book,
when they go wrong, but by those who will take the trouble
to understand them."
—*Learned Hand*

THE LAW SCHOOL

THE UNIVERSITY OF CHICAGO

Supreme Court Review

EDITED BY

PHILIP B. KURLAND

GERHARD CASPER

AND DENNIS J. HUTCHINSON

 THE UNIVERSITY OF CHICAGO PRESS

CHICAGO AND LONDON

INTERNATIONAL STANDARD BOOK NUMBER: 0-226-46439-3

LIBRARY OF CONGRESS CATALOG CARD NUMBER: 60-14353

THE UNIVERSITY OF CHICAGO PRESS, CHICAGO 60637

THE UNIVERSITY OF CHICAGO PRESS, LTD., LONDON

© 1987 BY THE UNIVERSITY OF CHICAGO, ALL RIGHTS RESERVED, PUBLISHED 1987

PRINTED IN THE UNITED STATES OF AMERICA

TO
CARL McGOWAN

Friend, Lawyer, Teacher,
Statesman, Jurist

CONTENTS

PHILIP B. KURLAND

POSADAS de PUERTO RICO
v. TOURISM COMPANY:
" 'TWAS STRANGE, 'TWAS
PASSING STRANGE;
'TWAS PITIFUL, 'TWAS
WONDROUS PITIFUL."*

The Burger Court came to its end shortly before the dog days of
1986 not with a whimper but with a bang. June-July 1986 saw
Supreme Court precedents strewn about like bodies at Gettysburg,
except that more were seriously wounded than totally destroyed.
The press had a field day reporting on the tantalizing opinions
dealing with affirmative action, abortion, gerrymander, sodomy,
Gramm-Rudman, juvenilia in the high school press, sales of legitimate literature on illegitimate premises, sex discrimination, libel
law, etc., etc.[1] Almost lost in this profusion of decisions was the

Philip B. Kurland is William R. Kenan Distinguished Service Professor in The College
and Professor in The Law School, The University of Chicago.

*Shakespeare, Othello I:3:159–60.

[1]See, *e.g.*, Anderson v. Liberty Lobby, 106 S.Ct. 2505 (1986) (libel summary judgment);
Arcara v. Cloud Books, 106 S.Ct. 3172 (1986) (book store as nuisance); Bethel School Dist.
v. Fraser, 106 S.Ct. 3159 (1986) (student obscenity); Bowsher v. Synar, 106 S.Ct. 3181
(1986) (budget-balancing act); Dept. of Transportation v. Paralyzed Veterans, 106 S.Ct. 2705
(1986) (discrimination against handicapped); Kuhlman v. Wilson, 106 S.Ct. 2616 (1986)
(Massiah v. United States, 377 U.S. 201 (1964), revisited); Local 93 v. City of Cleveland,
106 S.Ct. 3063 (1986) (affirmative action); Local 28 v. EEOC, 106 S.Ct. 3019 (1986) (affirmative action); MacDonald, Sommer & Frates v. Yolo County, 106 S.Ct. 2561 (1986) (taking

© 1987 by The University of Chicago. All rights reserved.
0-226-46439-3/87/1986-0001$01.00

1

case of *Posadas de Puerto Rico* v. *Tourism Co.*,[2] which may contain
some startling new First Amendment jurisprudence. The last days
of the Burger Court were reminiscent of "The Last Train from
Paris," frenzied, noisy, crowded, with a mixed baggage of virtues
and vices, individuals and freight.

The *Posadas* opinion makes a reader think, too, of Lewis Carroll's
Alice in Wonderland and Franz Kafka's *The Castle*, as words take on
new meanings and bureaucracy triumphs over the rule of law. Admittedly, the oral arguments and briefs in the case were something
less than pellucid: the language, especially for appellant, was Island
English. The basis for the Court's jurisdiction was suspect, if the
reasons for limits on advisory opinions were kept in mind. And the
rush to judgment at the end of the Term provided its usual confusion
and haste-made waste. If, however, the Supreme Court is to afford
guidance for future decisions, lower courts and future litigants are
entitled to more cogent or at least more lucid reasoning than was
afforded here. As it stands, one is relegated to the faith that Justice
Field once expressed when he wrote in dissent: "I have an abiding
faith that this, like other errors, will, in the end 'die among the
worshippers.' "[3]

The *Posadas* case involved a statute and regulations of the Commonwealth of Puerto Rico that "restrict expression because of its
message, its ideas, its subject matter or its content."[4] Heretofore,
it was thought that it was beyond the power of an American government to inhibit speech that advocated legal activities and was
neither false nor fraudulent because of the adverse, but legal, effects
of allowing ideas or information to be disseminated. To choose
between "the dangers of suppressing information and the dangers
of its misuse if freely available" had been held to be a choice "that
the First Amendment makes for us."[5] It was also generally believed
that a government that impinged directly rather than indirectly on

---

clause); Meritor Savings Bank v. Vinson, 106 S.Ct. 2399 (1986) (sexual harassment); Thorn-
burgh v. American College of Obstetricians & Gynecologists, 106 S.Ct. 2169 (1986) (abortion).

[2]106 S.Ct. 2968 (1986).

[3]Baltimore & Ohio R.R. v. Baugh, 149 U.S. 368, 403 (1893) (dissenting). Compare Erie
R.R. v. Tompkins, 304 U.S. 64 (1938).

[4]Police Dept. of Chicago v. Mosley, 408 U.S. 92, 96 (1972).

[5]Virginia State Board of Pharmacy v. Virginia Citizens Consumer Council, 421 U.S. 748,
770 (1976).

speech has a heavy burden to justify its regulation.[6] Even in the judicially created category of second-class, *i.e.*, "commercial," speech: "The party seeking to uphold a restriction on commercial speech carries the burden of justifying it."[7] Or so it was believed before *Posadas*.

I. THE FACTS

In 1948, as part of its economic development program seeking to increase tourism in the Island, Puerto Rico legalized casino gambling on licensed premises under strict surveillance in deluxe hotels expected to be constructed to attract a deluxe tourist clientele. Under the 1948 law, roulette, dice, card games and bingo, and later slot machines, were legitimated.[8] The stated purpose of the casino statute was the attraction of tourists and the direct and indirect enhancement of Puerto Rican revenue. The statute also provided: "No gambling room shall be permitted to advertise or otherwise offer their facilities to the public of Puerto Rico."[9]

The regulatory powers of the Economic Development Administration of Puerto Rico under the casino statute were delegated to a public corporation, Tourism Company of Puerto Rico. Two regulations of the Tourism Company came into issue in this case. The first iterated the statutory language prohibiting advertising. The second read in relevant part:[10]

> No concessionaire, nor his agent or employee is authorized to advertise the gambling parlors to the public in Puerto Rico. The advertising of games of chance is hereby authorized through newspapers, magazines, radio, television and other publicity media outside of Puerto Rico subject to the prior editing and approval by the Tourism Development Company of the advertisement to be submitted in draft to the Company.

The first regulation purported to ban all advertising "to the public of Puerto Rico." The second created an elaborate system of censorship of media advertising outside of Puerto Rico.

---

[6]Linmark Associates, Inc. v. Township of Willingboro, 431 U.S. 85 (1977).

[7]Bolger v. Youngs Drug Products Corp., 463 U.S. 60, 71 n.20 (1983).

[8]P.R. Laws Ann., Tit. 15, §71 (1972).

[9]P.R. Laws Ann., Tit. 15, §77 (1972).

[10]106 S.Ct. at 2972.

The appellant corporation, *Posadas*, a Delaware company, obtained a license in 1975 to operate a gambling casino in the Condado Holiday Inn Hotel and Sands Casino. It soon was found wanting for allegedly failing to observe the advertising ban as construed by the Tourism Company although it had placed no ads in or out of Puerto Rico. The first violation alleged consisted of a pictorial page in a local newspaper supplement given over to a revelation of the grandeurs of the hotel including the casino. (It was rather like the puff piece on Harvard that was featured in the New York Times Magazine for 21 July 1986.) The appellant had neither sponsored nor paid for the supplement. A second alleged violation resulted from a labor dispute in which union pickets had carried signs outside the casino stating that "the Casino is closed." The appellant attempted to stem the resulting loss of business by posting a sign that "the Casino is open." A third involved a protest to the legislature over a short-lived limit on slot-machines which pictured some machines draped in black. A fourth violation was found in the fact that a letter addressed to the Tourism Company by Posadas was written under a letterhead which contained the forbidden word "Casino."

The appellant found itself threatened with a revocation of its franchise for failing to pay the fines imposed for these violations and was threatened with the withdrawal of its license in New Jersey for failing to comply with the Puerto Rican gambling laws. It paid the fines under protest and brought suit in the Puerto Rican Superior Court for a declaratory judgment that § 8 of the statute and the relevant regulations were unconstitutional under the First and Fourteenth Amendments. The record is fuzzy as to which constitutional provisions were properly invoked and how. But "A careful review of the record in this case reveals that appellant's federal constitutional claims were adequately raised at every stage of the proceedings below."[11] That proved to be too bad for the appellant.

The Puerto Rico Superior Court held in appellant's favor:[12] "After a trial, the Superior Court ruled that '[t]he administrative interpretation and application has been capricious, arbitrary, erroneous and unreasonable, and has produced absurd results which are contrary to law.' " The court therefore determined that it must "ov-

---

[11]*Id.* at 2975.

[12]*Id.* at 2973.

erride the regulatory deficiency to save the constitutionality of the statute." At this point, instead of fulfilling the judicial function by finding that the statute and regulations were invalid on their face and as applied to appellant, the Puerto Rico Court undertook the role of legislature and administrative agency. It rewrote the regulation and undertook itself to determine what advertising was to be allowed.[13] The objective of the judicial revision was defined:[14] "[W]hat the legislator foresaw and prohibited was the invitation to play at the casinos through publicity campaigns of advertising in Puerto Rico addressed to the resident of Puerto Rico. He wanted to protect him." In sum, it was sought to license the casinos to take advantage of the cupidity of visitors not residents, of aliens and citizens of the United States but not of those United States citizens who were also residents of Puerto Rico.

The newly written regulation was hardly less detailed and certainly no less restrictive of speech than was the old one; and it apparently left intact the administrative authority to censor any ads to be placed in the media, foreign or domestic.[15]

The trial court, by holding that the restrictions were not facially unconstitutional and could be sustained as modified by the court, fully satisfied appellant's rights to a declaratory judgment. But since appellant had never asked for any relief, not even an advisory opinion, under the rewritten rules of the trial court, nor had it engaged in or alleged facts of violation or threats of violation of the limitations in the judicially rewritten rule, there would seem to have been, at this time no case or controversy ripe for adjudication. "Nothing in this record shows that appellants had suffered any injury [under the revised law and regulations] therefore, and the law's future effect remains wholly speculative."[16]

According to the Court, the *Posadas* case purported to turn on "the restriction of pure commercial speech which does 'no more than propose a commercial transaction.' "[17] The fact is that we know

---

[13]*Id.* at 2973–74.

[14]*Id.* at 2973.

[15]*Id.* at 2986 (Stevens, J., dissenting). See Appendix, page 15 *infra.*

[16]Socialist Labor Party v. Gilligan, 406 U.S. 583, 589 (1972); *cf.* Rescue Army v. Municipal Court of Los Angeles, 331 U.S. 549 (1947).

[17]106 S.Ct. at 2976 (citing Virginia State Board of Pharmacy v. Virginia Citizens Consumer Council, 421 U.S. 748, 762 (1976)).

not what speech was in controversy, particularly since both the original and revised rules encompassed much more than advertising merely proposing a commercial transaction. None of the instances that got apellant into trouble and into court in the first place was speech that did no more than propose a commercial transaction. Indeed, the instances for which appellant was fined proposed no commercial transaction whatsoever.

II. The Opinion

When Oliver Wendell Holmes told us that: "The life of the law has not been logic; it has been experience,"[18] he was not suggesting the abandonment of reason. Nor, I submit, was he advocating the substitution of what Professor Nathaniel Nathanson used to call "the fallacy of the undistributed muddle" for the syllogism. But anyone versed in recent Supreme Court opinions will find Professor Bickel's and Professor Wellington's analysis of thirty years ago more and more fitting of the Court's decisions:[19]

> The Court's products has shown an increasing incidence of the sweeping dogmatic statement, of the formulation of results accompanied by little or no effort to support them in reason, in sum, of opinions that do not opine and of [judgments] that quite frankly fail to build the bridge between the authorities they cite and the results they decree.

The *non sequitur* has become a dominant feature of a very large portion of the High Court's opinions. *Posadas* is among them.

The Rehnquist opinion starts with an unimpeachable statement of the governing law about freedom of commercial speech. Although the dimensions of commercial speech are nowhere really clearly defined,[20] the rules applicable to it are:[21]

---

[18]Holmes, The Common Law 5 (Howe ed. 1963).

[19]Bickel & Wellington, Legislative Purpose and the Judicial Process: The Lincoln Mills Case, 71 Harv. L. Rev. 1, 3 (1957).

[20]See text at note 17 *supra*.

[21]106 S.Ct. at 2976. The court construed the State court's reconstruction of the Puerto Rican law as limiting it to "ensure that the advertising restrictions cannot be used to inhibit either the freedom of the press in Puerto Rico to report on any aspect of casino gambling, or the freedom of anyone, including casino owners, to comment publicly on such matters as legislation relating to casino gambling." *Id.* at note 7. Whether a fair reading of the court'substituted regulations truly confines the statute to proposals for commercial trans-

Because this case involves the restriction of pure commercial speech which does "no more than propose a commercial transaction," *Virginia Pharmacy* v. *Virginia Citizens Consumer Council, Inc.*, 425 U.S. 748, 762 (1976), our First Amendment analysis is guided by the general principles identified in *Central Hudson Gas & Electric Corp.* v. *Public Service Comm'n*, 447 U.S. 557 (1980). See *Zauderer* v. *Office of Disciplinary Counsel*, 471 U.S. ——, —— (1985). Under *Central Hudson*, commercial speech receives a limited form of First Amendment protection so long as it concerns a lawful activity and is not misleading or fraudulent. Once it is determined that the First Amendment applies to the particular kind of commercial speech at issue, then the speech may be restricted only if the government's interest in doing so is substantial, the restrictions directly advance the government's asserted interest, and the restrictions are no more extensive than necessary to serve that interest.

What the Court does not say is what the case law reveals that once it is determined that the speech in question "concerns a lawful activity and is not misleading or fraudulent," the burden is on the government not merely to assert that it has a "substantial" interest, but to demonstrate the nature of that interest by something more than an *ipse dixit*.[22] So, too, is it the government's obligation to demonstrate, not merely to assert, that the means it has chosen—suppression of speech—will be effective to secure the ends it seeks, and that there are no alternate reasonable means to the ends sought not involving censorship of speech. These burdens were clearly not met in *Posadas*. Indeed, there is no clear indication at all of any legislative purpose except so patently sophistical as to be incredible; there is no demonstration that the means, cutting off speech, will effectuate any of the hypothetical ends; and there is no showing that alternative means to these hypothetical ends were not available. Indeed, the Court chooses to rely entirely on assertions by Puerto

---

actions is highly doubtful. See the regulations as rewritten by the Puerto Rican court which are set out in the Appendix *infra*. Certainly, Justice Rehnquist's narrow reading is not shared by Justice Stevens in his dissent.

[22]See generally Bigelow v. Virginia, 421 U.S. 809 (1975); Virginia State Board of Pharmacy v. Virginia Citizens Consumer Council, 421 U.S. 748 (1976); Linmark Associates, Inc. v. Township of Willingboro, 431 U.S. 85 (1977); Carey v. Population Services Int'l., 431 U.S. 678 (1977); Bates v. State Bar of Arizona, 433 U.S. 350 (1977); Consolidated Edison Co. v. Public Service Commission, 447 U.S. 530 (1980); Central Hudson Gas & Electric Corp. v. Public Serv. Comm'n, 447 U.S. 557 (1980); In re R.M.J., 455 U.S. 191 (1982); Bolger v. Youngs Drug Products Corp., 463 U.S. 60, 71, n.20 (1983); Zauderer v. Office of Disciplinary Counsel, 105 S.Ct. 2265 (1985).

Rico's counsel as to what the legislative objective might have been, as to why the censorship would accomplish the speculated goals, and as to why alternative available means not involving government censorship need not have been used.

The Court first states the legislative purpose to be "the reduction of demand for casino gambling by the residents of Puerto Rico."[23] Since the same statute that authorized the censorship in the first place was the one legalizing casino gambling in the Island, it was not so much a reduction in demand as a foreclosure of demand that must have been in mind. Except for a desire by Puerto Rico to play the mythical role of Robin Hood, stealing only from the unworthy, a highly doubtful constitutional classification, what was the state interest? What were the evils to be feared from domestic gaming that were not also implicit in "tourist" attendance at the tables? We know only that Justice Rehnquist quotes someone in authority attributing to the legislature the stated goal that " 'The legislators wanted the tourists to flock to the casinos to gamble, but not our own people.' "[24]

The explanation cannot lie in Puerto Rico's aversion to native gambling, or its real unwillingness to pluck its own citizens. Horse racing, "picas," cockfighting, dog racing and the Puerto Rican lottery were all legislatively authorized.[25] Moreover, as Justice Brennan points out: "There is no suggestion that discouraging residents from patronizing gambling casinos would further Puerto Rico's interests in developing tourism, ensuring safeguards for tourists, or producing additional revenues," which were the Act's published Statement of Motives.[26] But, Rehnquist tells us: "The Tourism Company's brief before this Court explains the legislature's belief that '[e]xcessive casino gambling among residents . . . would produce serious harmful effects on the health, safety and welfare of the Puerto Rican citizens, such as the disruption of moral and cultural patterns, the increase in local crime, the fostering of prostitution, the development of corruption, and the infiltration of organized crime.' "[27] Now there is a parade of horribles to conjure with! And it may well be that casino gambling brings all such evils with it. But if it does,

---

[23] 106 S.Ct. at 2977.

[24] *Ibid.*

[25] *Id.* at 2978 n.8.

[26] *Id.* at 2983.

[27] 106 S.Ct. at 2977.

why will it be less because the tables are dominated by Yanquis
and Anglos? Is crime, prostitution, corruption, and the infiltration
of organized crime, diminished by refusing to allow natives to pa-
tronize the casinos? Is it sufficient that the censorship program was
a sop to government consciences concerned about imposing on pas-
toral Puerto Rico a new Monte Carlo, a new Las Vegas, a new
Atlantic City? And does the discrimination between natives and
foreigners favor or burden the one or the other?

The second question about means and ends was answered by
the Court as it answered the first: *a priori*. It said as to the first,
the substantial interest of the State was demonstrated by the words
uttered by the State's agents in the Court. It was "reasonable" for
the legislature to believe that Pandora's ills could be kept in the
box, if only the media were precluded from telling the people of
Puerto Rico about the existence of casinos in newspaper ads and
radio and television commercials. Keep the people of Puerto Rico
in ignorance—or pretend to—and they will voluntarily abstain from
adding their contributions to the earnings of the wheel, the crap
games, blackjack, poker, and the one-armed bandits. Their moral
and cultural patterns would be preserved by confining them to the
race tracks, the cock fights, "picas," and, not least, the lottery. If
this is a credible argument, it is so only to the credulous, among
which the Supreme Court and its readers are not to be numbered.

So, too, the legislature could reasonably believe that advertising
the casinos to natives would necessarily have the effect of increasing
native patronage at the casinos. This, the Court tells us, is obvious.
The obvious, however, is not always the true. Advertising might
have the effect of increasing the share of one competitor against
another without increasing the demand for the product at all. What
is the evidence that local casino advertising increases the play of
natives? Absent advertising, the Puerto Rican patronage is esti-
mated at 5 percent. What is the percentage of locals patronizing
the casinos at Monte Carlo, or Las Vegas, or Atlantic City, or any
other resort area that has given in to the temptation to support its
economy by mulcting avaricious tourists? The new saint of con-
servative American jurisprudence, Edmund Burke, once told us
that gaming is instinctive and presumably requires no artificial stim-
ulation by Madison Avenue devices: "Gaming is a principle inherent
in human nature. It belongs to us all."[28] But the point here is only

---

[28]Speech, House of Commons, 11 Feb. 1780, reproduced in II Works 293 (9th ed. 1889).

that, if there was an obligation on the part of the State to demonstrate a substantial state interest sufficient to warrant suppression
of speech and to demonstrate that the suppression of speech would
substantially contribute to the effectuation of the State interest, the
obligation was not met on either score in *Posadas*. The Court was
satisfied without evidence of record on the basis of mere represen-
tations of the State, which fortunately need not meet the Court's
commercial speech standards for truth and honesty. But a "reasonable belief" of countervailing interest ought not to suffice to justify
substantial inroads on the First Amendment rights of Americans
to speak.

When it comes to the fourth element of the *Central Hudson* test,
Posadas is even more deficient. If the objective of the statute truly
was to preclude access to the tables by native Puerto Ricans, either
because casino gaming is instinct with all the evils detailed by
Rehnquist or because Puerto Ricans have to be protected against
squandering their money in casinos rather than at racetracks, cock-
fights, dog races, picas, and the state lottery, why did the legislature
not simply act in accordance with its alleged purposes? It could
have denied legitimacy to casinos altogether, for both tourists and
natives; the natives thus would be better protected than by a ban
on advertising. Or the Commonwealth could have forbidden casinos
to serve native customers. Both alternatives would have avoided
conflict with the First Amendment, whether or not the second was
invalid under the Fourteenth Amendment. But, if the second alternative were unconstitutionally discriminatory, so too should be
the advertising ban. Justice Rehnquist suggests that the total ban
alternative would not satisfy the appellant, since it would put him
out of business. "It would surely be a Pyrrhic victory for casino
owners such as appellant to gain recognition of a First Amendment
right to advertise their casino to the residents of Puerto Rico, only
to thereby force the legislature into banning casino gambling to
residents altogether."[29] To say, however, that the appellant might
prefer the loss of constitutional rights to the loss of business if the
casinos were to be closed is not a valid justification for the government's unconstitutional behavior. And, in terms of Rehnquist's bar-
gains, it is far more likely that the Commonwealth would be prepared to give up its ban on advertising to natives rather than surrender

[29]106 S.Ct. at 2979.

the benefits from its licensed tourist traps. But neither is that a constitutional argument. Free speech is not to be violated because victims can be coerced into acquiescence, at least in a free society.

But why should the state not simply foreclose the gambling casinos to natives if its overriding purpose was truly to protect them against incitement to gamble? This would not invoke press censorship. Rehnquist asserts, whatever Justice Stevens' dissent may say, "the Puerto Rico legislature surely could have prohibited casino gambling by the residents of Puerto Rico altogether."[30] If Puerto Rico was sincere in its desire to keep Puerto Ricans out of the casinos, was the direct regulation not also the most efficient? The mechanism for doing so was easy enough, since it must have been the same one as required by the Commonwealth's eighteen-year old limit: the requirement of identification, which need not be a passport since a driver's license would do. But the only alternative to censorship that the majority of the Court thought feasible was a requirement of requiring warnings—counterspeech materials—in the advertising. It agreed that the legislature could reasonably believe that "counterspeech" would not have been adequate to keep Puerto Ricans away, and besides, as the Court did not say, compulsory speech carries with it some of its own First Amendment problems.[31]

If the Puerto Rico legislature wanted to keep the Puerto Ricans from the tables, legislation forbidding the gambling operatives from giving the natives access would surely have abated all the evils and more than the ban on advertising was supposed to accomplish. If all that the legislature wanted was the appearance of concern for their wards, the Supreme Court, in *Posadas*, indulged it in its hypocrisy. But which was the greater hypocrite?

What must be kept in mind about *Posadas* is that the issue is not the desirability or undesirability, validity or invalidity of state licensed gambling. That question presumably is a matter of legislative discretion; and, it appears, forty-eight states have made casino gambling illegal, apparently without falling afoul the national Constitution. So far as is revealed, none has attempted to legalize casino gambling for one caste but not for another. None has attempted to

---

[30]*Ibid.*

[31]Miami Herald Pub. Co. v. Tornillo, 418 U.S. 241 (1974); Pacific G. & E. v. Public Utilities Comm'n of California, 106 S.Ct. 903 (1986).

keep its own citizens in the dark about the existence of casinos. The problem here is not gambling but speech. The issue is not when gambling can be made illegal but when speech can be made illegal. And until now, as Justice Rehnquist announced at the outset of his opinion, speech could be inhibited by government only when the government could sustain its burdens under the standards of *Central Hudson Gas & Electric*. As Justice Brennan's dissent details, the *Posadas* statute and regulations did not conform to the Court's heretofore announced First Amendment standards, although a majority of the Justices in *Posadas* pretended that it did.

If the *Posadas* opinion had done no more than patently to misapply its own established commercial speech doctrine to what is concededly an idiosyncratic set of facts, it would simply be another example of the Court's frequently cavalier treatment of precedents in the service of desire. We have become more or less acclimated over recent years to these kinds of judicial machinations. In the course of distinguishing in *Posadas* two indistinguishable precedents, however, the Court seemed to create a novel principle that is violative of every notion of what the Free Speech Clause has stood for, from the limited Blackstonian notion of "prior restraint"[32] through Mr. Justice Black's "absolutism."[33]

In *Carey* v. *Population Services Intl.*,[34] "this Court struck down a ban on 'any advertisement or display' of contraceptives."[35] In *Bigelow* v. *Virginia*,[36] "we reversed a criminal conviction based on the advertisement of an abortion clinic."[37] The Court's argument in *Posadas* was that the advertisements in *Carey* and in *Bigelow* related to constitutionally protected activities and thus derived their constitutional protection from that protection which was afforded the subject matter of the advertising. The subject of gambling enjoyed no similar constitutional protection and, therefore, casino advertising was not protected speech but unprotected conduct.

The announced principle was that advertising of any economic activity that was not itself constitutionally protected activity, how-

---

[32]Kurland, The Original Understanding of the Freedom of the Press Provisions in the First Amendment, 55 Miss. L. J. 225 (1986).

[33]A Constitutional Faith (1968).

[34]431 U.S. 678, 700–02 (1977).

[35]106 S.Ct. at 2979.

[36]421 U.S. 809 (1975).

[37]106 S.Ct. at 2979.

ever legal that activity might be, was properly subject to government censorship. The argument bears a great similarity to that long since rejected under the rubric of unconstitutional conditions.[38] If the activity was subject to government ban but was not banned, advertising of that activity could be subject to ban, because advertising was only a lesser included part of the whole activity. The grossness of this perversion of First Amendment law may be realized through the recognition that, since the death of "substantive due process," there is almost no area of economic activity which is not subject to government regulation.[39] Presumably, then, under *Posadas*, there is no advertising that is not subject to government censorship. Truthful speech that does not conduce to crime and is not itself an assault may thus be made illegal at the discretion of any bureaucrat with legislative license drawn in as broad terms as that given to the Tourism Company in *Posadas*.

Justice Stevens recognized the holding of the majority for what it was, but refused to deal with it because he found so many other constitutional deficiencies in the Puerto Rico scheme which the Court sanctions:[40] "The court concludes that 'the greater power to completely ban casino gambling necessarily includes the lesser power to ban advertising of casino gambling,' . . . ." Whether a State may ban all advertising of an activity which it permits but could prohibit—such as gambling, prostitution, or the consumption of marijuana or liquor—is an elegant question of constitutional law." Why Stevens finds gambling, prostitution, marijuana, and liquor in a special and, presumably, separate category is not clear. Nor is it clear what he means by saying the question is "elegant."[41]

Perhaps Justice Stevens had in mind that Justice Rehnquist's formula for the Court in effect destroyed one long-standing dichotomy that has permeated much of the constitutional law in the

---

[38]Frost & Frost Trucking Co. v. Railroad Comm'n, 271 U.S. 583, 593–94 (1926); Speiser v. Randall, 357 U.S. 513 (1958); *cf.* Pickering v. Bd. of Education, 391 U.S. 563 (1968).

[39]Williamson v. Lee Optical Co., 348 U.S. 483 (1955); Ferguson v. Skrupa, 372 U.S. 726, 730–31 (1963); City of New Orleans v. Dukes, 427 U.S. 297 (1976).

[40]106 S.Ct. at 2986.

[41]The Oxford Universal Dictionary defines "elegant" thus: "1. Tastefully ornate in dress. 2. Characterized by refinement, grace, propriety 1658. 3. Of scientific processes, formulae, etc.: Neat 1668. 4. Of persons: Correct and delicate in taste. Now only in *e. scholar*, 1667. 5. Graceful, polite, appropriate to persons of cultivated taste 1705. 6. *U.S.* Excellent, first rate 1772." None of these denotations seem enlightening and American dictionaries offer no better guidance.

field of freedom of speech. By transmogrifying speech into behavior, it becomes subject to a different—more limited—set of constitutional principles. Actions have long been subject to government regulation that could not validly reach speech.[42] If all that is needed to erase the protections that Cardozo[43] once described as fundamental to all our liberties is to subsume speech under actions, our liberties are truly endangered.

In the *Northern Securities* case,[44] Mr. Justice Holmes told us:

> Great cases, like hard cases, make bad law. For great cases are called great not by reason of their real importance in shaping the law of the future, but because of some accident of immediate overwhelming interest which appeals to the feelings and distorts the judgment. These immediate interests exercise a kind of hydraulic pressure which makes what previously was clear seem doubtful, and before which even well-settled principles of law will bend.

In Holmes's terms, *Posadas* was neither a great case nor a hard case. And yet there must have been some "overwhelming interest which appeals to the feelings and distorts the judgment" to explain the Court's willingness to make doubtful what was previously clear and to bend well-settled principles. Of course, probably none knows the "hidden agenda" behind any Supreme Court opinion except its author. Yet a judicial sport, like a biological sport, necessarily evokes speculation as to its cause.

What caused so dreary an exercise in small-time authoritarianism to be treated as a vehicle for emendation and reformulation of free speech doctrine? The likely and happiest answer would be that no major change of doctrine or application of existing law was intended. This was only an ad hoc response to an ad hoc issue. The opinion was only the result of accidents of composition in an attempt to accommodate the views of an unstable majority at the end of a Term bristling with hard questions and brittle majorities.[45] If so, *requiescat in pace.*

---

[42]Adderley v. Florida, 385 U.S. 9 (1966); United States v. O'Brien, 391 U.S. 369 (1968).

[43]"Of that freedom one may say that it is the matrix, the indispensable condition, of nearly every other form of freedom. With rare aberrations a pervasive recognition of that truth can be traced in our history, political and legal." Palko v. Connecticut, 302 U.S. 319, 327 (1937).

[44]Northern Securities Co. v. United States, 193 U.S. 197, 400-01 (1904) (dissenting).

[45]*Cf.* Douglas, J., in Camarano v. United States, 358 U.S. 498, 514 (1959) (concurring).

Perhaps *Posadas* was intended to further a new moral code, which tolerates government restraint not only on speech that is conducive to illegal behavior but also on speech that may lead to immoral though legal conduct. The difficulty here is that we know or can find out, more or less, what has been made illegal. We cannot know what the courts will determine to be immoral until they tell us. Is gambling immoral? Only casino gambling? Is wine drinking immoral? When do purchases of luxuries become immoral? Doing any business with South Africa, Libya, Syria? If immorality is to be the guide to legitimating censorship, we have entered on a long and rocky road indeed.

Or it may be that this opinion is just another facet of the new federalism, freeing the states from the rigidities of the Bill of Rights, whether on the grounds of "original intent" or based on the notion that government is best for the people that is closest to the people. Or can it be a return to substantive due process which requires a judicial imprimatur as to the wisdom of legislation. Or is it Rehnquist's movement back to his original position that "commercial speech" is not protected speech at all.[46] Suppose the censorship was imposed on advertising cereals with high sugar contents or advertising automobiles with high fuel consumption or advertising inexpensive air flights to Las Vegas or Atlantic City?

Obviously speculation as to the reach of a judicial opinion is a law professor's game best played only with his law students. Only the future can reveal the effects of *Posadas*. Meanwhile, it is to be hoped that it will be read by lower courts and legislatures in its narrowest rather than its broadest dimensions. A commitment to our most fundamental liberty demands no less.

APPENDIX

Regulation 76a-1 (as rewritten by the Puerto Rico Superior Court):

"Advertisements of the casinos in Puerto Rico are prohibited in the local publicity media addressed to inviting the residents of Puerto Rico to visit the casinos.

---

[46]See Virginia Board of Pharmacy v. Virginia Citizens Consumer Council, 425 U.S. at 781 (Rehnquist, J., dissenting).

•   •   •   •   •   •   •   •

"We hereby allow, within the jurisdiction of Puerto Rico, advertising by the casinos addressed to tourists, provided they do not invite the residents of Puerto Rico to visit the casino, even though said announcements may incidentally reach the hands of a resident. Within the ads of casinos allowed by this regulation figure, for illustrative principles only, advertising distributed or placed in landed airplanes or cruise ships in jurisdictional waters and in restricted areas to travelers only in the international airport and the docks where tourist cruise ships arrive since the principal object of said announcements is to make the tourist in transit through Puerto Rico aware of the availability of the games of chance as a tourist amenity; the ads of casinos in magazines for distribution primarily in Puerto Rico to the tourist, including the official guide of the Tourism Company 'Que Pasa in Puerto Rico' and any other tourist facility guide in Puerto Rico, even though said magazines may be available to the residents and in movies, television, radio, newspapers and trade magazines which may be published, taped, or filmed in the exterior for tourism promotion in the exterior even though they may be exposed or incidentally circulated in Puerto Rico. For example: an advertisement in the New York Times, an advertisement in CBS which reaches us through Cable TV, whose main objective is to reach the potential tourist.

"We hereby authorize advertising in the mass communication media of the country, where the trade name of the hotel is used even though it may contain a reference to the casino provided that the word casino is never used alone nor specified. Among the announcements allowed, by way of illustration, are the use of the trade name with which the hotel is identified for the promotion of special vacation packages and activities at the hotel, in invitations, 'billboards,' bulletins and program or activities sponsored by the hotel. The use of the trade name, including the reference to the casino is also allowed in the hotel's facade, provided the word 'casino' does not exceed in proportion the size of the rest of the name, and the utilization of light and colors will be allowed if the rest of the laws regarding this application are complied with; and in the menus, napkins, glasses, tableware, glassware and other items used within the hotel, as well as in calling cards, envelopes and letterheads of the hotel and any other use which constitutes a means of identification.

"The direct promotion of the casinos within the premises of the hotel is allowed. In-house guests and clients may receive any type of information and promotion regarding the location of the casino, its schedule and the procedure of the games as well as magazines, souvenirs, stirrers, matchboxes, cards, dice, chips, T-shirts, hats, photographs, postcards and similar items used by the tourism centers of the world.

"Since a *clausus* enumeration of this regulation is unforeseeable, any other situation or incident relating to the legal restriction must be measured in light of the public policy of promoting tourism. If the object of the advertisement is the tourist, it passes legal scrutiny."

D A V I D   P.   C U R R I E

THE DISTRIBUTION OF POWERS AFTER BOWSHER

Article I of the Constitution entrusts the legislative power of the United States to Congress, so that democratically elected representatives will determine national policy. Article II vests the executive power in the President, in the interest of unified administration by an elected officer. Article III places the judicial power in judges appointed for life and removable only for high crimes and misdemeanors, so that cases may be decided without fear of reprisal. Above all, the distribution of these powers among three separate branches serves as a powerful check against arbitrary action, for it means that three distinct bodies must concur before the individual is effectively deprived of his liberty or property: Congress must pass a law, the President must seek to enforce it, and the courts must find a violation.[1]

One would scarcely suspect all this from observing the current operations of the national government. Executive departments as well as independent agencies promulgate regulations that look for all the world like statutes. Violations of law are prosecuted by officials independent of presidential control. Administrators and "non-Article III judges" decide cases within the federal judicial power. Most strikingly, sometimes all three functions are combined

---

David P. Currie is Harry N. Wyatt Professor of Law, University of Chicago.

Author's Note: The author wishes to thank Paul M. Bator, Larry B. Kramer, Michael W. McConnell, Geoffrey P. Miller, and Richard B. Stewart for valuable suggestions and criticism.

[1]The Due Process Clause of the Fifth Amendment, as I shall explain, reinforces to some extent this separation of powers.

in a single agency largely independent of all three branches and enjoying none of their attributes. The Federal Trade Commission, whose members are appointed for seven years and removable for "inefficiency, neglect of duty, or malfeasance in office," adopts regulations defining unfair methods of competition, institutes proceedings against purported offenders, and passes on the merits of its own complaints in a "quasi-judicial" proceeding.[2]

Reconciling this state of affairs with the Constitution has not been easy. Yet the Supreme Court, in a collection of decisions culminating in the 1930s and '40s, went a long way toward giving the new system a clean bill of health. Broad delegations of rule-making authority were upheld in such cases as *Yakus v. United States* and *Lichter v. United States*,[3] law enforcement by independent agencies in *Humphrey's Executor v. United States*,[4] tribunals without tenured judges in *Ex parte Bakelite Corp.* and *Crowell v. Benson*.[5] In *Marcello v. Bonds* the Court seemed to say the Constitution did not even require the separation of prosecutor and judge.[6]

In the last few years, however, the Court has displayed increasing concern for the distribution of powers. Despite its permissive precedents, the Court made clear in *INS v. Chadha* that Congress could not delegate lawmaking authority to one of its Houses,[7] and there have been hints that delegations to administrators may also be scrutinized more closely.[8] Despite *Crowell v. Benson*, the Court held in *Northern Pipeline Construction Co. v. Marathon Pipeline Co.* that bankruptcy judges without tenure could not decide certain controver-

---

[2] See 15 U.S.C. §45 *et seq.*

[3] 321 U.S. 414 (1944); 334 U.S. 742 (1948).

[4] 295 U.S. 602 (1935).

[5] 279 U.S. 438 (1929); 285 U.S. 22 (1932).

[6] 349 U.S. 302 (1955) (upholding a statutory provision for trial of deportation proceedings before an officer subject to supervision by the Attorney General). See also Withrow v. Larkin, 421 U.S. 35, 56 (1975) (dictum), where in upholding a state procedure combining *investigative* and adjudicatory functions the Court added that it saw no due-process objection to the "typical" situation in which "the members of administrative agencies . . . . receive the results of investigations, . . . approve the filing of charges or formal complaints instituting enforcement proceedings, and then . . . participate in the ensuing hearings."

[7] 462 U.S. 919 (1983).

[8] See National Cable Television Ass'n v. United States, 475 U.S. 336 (1974); Industrial Union Dep't v. American Petroleum Inst., 448 U.S. 607, 671–88 (1980) (Rehnquist, J., concurring); American Textile Mfrs. Inst. v. Donovan, 452 U.S. 490, 543–48 (1981) (Rehnquist, J., dissenting).

sies.[9] Despite *Humphrey's Executor*, the Court held in *Buckley v. Valeo* that Congress could not appoint officers with executive duties.[10] Last Term, in *Bowsher v. Synar*, the Court took another step in the same direction: Congress cannot remove such officers either.[11]

The individual decisions have been dissected in detail elsewhere. My aim is to be neither bibliographic nor repetitive but to present a concise general view of the distribution of powers.

I. LEGISLATIVE POWER

"All legislative powers herein granted," says Article I, "shall be vested in a Congress of the United States. . . ."[12]

Historically the transfer of legislative power from monarch to representative assembly was, as Montesquieu observed, an important step toward self-government.[13] It was also a significant means of protecting liberty and property. Long before there were limitations on the power of the state as a whole, liberty and property were safeguarded by requiring the consent of the people themselves, through their representatives, before their interests could be invaded.[14]

Of course, as Mill explained, the people themselves could not be trusted to respect the rights of minorities; the Bill of Rights demonstrates that eighteenth-century American reformers, unlike their nineteenth-century German counterparts, did not think popular control of public policy adequate to protect liberty.[15] Moreover, the Convention's decision to provide for an elected executive diminished to some extent the original justifications for vesting legislative powers in a popular assembly. Since the President as well as Congress was subject to popular control, both self-determination and

---

[9]458 U.S. 50 (1982).

[10]424 U.S. 1 (1976).

[11]106 S.Ct. 3181 (1986).

[12]U.S. Const. Art. I, §1.

[13]L'Esprit des Lois, bk. xi, ch. 6 (1748).

[14]See Schmitt, Verfassungslehre 130–31, 147–50 (1928).

[15]See Mill, On Liberty, in Burtt, The English Philosophers from Bacon to Mill 949, 951 (1939) (" '[T]he tyranny of the majority' is now generally included among the evils against which society requires to be on its guard"); Schmitt, note 14 *supra*, at 148–50; 2 Maunz, Dürig, & Herzog, Grundgesetz, Art. 20, pp. 264–65 (revised to 1985).

the safeguard of popular consent could have been assured to some extent without placing legislative power in Congress.

Nevertheless the debate on the Constitution was replete with explanations why it was desirable to place legislative powers in a representative assembly. First was the conviction that, notwithstanding ultimate popular control of other organs of government, it was important to give some substantial role in lawmaking to a body directly elected by the people. In arguing for direct popular election of the House of Representatives, for example, Mason urged among other things that that body should be "the grand depository of the democratic principle," and Madison that one body should be subject to direct popular control.[16] In urging that only the House be permitted to initiate revenue bills, Gerry, Mason, and Franklin emphasized that that chamber was composed of the "immediate[ ] representatives of the people."[17]

Gerry appeared to suggest that self-government was an end in itself: "It is a maxim that the people ought to hold the purse strings."[18] Franklin and Madison saw it as a means of protecting the interests of the people, the former insisting that "those who feel, can best judge,"[19] the latter that without a direct role in selection of the House "the people would be lost sight of altogether."[20] Wilson saw direct election of the House as contributing to "the confidence of the people," without which [n]o government could long subsist."[21]

Apart from the democratic nature of the House, a second pervasive theme of the debates was the value of having legislative decisions made by a collective body in which various interests were represented. "[A] numerous legislature," wrote Hamilton, was "best adapted to deliberation and wisdom, and best calculated to conciliate the confidence of the people and to secure their privileges and interests."[22] Mason echoed Montesquieu in sug-

---

[16] 1 Farrand, ed., Records of the Federal Convention of 1787 48, 50 (1911) (hereinafter cited as Farrand by volume number). This argument has only been strengthened by the democratization of the Senate as well through the 17th Amendment.

[17] 1 Farrand 233, 544, 546.

[18] *Id.* at 233.

[19] *Id.* at 546.

[20] *Id.* at 50.

[21] *Id.* at 49. See also *id.* at 50 (Madison): "[T]he great fabric to be raised would be more stable and durable if it should rest on the solid foundation of the people themselves. . . ."

[22] The Federalist, No. 70.

gesting that the House should "know & sympathise with every part of the community."[23] And Madison's famous argument that a diversity of views was a protection for minorities seems as applicable to the composition of the lawmaking body itself as to the size of the nation.[24]

The final theme, independent of the virtues of a particular lawmaking body, was the more general one of separation of powers: It was important to liberty that the legislative power not be in the same hands as the executive. This of course had been a central point for Montesquieu, whom Madison explicitly invoked during the Convention.[25] "The accumulation of all powers legislative, executive, and judiciary in the same hands," Madison repeated in the Federalist Papers, "whether few or many, and whether hereditary, self appointed, or elective, may justly be pronounced the very definition of tyranny."[26]

In short, despite the fact that the new Constitution provided for indirect popular control of the executive, the Framers were insistent that it was important to entrust the legislative power to Congress. For the more democratic nature of the House, the sheer numbers and representative nature of an assembly, and the mere separation of legislative from executive power were seen as important means of strengthening self-government, protecting against ill-founded or oppressive legislation, and securing the confidence of the people.[27]

---

[23]1 Farrand 48. *Cf.* Montesquieu, note 13 *supra*, at 204: "The inhabitants of a particular town are much better acquainted with its wants and interests, than with those of other places, and are better judges of the capacity of their neighbors, than of that of the rest of their countrymen." Both Montesquieu and Mason carried this principle to the point of advocating districting of the legislature to assure that various interests were represented.

[24]The Federalist, No. 51: "[T]he society itself will be broken into so many parts, interests and classes of citizens, that the rights of individuals or of the minority, will be in little danger from interested combinations of the majority."

[25]See 2 Farrand at 34–35; Montesquieu, note 13 *supra*, at 202: "When the legislative and executive powers are united in the same person, or in the same body of magistracy, there can be then no liberty; because apprehensions may arise, lest the same monarch or senate should enact tyrannical laws, to execute them in a tyrannical manner."

[26]The Federalist, No. 47. In the following paper he quoted Jefferson's Notes on the Commonwealth of Virginia to the same effect.

[27]Illustrative of the prevailing attitude was Hamilton's response to the objection that the proposed Constitution did not forbid standing armies: The interests of the people were adequately safeguarded by lodging the authority to raise them not in the executive but in

A. THE SUPREMACY OF STATUTES

The first and most obvious consequence of vesting legislative authority in Congress is the supremacy of statutes validly enacted.

That congressional enactments bind the public at large is implicit in the concept of law and confirmed by history: The Framers meant to create not a debating society but a maker of public policy. That statutes bind other organs of government as well had been made clear in England by the Bill of Rights in 1688, which forbade even the King to suspend or dispense with the laws.[28] In this country the binding effect of statutes on other branches is indispensable to effectuation of the expressed purpose of parliamentary control of public policy and thus implicit in the grants of legislative power in Article I, reinforced by the declaration of Article VI that "laws of the United States . . . shall be the supreme law of the land"[29] and by Article II's command that the President "take care that the laws be faithfully executed."

Marbury v. Madison made this clear in concluding that an Act of Congress required the Secretary of State to deliver Marbury's commission.[30] So did at least four Justices in *Youngstown Sheet & Tube Co. v. Sawyer,* in enforcing what they viewed as a congressional prohibition on executive seizure of steel mills.[31] There is no doubt that validly enacted laws bind other agencies of government.

"a popular body, consisting of the representatives of the people." The Federalist, Nos. 24, 26, 28.

[28]1 William & Mary, c. 36 (1688–89). In West Germany the fundamental law explicitly declares the executive and legislative branches bound by statute. Grundgesetz für die Bundesrepublik Deutschland (hereinafter cited as GG), Art. 20 III: "Die Gesetzgebung ist an die verfassungsmässige Ordnung, die vollziehende Gewalt und die Rechtsprechung an Gesetz und Recht gebunden." The Germans call this principle "Gesetzesvorrang." See Maunz, Dürig, & Herzog, note 15 *supra,* at 220.

[29]As its further language shows, this provision was principally designed to subordinate conflicting state laws. In declaring state judges "bound" by federal law, however, it appears to assimilate them to federal officials whose subordination to that law was unquestioned.

[30]1 Cranch 154–62 (1803). Similarly, the next year the Court enforced a congressional limitation on Presidential authority to seize vessels for violating the trade laws. The Flying Fish, 2 Cranch 170 (1804).

[31]Youngstown Sheet & Tube Co. v. Sawyer, 343 U.S. 579 (1952) (opinions of Frankfurter, Jackson, Burton, and Clark, JJ.). This was also the lesson of the impoundment controversy of the 1970s, which resulted in a decision requiring the Environmental Protection Agency to spend money appropriated by Congress. Train v. New York, 420 U.S. 35 (1975). The executive's duty to obey a valid statute was assumed.

B. THE NECESSITY FOR LEGISLATION

The second implication of vesting legislative authority in Congress is that no other branch may legislate. With rare exceptions, moreover, the executive may act only on the basis of law.

It is clear enough that executive officers cannot make laws, and in general federal courts cannot either.[32] The common law tradition in both England and the states does show that interstitial lawmaking by other branches subject to legislative correction is not wholly incompatible with the ultimate policymaking authority of the legislature. That tradition, however, is based on necessity; judges must decide cases whether or not the legislature has laid down a rule of decision. To extend such authority to the executive branch would poorly serve the goals of the Framers, for to require affirmative congressional action to undo bad laws made by others combines the weight of inertia with the certainty of interim harm.[33]

Hamilton's insistence that placing the power to raise armies in Congress was adequate protection against its arbitrary exercise[34] makes clear the understanding that the executive could not raise them; legislative powers were given to Congress because the Framers did not want other federal officers exercising them. The absence of lawmaking power in executive officers is thus implicit both in the grant of that authority to Congress and in the limited enumeration of executive powers, as Justice Black suggested in *Youngstown*: "[T]he Constitution is neither silent nor equivocal as to who shall make laws which the President is to execute."[35]

Apart from the Constitution's independent grants of Presidential authority in such fields as foreign affairs and defense, it follows

---

[32]Erie R.R. v. Tompkins, 304 U.S. 64 (1938); United States v. Hudson, 11 U.S. (7 Cranch) 32 (1812). In exceptional cases common law powers have been found conferred by particular jurisdictional grants of Article III (*e.g.*, admiralty, Southern Pac. Co. v. Jensen, 244 U.S. 205 (1917); interstate suits, Texas v. New Jersey, 379 U.S. 674 (1965)), or by statute (*e.g.*, §301 of the Taft-Hartley Act, Textile Workers' Union v. Lincoln Mills, 353 U.S. 448 (1957)).

[33]In the event of a Presidential veto it would mean that Congress could prevent others from making ultimate policy on matters entrusted to its care only by a two-thirds vote of both Houses.

[34]See note 27 *supra*.

[35]343 U.S. at 587. A presidential power to make laws would also be inconsistent with the carefully circumscribed role in lawmaking assigned to him by the veto clause of Art. I, §7. *Ibid*.

that executive officers can act only on the basis of legislation.[36] An undeclared executive war undermines the purposes of the Framers just as seriously as a declared one.[37] The lesson of Hamilton's essay on armies[38] was not only that the President could not pass laws raising them, but that he could not raise them at all. This was likewise the purport of Justice Black's opinion for the Court in the *Youngstown* case, for the executive had not professed to pass a law seizing the steel mills; he was forbidden to act without congressional authorization.[39] Since its purpose was to assure legislative control of policy, the congressional monopoly of federal legislative power inherent in Articles I and II implies a monopoly of policymaking with respect to the subjects confided to congressional care.[40]

---

[36] In England it has been clear for nearly 400 years that the Executive cannot create new offenses by proclamations unauthorized by Parliament, 12 Co. Rep. 74, 77 E.R. 1352 (160x), and German courts have held since the nineteenth century that the executive can invade liberty or property only on the basis of statutory authority. See Maunz, Dürig, & Herzog, note 15 *supra*, at 230–45. Only in part can this principle (Gesetzesvorbehalt) be attributed to explicit constitutional provisions such as those of the present Arts. 2, 5, and 14 GG, which provide that certain interests may be limited only "pursuant to a law." There have not always been such provisions; it is not clear that even now they cover all situations in which statutory authority is required. The more general principle is viewed as implicit in the rule of law (Rechtsstaatsprinzip) or in the distribution of powers among three distinct branches (Art 20 II GG).

[37] It is hard to believe Congress was meant to make only the relatively minor decision whether to incur the ancillary consequences of a formal declaration and not the fundamental choice between peace and war. See the War Powers Resolution, 87 Stat. 555 (1973), *passim*. That the text of Article I was altered to avoid precluding the President from repelling "sudden attacks" reinforces the inference that only Congress was meant to have power to initiate hostilities. See 2 Farrand at 318.

[38] See note 27 *supra*.

[39] A majority concurred in this opinion despite the narrower arguments, noted in text at note 31 *supra*, above, of several of its members.

[40] As Justice Jackson argued in *Youngstown*, this conclusion is also implicit in a very early understanding of the Due Process Clause, whose language was a paraphrase of Magna Carta's requirement that the King could deprive his subjects of life, liberty, or property only in accordance with the law of the land. Whatever the signification of this phrase in 1215, when legislative authority was apparently still exercised by the King (see McKechnie, Magna Carta (2d ed. 1914)), it developed into a requirement that executive action be authorized by law. See Youngstown Sheet & Tube Co. v. Sawyer, 343 U.S. 579, 643 (1952) (Jackson, J., concurring, comparing the requirement that the President take care that the laws be faithfully executed with the Due Process Clause): "One gives a governmental authority that reaches so far as there is law, the other gives a private right that authority shall go no farther. These signify about all there is of the principle that ours is a government of laws, not of men . . ."; Mayo v. Wilson, 1 N.H. 53, 57 (1817): The law of the land provision was "not intended to

C. THE NONDELEGATION DOCTRINE

The third consequence of the vesting of legislative power in Congress is that it cannot be further delegated. The debates fully support Justice Black's insistence, in protesting what he viewed as a delegation of legislative power, that "Congress was created on the assumption that enactment of this free country's laws could be safely entrusted to the representatives of the people in Congress, and to no other official or government agency"[41] As Justice Harlan observed, the nondelegation doctrine "insures that the fundamental policy decisions in our society will be made not by an appointed official but by the body immediately responsible to the people," as the Framers intended.[42]

---

abrogate the power of the legislature, but to assert the right of every citizen to be secure from all arrests not warranted by law"; Corwin, The Doctrine of Due Process of Law Before the Civil War, 24 Harv. L. Rev. 366 (1911).

[41]Zemel v. Rusk, 381 U.S. 1, 22 (1965) (dissenting).

[42]Arizona v. California, 373 U.S. 546, 626 (1963) (dissenting).

Experiences from other countries support this conclusion. Those English writers, for example, who viewed the short-lived grant of limited royal authority to designate additional offenses (Statute of Proclamations, 31 Hen. 8, c. 8 (1539)) as conveying more than authority to fill in "details" (see *e.g.*, Plucknett, A Concise History of English Law 45–46 (5th ed. 1956)), considered it a grave breach of parliamentary sovereignty. See Dicey, The Law of the Constitution 48–52 (6th ed. 1902); 2 Stubbs, Constitutional History of England 619–20 (1929 ed.), arguing that the statute "employs the legislative machinery which by centuries of careful and cautious policy the parliament had perfected in its own hands, to authorise a proceeding which was a virtual resignation of the essential character of parliament as a legislative body."

In Germany, after Adolf Hitler had been authorized by the infamous Ermächtigungsgesetz of 1933 to govern by decree ("Reichsgesetze können ausser in dem in der Reichsverfassung vorgesehenen Verfahren auch durch die Reichsregierung beschlossen werden," RGB1. 1933, Teil I, S. 141), the founders of the postwar Federal Republic reacted by explicitly limiting legislative power to authorize the executive to promulgate regulations; and the Constitutional Court has generalized the underlying principle to forbid the grant of overly broad discretion in taking any administrative action. Revealingly, the Germans view this as a second aspect of the Gesetzesvorbehalt discussed in note 36 *supra:* It follows from the reservation of lawmaking power to the parliament that that body cannot give the power to anyone else. See Art. 80 I GG; BVerfGE 8, 274 (325–56) (1958) (Preisgesetz) (describing the doctrine as an aspect of the Rechtsstaatsprinzip (rule of law) and of the separation of powers); Maunz, Dürig, & Herzog, note 15 *supra*, at 245–47; Götz, Klein, & Starck, Die öffentliche Verwaltung zwischen Gesetzgebung und richterlicher Kontrolle 9–130 (1985). The German court's explanation of the basis of this rule echoes that of Justices Black and Harlan: The Basic Law "entrusts to the lawmaker in the first instance the decision which public interests are so important that the liberty of the individual must be subordinated. From this duty of decision the democratic lawmaker may not withdraw at pleasure." BVerfGE 33, 125 (159) (1972) (Fachärzte).

Thus it is not surprising that the Supreme Court has repeatedly made clear that Congress cannot delegate legislative power.[43] It is of course immaterial whether the authorizing Act explicitly empowers the delegate to enact "laws," as did the 1933 German statute empowering Adolf Hitler to govern by decree;[44] the essence is that, in accordance with the purposes of the Framers, Congress may not leave the fundamental policy decisions to others.[45] This does not preclude Congress from leaving details to another agency, for filling gaps in applying inevitably imprecise legislation is inseparable from the executive function. But the purposes of the Framers in granting legislative power to a representative assembly cannot be attained unless the lawmakers themselves lay down, as the Supreme Court has said, a "primary standard" or an "intelligible principle."[46]

Fifty years ago, in *Panama Refining Co. v. Ryan* and in *Schechter Poultry Corp. v. United States*, the Supreme Court found two instances in which Congress had failed to heed this important limitation.[47] These decisions were no reactionary aberrations. Both were joined by such respected liberals as Brandeis and Stone, the second—rendered without dissent—also by Cardozo. It was obviously inconsistent with the constitutional plan to authorize the President, in *Schechter*, to require whatever was good for the economy.[48] And even Cardozo, the sole Justice to dissent in the *Panama* case, was able to do so only after performing major surgery to show that the President's discretion whether to ban interstate shipment of oil

---

[43]See, *e.g.*, Field v. Clark, 143 U.S. 649, 692 (1892): "That Congress cannot delegate legislative power to the President is a principle universally recognized as vital to the integrity and maintenance of the system of government ordained by the Constitution."

[44]See note 42 *supra*.

[45]Congress's authority to revoke a delegation or to overturn the product of its exercise is as inadequate a substitute for the retention of the exclusive power of initial decision as its authority to overturn lawmaking by other branches is for its lawmaking monopoly, and for the same reasons. See text at notes 32–33 *supra*.

[46]Buttfield v. Stranahan, 192 U.S. 470, 496 (1904); J.W. Hampton Co. v. United States, 276 U.S. 394, 409 (1928). As the German court says, the legislature must answer the essential questions. BVerfGE 33, 125 (159) (1972) (Fachärzte); see Maunz, Dürig, & Herzog, note 15 *supra*, at 245–47.

[47]293 U.S. 388 (1935); 295 U.S. 495 (1935).

[48]The statute empowered the President to promulgate "codes of fair competition," without significantly limiting their content. As Cardozo observed, in essence he was authorized to include "whatever ordinances may be desirable or helpful for the well-being or prosperity of the industry affected." 295 U.S. at 552–53 (concurring).

produced in excess of state quotas actually was quite narrowly limited.[49]

Later decisions seemed lenient in reviewing claims that legislative power had been invalidly delegated. During the 1940s, for example, the Court upheld grants of authority to set "fair and equitable" maximum prices, to appoint receivers for national banks, and to recapture "excessive profits" from government contractors.[50] Such decisions have led some observers to the unsettling conclusion that the nondelegation doctrine is dead.[51]

In no case, however, has the Court repudiated the principle. In the decisions just noted, for example, the Justices emphasized that there was no absence of standards to guide the exercise of delegated authority. The price-control statute essentially required preservation of preexisting price levels with adjustments for changing costs; the experience of state regulators had established "well-defined practices" governing the appointment of bank receivers; "the purpose" of the statute and "its factual background," including experience under prior laws, had established "a sufficient meaning" for excessive profits.[52] In 1974, in *National Cable Television Ass'n v. United States*, the Court explicitly reaffirmed the nondelegation doctrine in narrowly interpreting an authorization to charge fees to the recipients of government services in order to avoid a question of its constitutionality.[53] In two subsequent cases Justice Rehnquist argued that the not very sweeping authority to carry out a congressional policy of all feasible protection from certain workplace health hazards went too far.[54]

---

[49]293 U.S. at 433–48 (Cardozo, J., dissenting).

[50]Yakus v. United States, 321 U.S. 414 (1944); Fahey v. Mallonee, 332 U.S. 245 (1947); Lichter v. United States, 334 U.S. 742 (1948).

[51]See, *e.g.*, 1 Davis, Administrative Law Treatise, ch. 3 (2d ed. 1978).

[52]See *Yakus*, 321 U.S. at 421–27; *Fahey*, 332 U.S. at 249–50; *Lichter*, 334 U.S. at 778–86.

[53]415 U.S. 336, 342 (1974), quoting the criterion set forth in the *Hampton* case, note 46 *supra*: " 'If Congress shall lay down by legislative act an intelligible principle to which the person or body authorized to fix such rates is directed to conform, such legislative action is not a forbidden delegation of legislative power.' " See also Kent v. Dulles, 357 U.S. 116, 129 (1958), construing a grant of authority to deny passports narrowly to avoid constitutional questions: "[T]he right of exit is a personal right included within the word 'liberty' as used in the Fifth Amendment. If that 'liberty' is to be regulated, it must be pursuant to the lawmaking functions of the Congress. . . . And if that power is delegated, the standards must be adequate to pass scrutiny by the accepted tests."

[54]Industrial Union Dept. v. American Petroleum Inst., 448 U.S. 607, 671–88 (1980)

In sum, individual decisions over the years may have stretched the nondelegation doctrine; but it remains the law that delegated authority must be confined in order to preserve the responsibility of the legislature to make basic policy.[55]

D. THE LEGISLATIVE VETO

It is clear enough that the directly elected House of Representatives was meant to play a central role in the lawmaking process. It is equally clear, however, that the House was not to make law on its own; Article I, § 7 provides for the enactment of laws by the concurrence of both Houses, subject to an overridable Presidential veto. Apart from the obvious safeguard against ill-considered action provided by any bicameral legislature, the history reveals a deliberate decision to give the states equal voices in one chamber and to require the consent of a body partly insulated by a six-year term from the fickle popular will.[56] The President's veto was designed both to protect the executive from legislative encroachments and as an additional safeguard "against the enaction of improper laws."[57]

When Congress began passing laws authorizing one or both of its Houses to block executive action, it undermined these provisions. Nowhere is Congress given power to reverse executive policy except by legislation; and Congress has only the powers given it by the Constitution.[58] The Supreme Court recognized this in *INS v. Chadha* in 1983.[59] It was not really a hard case.[60]

(concurring); American Textile Manufacturers Inst. v. Donovan, 452 U.S. 490, 543–48 (1981) (dissenting).

[55]The district court in Synar v. United States, 626 F. Supp. 1374, 1382–91 (D.D.C. 1986), was wholly consistent with this principle in concluding that the Gramm-Rudman Act's delegation of authority to the Comptroller General with respect to spending reductions did not go too far. Congress itself had made the basic policy decision that the federal budget must be balanced. As the court said, the statute left to the administrator only the task of estimating revenue and expenditures and plugging the numbers into a legislatively prescribed formula. Because the Supreme Court found the challenged provision invalid on other grounds, see text at notes 65–70 *infra*, it did not review this conclusion. See Bowsher v. Synar, 106 S.Ct. 3181, 3193 n. 10 (1986).

[56]See, *e.g.*, The Federalist, Nos. 51, 62, 63; 1 Farrand at 254 (Mr. Wilson).

[57]See, *e.g.*, The Federalist, No. 73.

[58]The only congressional powers not requiring the agreement of both Houses subject to Presidential veto—such as impeachment, consent to appointments and treaties, the proposal of constitutional amendments, and purely internal matters like the adoption of procedural

II. EXECUTIVE POWER

"The executive Power," says Article II, "shall be vested in a President of the United States of America."[61]

Three critical concerns underlie this provision. The first is the democratic principle that the executive should be elected and thus responsive to the people: "It was desirable, that the sense of the people should operate in the choice of the person to whom so important a trust was to be confided."[62] The second was once again the desire to separate the executive and legislative powers in order to reduce the risk of invasions of liberty: "[A] dependence of the Executive on the Legislature, would render it the Executor as well as the maker of laws; & then according to the observation of Montesquieu, tyrannical laws may be made that they may be executed in a tyrannical manner."[63] The third was the need to concentrate executive power in the hands of a single person. Rutledge argued that "[a] single man would feel the greatest responsibility and administer the public affairs best"; Wilson "preferred a single mag-

---

rules and the election of legislative officers—were plainly inapplicable. The necessary and proper clause, of course, does not empower Congress to amend the Constitution.

[59]462 U.S. 910 (1983).

[60]Justice White argued in dissent that it was no worse for Congress to delegate authority to its own Houses than to executive agencies. Apart from the fact that the provision for legislative veto in *Chadha* lacked the standards to limit the delegate's action that are necessary to sustain any delegation, the theory of the delegation cases is that filling in the details of congressional policy is a normal executive task. Congress, of course, has no executive powers.

Justice White also contended that the effect of the legislative veto was the same as if the executive had proposed a private bill and a single House had rejected it. But the Attorney General had not merely made a proposal that failed for want of legislative approval; as a result of the Attorney General's action Chadha would have become a permanent resident alien but for the affirmative intervention of a single House. The Constitution is not to be judically amended by arguing that what the Framers did not authorize is no more dangerous than what they did.

[61]U.S. Const. Art II, §1.

[62]The Federalist, No. 68 (Hamilton).

[63]2 Farrand at 34 (Madison). See also *id.* at 29–31, 52–53, 56 (Morris, Wilson, and Madison); The Federalist, No. 68. It was for this reason that the President's salary was protected against congressional alteration and his election by the legislature (absent a deadlock in the electoral college) rejected, see 2 Farrand at 29–36, 52–59; The Federalist, Nos. 71, 73. Morris and Madison even thought that the limited power of impeachment conferred by Article I rendered the President too dependent on the legislature. 2 Farrand at 53, 550–51. See generally 3 Story, Commentaries on the Constitution 279 (1833).

istrate, as giving most energy dispatch and responsibility to the office."[64] "The persons . . . to whose immediate management [the administration of government is] committed," wrote Hamilton, "ought to be considered as the assistants or deputies of the chief magistrate; and, on this account, they ought to derive their offices from his appointment, or at least from his nomination, and ought to be subject to his superintendence."[65]

The consequences of vesting the executive power in a single, independent, elected President are several.

A. CONGRESS MAY NOT EXECUTE THE LAWS

Apart from such matters as impeachment and consent to appointments, where it functions as a check on other branches, Congress has been given only legislative powers. The debates show that the withholding of executive authority from Congress was, among other things, a deliberate means of protecting against the dangers that arise when the same persons both make and carry out the laws. The limited enumeration of congressional powers and the explicit vesting of the executive power in the President preclude Congress from administering spending programs, prosecuting offenses, or giving orders to armies in the field.[66]

It follows that Congress cannot effectively control the exercise of executive power by making the tenure of those who administer the laws dependent upon congressional whim. "If it be essential to the preservation of liberty that the Legisl[ative,] Exec[utive,] & Judiciary powers be separate," said Madison, "it is essential to a maintenance of the separation, that they should be independent of each other."[67] To grant executive power to an officer removable at the discretion of Congress would undermine all the reasons for creating an independent executive. For, as Hamilton wrote in con-

---

[64]1 Farrand at 65. See also The Federalist, Nos. 70, 74; 3 Story, note 63 *supra*, at 284–91, 340–41. The alternative they were opposing was a collegial executive; no one even suggested that executive authority be dispersed among departments independent of one another.

[65]The Federalist, No. 72.

[66]See, *e.g.*, Ex parte Milligan, 4 Wall. 2, 139–40 (1866) (Chase, C.J., concurring).

[67]2 Farrand at 34.

nection with judges, "A power over a man's subsistence amounts to a power over his will."[68]

This unsurprising conclusion informs the decision in *Bowsher v. Synar* that Congress could not empower the Comptroller General to administer the Gramm-Rudman law requiring a balanced federal budget.[69] As the dissenters noted, Congress could discharge that official only upon a finding of "disability, . . . inefficiency, . . . neglect of duty, . . . malfeasance, . . . felony or . . . moral turpitude"; but that is a far cry from the degree of control the Framers grudgingly afforded Congress in the impeachment clauses.[70]

Finally, for similar reasons, Congress may not appoint those who execute the laws. As *Buckley v. Valeo* held, Article II makes this plain by authorizing Congress to vest appointing power in almost anybody except itself;[71] and in any event the default provision for

---

[68]The Federalist, No. 79.

[69]106 S.Ct. 3181 (1986). There was no serious doubt that the authority granted the Comptroller General was executive. It involved neither legislation nor adjudication, but rather was part of the process for carrying the law into effect. See 106 S.Ct. at 3192: "Interpreting a law enacted by Congress to implement the legislative mandate is the very essence of 'execution' of the law."

[70]See 106 S.Ct. at 3187; U.S. Const. Art. II, §4: "The President, Vice President and all Civil Officers of the United States shall be removed from Office on Impeachment for, and Conviction of, Treason, Bribery, or other high Crimes and Misdemeanors." Removal on a finding of "maladministration," Madison successfully argued, would be "equivalent to a tenure during pleasure of the Senate." 2 Farrand at 550. See also 106 S.Ct. at 3191, quoting Mansfield, The Comptroller General: A Study in the Law and Practice of Financial Administration 65 (1939): "Congress created the office because it believed that it 'needed an officer, responsible to it alone, to check upon the application of public funds in accordance with appropriations.' " The impeachment clauses do not forbid Presidential removal of executive officials, see Myers v. United States, 272 U.S. 52 (1926). The debates demonstrate, however, that they were meant to limit the degree of legislative interference with the independent executive.

Indeed, as the Court recognized (106 S.Ct. at 3188), *Bowsher* was inevitable after *Myers*, which struck down a provision forbidding the President to discharge a postmaster without Senate consent. In *Myers* congressional control was much more attenuated, for the Senate could not discharge the official on its own; the mere authority to block the President from firing his subordinate gave legislators more influence over the executive than was consistent with the constitutional plan. See 272 U.S. at 161: For Congress "to draw to itself, or to either branch of it, the power to remove or the right to participate in the exercise of that power . . . would be to infringe the constitutional principle of the separation of governmental powers."

[71]See U.S. Const. Art. II, §2: "The President . . . shall nominate, and by and with the Advice and Consent of the Senate, shall appoint Ambassadors, other public Ministers and Consuls, Judges of the supreme Court, and all other Officers of the United States, whose

nomination by the President and confirmation by the Senate marks the degree of intended legislative control over appointments. If there had been no such provisions, the debates explaining that simple congressional selection of the President was incompatible with his independence would have confirmed in the national context the Court's earlier decision in *Springer v. Philippine Islands* that legislative appointment of nonlegislative officers was forbidden by provisions vesting legislative and executive powers in separate branches.[72]

In short, congressional execution of the laws and congressional appointment or removal of executive officers would make the executive more dependent upon the legislature than is consistent with the constitutional plan.

B. THE PRESIDENT MUST CONTROL EXECUTION OF THE LAWS

Although the Court properly refrained from so deciding in *Bowsher*, it should be equally plain that Congress cannot deprive the President of the executive power. For the Constitution not only denies executive authority to Congress, in the interest of separation of powers; it also vests that authority in the democratically elected President, in order to concentrate executive authority in a single responsive official.

Thus the Court was plainly right in *Myers v. United States* that Congress could not forbid the President to discharge a postmaster.[73] The aggravating circumstance that Congress had purported to give one of its Houses a veto power over removal played a minor role in the decision; the essence of the argument was that the President could not fulfill his duty to see that the laws were faithfully executed if he could not control those executing them.[74] *Myers* was the converse of *Bowsher:* as one with power to discharge can control, one without that power cannot.

This does not mean that ordinary civil service limitations on groundless discharges are invalid; so long as the President retains

---

Appointments are not herein otherwise provided for, and which shall be established by Law; but the Congress may by Law vest the Appointment of such inferior Officers, as they think proper, in the President alone, in the Courts of Law, or in the Heads of Departments." See also Buckley v. Valeo, 424 U.S. 1, 109–43 (1976).

[72]277 U.S. 189 (1928) (construing the statute setting up a government for the Philippine Islands); 2 Farrand at 29–36, 52–59.

[73]272 U.S. 52 (1926).

[74]272 U.S. at 117, 131, 135.

authority to give orders, their disobedience will be cause for discharge.[75] But the President has no such authority over Federal Trade Commissioners; a central purpose of the legislation was to create a body independent of Presidential control.[76] Thus the 1935 decision in *Humphrey's Executor v. United States*,[77] upholding the statute forbidding dismissal of such a Commissioner without cause, was grievously wrong. The filing of complaints, as the Court emphasized in *Buckley*, is an executive function;[78] and the Constitution requires the President to control the execution of the laws.

It is no answer that, as the Court argued in *Humphrey's*, the Commission's prosecuting function is in some sense incidental to other activities that may be characterized as "quasi-legislative" or "quasi-judicial."[79] *Buckley* makes that clear as to appointments,[80] and it is no less true as to removal. The Constitution recognizes only three kinds of federal powers: legislative, executive, and judicial. If the power either to "fill[ ] in . . . the details" of the congressionally prescribed prohibitions[81] or to adjudicate disputes arising under federal law can properly be lodged outside Congress and the courts, it is only on the theory that they pertain to the implementation of law;[82] and this means that they too must be subject to Presidential control. To uphold the Commission's independence on the ground

---

[75]This consideration, rather than the artificial distinction between officers appointed by the President with Senate consent and those appointed by heads of departments invoked by the opinion (272 U.S. at 162), explains why *Myers* is consistent with Perkins v. United States, 116 U.S. 483 (1886), which properly upheld a statute forbidding the discharge of naval officers without court-martial.

[76]See Humphrey's Executor v. United States, 295 U.S. 602, 625–26 (1935).

[77]295 U.S. 602.

[78]424 U.S. at 138.

[79]295 U.S. at 628: "To the extent that [the Commission] exercises any executive function . . . it does so in the discharge and effectuation of its quasi-legislative or quasi-judicial powers. . . ." See also *id.* at 624: "Its duties are neither political nor executive, but *predominantly* quasi-judicial and quasi-legislative" (emphasis added).

[80]See 424 U.S. at 137–41, invalidating congressional appointment of election commissioners with executive duties, although they also had been given unassailable authority to inform Congress.

[81]295 U.S. at 628.

[82]See 295 U.S. at 628: "The Federal Trade Commission is an administrative body created by Congress to carry into effect legislative policies embodied in the statute in accordance with the legislative standard therein prescribed. . . ." *Cf.* Bowsher v. Synar, 106 S.Ct. at 3192: "Interpreting a law enacted by Congress to implement the legislative mandate is the very essence of 'execution' of the law."

that these powers are not executive, on the other hand, is to argue that Congress may violate Article II whenever it is willing to violate Articles I and III as well.[83] *Bowsher* should therefore have come out the same way if authority to administer the budget law had been given to an officer independent of congressional as well as Presidential control.[84]

Finally, an examination of the reasons for lodging executive power in the President supports the Court's 1839 dictum that the clause of Article II empowering Congress to provide for the appointment of inferior officers by "the President alone, . . . the Courts of law, or . . . the Heads of Departments" permitted appointments only by "the department of the government to which the officer to be appointed most appropriately belonged."[85] For judges to appoint their own clerks makes obvious sense; for them to appoint State Department officials would seem quite inconsistent with the Framers' notions of unified executive power.[86] For them to appoint prosecutors, as they were authorized to do in the wake of the Nixon Administration scandals,[87] offends the separation of powers as well by giving judges too much influence over the prosecution.[88]

---

[83]Contrary to the Court's conclusion, combining these three powers in a single agency only compounds the evil. In addition to offending Articles I, II, and III individually, it offends the principle of fair trial the Court has found in due process and makes a mockery of the separation of powers.

[84]For a more detailed analysis leading to the same conclusion see Miller, Independent Agencies, 1986 Supreme Court Review, *infra.* x. It is not inconsistent to conclude that an officer removable for inefficiency, malfeasance, and neglect is both too independent of the President and not independent enough of Congress; for the President is to have complete control of executive officers and Congress none at all.

[85]U.S. Const. Art. II, §2; In re Hennen, 13 Pet. 230, 257–59 (1839). Later Justices in Ex parte Siebold, 100 U.S. 371, 397–98 (1880), disputed this conclusion on the basis of the language of the Clause, but the Court added that no branch was more appropriate than the courts to appoint federal election supervisors.

[86]Appointment by a department head subject to the President, in contrast, poses no threat to this principle; the President can control the appointment by controlling the appointing officer.

[87]28 U.S.C. §§591 *et seq.*, added by 92 Stat. 1824 (1978).

[88]This point is illustrated in more extreme form by United States v. Cox, 342 F.2d 167 (5th Cir. 1965), which held a district court could not order a United States Attorney to draft or sign indictments as requested by the grand jury: "It follows, as an incident of the separation of powers, that the courts are not to interfere with the free exercise of the discretionary powers of the attorneys of the United States in their control over criminal prosecutions." That the appointing and presiding judges are not the same is no answer; the risk that both may be subject to influence by the same Judicial Conference or Council illustrates why the Framers insisted that executive and judicial powers be placed in separate branches.

III. JUDICIAL POWER

"The judicial Power of the United States," says Article III, "shall be vested in one Supreme Court, and in such inferior Courts as the Congress may from time to time ordain and establish."[89]

There is no doubt why. The judges of these courts, according to Article III, "shall hold their Offices during good Behaviour," and their "Compensation . . . shall not be diminished"—in order, as Hamilton made clear, to guarantee their independence. "That inflexible and uniform adherence to the rights of the constitution and of individuals, which we perceive to be indispensable in the courts of justice, can certainly not be expected from judges who hold their offices by a temporary commission. . . . [W]e can never hope to see realised in practice the complete separation of the judicial from the legislative power, in any system, which leaves the former dependent for pecuniary resources on the occasional grants of the latter."[90]

The Supreme Court has been alert to enforce these provisions to prevent reductions in the salary of judges appointed pursuant to Article III.[91] In one of its most courageous and admired decisions it invoked the same provisions to invalidate the military trial of civilians during the Civil War: "One of the plainest constitutional provisions was, therefore, infringed when Milligan was tried by a court not ordained by Congress, and not composed of judges appointed during good behavior."[92]

Unfortunately the Court has not always been so attentive. John Marshall himself allowed the creation of courts without Article III protections in the territories, and his successors extended his conclusion to the District of Columbia, reasoning mistakenly that the absence of federalism concerns in those areas justified dispensing with the distinct requirements of the separation of powers.[93] *Ex*

---

[89]U.S. Const. Art. III, §1.

[90]The Federalist, Nos. 78, 79. See also 2 Farrand at 34, 428–29; 3 Story, note 63 *supra*, at 425 *ff*.

[91]*E.g.*, United States v. Will, 449 U.S. 200, 224–26 (1980).

[92]Ex parte Milligan, 4 Wall. 2, 122 (1967) (also holding that Milligan had been deprived of his right to trial by jury). See also Glidden Co. v. Zdanok, 370 U.S. 530, 533 (1962) (opinion of Harlan, J., for three Justices), recognizing that Article III gave litigants in Article III courts the right to be tried by Article III judges. The other Justices appeared to agree with this conclusion. *Id.* at 585–606.

[93]American Ins. Co. v. Canter, 26 U.S. (1 Pet.) 511, 546 (1828); Palmore v. United States,

parte Bakelite Corp. in 1929 swallowed the unconvincing argument that because Congress need not provide for judicial resolution of certain customs disputes it could entrust them to judges lacking the tenure and salary protections of Article III.[94] A 1932 dictum in *Crowell v. Benson*, basically approving administrative decision of workmen's compensation cases subject to appellate judicial review, went even further in suggesting in the teeth of Article III's requirement that all federal judges be independent that trial judges need not be.[95]

The Court took a long step in the right direction by holding in *Northern Pipeline Construction Co. v. Marathon Pipe Line Co.* that bankruptcy judges appointed for fourteen-year terms could not determine state law claims by the bankrupt against another party.[96] There was no majority opinion, and Justice Brennan's attempt to distinguish *Crowell* as a case arising under federal statute rested in part upon *Bakelite*'s unfortunate notion that the greater power included the lesser.[97] More faithful to Article III, though hardly to precedent, was Justice Brennan's suggestion that *Crowell* had approved only

---

411 U.S. 389, 403, 410 (1973). Earlier the Court had held the tenure and salary provisions applicable in the District of Columbia. O'Donoghue v. United States, 289 U.S. 516 (1933).

[94]279 U.S. 438 (1929). Article III may not require that courts be used at all, but it leaves no doubt as to how they are to be constituted if they are. *Cf.* Curtis v. Loether, 415 U.S. 189 (1974) (constitutional right to jury trial in statutory action Congress not obliged to create); Arnett v. Kennedy, 416 U.S. 134 (1974) (due process requires certain procedures to terminate property interest state not required to confer).

[95]285 U.S. 22 (1932). See U.S. Const. Art III, §1: "The Judges, both of the supreme and inferior Courts, shall hold their Offices during good Behaviour. . . ." The holding was that certain "jurisdictional" determinations by an agency deciding workers' compensation cases had to be reviewed de novo by an Article III court; the dictum was that other determinations by the agency did not. The Court's analogy to jury trial and the dissent's to concurrent state court jurisdiction were misplaced: Jury trial cannot offend the Constitution that requires it, and state judges are not subject to pressure from other federal branches. On the importance of a trustworthy trial tribunal see Osborn v. Bank of the United States, 9 Wheat. 738, 822–23 (1824), upholding a grant of federal question jurisdiction to a trial court: To rely only upon appellate review of state court decisions would afford "the insecure remedy of an appeal, upon an insulated point, after it has received that shape which may be given to it by another tribunal, into which [a litigant] is forced against his will"; England v. Louisiana State Bd. of Medical Examiners, 375 U.S. 411, 416 (1964); 1 Farrand at 124 (Madison).

[96]458 U.S. 50 (1982).

[97]"[W]hen Congress creates a federal substantive right, it possesses substantial discretion to prescribe the manner in which that right may be adjudicated. . . ." 458 U.S. at 80. This distinction was disapproved in Commodity Futures Trading Commission v. Schor, 106 S. Ct. 3245, 3259 (1986): "[T]here is no reason inherent in separation of powers principles to accord the state law character of the claim talismanic power in Article III inquiries."

agency powers subject to plenary court review: "[W]hile orders issued by the agency in *Crowell* were to be set aside if 'not supported by the evidence,' the judgments of the bankruptcy courts are apparently subject to review only under the more deferential 'clearly erroneous' standard."[98]

Two subsequent decisions have limited the progress made in *Northern Pipeline*. *Thomas v. Union Carbide Agricultural Products Co.* upheld a provision requiring arbitration of disputes over the allocation of pesticide registration costs among various manufacturers, subject to very limited judicial review.[99] *Commodity Futures Trading Comm. v. Schor* allowed the nontenured members of a federal commission to pass upon a state law counterclaim to a complaint seeking reparations for violations of federal law.[100]

Fortunately, the reasoning of both decisions is narrow. Rightly or wrongly, *Thomas* assimilated the provision for compulsory cost arbitration to *Bakelite*'s long-standing and limited category of matters such as claims against the United States, which " 'could be conclusively determined by the Executive and Legislative Branches.' "[101] *Schor* relied heavily upon the fact that both parties had agreed to the Commission's jurisdiction: The objecting party had "waived any [personal] right" to an Article III trial, and "separation of powers concerns" were "diminished" because "the decision to invoke this forum is left entirely to the parties."[102] It may be, as several of our most thoughtful judges have argued, that the requirement of an independent tribunal serves purposes beyond protection of the immediate parties;[103] but the Court's reasoning

---

[98]458 U.S. at 85. *Cf.* United States v. Raddatz, 447 U.S. 667 (1980), upholding the adjudicatory authority of nontenured magistrates subject to de novo court review. In such a case the purposes of Article III are satisfied; full power to decide is reserved to an independent judge.

[99]105 S.Ct. 3325 (1985). The arbitrator's decision was reviewable only for "fraud, misrepresentation or other misconduct." 7 U.S.C. §136a(c)(1)(D)(ii).

[100]106 S.Ct. 3245 (1986).

[101]105 S.Ct. at 3337–38. What was new was the addition of the cost dispute to that category and the express elimination of the additional requirement that the Government be a party, which was if anything backwards in terms of the relevant considerations: Independence is most essential when the Government is a party. See *id.* at 3336.

[102]106 S.Ct. at 3256–57, 3260.

[103]See Geras v. Lafayette Display Fixtures, Inc., 742 F.2d 1037, 1051–52 (Posner, J., dissenting); Lehman Bros. v. Clark Oil & Ref. Corp., 739 F.2d 1313, 1318–19 (Lay and Arnold, JJ., dissenting); Pacemaker Diagnostic Clinic v. Instromedix, Inc., 725 F.2d 537,

preserves the parties' all-important right to insist on trial before a tenured judge.[104]

IV. Conclusion

It would be unnecessary to point out that the Constitution vests legislative, executive, and judicial powers in separate and deliberately constituted branches, if it were not that today's Government bears so little resemblance to the constitutional model. With considerable encouragement from the Supreme Court, independent agencies commonly exercise powers that Articles I, II, and III grant to Congress, the President, and the courts.

I do not expect the Court to restore the original distribution of powers in a single blow. I do take comfort from a marked increase in recent years in the Court's willingness to stand up against infringement of that plan.[105]

It may be obvious that the Emperor is not wearing clothes; but there is traditional support for the conclusion that it may be worth pointing it out if nobody seems to notice.

---

549 (9th Cir. 1984) (Schroeder, J., dissenting). Arbitration, Judge Posner argued, was not analogous to decision by a nontenured magistrate: Arbitrators' decisions have less impact on third parties; arbitrators "are not public officials"; "[t]heir decisions carry no official imprimatur"; and "they do not rule on questions of law at all." 742 F.2d at 1051–52. Justices Brennan and Marshall, dissenting in *Schor*, also argued that "consent is irrelevant to Article III analysis." 106 S.Ct. at 3266. The majority agreed that consent could not cure "structural" objections "to the extent" they are "implicated in a given case," 106 S.Ct. at 3257, but went on to find the voluntary nature of the Commission's jurisdiction reduced structural as well as personal objections.

[104]For more detailed discussion of the issues considered in this section see Currie, Bankruptcy Judges and the Independent Judiciary, 16 Creighton L. Rev. 441 (1983).

[105]Cause for comfort in respect to the due process implications of combining prosecutor and judge is found in Ford v. Wainwright, 106 S.Ct. 2595, 2605 (1986), where in concluding on statutory grounds that a Governor's decision whether a condemned felon had become insane did not preclude a de novo inquiry on federal habeas corpus the Court noted that "[t]he commander of the prosecutors cannot be said to have the neutrality that is necessary for reliability in the factfinding process." For earlier statements to this effect see In re Murchison, 349 U.S. 133, 137 (1955) ("Fair trials are too important a part of our free society to let prosecuting judges [except in emergencies involving contempt in open court] be trial judges of the charges they prefer"); Wong Yang Sung v. McGrath, 339 U.S. 33, 44 (1950) (quoting a Labor Department study: " 'A genuinely impartial hearing . . . is psychologically improbable if not impossible, when the presiding officer has at once the responsibility of appraising the strength of the case and seeking to make it as strong as possible' ").

GEOFFREY P. MILLER

INDEPENDENT AGENCIES

I. Introduction

The bicentennial of the United States Constitution cele-
brates the first self-conscious attempt to establish a national government on the principle of separation of legislative, executive, and
judicial powers. The same year, 1987, marks, too, the centennial
of another event that profoundly altered the system of separated
powers—the birth of the federal administrative state in the Interstate Commerce Act of 1887.[1] The Interstate Commerce Commission created by that statute was something new in the American
system of government: a strange amalgam of executive, legislative,
and judicial powers, combining functions of all three branches yet
the creature of none. As many in the Congress of 1887 understood,
the Commission posed a serious challenge to the integrity of the
tripartite structure of government established by the Framers. In
the words of one opponent, the bill was "absolutely unconstitutional
and void, because . . . it is a blending of the legislative, the judicial,
and perhaps, the executive powers of the government in the same
law."[2] These constitutional misgivings gave way to "the practicalities
of the situation."[3] Congress created the proposed hybrid agency and

---

Geoffrey P. Miller is Assistant Professor of Law, University of Chicago Law School.

Author's Note: The John M. Olin Foundation provided financial assistance for this
project. I would like to thank Paul Bator, David Currie, Larry Kramer, Lee L. Liberman,
Richard A. Posner, Richard Stewart, Peter Strauss, and Cass R. Sunstein for helpful comments and Brian Hedlund for valuable research assistance. I profited from conversations on
this subject with Michael W. McConnell.

[1]Act of Feb. 4, 1887, 24 Stat. 379.

[2]18 Cong. Rec. 848 (1887) (Rep. Oates).

[3]Landis, The Administrative Process 2 (1938) (hereinafter cited as Landis).

brid agency and proceeded to enhance its powers substantially in subsequent legislation.

Since then the independent regulatory agencies have become an integral part of our national political life. The Board of Governors of the Federal Reserve System (established in 1913) regulates segments of the banking industry and controls the nation's money supply.[4] The Federal Trade Commission (1915) polices against false and deceptive commercial practices and, in conjunction with the Department of Justice, oversees the structure of the nation's industries under the antitrust laws.[5] The Securities and Exchange Commission (1934) regulates the issuance and subsequent resale of securities on national exchanges and over-the-counter markets.[6] The Federal Communications Commission (1934) controls many aspects of the nation's telephone, radio, and television industries.[7] The National Labor Relations Board (1935) oversees the relationship between organized labor and management in all but the smallest businesses.[8] The list is long.[9] And Congress has not lost enthusiasm for the independent agency form. In 1977 it established the Federal Energy Regulatory Commission to oversee certain aspects of energy pricing and distribution,[10] and in 1983 it declared the independence of the Commission on Civil Rights.[11] Proposals to establish new independent commissions, or to enhance the independence of ex-

---

[4]See Board of Governors of the Federal Reserve System, The Federal Reserve System: Purposes and Functions (1974).

[5]See generally Clarkson & Muris, eds., The Federal Trade Commission since 1970 (1981). The Federal Trade Commission Act was passed in 1914 but the Commission did not come into existence until 1915.

[6]See Lamden, The Securities and Exchange Commission 83–97 (1978); Gadsby, Historical Development of the SEC—the Government View, 28 Geo. L. Rev. 6 (1959).

[7]See generally Rosen, The Modern Stentors: Radio Broadcasters and the Federal Government 1920–1934 (1980). The FCC evolved out of the earlier Federal Radio Commission (1927).

[8]See generally Meltzer, Cases and Materials on Labor Law (1985).

[9]See generally Strauss, The Place of Agencies in Government: Separation of Powers and the Fourth Branch, 84 Colum. L. Rev. 573 (1984).

[10]See Department of Energy Organization Act, Pub. L. 95-91 §401(d), 91 Stat.565 (1977). The Commission succeeded to many of the powers of a predecessor agency, the Federal Power Commission. Other independent agencies established since 1970 include the Commodity Futures Trading Commission, the Consumer Product Safety Commission, the Nuclear Regulatory Commission, and the Federal Election Commission.

[11]United States Commission on Civil Rights Independence Act of 1983, Pub. L. No. 98–183, 97 Stat. 1301 (1983).

isting agencies, are introduced in virtually every session of Congress.[12]

Despite their undoubted integration into the national political culture, independent agencies have never quite overcome the constitutional questions that dogged the drive to establish the Interstate Commerce Commission a century ago. The notion of an agency that is neither legislature nor court, yet is independent of the executive branch, is exceedingly difficult to reconcile with a tripartite structure of government. Even fervent admirers of independent agencies have recognized this fact, conceding that they were created "[w]ithout too much political theory."[13] And although the Supreme Court apparently endorsed the constitutionality of independent agencies in *Humphrey's Executor v. United States*[14] and *Wiener v. United States*,[15] these cases did not involve attempts by the President to remove agency heads on grounds of disobedience to a presidential directive.

Today the independent agency is again coming under attack. Indeed, a number of cases currently on file in the federal courts have mounted a facial challenge to the constitutionality of these agencies.[16] The storm clouds are building for a major constitutional controversy raising basic questions about the nature of the government established by the Framers.

It would be unfortunate if the debate in this controversy focused only on the general concept of agency "independence" without breaking the question down into an analysis of the specific powers at issue. Agencies throughout the federal government, even traditional "executive branch" agencies, enjoy greater or lesser amounts of independence from direct presidential control; and, conversely, even classic "independent" agencies such as the Interstate Commerce Commission are subject to a substantial amount of presidential influence. A more useful analytic approach is to undertake

---

[12]See, *e.g.*, Regulatory Commissions' Independence Act, S. Rep. No. 1319, 93d Cong., 2d Sess. (1974). Congress recently took the unusual step of disbanding an independent agency, the Civil Aeronautics Board. See 49 U.S.C. §1551 (Supp. 1985). This action, however, reflected a loss of confidence in the agency's substantive mandate rather than any congressional qualms about its independence.

[13]Landis at 2.

[14]295 U.S. 602 (1935).

[15]357 U.S. 349 (1958).

[16]See text at notes 37–41 *infra*.

a detailed study of the particular form of presidential oversight and control that is being asserted. A first step toward evaluating the constitutionality of independent agencies, in other words, is to "deconstruct" the agencies into their constituent elements of independence. This article follows these analytical lines by looking specifically at the matter of removal. Other aspects of agency independence, such as control over budget, relations with Congress, and the like, are not treated except in passing; nor have I attempted a complete theory of agency independence. The question of removal, however, is, I believe, an important starting place for analysis.

The thesis of this article is that Congress may not constitutionally deny the President the power to remove a policy-making official who has refused an order of the President to take an action within the officer's statutory authority.[17] This thesis rests on a model of the President's relationship to the federal administrative state. Congress, in this model, has power to create federal agencies, to vest substantial discretion in agency heads, and to provide that action by the agency head is a necessary precondition to the effective exercise of the authority in question. The President retains the constitutional power to direct the officer to take particular actions within his or her discretion or to refrain from acting when the officer has discretion not to act. Such presidential directives can either be specific to the action in question or general programmatic instruction applicable to a range of actions or agencies. Congress may not constitutionally restrict the President's power to remove officials who fail to obey these presidential instructions, but may prohibit the President from removing officers for other reasons, such as personal animus or refusing to obey an order to do something outside the officer's statutory authority.

---

[17]The literature on the constitutionality of independent agencies is quite sparse, probably because of the widely shared assumption that the issue was definitively settled in *Humphrey's Executor*. An outstanding early article is Cushman, The Constitutional Status of the Independent Regulatory Commissions, 24 Cornell L. Q. 13, 163 (1938–39). Criticism of limits on presidential removal is found in Donovan & Irvine, The President's Power to Remove Members of Administrative Agencies, 21 Cornell L. Q. 215 (1936); compare Corwin, Tenure of Office and the Removal Power under the Constitution, 27 Col. L. R. 353 (1927). More recent discussion is found in Parker, The Removal Power of the President and Independent Administrative Agencies, 36 Ind. L. J. 63 (1960); Bruff, Presidential Power and Administrative Rulemaking, 88 Yale L. J. 451 (1979); Strauss, note 9 *supra;* and Tribe, American Constitutional Law § 4-8 (1978). The only recent works taking a position similar to that suggested in this article are Currie, The Distribution of Powers after *Bowsher*, 1986 Supreme Court Review 19 (1986) and Note, Incorporation of Independent Agencies into the Executive Branch, 94 Yale L. J. 1766 (1985).

This thesis—that the President may not be denied the power to remove an officer who has failed to comply with a presidential directive to take an action within the scope of the officer's discretion—may sound revolutionary. In fact, the thesis could be implemented without wholesale invalidation of federal statutes. Most statutes establishing independent agencies can easily be construed as including disobedience of the President's lawful instructions within the varieties of "cause" for which presidential removal is already authorized. In the relatively infrequent cases where the statutes cannot be so construed, the unconstitutionality of the removal provision would not ordinarily invalidate the agency's substantive and enforcement powers. And the President can be expected in some cases voluntarily to eschew the power to remove particular officers who now head "independent" agencies, either by means of a formal commitment or by informal policy.

This is not to deny that the proposal would have a potentially significant impact. Its effect would be to increase, in more or less important ways, the control that the President is able to exercise over the federal bureaucracy. Such a change, however, might well be a beneficial development.

II. INDEPENDENT AGENCIES UNDER ATTACK

Despite the long-standing constitutional doubts about independent agencies, the executive branch has long accepted these agencies as a fact of life, an annoyance perhaps, but one which was inherent in the scheme of things. In the past five or ten years, however, Presidents have been increasingly aggressive in asserting their constitutional powers over the administrative state.[18]

President Reagan asserted control over rule making by executive agencies, first by postponing proposed or pending regulations left over from the Carter presidency[19] and later by promulgating Executive Order 12291,[20] a comprehensive program of White House

---

[18]This revival of presidential power represents a dramatic change from the dark days of the Watergate period, in which the President's authority was circumscribed by developments such as the Budget and Impoundment Control Act of 1974, Pub. L. 93–344, 88 Stat. 297, the War Powers Resolution of 1973, Pub. L. 93–148, 87 Stat. 555, and the effective political nullification of executive privilege, which had previously been in public favor because of its role in the struggle against McCarthyism in the 1950s.

[19]Postponement of Pending Regulations, 46 Fed. Reg. 11227 (January 29, 1981).

[20]Codified at 3 C.F.R. 127 (1982). This program built upon an earlier, less comprehensive

oversight of rule making by executive agencies. The President asserted executive privilege against congressional demands for the papers of Interior Secretary James Watt and Environmental Protection Agency Administrator Anne Gorsuch Burford[21] on grounds rather clearly reflecting an intent to resist congressional influence over the executive branch's administration of the laws.[22] He opposed the constitutionality of legislative vetoes,[23] a position vindicated by the Supreme Court in *Immigration and Naturalization Service v. Chadha*.[24] He made recess appointments to agencies when he wanted to avoid a confirmation battle in the Senate,[25] and freely removed officials[26] despite the threat of judicial challenge.[27] And he objected to provisions of the Gramm-Rudman Act that vested executive powers in an officer removable by Congress, winning another important Supreme Court victory in *Bowsher v. Synar*.[28]

---

program instituted by the Carter Administration. See Executive Order 12044, 3 C.F.R. 152 (1978). President Reagan further strengthened the regulatory oversight program in Executive Order 12498, 50 Fed. Reg. 1036 (1985).

[21]The history of the Watt dispute is documented in Contempt of Congress: Hearings on the Congressional Proceedings against Interior Secretary James G. Watt before the Subcommittee on Oversight and Investigation of the House Committee on Energy and Commerce, 97th Cong., 2d Sess. (1982); Contempt of Congress, Report of the Committee on Energy and Commerce, H. Rep. No. 898, 97th Cong., 2d Sess. (1982). The Gorsuch controversy is detailed in EPA: Investigation of Superfund and Agency Abuses, Hearings before the Subcommittee on Oversight and Investigations of the House Committee on Energy and Commerce, 98th Cong., 1st Sess. (1983); Investigation of the Environmental Protection Agency, Report on the President's Claim of Executive Privilege over EPA Documents, Abuses in the Superfund Program, and Other Matters, Comm. Print 99-AA, 99th Cong., 2d Sess. (1984). The Justice Department's handling of the Gorsuch controversy is exhaustively documented in Report of the House Committee on the Judiciary on Investigation of the Role of the Department of Justice in the Withholding of Environmental Protection Agency Documents from Congress in 1982–83, H. Rep. No. 435, 99th Cong., 1st Sess. (1985).

[22]This concern is explicit in the Attorney General's opinion recommending the assertion of privilege in the Watt controversy. See Assertion of Executive Privilege in Response to a Congressional Subpoena, 5 Op. O.L.C. 27 (1981).

[23]See The Legislative Veto and Congressional Review of Agency Rules, 5 Op. O.L.C. 294 (1981); Congressional Disapproval of AWACS Arms Sale, 5 Op. O.L.C. 308 (1981).

[24]462 U.S. 919 (1983).

[25]See Taylor, 4 Named to Board of Legal Aid Unit—Reagan Acts While Congress Is in Recess So Men Can Take Jobs Immediately, New York Times, January 22, 1983, at 6, col. 1; Legal Services Outside the Law, New York Times, Jan. 27, 1983, at 18, col. 1.

[26]See The President's Power to Remove Members of the Federal Council on Aging, 5 Op. O.L.C. 337 (1981).

[27]See Martin v. Reagan, 525 F. Supp. 110 (D. Mass. 1981).

[28]106 S.Ct. 3181 (1986).

To date, the President has not squarely challenged the constitutionality of independent agencies. These bodies were exempted from the regulatory review procedures of Executive Order 12291, although the Vice President invited them to participate voluntarily.[29] The President has not removed any commissioner of a recognized independent agency, despite what must have been a considerable temptation to do so in order to still the carping voices of holdover Carter appointees.[30] He has neither sought to control congressional access to papers of the independent agencies, nor has he insisted that all independent agency communications to Congress be cleared with the Office of Management and Budget to ensure that they are not objectionable "from the standpoint of the President's program."

It was inevitable, however, that a resurgent presidency would begin to resent the limitation on its powers represented by independent agencies. A first glimmering that the Reagan Administration had designs on regulatory independence came when the Justice Department advanced the position in court that there was no difference in constitutional principle between legislative vetoes of informal executive action—the matter at issue in *Chadha*—and legislative vetoes of rule making by independent agencies.[31] The argument at least implied that Congress did not have special prerogatives with respect to overseeing and guiding the activities of independent agencies.

More recently the Justice Department has been much franker about its hostility toward agency independence. Attorney General Meese, in a widely reported speech, questioned the constitutionality

---

[29]See Role of the Office of Management and Budget in Regulation: Hearings before the Subcommittee on Oversight and Investigations of the House Committee on Energy and Commerce, 97th Cong., 1st Sess. 315 (1981).

[30]Michael Pertschuk, a Carter appointee to the Federal Trade Commission, proved particularly nettlesome. See, *e.g.*, Mattel, Inc. and Carson-Roberts, Inc., 104 F.T.C. 555, 560–61 (1984) (Pertschuk, dissenting); General Motors Corp., 103 F.T.C. 641, 702–04 (1984) (Pertschuk, dissenting); Texaco Inc. and Getty Oil Co., 104 F.T.C. 241, 261–63 (1984) (Pertschuk, dissenting); Champion Spark Plug Company, 103 F.T.C. 546, 631–39 (1984) (Pertschuk, dissenting); General Motors Corp., 103 F.T.C. 374, 388–91 (1984) (Pertschuk, dissenting); Cliffdale Associates, Inc., 103 F.T.C. 110, 184–89 (1984) (Pertschuk, concurring and dissenting); Schlumberger, Ltd.,103 F.T.C. 78, 81–83 (1984) (Pertschuk, dissenting); General Motors Corp., 103 F.T.C. 58, 72–76 (1984) (Pertschuk, dissenting).

[31]The Justice Department articulated this position in Consumer Energy Council of America v. Federal Energy Regulatory Commission, 673 F.2d 425 (D.C. Cir. 1982), aff'd *sub nom.* Process Gas Consumers Group v. Consumer Energy Council of America, 463 U.S. 1216 (1983).

of independent agencies.[32] Meese argued that the notion of agencies outside the executive branch should be abandoned: "federal agencies performing executive functions are themselves properly agents of the executive. They are not 'quasi' this, or 'independent' that. In the tripartite scheme of government a body with enforcement powers is part of the executive branch of government. Power granted by Congress should be properly understood as power granted *to the Executive*."[33]

And in the government's brief in the Gramm-Rudman Act case, the Solicitor-General came within an eyelash of launching a frontal attack on independent agencies. The budget-cutting authority of that statute was vested in the Comptroller General of the United States, an officer removable by Congress through joint resolution. The simplest and most obvious objection to the statute was to assert that no official exercising the powers vested in the Comptroller General could be removable by Congress. Solicitor General Fried took this line in his brief; but he also advanced the alternative position that the statute was unconstitutional because the Comptroller General was not removable "at the pleasure of the President."[34] This was close to a challenge to independent agencies in general. The Solicitor General's argument could not easily be limited to the Comptroller General, a point pressed by Justice O'Connor during oral argument;[35] and Fried's disavowal of an intent to challenge independent agencies generally was unconvincing.[36]

These increasingly aggressive actions and statements by the executive branch—in conjunction with the notable victories in *Chadha* and *Bowsher*—have not gone unnoticed by the bar. It is somewhat remarkable that the independent agencies have survived for a century without serious constitutional challenge from any private party. In theory at least it has always been possible for someone adversely

---

[32]See Address of Edwin Meese III before the Federal Bar Association, Friday, September 13, 1985.

[33]*Id.* at 9–10. The speech received notice in the New York Times, see Taylor, A Question of Power, a Powerful Questioner, New York Times, Nov. 5, 1985, and sparked a heated rejoinder in Congress, see 131 Cong. Rec. S 15177–79 (daily ed., Nov. 12, 1985) (Senator Proxmire).

[34]Brief for the United States, in Bowsher v. Synar, No. 85-1377, October Term 1985, at 44.

[35]See 54 U.S.L.W. 3709–10 (April 29, 1986).

[36]See *Id.* at 3710.

affected by an agency's action to challenge that action in court on the ground that the agency was unconstitutionally organized. Yet lawyers did not make this argument. In most cases they probably never even considered the possibility. The more a lawyer becomes steeped in practice before an agency, the less likely is it that he or she will consider basic questions going to the agency's authority. The few lawyers who may have focused on the issue had good reason to reject it. So firmly entrenched were independent agencies that lawyers judged, undoubtedly correctly, that a facial challenge to the legality of an agency had zero chance of success and could only harm the client's prospects on other grounds.

The changed legal environment has precipitated several private suits that squarely raise the constitutional issue. A leading case is *Ticor Title Insurance Company v. FTC*,[37] a dispute growing out of an FTC challenge to pricing practices by title insurance companies. The title companies contested the charges before an administrative law judge, but also brought an action in federal district court challenging the constitutionality of the Commission's activities.[38] They argued that law enforcement is an executive function; that the Commission is not in the executive branch since its members do not serve at the President's pleasure; and, accordingly, that the Commission could not legally exercise the law enforcement activities purportedly conferred by the statute. The district court dismissed the case on ripeness grounds.[39] The case was appealed to the Court of Appeals for the District of Columbia Circuit, where the constitutional issue was fully briefed and argued.

Similar arguments have been made in other lawsuits.[40] Although there are substantial impediments to the decision of the constitutional issue in these cases,[41] it is virtually certain that constitutional challenges to independent agencies will continue to be made until the issue is definitively resolved by the Supreme Court.

---

[37]No. 86-5078 (D.C. Cir.), appeal docketed Feb. 11, 1986.

[38]See Brief for Plaintiffs-Appellants at 6.

[39]Ticor Title Insurance Company v. FTC, No. 84-3089 (D.D.C. January 2, 1986).

[40]See Hospital Corporation of America v. FTC, No. 85-3185 (7th Cir.); FTC v. American National Cellular, Inc., Civ. No. 85-7375 WJR (PX) (C.D. Cal., filed Nov. 12, 1985); American Board of Trade v. SEC (S.D.N.Y., filed April 24, 1986).

[41]Among other things, they are subject to the objection that an order voiding the challenged removal provisions would not affect the legality of the enforcement actions. See text at notes 171–75 *infra*.

III. Preliminary Considerations

A. THE REMOVAL POWER

An initial problem with assessing the constitutionality of independent agencies is the lack of any set meaning to the term "independent." A wide variety of different agencies might be considered independent in some sense of the word. For example, Congress has created a substantial number of institutions as "independent agencies within the executive branch."[42] These agencies resemble traditional executive departments in that they are headed by a single administrator appointed by the President (usually with the advice and consent of the Senate) and subject to removal at the President's pleasure. They are "independent" only in the sense that they are not placed within one of the old-line executive departments, a feature that gives them a degree of administrative autonomy and a measure of direct access to the President. Second, there are legislative, or "Article I" courts of various types that perform adjudicative services but do not otherwise execute the law or engage in policy formulation through rule making.[43] These institutions are typically headed by panels of judges, appointed by the President subject to the advice and consent of the Senate, who serve for lengthy terms during which they can be removed by the President only for cause. Legislative courts operate quite free of presidential supervision (although they may be subject to review by the federal courts), and in this sense can be considered "independent" of the President. Third, there is a panoply of governmental and quasi-governmental corporations and boards that perform specialized administrative tasks. These agencies are structured in a variety of different ways, often taking a traditional corporate form[44] or operating in some type of council structure.[45] These agencies often operate with substantial freedom from presidential oversight and control, and accordingly may be termed "independent" in some sense.

---

[42]*E.g.*, 12 U.S.C. §1752a (1982) (National Credit Union Administration); 12 U.S.C. §2241 (1982) (Farm Credit Administration); 42 U.S.C. §1861 (1982) (National Science Foundation).

[43]*E.g.*, 26 U.S.C. §7441 (1982) (United States Tax Court).

[44]Examples abound in the banking field, *e.g.*, the Federal National Mortgage Association, the Federal Reserve district banks, the federal home loan banks, and the federal land banks.

[45]*E.g.*, Fishery Conservation and Management Act of 1976, 16 U.S.C. §§1801 et seq. (1982) (Regional Fishery Management Councils).

These different agencies raise a variety of questions under the doctrine of separation of powers. To simplify analysis, however, this article concentrates on the traditional independent regulatory agencies, such as the SEC, ICC, FCC, Federal Reserve Board, and NLRB. This limitation raises a problem. It is not entirely clear exactly what features of the independent regulatory commissions are essential and what are merely incidental. Almost uniformly they display the following characteristics: (1) leadership by a multi-member panel; (2) political criteria for appointment, with no more than a majority allowed to come from one party; (3) broad rule making authority; (4) power to conduct on-the-record adjudicative hearings; (5) power to conduct investigations and to bring enforcement actions either in court or within the agency itself or both; (6) a specialized mandate directing the agency to focus either on particular industries or on specific cross-cutting problems; and (7) restrictions on the presidential removal power. In addition, most independent agencies enjoy a measure of discretionary authority over matters such as budget, relations with Congress, and positions taken in litigation.

The limits on presidential removal are distinctive. Some features—leadership by multi-member panels and specialized mandates—are significant from the standpoint of political science but do not raise constitutional issues. Other features—the broad rule making, adjudicatory, and prosecutorial powers—do raise issues about the permissibility of combining legislative, judicial, and executive functions in a single body.[46] These questions, however, have receded in importance over the past fifty years.[47] And these features do not distinguish independent agencies from traditional executive branch agencies, at least under present conditions in which executive departments exercise broad rulemaking and adjudicatory au-

---

[46]See Currie, The Distribution of Powers after *Bowsher*, 1986 Supreme Court Review 19 (1986). Robert Cushman's excellent analysis of the constitutional status of independent regulatory commissions, published in 1938 and 1939, focused primarily on agency exercise of what appeared to be judicial, legislative, or executive powers; the problem of presidential control and removal was treated as a secondary issue. See Cushman, note 17 *supra*.

[47]This is not to say problems of agencies exercising apparently legislative or judicial authorities have been altogether eliminated. See Industrial Union Department, AFL-CIO v. American Petroleum Institute, 448 U.S. 607, 674 (1980) (Rehnquist, J., dissenting) (delegation); American Textile Manufacturers Institute v. Donovan, 452 U.S. 490, 543–48 (1981) (Rehnquist, J., joined by Burger, C.J., dissenting) (delegation); Northern Pipeline Construction Co. v. Marathon Pipeline Co., 458 U.S. 50 (1982) (Article III); Commodity Futures Trading Commission v. Schor, 106 S.Ct. 3245, 3262 (1986) (Brennan, J., dissenting)(Article III).

thority.[48] Thus, problems of combination of functions, to the extent they remain current, are not peculiar to independent agencies. The political limitations on presidential appointment raise serious separation of powers concerns under the Appointments Clause, but the executive branch has not strongly disputed these provisions. Finally, the pattern of independent agency control over budget, congressional relations, and litigation is so varied as to suggest the value of concentrating, at least initially, on the more distinctive question of removal.[49]

B.   AN APPROACH TO SEPARATION OF POWERS ANALYSIS

Before analyzing the specific problem of removal, it is useful to establish a framework for evaluating separation of powers issues generally. Here we may distinguish two general analytical approaches: the pragmatic and the neoclassical approaches. The pragmatic view, championed by Holmes and Brandeis and dominant on the Court between the 1930s and the 1970s,[50] tends to view the separation of powers as a practical approach to government, such that the division of powers between the branches, and the system of checks and balances by which those powers are related to one another, can stand considerable stretching in order to accommodate the changing needs of a modern society.[51] As Holmes said in a

---

[48]See, e.g., Chevron, U.S.A. v. Natural Resources Defense Council, 104 S.Ct. 2778 (1984) (rule making); Mashaw, Bureaucratic Justice (1983) (adjudications).

[49]Focusing on the particular contours of the removal power has the added benefit of relaxing the mysteriously powerful grip that the notion of "independent" agencies seems to exercise on the imagination. When the idea of independent agencies is taken as having some content other than the various specific restrictions on presidential control, then it becomes extremely tempting to draw broader—and misleading—distinctions between independent and executive branch agencies.

[50]In addition to *Humphrey's Executor* and *Wiener*, more or less explicit formulations of the pragmatic approach can be found in the concurring opinions of Justices Frankfurter and Jackson in the *Steel Seizure* case, 343 U.S. 579 (1952); Yakus v. United States, 321 U.S. 414 (1944); and FTC v. Ruberoid Co., 343 U.S. 470 (1952).

[51]The pragmatic approach to separation of powers reflected the prevailing view among students of administrative law in the 1930s and 1940s that the traditional tripartite system of government was not adequate to cope with the problems of governing a modern industrial state. In the words of James Landis, the most prominent spokesman of this view, "[i]n terms of political theory, the administrative process springs from the inadequacy of a simple tripartite form of government to deal with modern problems. It represents a striving to adapt governmental technique, that still divides under three rubrics, to modern needs and, at the same time, to preserve those elements of responsibility, and those conditions of balance that

famous dissent in *Springer v. Philippine Islands*,[52] "[w]hen we come to the fundamental distinctions it is obvious . . . that they must be received with a certain latitude or our government could not go on. . . . It does not seem to need argument to show that however we may disguise it by veiling words we do not and cannot carry out the distinction between legislative and executive action with mathematical precision and divide the branches into watertight compartments."[53]

Contrasting with this pragmatic approach is what we might call a "neoclassical" approach, which has recently come to the fore in *Buckley v. Valeo*,[54] *INS v. Chadha*,[55] and other cases.[56] The neoclassical approach, which resembles the Court's approach to these matters prior to the 1930s, takes seriously both the distinctions between the branches of government and the specific structure of checks and balances outlined in the Constitution. This approach de-emphasizes the importance of convenience and efficiency, as not being the "hallmarks . . . of democratic government," and emphasizes instead the "constitutional design for the separation of powers" and the "struc-

---

have distinguished Anglo-American government." Landis at 1. Landis eventually came to a less glowing view of the virtues of agency independence. See Landis, Report on Regulatory Agencies to the President-Elect, reprinted in Committee Print, Senate Judiciary Committee, 86th Cong., 2d Sess. 84 (1960) (consolidation of independent agencies into executive departments "might eventually be the right answer").

Academic support for the pragmatic approach remains strong today. For recent expositions, see Strauss, note 9 *supra* (suggesting that all government agencies—not just independent agencies—should be seen as falling outside the constitutionally described schemata of the three named branches); Casper, The Constitutional Organization of the Government, 26 W. & M. L. Rev. 177 (1985) (endorsing use of "framework legislation" that supports the organizational skeleton of the Constitution with more detailed arrangements for governmental decision making); Bruff, note 17 *supra*, at 470–71 (advocating a "complicated theory of shared but reciprocally limiting powers").

[52]227 U.S. 189 (1928). The case was a construction of the Philippine Organic Act, a constitution adopted by Congress for the Philippines that divided the government of the islands into executive, legislative, and judicial departments. At issue was whether the Philippine legislature could validly vest voting power over certain government-owned corporations in legislative officers.

[53]*Id.* at 210–11.

[54]424 U.S. 1 (1976)(per curiam).

[55]462 U.S. 919 (1983).

[56]E.g., *Bowsher*, 106 U.S. 3181 (1986); Northern Pipeline Co. v. Marathon Pipe Line Co., 458 U.S. 50, 57 (1982) (plurality opinion). The Court's return to an older style of analysis in separation of powers cases has been noted elsewhere. See, *e.g.*, Stone, Seidman, Sunstein and Tushnet, Constitutional Law 385 (1986); Strauss, note 9 *supra*, at 625–40; Note, Incorporation of Independent Agencies into the Executive Branch, 94 Yale L. J. 1766 (1985).

ture of the articles delegating and separating powers under Acts I, II, and III."[57]

These two approaches are distinguishable principally in terms of emphasis and nuance. The pragmatic approach does not deny the importance of text and structure; it merely tends to give these factors less weight than does the neoclassical approach. The neoclassical approach, on the other hand, does not dispute that pragmatic considerations have a role to play in the constitutional analysis; it merely gives these considerations secondary, although not insignificant, importance. Nevertheless, the differences between the approaches are unmistakable, and have been noted on the Court. In the words of Justice White, the most vigorous dissenter from the new approach, the Court has recently adopted a "distressingly formalistic" view of separation of powers, resting on "rigid dogma" and "unyielding principle[s]" that are, according to White, both "misguided" and "insensitive to [the Court's] constitutional role."[58]

Justice White to the contrary notwithstanding, I believe that the neoclassical approach is the superior mode for analyzing separation of powers questions, for several reasons. First, it is congenial to the purposes of the Framers. If the history of the framing of the Constitution shows us anything, it is that the Framers viewed the separation of powers as the single greatest protection against the danger of tyranny that inheres in the process of government itself. To this end they divided the government among three branches and carefully worked out the system of checks and balances among them.[59] The Framers were children of the Enlightenment; they took seriously the Newtonian structure of attractive and repulsive political forces that they were creating. They would have applauded the adherence to principle that Justice White finds so distressing in the Court's recent opinions.

The neoclassical approach also comports with the notion of a written Constitution. Advocates of the pragmatic approach often

---

[57] *Chadha*, 462 U.S. at 946. Chief Justice Burger's opinion is criticised in Elliott, INS v. Chadha: The Administrative Constitution, the Constitution, and the Legislative Veto, 1983 Supreme Court Review 125; Strauss, Was There a Baby in the Bathwater? A Comment on the Supreme Court's Legislative Veto Decision, 1983 Duke L. J. 789; and Tribe, The Legislative Veto Decision: A Law by Any Other Name?, 21 Harv. J. Legis. 1 (1984).

[58] *Bowsher*, 106 S.Ct. at 3205, 3214 (White, J., dissenting). See also *Northern Pipeline*, 458 U.S. at 92–118 (White, J., dissenting); *Chadha*, 462 U.S. at 967–1003 (White, J., dissenting).

[59] See the synoptic discussion in Currie, The Distribution of Powers After *Bowsher*, 1986 Supreme Court Review 19 (1986).

use a de minimis argument, observing that many of the particular mechanisms of government could be altered or abandoned without fundamentally changing our system of government or creating dangers of tyranny. It would be possible to write a constitution along the lines contemplated by this argument: such a document would set up an initial structure of legislative, executive and judicial branches, and would then allow Congress to alter this arrangement as it sees fit, provided that power is not concentrated in such a manner as to create a danger of tyranny. But the Framers did not adopt such a Constitution. They set forth a detailed structure of checks and balances among the branches of government. Any one of these specific powers or immunities could perhaps be abandoned without threatening the basic structure of the system as a whole; but if all were abandoned—if the pragmatic constitution were adopted—there is little doubt that our government would evolve into something far different from what it has been for the past two centuries. The government that developed would not necessarily be a bad government; in Britain, without a written constitution, the system of separation of powers established by the Glorious Revolution evolved into a Parliamentary system that appears to govern quite adequately. But it would not be our government—a government under a written Constitution that is constrained in the degree to which it can evolve in the absence of constitutional amendment.

The neoclassical approach is consistent with the profound changes that have altered the shape of American society over the past two hundred years. The pragmatic approach sometimes invokes an argument from changed circumstances, to the effect that the rise of the administrative state has so altered the landscape of government that new roads must be cut to enable government to function according to the basic goals of the Framers: vigor and efficiency in government and the avoidance of tyranny and faction. And because administrative government vests unparalleled power and discretion in the executive branch, the balance of power among the branches that lies at the core of separation of powers requires that new governmental mechanisms be devised in order to check and limit the President's authority. At the outset, the changed circumstances argument faces the burden of showing that the world is actually different in a way that matters. It would be unwise to abandon structures of government that have proved serviceable unless the need to revise and experiment is clearly established. It is doubtful, however, that this burden can be met. The pragmatic position may well understate the degree to which the neoclassical approach is backed by real purposes that are of present concern in government as it exists today. With respect to vigor in government, it is evident that a President committed to implementing a program—whether it be a New Deal, a Fair Deal, a Great Society, or a New Federalism—can govern more energetically to the extent that he or she is not hampered by technologies of government that check and limit executive powers. As to efficiency, the centralization and coordination that a unitary executive makes possible are likely to be more conducive to efficient government than is a splintered executive branch subject to various checks and balances beyond those set forth in the text of the Constitution. As to the danger of tyranny, the analysis is ambiguous: although it could be argued that a powerful and unified executive branch poses the threat of tyranny, the system of checks and balances has proved outstandingly effective at limiting the power of Presidents when they begin to govern in an "imperial" fashion. Moreover, the benefits of splintering power are themselves ambiguous, since the abandonment of a tripartite system of government may possibly undermine the stability of the structure as a whole. As to the danger of faction, there is reason to believe that a President accountable to the entire nation is less likely to be subject to the influence of discrete interest groups than is some extraconstitutional institution established purportedly to check presidential authority.[60] And the quid pro quo argument— that new mechanisms must be devised to check the radical increase in presidential power accompanying the rise of the administrative state—overlooks the fact that administrative government reflects an increase in the powers of *all* branches of the federal government, in particular the dramatically enhanced power of Congress under expansive interpretations of the Commerce Clause.

Finally, the neoclassical approach is desirable as a way of imposing discipline in government. The pragmatic approach too often

---

[60]The legislative veto, for example, is sometimes defended on the ground that it does not pose any threat to the fundamental values of the separation of powers. Yet legislative vetoes may in fact be subject to manipulation by faction in ways that a unitary executive is not. For a description of the ease with which the legislative veto can be manipulated by interest groups, see Bruff & Gellhorn, Congressional Control of Administrative Regulation: A Study of Legislative Vetoes, 90 Harv. L. Rev. 1369 (1977). On factions and independent agencies, see text at notes 126–28, 154–56 *infra*.

commits the error of confusing popularity with desirability or necessity. The legislative veto is a case in point. Justice White's critique of the Court's recent decisions might have more force if they seriously impeded the processes of government or interfered with the national welfare. To date, however, there has been no indication that these decisions have resulted in anything more than minor inconveniences. Almost two hundred legislative veto provisions were cast in doubt by the *Chadha* case. The government has shown no signs of falling or being shaken. Congress has begun to find alternative, constitutionally sound methods of controlling administrative discretion under broad delegations of statutory authority. New governmental technology such as legislative vetoes is often developed, not to enhance efficiency or accountability, but to avoid having to make hard decisions or to deny accountability for the decisions that are made. The neoclassical approach to separation of powers is a useful antidote to these bad habits of governing.

For these reasons, the neoclassical approach is the preferable framework for analyzing separation of powers issues, including the question of the removal power. The neoclassical approach suggests that the starting point for analysis is the text of the Constitution, interpreted in light of the tripartite structure established by the Framers. An additional factor is the history surrounding the framing and original implementation of the system of separated powers, which may help illuminate the meaning of the Constitution as it would have been understood by the Framers. At the same time the neoclassical approach does not rule out pragmatic considerations: at some margin principles must give way to practicalities. If limitations on presidential removal have come to serve a highly valuable function in our system, the benefits of which could not reasonably be obtained by other means, then this fact would not be insignificant in the constitutional analysis. Similarly, if Presidents have acquiesced in limitations on removal, that behavior could suggest that the intrusion on executive prerogatives may be less severe than might be inferred from an analysis of text, structure, and history alone. And if limitations on removal have inserted themselves so deeply into the fabric of American public law that their invalidation would work serious disruption on government processes, then this is an argument for treading carefully in considering whether they should be struck down. Finally, the impact of prior Supreme Court decisions should be considered. Other things being equal, it would be desirable if the rule to be adopted were one that could be squared with the Court's decisions in the area. Accordingly, the relevant considerations (listed in approximate order of importance) are these: (1) text; (2) structure; (3) history; (4) function; (5) prescription; (6) remedy; and (7) case law. The following section considers each of these factors in turn.

III. CONSTITUTIONALITY OF LIMITS ON THE REMOVAL POWER

A. TEXT

The starting point for textual analysis is the basic grant of authority to the President: "[t]he executive Power shall be vested in a President of the United States of America."[61] The Constitution is crystal clear that the "executive power"—whatever that might be—was to be vested in a single individual. The concept of a unitary executive[62] could, in principle, support theories of presidential authority far stronger than any advanced by advocates of presidential power today. It could be argued, for example, that only the President, and not Congress, has the power to establish executive agencies, on the ground that the President, as head of the executive branch, must have absolute discretion as to how that department of government is organized. This theory has never had much currency, partly because it stands in tension with the congressional authority to grant appointment power over inferior offices to courts or department heads[63], and partly because the first Congress established a number of executive departments by legislation without protest from President Washington.[64] But the construction is not logically ruled out by the constitutional text. It could also be argued that the concept of a unitary executive implies that the President should at least have the power to overrule any action by department heads. Otherwise the executive would effectively be split, contrary to the constitutional design, at least for purposes of that decision. Again this is a road not taken, it having been accepted early on that Congress could not only create executive departments but could make action by the agency head a precondition of the effective

---

[61]U.S. Const., Art. II, §1, cl. 1.

[62]See generally Corwin, The President: Offices and Powers (5th ed. 1984).

[63]See text at notes 69–72 infra.

[64]See generally text at notes 93–112 infra.

exercise of the power. What is significant about these alternative readings is not their current viability, but rather their logical plausibility. The fact that the constitutional text can without contradiction be read to support sweeping concepts of presidential authority over administration suggests that the President's power should not fall wildly short of what the text of the Constitution could sustain. Thus the unitary executive concept provides some support for the proposition that the President should at least have the authority to issue legally binding orders to officers instructing them to take some action within their statutory discretion (or to refrain from acting where they have authority not to act).[65] If the President has the authority to issue such instructions, it is reasonable to posit that the President should also be able to remove executive officials who for whatever reason refuse to follow these instructions, so long as the action in question is otherwise within the officer's statutory discretion.

Additional support for this construction might be found by comparing the language of Article II with that of Article III. Article III vests the judicial power "in one supreme Court and in such inferior Courts as the Congress may from time to time ordain and establish." This grant of judicial power to the Supreme Court is the chief textual basis for the argument that Congress may not restrict the Court's appellate jurisdiction over important categories of cases, since doing so would impermissibly interfere with the Court's role as the head of the judicial branch.[66] The textual argument for the unitary executive, however, is considerably stronger than the corresponding argument for a unitary Court. In the case of the judicial branch, the power of Congress to establish inferior courts is expressly set out, in contrast with the executive branch in which the congressional power to establish administrative agencies is conferred only by allusion and indirection. Moreover, the Constitution expressly vests some of the judicial power in inferior

---

[65]United States ex rel. Kendall v. Stokes, 12 Pet. 524 (1838), is not to the contrary. Although that case is sometimes read as holding that Congress can exclude the President altogether from participation in a decision committed to the discretion of an agency head, in fact the case stands only for the much narrower proposition that that President has no inherent authority to order an officer to take an action plainly contrary to the officer's statutory responsibilities—a proposition perfectly consistent with the argument in text.

[66]See, *e.g.*, Ratner, Congressional Power over the Appellate Jurisdiction of the Supreme Court, 109 U. Pa. L. Rev. 151 (1960).

courts if Congress chooses to establish them. Inferior courts are granted judicial power through the Constitution itself; the power does not flow by delegation from the Supreme Court. In contrast, the Constitution does not grant any of the executive power to administrative agencies, but rather expressly vests the entire executive power in "a President of the United States of America." The inference can be drawn that the executive power does not vest in administrative agencies simply by virtue of their creation by Congress, but rather must in some sense flow to those agencies out of the original font of executive power in President. Finally, the Constitution expressly grants Congress the power to insulate the inferior federal courts from the power of the Supreme Court—to establish a certain independence in those courts by creating exceptions to the Supreme Court's appellate jurisdiction.[67] No similar authority is provided for Congress to establish any form of independence for administrative agencies. To be sure, these arguments rest on an analogy between inferior federal courts and administrative agencies. There are clearly differences between these governmental bodies that undermine the analogy. Nevertheless, the comparison with Article III does appear to support the proposition that the President was to have a broad degree of authority over the administrative agencies.

The Constitution expressly mentions administrative departments in two principal provisions: the Appointments Clause and the Report Clause.[68] The Appointments Clause[69] provides that the President, by and with the advice and consent of the Senate, shall appoint "Officers of the United States, whose Appointments are not herein otherwise provided for, and which shall be established

---

[67]U.S. Const., Art. III, §2, cl. 2.

[68]In addition to these principal clauses, the Constitution twice mentions the power of the President to grant commissions to officers of the United States. See U.S. Const., Art. II, §2, cl. 3; *id.* §3. The power to issue commissions, however, was apparently considered, at the time of the framing of the Constitution, to be merely a ministerial act incident to the appointment of an officer by constitutional means. *Cf.* Marbury v. Madison, 1 Cranch. 137, 155 (1803): "The acts of appointing to office, and commissioning the person appointed, can scarcely be considered as one and the same; since the power to perform them is given in separate and distinct sections of the constitution. . . . [T]o issue a commission would apparently be a duty distinct from the appointment, the performance of which, perhaps, could not legally be refused." Accordingly, the President's power to issue commissions provides little, if any, evidence on the question under consideration.

[69]U.S. Const., Art. II, §2, cl. 2.

by Law: but the Congress may by Law vest the Appointment of such inferior Officers, as they think proper, in the President alone, in the Courts of Law, or in the Heads of Departments." This provision rather clearly grants Congress the power to create executive offices "by Law," thus undermining the interpretation that only the President can organize the executive branch agencies. But it is equally clear that administrative officials who qualify as "Officers of the United States" can only be appointed by the President (with Senate approval). Members of independent regulatory commissions, as heads of departments, are clearly "Officers of the United States," and, as such, can only be appointed by the President.[70] The fact that the President must have the power to appoint implies, albeit not unambiguously, that the President must also have broad power to remove members of regulatory agencies.[71] Moreover, the provisions regarding appointment of inferior officers implies that the "Departments" are in the executive branch of the government, since that term is used in contradistinction to the "Courts of Law."[72] On the other hand, the power of Congress to vest appointment of inferior officers in the heads of executive departments or the courts suggests that Congress could give some degree of autonomy to the departments.

A second reference to administrative agencies is the provision of Article II authorizing the President to "require the Opinion, in writing, of the principal Officer of each of the executive Departments, upon any Subject relating to the Duties of their respective Offices."[73] A narrow reading would suggest that the clause merely enables the President to remain informed as to the doings of the agencies, and that the fact the President was given the express power

---

[70]See *Buckley*, 424 U.S. at 138.

[71]This inference was the principal textual support for the *Myers* opinion, but was implicitly rejected as a hard-and-fast rule by the opinion in *Humphrey's Executor*. If Justice Sutherland had maintained the view that the appointment and removal powers are always vested in the same body, his conclusion that Congress could limit the President's power to remove the heads of regulatory commissions would have entailed the proposition that Congress could also limit the President's power to appoint them. Sutherland was at pains, however, to emphasize that the case did not authorize congressional limitations on the presidential appointment power. See *Humphrey's Executor*, 295 U.S. at 625–26.

[72]See *Buckley*, 424 U.S. at 127 (the phrase suggests that the departments "are themselves in the Executive Branch or at least have some connection with that branch.")

[73]U.S. Const., Art. II, §2, cl 1.

to require opinions from department heads negatives the inference text the President had greater inherent powers of control.[74] But this reading, although textually consistent, may be too limited. By this clause the administrative agencies were required to report to the President. The duty to report is meaningful only if the President retains a measure of substantive authority over the doings of the agency. This conclusion is buttressed by the fact that the President can demand the "opinion" of the department head. The word suggests that the report is not simply to inform the President as to the facts of a matter, but rather to provide him or her with input leading to executive decisions.[75] The Report Clause can easily be read to imply that the President should be able to instruct the official how to act on a matter within the official's statutory discretion, and to remove the official if he or she fails to carry out the President's directions.[76]

Finally, the Constitution instructs the President to "take Care that the Laws be faithfully executed."[77] In terms, this is the imposition of a duty; but it necessarily carries with it the authority to perform actions necessary and proper to the accomplishment of the duty. This clause does not itself mention administrative agencies; but such agencies are implicitly alluded to by its grammatical structure. The clause does not contemplate that the President will personally execute all of the laws. The President's job is to "take care" that the laws be faithfully executed by persons unnamed—a category that no doubt includes the President but also is broad enough to encompass the heads of administrative departments as well. The President's role is one of supervision. The Take Care Clause supports the proposition that there can be some distance between the President, as supervisor, and the agency heads who actually execute the law. The President's duty to take care that the laws be faithfully executed implies the power to "supervise and

---

[74]See Strauss, note 9 *supra*, at 600.

[75]This reading is supported by the history of cabinet government under President Washington. See text at notes 109–12 *infra*.

[76]The Report Clause was the chief textual support cites by the House of Delegates of the American Bar Association as the basis for their conclusion that the requirements of Executive Order 12291, see text at notes 19–20 *supra*, should be extended to independent agencies. See American Bar Association, Section on Administrative Law, Report to the House of Delegates (Resolution 100, passed February 10, 1986).

[77]U.S. Const., Art. II, §3.

guide"[78] the actions of the administrative agencies. Without such disciplinary powers the President would be helpless to prevent the agencies from failing to execute the law as Congress intended. Thus, the clause at least implies that the President must have power to remove an agency head who the President deems to have been faithless in his execution of the law. Left open by this construction of the Take Care Clause is the situation, so common today, in which the agency is given a broad statutory mandate that permits a wide range of discretionary action. In these circumstances the agency head may act in a manner that is consistent with the broad terms of the enabling statute but which conflicts with the President's program. It is unclear whether the Take Care Clause is sufficiently broad to authorize removal simply on the ground that the officer has failed to comply with the President's instructions. When the Take Care Clause is considered in conjunction with the other clauses, however, the inference seems relatively strong that the Constitution guarantees the President the power to remove officers when they fail to follow the President's directions to take actions otherwise within their statutory discretion.

B. STRUCTURE

The Constitution establishes branches of the government and divides and allocates powers among the branches in various ways. If independent agencies are constitutional they must fit within the structure of government in some way that does not do violence to the basic architecture of the system.

1. *The "arm of Congress" theory.* One of the principal structural approaches used to justify independent agencies is what might be called the "arm of the Congress" theory. According to this view, independent agencies function essentially as agencies of Congress and should be located within the legislative branch of government. Because they are within the legislative branch, so this argument goes, there is no violation of the tripartite principle of separation of powers. Support for this view traces back to dicta in *Humphrey's Executor* that the Federal Trade Commission is an "agency of Congress."[79] This argument is a particular favorite of congressmen and

---

[78]*Myers*, 272 U.S. at 135.

[79]295 U.S. at 628, 630.

congressional committees.[80] Similar statements can be found in the congressional testimony of agency heads.[81]

The "arm of Congress" theory is typically unsupported by argument. For its proponents, it suffices to label independent agencies as part of the legislative branch, without exploring the justifications for applying such a label or the implications of the categorization from the standpoint of separation of powers. The closest thing to argument is the "creation" theory: because Congress creates the independent agencies, they are "creatures" of Congress and therefore part of the legislative branch.[82] The fallacy in the argument is too grotesque to bear elaboration.[83] Moreover, if independent agencies are, in fact, arms of the Congress, it is evident that many of their actions must be unconstitutional. These agencies have rule making and enforcement authorities that, when exercised, "alter[ ] the legal rights, duties, and relations of persons."[84] Such actions are "essentially legislative in purpose and effect," and, as such, ought to comply with the procedures for enacting legislation set out in Article I, § 8 of the Constitution.[85] The "arm of Congress" theory has little cogency as a constitutional justification for independent agencies.

2. *The "fourth branch" theory.* The principal competing theory to justify the status of independent agencies within a tripartite structure of government is the view that these agencies are not part of any of the existing three branches.[86] They are completely "independent" of the political and the judicial branches. Together they make up a "fourth branch" of government which has evolved by constitutional usage. This model has some vitality as a descriptive

---

[80]See, *e.g.*, Senate Committee on Governmental Affairs, Study on Federal Regulation, 95th Cong., 1st Sess., Vol. V. p. 31 ("[u]nquestionably the 'arm of Congress' notion has continuing vitality").

[81]See, *e.g.*, Hearings before the Select Comm. on Government Operations, 75th Cong., 1st Sess. 179 (1937) (ICC Commissioner Eastman).

[82]See, *e.g.*, Cushman, The Independent Regulatory Commissions 114 (1941) (quoting statement by a congressman that "the [ICC] is a creature of Congress. . . . It is certainly an erroneous statement to say that the Commission is a creature of the President. . . . It is an independent body, created by act of Congress of the United States").

[83]See Robinson, The Federal Communications Commission: An Essay on Regulatory Watchdogs, 64 Va. L. Rev. 169, 173 (1978).

[84]*Chadha*, 462 U.S. at 952.

[85]See also *Bowsher*, 106 S.Ct. at 3189.

[86]For an outstanding example of this approach, see 2 Sharfman, The Interstate Commerce Commission 453–58 (1931).

theory. And were it not for the written Constitution, it might be accurate to state that a fourth branch of government has been evolving out of the executive branch in much the same way as Parliament evolved from the status of advisor of the Crown into a separate and autonomous organ of government.[87]

The fourth branch theory, however, cannot be reconciled with the written Constitution. The first three articles of the Constitution establish three and only three branches of the government. The overall philosophy of the Constitution is that the national government was a government of limited powers. It would be anomalous to presume that the Framers would have approved the establishment of an independent fourth branch of government. The only justification for such a theory is an extreme version of the pragmatic approach to separation of powers, under which the system of checks and balances set forth in the Constitution is taken as illustrative of a broader universe of arrangements which are permissible so long as some sort of a division and balance of governmental powers is maintained.[88] Otherwise, there is no place for an agency exercising federal governmental powers outside the boundaries of the three branches explicitly established in the Constitution.

3. *Independent agencies as executive agencies.* What remains is the obvious and sensible view that independent agencies are part of the executive branch. It may seem somewhat odd that constitutional theory has such trouble with this approach. A partial explanation lies in the history of administrative law. Before the twentieth century, government operated without such agencies. Most federal legislation was extremely detailed, leaving the President and the department heads only the task of carrying out specifications elaborately set forth by the legislative branch. Congress was able to maintain its control of administration, despite the increasing complexity of American society during the latter part of the nineteenth century, because of the development of the system of standing committees with expertise over matters within their jurisdictions.[89]

---

[87]See generally Smith, History of the English Parliament 54—180 (1892).

[88]See, *e.g.*, Landis at 46: "If the doctrine of separation of powers implies division, it also implies balance, and balance calls for equality. The creation of administrative power may be the means for the preservation of that balance, so that, paradoxically enough, though it may seem in theoretic violation of the doctrine of separation of powers, it may in matter of fact be the means for the preservation of the content of that doctrine."

[89]On standing committees of Congress, see Casper, The Committee System of the United States Congress, 26 (Suppl.) Am. J. Comp. L. 359 (1978).

It was this elaborate system of legislative control that Woodrow Wilson decried in *Congressional Government*.[90]

Against this historical backdrop it may be possible to see why administrative agencies seemed at first to pose such grave constitutional problems. The typical enabling statute gave the agency a degree of authority to establish rules of conduct and to determine whether those rules had been observed in particular cases. These powers may have been so unlike the "executive" powers that Presidents and department heads had typically exercised as to seem different in kind. The rule-making authority seemed legislative, rather than executive, for the agency was not "executing" a rule but making up the standard of conduct *ab initio*. And the authority to determine whether the rules had been violated seemed not to be executive but judicial, in the sense that it involved the application of broad standards to particular actions. Hence these agencies seemed to be agents of the judicial or legislative branches rather than traditional "executive" departments.

In retrospect this difficulty appears less troubling. Today administrative agencies routinely operate under broad grants of delegated authority. It is not nearly as difficult to understand that their actions under these statutes can be purely executive in nature. The agencies are simply executing broad and general, rather than narrow and detailed, statutory instructions. This is not to deny the vast increase in the scope of discretionary executive power over the past fifty years. But the difference may be more one of degree than of kind. Even under the most detailed statute it will occasionally be necessary for the executive to interpret the legislative mandate and to develop formal or informal rules to guide future action. And it will be necessary to apply those rules to particular instances, with or without formal procedural protections for the affected parties. In short, the functions which in the early days of administrative law were conceptualized as "quasi-legislative" or "quasi-judicial" are for the most part nothing more than highly developed aspects of traditional executive action.[91]

---

[90]Wilson, Congressional Government (1887).

[91]See *Chadha*, 462 U.S. at 953 n.16 (action by the Attorney General under broad grant of statutory authority is an Article II power even though in some sense it resembles lawmaking). This is not to say that there are no limits to executive power in rule making or adjudication. See note 46 *supra*.

There is no indication that any of the Justices on the Supreme Court today, even those who espouse a pragmatic notion of separation of powers, would view independent agencies as located anywhere but within the executive branch of government. The structural analysis of the Constitution compels this result. And this conclusion, in turn, supports the inference that the President, as head of the executive branch, must have a considerable degree of constitutional authority to supervise and guide the activities of administrative agencies. Yet concluding that independent agencies are executive branch agencies does not definitively resolve the question of the constitutionality of limitations on the President's removal authority. There is no logical inconsistency in concluding that Congress may constitutionally limit the President's power to remove even purely executive officials.[92] The structural analysis supports the President's constitutional authority to remove officers who have disobeyed presidential directives, but it does not logically compel this result.

C. HISTORY

Much of the history of the constitutional provisions relating to the President's removal power is exhaustively—even turgidly—documented in Chief Justice Taft's opinion in *Myers*. Taft demonstrated that the First Congress, after extensive debate in which many of the Framers participated, decided that the President alone had power to remove the head of the Department of Foreign Affairs. This fundamental decision received nearly universal acquiescence from both Congress and the Executive until the passage of the Tenure in Office Act of 1867, which Taft characterized as an "extreme" measure adopted by a reconstruction Congress in the wake of the convulsion of the Civil War. The early history of acquiescence in the President's removal power was the principal evidence adduced by the Chief Justice to support his conclusion that Congress could not constitutionally limit the President's power to remove federal postmasters. No purpose would be served by reiterating the discussion in *Myers*, other than to note that the decision of the First Congress provides evidence for presidential removal authority, even if the case is not as powerful as Chief Justice Taft implied.[93] There

---

[92] A point made in Cushman, note 17 *supra*, at 42.

[93] Among other things, Taft failed to give sufficient weight to the closeness of the decision,

are, however, certain other elements in the historical record, left out of the *Myers* opinion, that bear on the constitutionality of independent agencies.

First, it is useful to consider the forms of administration adopted under the Continental Congress. Just as the general experience of government since 1776 informed every aspect of the Constitution of 1787, so it is highly likely that the particular experience of administrative government would inform the views of the Framers on the question of presidential control over the executive departments. The system of administration that evolved during the Revolutionary War and its aftermath was one of steadily increasing executive power. The pattern, with minor variations, was discernible across each of the important areas of administration during this formative period: war, finance, foreign affairs, the navy, and so on.[94] Perhaps the clearest example is in the area of military affairs. The conduct of the Revolutionary War was originally entrusted to a variety of different congressional committees, each performing a specific and narrow duty—a system that proved an utter failure because the committees "neither took pains to render mutual assistance to each other nor to preserve peace within their own ranks."[95] In 1776, at Washington's request, Congress established a Board of War and Ordnance, consisting of five members of Congress, with overall responsibility for overseeing the war effort.[96] This arrange-

---

or to consider the fact that James Madison, a chief proponent of the proposition that Congress could not limit the President's power to remove the Secretary of the Department of Foreign Affairs, also suggested in the first Congress that the Comptroller of the Treasury, a subordinate official in the Treasury Department, should not hold office at the pleasure of the President. See 1 Annals of Congress 635–36 (1789). Although Congress rejected the proposal, Madison's statement suggests that many of the Framers and their contemporaries in Congress may have been somewhat less certain about the removal issue than the debate on the Department of Foreign Affairs might imply if taken in isolation. Madison's proposal for the Comptroller, however, could be reconciled with the Taft analysis if the Comptroller is seen as an inferior officer as to whom Congress may vest appointment (and, presumably, removal) power in the heads of departments or the courts of law. For discussion of some of the ambiguities in the Decision of 1789, see Grundstein, Presidential Power, Administration and Administrative Law, 18 Geo. Wash. L. Rev. 285, 294–300 (1950).

[94]See generally Thach, The Creation of the Presidency, 1775–1789: A Study in Constitutional History 59–70 (1969).

[95]Guggenheimer, The Development of the Executive Departments, 1775–1789, in Jameson, ed., Essays in the Constitutional History of the United States in the Formative Period 116, 120 (1970).

[96]*Id.* at 122. The first chairman of this board was John Adams. *Ibid.*

ment had the advantage of concentrating the task of administration in a single committee; but it too failed because of the inability or unwillingness of members other than Adams to attend to their tasks. Congress amended the system again in 1777, this time creating a Board of War comprised of five members who were not to be delegates in Congress.[97] The removal of members of Congress from the war board was something of an improvement; but the attempt to operate the war through a multi-member board remained unsatisfactory. The obvious solution was to substitute single executive officers for the clumsy and irresponsible boards—a step that Congress did not take lightly because of its fear of vesting excessive power in a single hand.[98] In 1781, however, Congress provided for the appointment of a Secretary of War who, although still required to report to Congress, was given a generous measure of executive powers.[99] Among other things, Congress provided in 1785 that the Secretary of War should "appoint and remove at pleasure all persons employed under him, and [should] be responsible for their conduct in office"[100]—a move reflecting the recognition that "the power to appoint and remove subordinates is essential to control and responsibility on the part of the real head."[101] This arrangement apparently proved satisfactory and was maintained until the establishment of the Constitution in 1787.[102] Thus the pattern was one of movement from congressional towards executive government. Congress, although loath to cede any of its powers to an executive, was compelled by the exigencies of war and the needs of government to do so. By the time of the Constitution, the principle of administrative management by single executive officials had been firmly established. This concept of a single executive with authority to supervise, guide, and coordinate a variety of disparate tasks and responsibilities was projected into the institution of the President of the United States, a single official with overall responsibility for

---

[97]*Id.* at 125. The predecessor Board of War and Ordnance continued in existence in a supervisory capacity.

[98]*Id.* at 126.

[99]The same year Congress established departments of foreign affairs, treasury and marine. *Ibid.*

[100]Thach, note 94 *supra*, at 68.

[101]*Id.* at 74.

[102]Guggenheimer, note 95 *supra*, at 154.

all executive actions. The model of administration that developed under the Continental Congress, in other words, provided an exemplar for the Framers as they struggled to form a new government.

Additional evidence on the President's responsibility for administration can be found in the events in the Constitutional Convention. Much of the Convention's deliberations over the powers of the Presidency centered around sundry proposals to establish some kind of council to oversee and check the President's executive powers. The council idea apparently grew out of English practice, and out of the model of states in which the administrative function was exercised by a weak executive in conjunction with a council of state.[103] Proposals to establish checks and balances within the executive branch through the establishment of a council were supported by Madison, Wilson, Ellsworth, and Franklin, among others.[104] None of these proposals, however, succeeded. The decision not to include a council within the executive branch suggests that the President was not to be subject to internal checks over his or her responsibility to see that the laws be faithfully executed.[105] The success of the unitary executive represents a victory for the proponents of executive power at the Convention—men like Wilson, Morris, and Pinckney—who believed that the President was to be the "active chief of administration."[106] In their view, the department heads were to be completely subordinate to the chief executive, since they were to be appointable by the President alone and to hold office at his pleasure.[107] And it was clear that this principle was to apply across the board to all executive departments regardless of function: "Nor is there any distinction made between departments on any basis of special relationship to the President."[108]

A final piece of historical evidence not discussed in the *Myers* opinion concerns the actual administrative practice in the Washington administration. President Washington regularly consulted

---

[103]See Pious, The American Presidency 23 (1979).

[104]See *id*. at 31.

[105]See Thach, note 94 *supra*, at 89 (abandonment of council idea was "of greatest importance" because it deviated from practice of virtually every state and of Great Britain). The classic justification of the unitary executive, Federalist No. 70, specifically discusses the defects of the plural executive under state constitutions.

[106]Thach, note 94 *supra*, at 122.

[107]See *ibid*.

[108]*Ibid*.

with the heads of the administrative departments and only infrequently overruled them.[109] But he was not afraid to do so on matters of great public moment.[110] None of the cabinet secretaries, not even Hamilton, settled any matter of importance without consulting the President.[111] In Washington's administration "the power to govern was quietly but certainly taken over by the President. The heads of departments became his assistants. In the executive branch . . . the President was undisputed master."[112] This early history of internal executive management provides some support for the inference that the President was to be in charge of the administration of the government—although, to be sure, practice within the executive branch supporting an executive power is less persuasive than practice and understandings outside the executive branch. Nevertheless, experience under the Washington Administration does cast some question on the notion of an agency operating within the executive branch and performing executive functions free of presidential supervision and control in the form of the power to remove an official who fails to comply with a presidential directive to take an action that is otherwise within the officer's statutory discretion.

D. FUNCTION

Additional evidence on the constitutionality of limitations on the President's removal authority can be obtained through an analysis

---

[109]See Charles, The Origins of the American Party System 41 (1956).

[110]A telling example is Washington's decision to sign the bill establishing the First Bank of the United States notwithstanding the formal opinion of Attorney General Randolph that the bank was unconstitutional. See Symonds & White, Banking Law 12 (2d ed. 1984); Hammond, Banks and Politics in America from the Revolution to the Civil War 118–22 (1957).

[111]See White, The Federalists: A Study in Administrative History 27 (1948). Jefferson admiringly described Washington's style of governing as follows: "[He] was always in accurate possession of all facts and proceedings in every part of the Union, and to whatsoever department they related; he formed a central point for the different branches; preserved an unity of object and action among them; exercised that participation in the suggestion of affairs which his office made incumbent on him; and met himself the due responsibility for whatever was done." Jefferson, The Complete Jefferson 306 (Padover, ed., 1939). Washington's approach to the Presidency, in Jefferson's view, was undoubtedly preferable to that of Adams, who, due to frequent absences from the seat of government, "rendered this kind of communication impracticable, removed him from any share in the transaction of affairs, and parcelled out the government, in fact, among four independent heads, drawing sometimes in opposite directions." Ibid.

[112]White, note 111 supra, at 37.

of the functional justifications for those entities. Deviations from the classical model of separation of powers may be justified by sufficiently compelling considerations of policy. The burden of proof, however, should rest heavily on the proponents of new technologies of government to establish their convenience and necessity. If the goals of agency independence themselves are questionable, or if independence is a dubious means of achieving the goals, then the argument in favor of the constitutionality of independent agencies is considerably eroded.

1. *The haphazard pattern of agency independence.* Perhaps the single most telling rebuttal to the functional justification for independent agencies is the fact that Congress has been extremely inconsistent in its use of limitations on the President's removal power. Sometimes it creates an independent agency with express limits on presidential removal; sometimes it establishes an office in the executive branch performing apparently identical functions. The Federal Trade Commission, an independent agency, polices against violations of the antitrust laws.[113] So does the Department of Justice, a traditional executive branch department.[114] The Federal Reserve Board, an independent agency,[115] the Federal Deposit Insurance Corporation, a hybrid institution with certain independent features,[116] and the Comptroller of the Currency, a subordinate official in the Department of the Treasury,[117] regulate different segments of the commercial banking industry; and if a bank is dissatisfied with one regulator it can simply switch to another with no essential change in function.[118] Dangers at the workplace are regulated at the federal level by the Occupational Safety and Health Administration, an executive branch agency,[119] and by an independent commission, the Occupational Safety and Health Review Commission.[120] Nuclear safety is under the control of an independent agency, the Nuclear

---

[113]15 U.S.C. §§45, 46 (1982).

[114]15 U.S.C. §§4, 25 (1982).

[115]12 U.S.C. §§241–42 (1982).

[116]See 12 U.S.C. §§1811–12 (1982 & Supp. 1984).

[117]12 U.S.C. §1 (1982).

[118]See Scott, The Dual Banking System: A Model of Competition in Regulation, 30 Stan. L. Rev. 1 (1977).

[119]29 U.S.C. §656 (1982).

[120]29 U.S.C. §661 (1982).

Regulatory Commission.[121] There is little rhyme or reason to these different allocations of authority. In the words of Peter Strauss, the diversity in agency forms "is characteristic of our pragmatic ways with government, reflecting the circumstances of the particular regulatory regime, the temper of presidential/congressional relations at the time, or the perceived success or failure of an existing agency performing like functions, more than any grand scheme of government."[122]

The failure of Congress to demonstrate a consistent approach to agency independence is mirrored at the theoretical level by the absence of any noncircular explanation for why independence is needed in a particular case. None of the leading proponents of independent agencies has provided any kind of a coherent theory as to when independence is desirable and when it is not. Independent agencies are sometimes justified with reference to formulae that are nothing more than descriptions of what the typical independent agency does. William Cary, for example, stated that independent agencies "formulate and carry out comprehensive regulatory programs for particular industries or segments of the economy."[123] James Landis described their activity as "either the orderly supervision of a specific industry or . . . an extension of a particular branch of the police work of the general government."[124] These statements are so broad as to include virtually any regulatory agency, independent or not; all of the great executive departments carry out comprehensive regulatory programs for particular industries or segments of the economy. Being merely discriptive, these statements do nothing to advance understanding as to when the independent agency form is needed. Nor are matters advanced by the various justifications advanced for agency independence, such as expertise, insulation from political pressures, and the like. These justifications typically apply to any administrative agency, and accordingly suggest that the entire administrative state ought to be comprised of independent agencies. Yet no proponent of agency independence has been willing to go this far.[125] Short of this extreme

---

[121]42 U.S.C. §§5841–51 (1982).

[122]Strauss, note 9 *supra*, at 584–85.

[123]Cary, Politics and the Regulatory Agencies 3, 133 (1967).

[124]Landis at 23.

[125]James Landis came closest to making this claim, suggesting rather unconvincingly that

claim, however, we are left with circular justifications: the independent form should be used when it is desirable to insulate agency action from politics, when expertise is a desideratum, and so on.

The single most economical explanation for why Congress uses the independent form in some cases and not in others is that agency independence provides a useful mechanism for compromise and accommodation among competing political interest groups. Independent agencies, in this respect, are quite similar to legislative vetoes. It is often the case that there is a political consensus in favor of regulation, but that Congress is unable to adopt any particular regulation because of the existence of blocking coalitions. The obvious solution is to formulate highly general standards that veil the areas of disagreement and give the matter to an administrative agency for decision. But members of Congress, or the interest groups they serve, may not want to give up this much power to the executive branch. An obvious solution to the dilemma, prior to the *Chadha* case, was to authorize the executive action subject to legislative veto, thus breaking the legislative deadlock without granting unfettered power to the executive. Agency independence performs something of the same function. Because independent agencies are not thought subject to executive oversight, they can be given the power to decide politically controversial matters without accentuating the power of the President. And although Congress does not have the power to reverse the actions of independent agencies (short of new legislation), it probably does exercise a greater degree of influence and control over the independent agencies than over the old-line executive departments.

This political function of agency independence has apparently been a feature of the regulatory state from the beginning. Congress created the Interstate Commerce Commission with limited rate setting authority for railroads. The matter of rates was thereby passed to another decision maker. The ICC, as originally established in 1887, was not an independent commission, but rather was in form (if not in function) a traditional executive branch agency.[126]

---

all agencies would be independent were it not for political considerations: "The effort to run a rational unifying thread through [administrative agencies] at first seems impossible. Certainly the effort to correlate and integrate them according to whether or not they happen to be independent is, to say the least, sterile. The lack of independence results sometimes from political maneuvering rather than from a deliberate theory of creation." *Id.* at 22.

[126]See Miller, The Legislative Evolution of the Interstate Commerce Act 219–220, 278–79 (1930); Cushman, The Independent Regulatory Commissions 60–61 (1941).

The independent features of the Commission were adopted two years later, when Congress, without hearing or debate, removed the Commission from the Department of the Interior and granted it sole authority over budget, personnel, and internal management.[127] The proponents of this measure evidently were not anxious to publicize the reasons for their action; but the motivation is not hard to infer. The statute granting independence to the ICC was adopted two days before the inauguration of Benjamin Harrison, a Republican railroad lawyer. The first independent commission may well have grown out of a desire on the part of the Democratic sponsors of the original legislation to insulate the agency from Harrison's influence.[128]

The political explanation for congressional decisions creating independent agencies provides scant support for the argument that such agencies are desirable because of their functional contribution to better government. If independent agencies are often established for reasons of political expediency rather than because of their clear superiority as devices for governing, the argument in favor of insulating the heads of these agencies from presidential removal is considerably undermined.

2. *The functional arguments.* The functional justification for independent agencies has tended to stress three main advantages which these agencies supposedly possess as compared with traditional executive departments: (1) focused agenda; (2) expertise; and (3) insulation from political pressures. These justifications are closely related, and in many respects are variations on the same overall theme. On analysis, each of the purported advantages turns out to be subject to serious doubt.

a). Focused agenda. One of the principal early justifications for independent agencies is that, because they operated under a specialized mandate, they would tend to have a focused regulatory agenda. In this respect the independent agencies were sharply contrasted with the great executive departments with their almost limitless range of duties. The proponents of independent agencies argued that their focused agendas would improve the efficacy and energy of government. The commissioners of specialized agencies would not be required to "dissipate their energies over a wide

---

[127]Act of March 2, 1889, 25 Stat. 861.

[128]This thesis is suggested in Study on Federal Regulation Prepared Pursuant to S. Rev. 71, Senate Committee on Governmental Affairs, 95th Cong., 1st Sess. Vol. 5, p. 28 (1977).

periphery,"[129] and could devote their full time and efforts to a single, focused task. Specialization would facilitate a high level of expertise.[130] It would, moreover, fix responsibility for outcomes in a way that was not possible in the executive departments.[131] Responsibility, in turn, would aid in attracting able individuals to government service and would encourage the vigorous performance of their tasks. A specialized mandate would also permit flexibility in organization, enabling the agency to adapt to the particular needs of its regulated industry and facilitating the casting off of "overhanging habits and traditions"[132] that would otherwise hamper effective operation.

Underlying these supposed practical advantages of focused agendas were certain deeper themes that were not always explicitly articulated. One such theme, applicable to the agencies with substantive responsibility over particular industries, was a model of administrative structure based on the organization of the regulated industry itself. This theme is explicit in the work of James Landis. Landis argued that the task of regulating large corporations is very similar to the job of managing them. And he observed that industries never organized themselves "along Montesquieu's lines" of separation of powers.[133] Accordingly, it is only "intelligent realism" for government to "follow the industrial rather than the political analogue."[134] When organized along industry lines, the independent agency form "vests the necessary powers with the administrative authority it creates, not too greatly concerned with the extent to which such action does violence to the traditional tripartite theory of governmental organization."[135]

This picture of independent agencies as homologues of their subject industries reflects a vision of the role of regulation. If the function of government in the nineteenth century had been conceptualized as police power, the role of agencies in the twentieth century was to be "management." The independent agencies were

---

[129]Landis at 27.

[130]*Id.* at 25–26.

[131]*Id.* at 29.

[132]*Id.* at 27.

[133]*Id.* at 10.

[134]*Id.* at 11–12.

[135]*Id.* at 12.

to "plan" and "promote" as well as to police. Thus, administrative power, "though it may begin as an effort to adapt and make efficient police protection within a particular field, moves soon to think in terms of the economic well-being of an industry."[136] The agencies, in short, were to be virtual partners in the management of their subject industries; their relationship with the private sector was to have strong elements of cooperation and even boosterism—attitudes that would be difficult to engender in government officials outside the context of agencies with mandates narrowly limited to particular industrial sectors.

A second broad theme underlying the agenda-focusing rationale of independent agencies has to do with executive power. The concept of prosecutorial discretion is an aspect of the theory of separation of powers; it describes the ability of the executive branch to vary the intensity with which it enforces statutes passed by the legislative branch. In the traditional executive department, therefore, regulatory statutes will not necessarily receive effective enforcement. Much will depend on the priorities of the agency head, who must allocate scarce prosecutorial resources among competing statutory responsibilities. The single-purpose agency circumvents this problem by establishing a unified set of bureaucratic incentives on the part of agency officials.[137] Thus, viewed through the perspective of separation of powers the function of agenda-focusing is nothing other than a form of substantive control by Congress of the discretion that the executive branch might otherwise exercise in enforcing the law.

The benefits of narrow regulatory agendas do not by themselves justify the establishment of agencies free from presidential supervision and direction. To the extent that there are benefits from this device, they can largely be obtained without the use of independent agencies. Congress may establish "independent agencies within the executive branch," which are unquestionably constitutional so long

---

[136]*Id.* at 15–16.

[137]This enforcement problem was well-understood by the late Nineteenth Century, and was particularly acute in the case of statutes promoted by the dairy industry which attempted to suppress the trade in oleomargarine. In states where enforcement of these statutes was vested in the state attorneys general they proved to be almost wholly ineffective. But the statutes were far more effective in states that had created a specialized administrative agency or commission to enforce the anti-margarine laws. See Miller, The Margarine War (1986) (unpublished manuscript).

as the President retains the power to remove agency heads who do not fit in with the President's program. The Environmental Protection Agency, for example, has an agenda limited to enforcing the federal environmental protection statutes. There is a natural tendency for the heads of these agencies to fight to protect their bureaucratic turf; and in the process of doing so they will tend vigorously to enforce their statutory mandates. To be sure, the agendas of independent agencies within the executive branch are likely to be somewhat less single-focused than the agendas of classical independent agencies because of the President's power to remove the officials of executive branch agencies and to engage in various subsidiary forms of supervision and guidance of their activities. Nevertheless, many of the benefits of focused agendas can be obtained without resort to the constitutionally questionable device of limiting the President's power to remove officers who fail to follow the President's program.

More fundamentally, the benefits of focused agendas are far from unambiguous. The justification for narrow agency mandates is implicitly premised on a compartmentalized view of the national economy in which particular industries operate virtually in isolation from other industries. Under this view, the operations of one independent agency in furthering the well-being of a particular industry do not create externalities affecting other industries. At most, proponents of independent agencies tend to content themselves with the simplistic view that actions that benefit a particular industry also benefit the nation as a whole.[138] But this is obviously an error. In a highly interdependent economy regulation of any one industry necessarily affects the well-being of any number of other industries. Energy price controls affect the cost of farming; limits on particulate emissions affect the mining industry; strip mining rules affect railroads; automobile safety rules affect the demand for steel, and so on. Agencies with highly specialized agendas will tend to focus solely on matters within their jurisdiction, thus often adopting regulatory policies with perverse consequences elsewhere in the economy. Moreover, there is a dark side to the idyllic vision of the competing segments of an industry peacefully coexisting under the benign supervision of an independent agency dedicated to further-

---

[138]See Landis at 16 (equating "economic well-being of an industry" with "efficient functioning of the economic processes of the state").

ing the industry's well-being. Everyone can be made better off within an industry to the extent that the governmental body limits competition or fixes prices. Government-sponsored cartels have been far from unknown in the history of regulation;[139] and the rosy picture of industry well-being that a government-sponsored cartel might present does not translate into net economic benefits for the society as a whole.

The problem with limited agendas, in short, is the complete lack of coordination which they create among different regulatory bodies. The problem has been understood for many years. It was the chief objection leveled against independent agencies by the Brownlow Committee in its report to President Roosevelt in 1937. The independent agencies, according to this committee, were "in reality miniature independent governments set up to deal with the railroad problem, the banking problem, or the radio problem." They constituted a "headless 'fourth branch' of the Government, a haphazard deposit of irresponsible agencies and uncoordinated powers."[140] This objection to independent agencies, so effectively stated by the Brownlow Committee, has been echoed in years since by a variety of Presidents and presidential commissions, and has even been endorsed by former agency commissioners.[141]

b). Expertise. A second functional justification for independent agencies is that they facilitate development of "expertise" in administration. The virtues of expertise are that it will lead to more efficient and effective regulations, and that it will tend to counteract the influence of politics on the regulatory process. Proponents of independent agencies suggest that these bodies are better suited to developing administrative expertise than are traditional executive departments. The reason, in part, is the focused agendas of independent agencies, which facilitate administrative specialization. In addition, the independence of the agency is said to be an important stimulus in drawing highly talented men and women into government service, since their actions are not subject to review and re-

---

[139]An egregious example is the regulation that until recently limited the amount of interest that banks and thrift institutions could pay for deposits. See Scott, The Uncertain Course of Bank Deregulation, Regulation 40 (May–June 1981).

[140]Report of the President's Committee on Administrative Management 39–40 (1937).

[141]For a former member's devastating critique of the Civil Aeronautics Board, see Hector, Problems of the CAB and the Independent Regulatory Commissions, 69 Yale L. J. 931 (1960).

versal by "young bureaucrats"[142] in some White House office.[143] Morever, the sustained tenure that the independent agency makes possible encourages the development of expertise through continuity in office.[144]

The expertise rationale for agency independence has a number of problematic features. There is no evidence that the level of expertise in independent agencies is any higher than it is in executive branch agencies.[145] The expertise that makes a difference in particular cases will be concentrated in the career staff of an agency; and for career officers it makes little difference whether their agency is independent or not. In either case the recommendations of the career officer will be reviewed by "policy-making" officials higher up in the chain of authority. And in the vast majority of cases, in both independent and executive agencies, the staff recommendations are accepted by the agency heads without change.

Moreover, the simplistic notion that "good men" (or women) will be more attracted to independent agencies is far from established even in theory. The premise of the argument is that highly qualified individuals seek out challenge and responsibility. If so, there are good grounds to suppose that independent agencies will be less attractive places of employment than executive agencies. The heads of independent agencies, after all, are members of panels with five, seven, or more fellow members each with equivalent powers. Even the chairman of an independent agency is in theory only first among equals.[146] Executive agencies, in contrast, are headed by single administrators or cabinet officers with general responsibility for the entire agency. The challenge and responsibility of the job is greater if one is the sole head of an agency than if power is shared among a panel of fellow administrators. Further, the narrow statutory mandate of independent agencies necessarily entails limitations on their powers. A highly talented young man or woman seeking responsibility might well be more attracted to a large executive department, such as the Department of State, with its broad au-

---

[142]Friendly, The Federal Administrative Agencies 154 (1962).

[143]See *id.* at 153–54; Landis at 28–30.

[144]Landis at 23.

[145]See Bernstein, Regulating Business by Independent Commission 17 (1955); Hector, note 141 *supra*.

[146]Agency chairmen, however, do often enjoy considerably greater powers because of their prestige in Congress, their access to the press, and their control over internal housekeeping matters such as staffing or budget.

thority over the nation's external relations, than to some specialized administrative agency such as the Federal Maritime Commission or the Interstate Commerce Commission. Aspiring bureaucrats, in short, might well have greater career opportunities in executive branch agencies than in independent agencies.

Finally, the deadening effects of lengthy job tenure and group decision making should not be disregarded. Officials who serve terms of ten or fourteen years, subject to removal only for serious malfeasance, may naturally become complacent or even lazy in their jobs.[147] In most cases members of independent regulatory commissions can look forward to lucrative positions in private industry upon completion of their term of service. They need not distinguish themselves while in office. Indeed, because decisions are typically made by majority vote, it is rare for their personal contributions to be singled out for admiration or criticism. Members of independent regulatory commissions can get by for years doing little more than attending meetings and voting to endorse the recommendations sent up by the staff. The heads of executive departments, in contrast, typically serve for much shorter periods. Because they are individually responsible for the affairs of the agency, they have an incentive to perform their duties with vigor and attention. And the possibility of falling into disfavor with the President is an ever-present goad to their energetic performance in implementing the President's program.

c). Insulation from political pressure. A third argument for agency independence is that independent agencies are relatively insulated from political pressures.[148] This insulation, it is said, will encourage decisions on the substantive merits of the case, thus enhancing the beneficial effects of agency expertise. More broadly, insulation from political pressures is calculated to reduce the influence of factions or interest groups, and thereby to serve the broad ideals that inspired the Framers of the Constitution.[149]

This argument also is not a convincing justification for independent agencies. First, the optimistic ideal of nonpolitical administration is itself coming under scrutiny. The naive faith of the New

---

[147]See Bernstein, note 145 *supra*, at 108.

[148]*E.g.*, Friendly, note 142 *supra*, at 156–57.

[149]See, *e.g.*, Federalist Nos. 10, 51 (Madison). See generally Sunstein, Naked Preferences and the Constitution, 84 Colum. L. Rev. 1689 (1984); Sunstein, Interest Groups in American Public Law, 38 Stan. L. Rev. 29 (1985).

Deal era administrative law theorists was that expertise alone could provide a means of deciding the fundamental questions of wealth distribution that must needs be resolved in implementating many ostensibly "neutral" statutory schemes. But today it is increasingly recognized that the broad discretionary authorities granted to administrative agencies cannot even in principle be implemented in the absence of political considerations. The Supreme Court implicitly accepted as much in *Chevron USA, Inc. v. Natural Resources Defense Council, Inc.*,[150] stating that "an agency to which Congress has delegated policymaking responsibilities may, within the limits of that delegation, properly rely upon the incumbent administration's views of wise policy to inform its judgments."[151] Thus, the argument that independent agencies are desirable because they are apolitical is subject to the skeptical refutation that in principle they cannot, nor should they, exclude politics as a consideration in determining how to implement their statutory mandates. The goal of administrative law, as perceived by many students of the subject today, is not to exclude politics altogether, but to find some means for allowing broadly political considerations to play a role in administrative decisions while at the same time protecting against undesirable forms of political influence, especially the wielding of excessive influence by special interest lobbies.[152]

Second, these theoretical considerations to one side, it is most definitely not the case that independent agencies are insulated from political pressures. The unanimous testimony of those who have served at the highest levels of such agencies is emphatically to the contrary. In the words of William Cary, a former Chairman of the Securities and Exchange Commission, "[g]overnment regulatory commmissions are often referred to as 'independent' agencies, but this cannot be taken at face value by anyone who has ever had any experience in Washington. In fact, government regulatory agencies are stepchildren whose custody is contested by both Congress and the Executive, but without very much affection from either one."[153]

---

[150]104 S.Ct. 2778 (1984).

[151]*Id.* at 2793.

[152]See, *e.g.*, Sunstein, The Decline of the New Deal Agency (1986) (unpublished manuscript).

[153]Cary, note 155 *supra*, at 4. See also Minow, Equal Time: The Private Broadcaster and the Public Interest (1964); Robinson, The Federal Communications Commission: An Essay on Regulatory Watchdogs, 64 Va. L. Rev. 169 (1978).

Independent agencies do not operate free of politics; they exist in a complex political environment in which they must attempt to remain on good terms with the White House, their oversight and appropriations committees in Congress, and their regulated industries without being subservient to any.

Moreover, many independent agencies are subject to a particularly insidious type of faction. In agencies serving the interests of particular industries, it is all too possible for them to pass over the line of objectivity and become the advocates of their industries. The phenomenon of agency "capture" has frequently been documented.[154] But capture by an industry is nothing else than the expression through the coercive arm of government of a particular form of faction. In this respect, the independent agencies, far from resisting the danger of faction, in fact may increase that danger as compared to the executive branch agencies. This is not to say, of course, that the President is immune from the danger of faction, or that executive branch agencies do not cater to the wishes of Congress or their regulated industries. The difference is one of degree; but to the extent it exists, it may suggest the desirability of presidential removal as a means of mitigating the force of special interests in the administration of national programs.

Finally, it is sometimes suggested that independence is necessary in order to preserve the impartiality of agency adjudications. Adjudications, however, routinely take place within "executive" agencies just as in independent agencies.[155] And presidential interference in ongoing adjudicatory proceedings could well create the kind of bias that would invalidate the results of the adjudication under the Due Process Clause.[156]

E. PRESCRIPTION

Yet another factor bearing on the constitutionality of independent agencies is the history of acquiescence or resistance to these agencies

---

[154]*E.g.*, Noll, Reforming Regulation 99–101 (1971); Bernstein, note 145 *supra*. For arguments that the problem of agency capture can be mitigated by enhanced judicial review of agency action, see Sunstein, Interest Groups in American Public Law, 38 Stan. L. Rev. 29, 60 (1985); Sunstein, In Defense of the Hard Look: Judicial Activism and Administrative Law, 7 Harv. J. L. & Pub. Pol. 51 (1984).

[155]See note 48 *supra*.

[156]*Cf.* Mathews v. Eldridge, 424 U.S. 319, 349 (1976)(due process in administrative proceedings).

on the part of Presidents. Essentially, this is a notion of prescription; it entails both a long and continued pattern of usage and a failure by the branch of government whose prerogatives are ostensibly infringed to protest against the custom.[157] If a practice of government has persisted for many years without significant controversy, then this is evidence that the practice is constitutional, or has become so by prescription.

There is no doubt that independent agencies have been part of the fabric of government long enough to achieve some form of prescriptive rights. What is less clear is the status of executive acquiescence. It is evident that merely signing a bill that establishes an independent agency does not constitute acquiescence in the agency's constitutionality. The needs of government often compel Presidents to accept provisions in legislation that they consider undesirable or even unconstitutional. If merely signing a statute were tantamount to acquiescence, then the legislative veto case might have been differently decided, since the President signed most or all of the nearly two hundred federal statutes containing such provisions. Probably, what is required to prevent a conclusion that the President has acquiesced is that the President make known his opposition to a practice and do nothing affirmative to enhance it. In the context of legislative vetoes, for example, Presidents have often included their views on the constitutionality of the device in signing statements.[158] And only in rare instances have Presidents proposed legislative vetoes or suggested that they might be acceptable across the board.[159]

Unlike the case of legislative vetoes, the executive branch has not consistently opposed independent agencies on constitutional grounds. A survey of signing statements for legislation establishing four randomly selected independent agencies disclosed not a single instance in which the President publically noted the difficulties under the separation of powers.[160] Moreover, Presidents have until

---

[157]See, *e.g.*, The Pocket Veto Case, 279 U.S. 655, 688–89 (1929).

[158]*E.g.*, Marine Protection, Research, and Sanctuaries Appropriations Bill, 16 Weekly Comp. Pres. Docs. 1592 (1980); Nuclear Non-Proliferation Act of 1978, 14 Weekly Comp. Pres. Docs. 500, 502 (1978).

[159]For a catalogue of cases in which Presidents failed to maintain a vigorous opposition to legislative vetoes, see *Chadha*, 462 U.S. at 969–70 n.5 (White, J., dissenting).

[160]The agencies were the Federal Trade Commission, the Securities and Exchange Commission, the Consumer Product Safety Commission, and the Commodities Futures Trading

now backed away from direct confrontations with Congress over the status of independent agencies.[161] And the Department of Justice has accepted the proposition that, under *Humphrey's Executor* and *Wiener*, "Congress has the authority to limit the President's power to remove quasi-judicial or quasi-legislative officers."[162]

On the other hand, Presidents and their advisors have never been partial to the independent agency form. The Brownlow Committee Report[163] is only one in a series of reports to Presidents raising serious questions as to the desirability of independent agencies.[164] And Presidents have challenged purported limits on their removal authority in a variety of settings.[165] Moreover, a close reading of the Department of Justice opinions reveals a strong degree of antipathy toward congressional efforts to limit the President's removal power.[166] Presidents and their lawyers have done little more than give lip service to the dicta in *Humphrey's Executor* and *Wiener* without actually taking affirmative action to enhance the position of independent agencies within the system of government. In these circumstances, the evidence of prescription is mixed, and probably

---

Commission. In one case—President Nixon's statement on the Consumer Product Safety Act—the President did criticize the statute for "tend[ing] to weaken budget control." Weekly Compilation of Presidential Documents, October 30, 1972, at 1582. But see 59 Cong. Rec. 8609–10 (1920) (veto message of President Wilson of statute establishing office of Comptroller General on the ground that "vesting [the] power of removal in the Congress is unconstitutional").

[161]See text at notes 29–36 *supra* for an account of the Reagan Administration's record on this score.

[162]*E.g.*, Memorandum Opinion for the Attorney General: Inspector General Legislation, 1 Op. O.L.C. 16, 18 (1977).

[163]See text accompanying note 140 *supra*.

[164]See, *e.g.*, President's Advisory Council on Executive Reorganization, A New Regulatory Framework: Report on Selected Independent Regulatory Agencies (1971); Landis, Report on the Regulatory Agencies to the President-Elect, Senate Judiciary Committee Print, 86th Cong., 2d Sess. (1960); Commission on Organization of the Executive Branch of the Government, Task Force Report on Regulatory Commissions (1949).

[165]In addition to the *Myers*, *Humphrey's Executor* and *Wiener* cases, see Morgan v. Tennessee Valley Authority, 115 F.2d 990, 993–94 (6th Cir. 1940), cert. denied, 312 U.S. 701 (1941); Ameron, Inc. v. Army Corps of Engineers, 787 F.2d 875, 885–87 (3d Cir. 1986); Martin v. Reagan, 525 F.Supp. 110 (D. Mass. 1981).

[166]See, *e.g.*, Memorandum Opinion for the President, 1 Op. O.L.C. 75 (1977) (proposals to establish an independent Attorney General are unconstitutional); Memorandum Opinion for the General Counsel, Civil Service Commission, 2 Op. O.L.C. 120 (1978) (Congress cannot restrict President's power to remove Special Counsel of the Merit Systems Protection Board); The President's Power to Remove Members of the Federal Council on the Aging, 5 Op. O.L.C. 337 (1981); Dixon, The Independent Commissions and Political Responsibility, 27 Ad. L. Rev. 1 (1975) (remarks by the Assistant Attorney General, Office of Legal Counsel).

is not strong enough to support the inference that the executive branch has forfeited its constitutional objections to independent agencies.

F. REMEDY

It may be useful to consider the practicalities of a decision, at this point in the history of administrative government, to strike down removal limitations on constitutional grounds. This factor should not be given excessive weight. In *Chadha*, for example, the Court did not hesitate to jeopardize nearly two hundred federal statutes. On the other hand there is an obvious and substantial interest in safeguarding the orderly functioning of government. If invalidating removal limitations were to work a hardship on private parties, or massively to distrupt ongoing governmental programs, this would be a substantial argument in favor of maintaining existing limits on the President's power to remove the heads of independent agencies.[167]

There is reason to suppose, however, that a decision consistent with the constitutional analysis set forth above might not be overly disruptive, for two reasons: (1) the organic statutes of independent agencies are often susceptible to interpretation saving them from constitutional attack; and (2) in those relatively infrequent cases where a statute cannot be saved through interpretation, the agency's overall powers and enforcement authority can usually be preserved through the principle of severability. Moreover, even when an entire agency is invalidated, Congress could reenact the statute creating the agency free of the objectionable removal provision.

1. *Saving through interpretation.* It may often be possible to save statutes from constitutional attack through interpretation of the "cause" requirement. Many statutes creating independent agencies do not clearly set forth the kinds of actions that constitute "cause" justifying removal by the President.[168] These statutes can rather

---

[167] *Cf. Northern Pipeline,* 458 U.S. at 88, in which the Court stayed its judgment invalidating the bankruptcy courts in order to give Congress time to repair the constitutional defect.

[168] Most such statutes do not specifically state the conditions under which the President may remove an agency head. See, *e.g.,* 47 U.S.C. §151 et seq. (1982) (Federal Communications Commission); 15 U.S.C. §78d(a)(1982) (Securities and Exchange Commission); 12 U.S.C. §1437(b)(1982) (Federal Home Loan Bank Board). At least one statute permits removal for "cause," without further elaboration. 12 U.S.C. §242 (1982) (Board of Governors of the Federal Reserve System).

easily be interpreted as including within the concept of cause the failure of an agency head to comply with the President's instructions to take some action otherwise within his or her statutory authority. So interpreted, they would limit the President's power to remove an officer who has either complied with the President's instructions, or who has refused to follow an instruction that would require the officer to act in a fashion plainly beyond the officer's discretion. They would also prohibit the President from removing an officer for reasons having nothing to do the President's responsibilities of government, such as personal animus or spite. Such limitations on the President's removal authority would be constitutional under the analysis presented above.

Other statutes purportedly set forth a detailed list of the actions that justify removal.[169] For these statutes the interpretative task is somewhat more difficult, since failure to follow a presidential directive is never stated as one of the permissible grounds. On the other hand a list can be interpreted as illustrative rather than exclusive. Thus, the failure of Congress expressly to include disobedience of a presidential order as a ground for removal does not necessarily rule it out. Moreover, it is not difficult to bring this ground of removal within the express terms of the statutes. A directive from the President requiring an officer to take an action otherwise within the officer's statutory discretion is a facially valid order. If the officer disagrees with the instruction, the proper course is resignation—a strategy that can impose considerable political costs on the President, as President Nixon discovered in the aftermath of the infamous "Saturday Night Massacre" in which the Attorney General and the Acting Attorney General resigned rather than comply with a presidential order to fire Special Prosecutor Archibald Cox. Because the President's order to an officer to take an action within the scope of the officer's discretion is a legally valid action, the officer's refusal to follow the order can easily be considered to be a form of "neglect of duty" or "malfeasance" for which removal is expressly provided under the terms of the statutes establishing purportedly "independent" agencies.[170]

---

[169]*E.g.*, 49 U.S.C. §11 (1982) (Interstate Commerce Commission) ("inefficiency, neglect of duty, or malfeasance in office"); 15 U.S.C. §41 (1982) (Federal Trade Commission) (same).

[170]Support for this approach is found in the majority opinion in *Bowsher*. The statute at issue in that case authorized Congress to remove the Comptroller for five specified grounds:

2. *Severability.* Even though the Court's power to save statutes through interpretation is very broad, there will remain cases where the text or legislative history unambiguously establishes that Congress intended to place strict limits on the President's removal authority. In such cases the constitutional analysis set forth above could mandate that the removal provision be struck down. Such a decision, however, would not necessarily disrupt ongoing agency powers, programs, or enforcement actions. Whether the other provisions of the agency's organic statute—establishing the agency, charging it with duties, and empowering it to take specified actions—would fall together with the removal provisions depends on whether these provisions are severable from the unconstitutional limitation of presidential removal. The severability inquiry, in turn, depends on whether Congress "would have enacted those provisions which are within its power, independently of that which is not."[171] Only if it is evident that the invalid provision is a but-for condition of the remaining provisions will the entire statute be declared invalid.[172]

In many cases the removal provision will clearly be severable from the remainder of the statute. In cases like *Wiener*, for example, the only indicia of legislative intent to establish an independent agency were the facts that Congress had vested the War Claims Commission with "quasi-judicial" powers and had specified a set term of office for its Commissioners. Where legislative intent to

---

disability, inefficiency, neglect of duty, malfeasance, and felony or conduct involving moral turpitude. Justice White, in dissent, contended that the statute permitted removal only for one of the five specified causes. 106 U.S. at 3211. The majority opinion rejected this analysis, finding it to be based on the "arguable" (*i.e.*, dubious) premise that "the enumeration of certain specified causes of removal excludes the possibility of removal for other causes." *Id.* at 3190. In support, the Court cited Shurtleff v. United States, 189 U.S. 311 (1903), an action for salary by an officer who had been summarily removed from office by President McKinley. The statute creating the office specified that the officer could be removed by the President for "inefficiency, neglect of duty, or malfeasance in office." 189 U.S. at 313. The Supreme Court held that the fact that the statute specified certain causes for removal did not exclude the President's right to remove for other causes. The *Bowsher* Court's approving reference to *Shurtleff* suggests that similar principles of interpretation may apply in the case of independent agencies.

[171]*Buckley*, 414 U.S. at 108, quoting Champlin Refining Co. v. Corporation Comm'n, 286 U.S. 210, 234 (1932).

[172]The more recent opinions seem to approve a presumption of severability. See Buckley, 424 U.S. at 108; *Chadha*, 462 U.S. at 931–35. But see Carter v. Carter Coal Co., 298 U.S. 238, 312 (1936) (in the absence of a severability provision the presumption is that the statute is not severable).

limit the President's removal authority is not clearly established either in the text of the statute or its legislative history, the requisite evidence of the importance of the removal limitation is lacking, and the statute should be deemed severable. In other cases, Congress will have expressly indicated its intent that if any provision of the statute is held unconstitutional the remainder will not be affected. Such severability provisions are routinely respected by the Court.[173] In still other cases the limitation of presidential removal will be express, and the act will contain no severability clause, but the legislative history will establish that agency independence was not a significant factor in the congressional consideration over the measure. In all these cases the standard rules on severability would dictate that if limits on the President's removal power are invalidated the only effect would be to strike out the objectionable part of the agency's organic statute.

What remains are a small number of difficult cases in which the legislative history clearly establishes that limitations on removal were an important part of the administrative scheme contemplated by Congress. It is unquestionable that there are such cases. As Marver Bernstein has observed, the legislative histories of several commissions "suggest that their enabling statutes might not have been enacted if Congress had not been able to delegate regulatory duties to agencies somewhat removed from continuing Presidential guidance. . . . [P]olitically speaking, some regulatory agencies would probably not exist at all if they were not independent."[174] In these hard cases the question will be whether there is sufficient evidence that the independence of the agency was indeed a sine qua non of the statute. Even here, however, the courts, reflecting a natural diffidence about broad-brush constitutional decisions, have tended to find statutes to be severable unless the contrary conclusion is irresistible.[175]

---

[173]See, *e.g.*, *Chadha*, 462 U.S. at 932. *Cf. Bowsher*, 106 S. Ct. at 3913 (fallback mechanism).

[174]Bernstein, note 145 *supra*, at 148–49.

[175]An extreme example is Consumer Energy Council of America, Inc. v. Federal Energy Regulatory Commission, 673 F.2d 425 (D.C. Cir. 1982), aff'd *sub nom.* Process Gas Consumers Group v. Consumer Energy Council of America, Inc., 463 U.S. 1216 (1983). The statute at issue in the case was so controversial that it took a conference committee ten months to work out a compromise bill, which then passed the House only by the narrowest of margins after its proponents gave assurances on the floor that agency rulemakings could be vetoed by either House of Congress. Despite the rather compelling evidence that the

It is of course true that a decision striking down limits on the President's removal authority would allow the President greatly to increase day-to-day White House control of agency operations, an eventuality that might disrupt ongoing programs at least in the short term. The disruption resulting from such a policy, however, would not be a necessary consequence of the constitutional ruling, but rather would result from discretionary actions by the President. Moreover, it would clearly be in the President's interest not to disrupt the functioning the executive branch through massive intrusion into traditional areas of agency discretion. In many cases the President can be expected to allow an official to remain in office until the conclusion of his or her statutory term, and even to reappoint officers initially placed in office by previous Presidents, without seeking to exert an unusual degree of influence over the officer's decisions. For example, despite the pronounced ideological differences between Presidents Reagan and Carter, President Reagan reappointed Federal Reserve Board Chairman Paul Volcker, a Carter appointee and, as head of the agency that regulates the nation's money supply, one of the most powerful officials in the government. It is unlikely that Presidents would use their removal power to destroy the functional independence of the Federal Reserve Board, since doing so would eliminate a convenient scapegoat for failed economic policies and would open the President to charges of manipulating the money supply during political campaigns.

G. CASES

Finally, it is useful to evaluate the implications of the Supreme Court's decisions on the removal power. *Myers v. United States*[176] was a suit for salary by a postmaster who had been summarily removed from office by the President. The plaintiff asserted that his firing was illegal because the President had failed to obtain Senate approval as required by the statute that established the

---

veto provision was important to the ultimate passage of the bill, the Court of Appeals found the provision to be severable, 673 F.2d at 440–45, a conclusion summarily affirmed by the Supreme Court.

Severability, however, cannot always be assumed. See, *e.g.*, Equal Employment Opportunity Commission v. Allstate Insurance Co., 570 F.Supp. 1224 (S.D. Miss. 1984), app. dismissed, 467 U.S. 1232 (1984); City of New Haven v. United States, 634 F.Supp. 1449 (D.D.C. 1986).

[176] 272 U.S. 52 (1926).

office.[177] Chief Justice Taft, a former President of the United States, upheld the President's action, finding that the statute in question was unconstitutional because it denied the President "the unrestricted power of removal."[178] To be sure, the President could not unilaterally direct the decisions of agencies established by Congress: some duties were "so peculiarly and specifically committed to the discretion of a particular officer as to raise a question whether the President may overrule or revise the officer's interpretation of his statutory duty in a particular instance."[179] And there might be duties "of a quasi-judical character" the discharge of which the President could not in a particular case influence or control.[180] But even in these instances, the President could remove the officer after the decision had been rendered, on the ground that the officer's discretion had "not been on the whole intelligently or wisely exercised."[181]

These *dicta* in *Myers* were much broader than what was needed to decide the case. The particular statute at issue required the consent of the Senate as a precondition to removal. Thus the case could have been decided on the narrow ground that the Senate does not have the power to advise and consent to removals—leaving open the important question whether Congress could debar the President from removing an officer without "cause." At the same time, the Court jumped rather too rapidly from its position that the Congress could not restrict the President's removal power to the holding that Myers should be denied his back pay. It would have been quite consistent to conclude that Congress, even though it does not have the power to restrict the President's power of removal, has at a minimum the power to guarantee that an official will receive his salary if removed. It was this issue—Myers's posthumous right to his salary—that was in dispute in the case; yet neither the massive opinion by Chief Justice Taft nor the dissents of Justices McReynolds, Holmes, or Brandeis gave any attention to this issue. The *Myers* opinion, by focusing on broad generalities, set the tone for the opinions that followed, which were similar in style of argument although quite different in philosophical orientation.

---

[177] *Id.* at 59.

[178] *Id.* at 176.

[179] *Ibid.*

[180] *Ibid.*

[181] *Ibid.*

The next case, *Humphrey's Executor v. United States*,[182] seemed to retract most of what the Court had said in *Myers*. Humphrey, a member of the Federal Trade Commission, was summarily removed by President Roosevelt on the ground that "your mind and my mind [do not] go along together on either the policies or the administering of the Federal Trade Commission."[183] Humphrey's executor brought suit in the Court of Claims for back pay between the time of his removal from office and his death. The matter came to the Supreme Court from the Court of Claims on two certified questions: whether the statute in question prohibited the President from removing Commissioners without cause; and whether the statute so construed was constitutional. Justice Sutherland, a former Representative and Senator, answered the questions in the affirmative.[184] In Sutherland's view, Congress intended "to create a body of experts who shall gain experience by length of service—a body which shall be independent of executive authority, *except in its selection*, and free to exercise its judgment without the leave or hindrance of any other official or any department of the government."[185] As to the constitutional question, Sutherland repudiated the broad dicta in favor of presidential authority in *Myers*, and limited the earlier opinion to "purely executive officers" such as postmasters.[186] The Federal Trade Commission, in contrast, "occupies no place in the executive department and . . . exercises no part of the executive power vested by the Constitution in the President."[187] Instead, it acts "as a legislative agency" and "as an agency of the judiciary."[188] To the extent that it exercises any executive functions, "as distin-

---

[182] 295 U.S. 602.

[183] *Id.* at 619. This statement was in a private letter from the President to Humphrey; the President's removal letter itself provided no grounds at all for the action. *Ibid.*

[184] All of the Justices except McReynolds joined Sutherland's opinion. McReynolds concurred in the result for the reasons stated in his dissenting opinion in *Myers*. On Sutherland's prior history, see Paschal, Mr. Justice Sutherland (1951). Despite his service in Congress, Sutherland appears to have come to his views on independent agencies rather late in life. While in Congress Sutherland bitterly opposed, on constitutional grounds, the bill to establish the Federal Trade Commission, see Cushman, note 17 *supra*, at 50; and even after coming to the Court he authored one of the most orthodox statements of the separation of powers doctrine ever written, see Springer v. Philippine Islands, 277 U.S. 189 (1928).

[185] 295 U.S. at 625–26.

[186] *Id.* at 628.

[187] *Ibid.*

[188] *Ibid.*

guished from executive power in the constitutional sense, . . . it does so in the discharge and effectuation of its quasi-legislative or quasi-judicial powers, or as an agency of the legislative or judicial departments of the government."[189]

Humphrey's Executor, as commentators have noted, is one of the more egregious opinions to be found on pages of the United States Supreme Court Reports.[190] It was nonsense to assert that the FTC did not act in an executive role. The Commission was, by its constitutive statute, instructed to prevent unfair methods of competition in commerce. To this end it was authorized to issue complaints setting forth charges of legal violations, to prosecute those charges in administrative proceedings, and to appeal for enforcement to the circuit courts of appeals.[191] These were law-enforcement functions of a quintessentially executive nature.[192] Moreover, Sutherland's description of the Commission as outside the executive branch of government was both confused and distorted. His analysis waffled between two inconsistent characterizations, one describing the Commission as an "agency" of Congress or the courts, the other describing its functions as "quasi"-legislative or "quasi"-judicial. If the Commission were an agency of Congress, then it would act in a purely legislative role, not one "softened with a quasi."[193] And the concepts of "quasi-legislative" and "quasi-judicial" themselves had no fixed content—a not-surprising consequence of the fact that the Constitution leaves no room for "quasi" anythings. The "quasi" rhetoric was merely a sophistical way of steering between the Scylla of viewing the Commission as an executive agency, and hence subject to unfettered presidential removal, and the Charybdis of viewing it as part of Congress or the Court, and hence unconstitutional on any number of other grounds.[194]

---

[189]*Ibid.*

[190]*E.g.*, Nathanson, Separation of Powers and Administrative Law: Delegation, the Legislative Veto, and the "Independent" Agencies, 25 Nw. L. Rev. 1064, 1101 (1981) ("unworkable and unsound"); Cushman, note 17 *supra*, at 173 ("extremely unsatisfactory"); Bruff, note 17 *supra*, at 479–80 ("unrealistic and oversimplified").

[191]295 U.S. at 620.

[192]See, *e.g.*, *Buckley*, 424 U.S. at 137; United States v. Nixon, 418 U.S. 683, 693 (1974); Confiscation Cases, 7 Wall. 454 (1869).

[193]Springer v. Philippine Islands, 277 U.S. 189, 210 (1928) (Holmes, J., dissenting).

[194]See FTC v. Ruberoid Co., 343 U.S. 470, 487 (1952) (Jackson, J., dissenting): "Administrative agencies have been called quasi-legislative, quasi-executive or quasi-judicial, as the

The exceptional weakness of the opinion can be attributed, at least in part, to the unusual circumstances of its creation. The case was decided in the thick of the bitter battle over the constitutionality of the New Deal. *Humphrey's Executor* may well have reflected reservations about the danger of overwhelming presidential power— a concern that had not inconsiderable force during the early days of the Roosevelt Administration. Within this context the idea of an independent agency had great appeal as providing a means of coping with the devastating economic conditions of the Depression without vesting excessive power in the President.

Humphrey's Executor has long been viewed as the fundamental constitutional charter of the independent regulatory commissions. This reading is, indeed, supported by the broad statements in the opinion. The dicta in *Humphrey's Executor* restricting presidential power are at least as expansive as were the pro-presidential comments in *Myers*. And there is no doubt that the intent of the Court was to sanction the constitutionality of agencies such as the FTC. But as in the earlier case the Court's broad statements were not strictly required by the facts. *Humphrey's Executor*, to be sure, presented the issues in an abstract context because of the nature of the questions certified to the Court. But the issue in *Humphrey's Executor* was not whether the President was disabled from removing a member of the Federal Trade Commission who had refused to comply with a presidential directive. The President had made no allegation that Humphrey had disobeyed any of his directives. Thus, *Humphrey's Executor* is not inconsistent with the thesis advanced in this article that the President must retain the constitutional authority to remove an officer who has failed to comply with a presidential directive to take an action otherwise within the officer's statutory authority.[195]

---

occasion required, in order to validate their function within the separation-of-powers scheme of the Constitution. The mere retreat to the qualifying 'quasi' is implicit with confession that all recognized classifications have broken down, and 'quasi' is a smooth cover which we draw over our confusion as we might use a counterpane to conceal a disordered bed."

[195]Indeed, on its facts the case can be read as raising no question of removal at all. A removal issue would have been presented had the plaintiff sought an injunction preventing his removal, or an order reinstating him to his position. Instead, the underlying dispute, as in *Myers*, was the right of Humphrey's estate to collect his back salary between the time he was fired and his death. There is, accordingly, some leeway for reading the opinion to hold merely that if Congress provides that a member of a regulatory commission may be removed only for cause, the officer has an action for salary if he or she is removed without cause.

The final case in this line is *Wiener v. United States*.[196] The petitioner had been summarily removed by President Eisenhower from his position on the War Claims Commission, a body established by Congress to adjudicate claims for harm inflicted by the enemy during World War II. He sued in the Court of Claims for back pay accrued between the time of his removal and the abolition of the Commission. The Supreme Court gave judgment to the petitioner in a unanimous opinion by Justice Frankfurter, holding that Congress had intended to limit the President's removal power, even though it had not said so explicitly in the statute establishing the Commission, and that this restriction on presidential power was constitutional, under *Humphrey's Executor*, because the Commission performed tasks of an "intrinsic [sic] judicial character."[197] The intent of the Court in *Wiener* was undoubtedly to reaffirm and even to extend the rule of *Humphrey's Executor*. But it is noteworthy, again, that the President stated no grounds for his removal of *Wiener*. The question whether the President could have removed Wiener for failing to follow a presidential directive to take an action within his statutory authority was simply not presented. Thus, *Wiener* also appears reconcilable with the position taken in this article.[198]

Last Term, in *Bowsher v. Synar*,[199] the Supreme Court ruled that the budget-cutting authority of the Gramm-Rudman Act could not constitutionally be vested in the Comptroller General, an officer removable by joint resolution of Congress. The case went off on the ground that Congress could not reserve removal authority over executive officials to itself, and accordingly the Court did not address the question of Congress' power to limit the President's removal

The possibility of reading *Humphrey's Executor* in this fashion is alluded to, but rejected, in Tribe, American Constitutional Law 4–9 (1978).

[196]357 U.S. 349 (1958).

[197]*Ibid*. at 385.

[198]Moreover, *Wiener*, like the two earlier cases, was a *post hoc* claim for salary. As such it did not directly address the President's power to remove the officer at all. That issue had been squarely raised in an earlier *quo warranto* proceeding brought by the petitioner, which challenged the makeup of the War Claims Commission under Eisenhower's replacement appointee. See *id*. at 351 n.*. But this claim was mooted with the abolition of the Commission. Thus, with respect to the constitutional aspect of the case, *Wiener*, like *Humphrey's Executor* before it, has the potential of being restricted in a subsequent case to the proposition that Congress could constitutionally guarantee the officer's right to salary in the event that he was removed by the President without cause.

[199]106 S.Ct. 3181 (1986).

authority. Indeed, Chief Justice Burger, writing for the Court, specifically stated that "no issues involving [independent] agencies are presented here."[200] As Justice White noted in dissent,[201] however, the status of independent agencies had been more or less squarely challenged by the Solicitor General in the brief of the United States.[202] And four of the Justices—Stevens, Marshall, White, and Blackmun—explicitly endorsed the power of Congress to limit the President's removal authority over members of independent agencies.[203] On the other hand, the silence of the remaining five Justices is perhaps not insignificant. The majority opinion could easily have joined the concurring and dissenting Justices in reaffirming *Humphrey's Executor* and *Wiener*. That it did not do so could support the inference that at least some of the Justices would be willing to reexamine those precedents in a future case.[204] Moreover, none of the Justices has indicated opposition to the limited proposition suggested in this article that Congress may not restrict the President's power to remove officers who have failed to follow a presidential directive to take an action within their statutory discretion.

V. Conclusion

The independent agency is a constitutional sport, an anomalous institution created without regard to the basic principle of

---

[200]*Id.* at 3188 n. 4.

[201]See 106 S.Ct. at 3206 (White, J., dissenting).

[202]See text at notes 34–36 *supra*.

[203]See 106 S.Ct. at 3195 (Stevens and Marshall, JJ., concurring in the judgment) ("it is universally accepted that [members of the Federal Trade Commission] are independent of, rather than subservient to, the President in performing their official duties"); *id.* at 3206 (White, J., dissenting) (Congress has power "to vest authority that falls within the Court's definition of executive power in officers who are not subject to removal at will by the President and are therefore not under the President's direct control."); *id.* at 3215 (Blackmun, J., dissenting). See also *Buckley*, 424 U.S. at 141 (affirming the rule of *Humphrey's Executor* in dictum).

[204]Chief Justice Burger's retirement removes a voice for executive authority from the Court. But President Reagan's replacement nominee, Antonin Scalia, shows every sign of being equally strong on presidential power. See, *e.g.*, Synar v. United States, 626 F. Supp. 1374 (D.D.C. 1986), aff'd, 106 S.Ct. 3181 (1986); To Renew the Reorganization Authority: Hearing before the Senate Committee on Government Operations, 95th Cong., 1st Sess. 50–51 (1977)(statement of Antonin Scalia). Scalia, like Chief Justice Rehnquist, is a former head of the Justice Department's Office of Legal Counsel, the office that formulates the legal defense of presidential and executive prerogatives.

separation of powers upon which our government was founded. Analysis of various factors bearing on the separation of powers analysis suggests that the President must have the power to remove policy-making officials of agencies, whether or not denominated as "independent," when the officials fail to follow a presidential instruction to carry out an action otherwise within their statutory discretion (or to refrain from carrying out an action when they enjoy discretion not to act). Although the President cannot personally take the action necessary to implement a statutory authority vested in particular agencies, the President can make his or her views known to the agency official and can remove the official if the ultimate decision is contrary to the President's instructions.

This conclusion suggests that the President must enjoy fairly broad powers to coordinate and guide the affairs of all federal agencies. It does not, however, necessarily resolve a number of important practical issues that have long simmered beneath the surface of the theoretical debate over independent agencies. For example, the fact that the President must have the power to remove agency heads for failing to obey presidential directives does not necessarily debar Congress from vesting litigating authority in agencies other than the Department of Justice. The issue of litigating authority is essentially a question of dividing governmental powers among executive agencies, a matter that has long been considered to fall largely within the discretion of Congress. Nor does a conclusion regarding removal necessarily imply that the President has the power to require White House clearance of communications to Congress, budget requests, or decisions to withhold or transmit information pursuant to congressional demand. These are practical questions that need to be addressed on their own terms rather than being lumped together with the logically separate question of removal.[205] Although the concept of the unitary executive tends to support a broad presidential power to centralize relations with Congress, the actual contours of that power would need to be explored in the context of an analysis of the specific matter at issue. In other words, once the misleading category of independent agencies is eliminated from legal thought, the next task is the particularized analysis of presidential powers over administrative agencies within the broad context of the theory of separation of powers.

---

[205]See Breyer & Stewart, Administrative Law and Regulatory Policy 123–26 (2d ed. 1985).

DAVID A. STRAUSS

THE MYTH OF
COLORBLINDNESS

Sometimes great slogans make bad law, or, more precisely, misunderstood law. For decades, colorblindness was the great slogan of the civil rights movement. That made it natural to believe that the movement's victories, such as *Brown v. Board of Education*,[1] established colorblindness as the central principle of the law governing racial discrimination. It was also natural for the notion of colorblindness to set the terms of the debate over affirmative action.[2]

Opponents of affirmative action, unsurprisingly, assert that *Brown* mandates colorblindness and that affirmative action is inconsistent with that mandate.[3] Proponents of affirmative action seem to be put on the defensive by the invocation of colorblindness. In general, they acknowledge that there is a tension between affirmative action and *Brown*'s prohibition against racial discrimination, but they insist

---

David A. Strauss is Assistant Professor of Law, The University of Chicago.

Author's Note: I am grateful to David P. Currie, Frank H. Easterbrook, Richard A. Epstein, Edwin S. Kneedler, Richard O. Lempert, Geoffrey P. Miller, Richard A. Posner, Stephen J. Schulhofer, Geoffrey R. Stone, and Cass R. Sunstein for their comments on an earlier draft. The Russell Baker Scholars Fund and the Bernard G. Sang Faculty Fund provided financial assistance for this project.

[1] 347 U.S. 483 (1954).

[2] By "affirmative action," I mean decisions based explicitly on race but justified on the ground that they help rather than hurt blacks. For the most part, I limit my discussion to affirmative action favoring, and racial discrimination against blacks; applying the arguments I make to groups other than blacks raises complex questions.

[3] See, *e.g.*, Bickel, The Morality of Consent 133–34 (1975); Abram, Affirmative Action: Fair Shakers and Social Engineers, 99 Harv. L. Rev. 1312 (1986); Van Alstyne, Rites of Passage: Race, the Supreme Court, and the Constitution, 46 U. Chi. L. Rev. 775 (1979).

that the tension can be adequately resolved, at least so that affirmative action is not always unconstitutional.[4]

Both approaches mistake a slogan for an analytical insight. The prohibition against discrimination established by *Brown* is not rooted in colorblindness at all. Instead, it is, like affirmative action, deeply race-conscious; like affirmative action, the prohibition against discrimination reflects a deliberate decision to treat blacks differently from other groups, even at the expense of innocent whites. It follows that affirmative action is not at odds with the principle of nondiscrimination established by *Brown* but is instead logically continuous with that principle. It also follows that the interesting question is not whether the Constitution permits affirmative action but why the Constitution does not require affirmative action.

Reduced to its simplest terms, my argument is as follows. The prohibition against racial discrimination prohibits—and must necessarily prohibit—the use of accurate racial generalizations that disadvantage blacks. But to prohibit accurate racial generalizations is to engage in something very much like affirmative action. Specifically, a principle prohibiting accurate racial generalizations has many of the same characteristics as affirmative action; and the various possible explanations of why accurate racial generalizations are unconstitutional lead to the conclusion that failure to engage in affirmative action may also sometimes be unconstitutional.

I

In *Palmore v. Sidoti*,[5] decided three Terms ago, the Supreme Court, unanimously and with no apparent difficulty, overturned a Florida state court decision that took custody of a white child away from the divorced mother when she remarried a black man. *Palmore* is a particularly good illustration of certain essential features of the prohibition against discrimination, features that are present in racial discrimination cases generally. But *Palmore* also shows that affir-

---

[4]See, *e.g.*, Ely, The Constitutionality of Reverse Racial Discrimination, 41 U. Chi. L. Rev. 723, 723–24 (1974); Sandalow, Preferences in Higher Education: Political Responsibility and the Judicial Role, 42 U. Chi. L. Rev. 653, 654–55 (1975); Greenawalt, Judicial Scrutiny of "Benign" Racial Preference in Law School Admissions, 75 Colum. L. Rev. 559 (1975). See also Brest, Foreword: In Defense of the Antidiscrimination Principle, 90 Harv. L. Rev. 1, 1–2, 16–23.

[5]466 U.S. 429 (1984).

mative action and nondiscrimination are, in important ways, the
same thing. On the one hand, what the Supreme Court did in
Palmore was plainly demanded by *Brown*; on the other hand, what
the Court did in *Palmore* is indistinguishable from affirmative action
in certain important respects. I am not suggesting at this point that
it is impossible to draw a commonsense distinction between affirmative action and nondiscrimination. But critics of affirmative action attack it on the ground that it causes innocent people to suffer,
and that instead of enforcing colorblindness, it draws attention to
race. *Palmore* shows that the prohibition against discrimination has
precisely these characteristics as well.

A

Linda and Anthony Sidoti are both white. When they were
divorced, Linda was awarded custody of their three-year-old daugh-
ter, Melanie. About eighteen months after the divorce, Linda mar-
ried Clarence Palmore, who is black. Anthony sued for custody of
Melanie in the Circuit Court of Hillsborough County, Florida.

Florida law required Judge Buck of the county court to apply
the traditional standard: he was to act in the best interests of the
child.[6] After hearing testimony, Judge Buck ordered that Anthony
be given custody of the child. Judge Buck apparently regarded
Anthony and Linda as equally fit parents. But he explained that
notwithstanding "the strides that have been made in bettering relations between the races in this country," racial prejudice was still
so pervasive, at least in central Florida, that a child raised by an
interracial couple was "sure" to "suffer from . . . social stigmatization." Because Melanie would be adversely affected if she were
raised in an interracial household, Judge Buck concluded that his
obligation to act in the best interests of the child required him to
divest Linda of custody and to award custody to Anthony.[7]

Although, as the Supreme Court noted, a child custody determination by an inferior state court is "not ordinarily a likely candidate for review by this Court,"[8] the Supreme Court granted certiorari, and, in a brief opinion delivered only two months after oral

---

[6]See 466 U.S. at 433.

[7]Appendix to Petition for Cert. at 26–27, Palmore v. Sidoti, No. 82-1734, O.T. 1982.

[8]See 466 U.S. at 431.

argument, unanimously reversed the Florida court. The Supreme Court did not question Judge Buck's factual conclusion that Melanie would suffer psychological harm if she were raised by an interracial couple. Nor could the Court reasonably have questioned that determination; after all, Judge Buck was far closer to the facts of life in central Florida, and his finding was entirely plausible. Indeed, the Court explicitly acknowledged that it was subjecting Melanie to potential psychological harm: "It would ignore reality to suggest that racial and ethnic prejudices do not exist or that all manifestations of those prejudices have been eliminated. There is a risk that a child living with a step-parent of a different race may be subject to a variety of pressures and stresses not present if the child were living with parents of the same racial or ethnic origin."[9]

The Court nonetheless thought it entirely clear that Judge Buck's decision had to be reversed:[10]

> The question . . . is whether the reality of private biases and the possible injury they might inflict are permissible considerations for removal of an infant child from the custody of its natural mother. We have little difficulty in concluding that they are not. The Constitution cannot control such prejudices but neither can it tolerate them. Private biases may be outside the reach of the law, but the law cannot, directly or indirectly, give them effect. . . .
>
> The effects of racial prejudice, however real, cannot justify a racial classification removing an infant child from the custody of its natural mother found to be an appropriate person to have such custody.

Considered from one angle, *Palmore* is the easy case that the Court thought it was. In other cases, the Court has refused to allow states to justify measures disadvantaging blacks on the ground that they were needed to avert evils that would be caused by private racial prejudice. In *Watson v. City of Memphis*,[11] for example, a city sought to delay the desegregation of its parks and recreational facilities on the ground that integration would lead to "interracial disturbances, violence, riots, and community confusion and turmoil";[12] the Court ruled that this was not an adequate justification.[13]

---

[9]466 U.S. at 422.

[10]*Id.* at 433–34 (footnote omitted).

[11]373 U.S. 526 (1963).

[12]*Id.* at 535.

[13]See also Wright v. Georgia, 373 U.S. 284, 293 (1963); Palmer v. Thompson, 403 U.S.

It is easy to see that this principle had to be established if *Brown* were not to become a dead letter. Desegregation was frequently disruptive, at least for a time. In some school systems the education of both black and white children was interrupted.[14] But if states could have invoked these harms—real as they were—as a reason for refusing to desegregate, *Brown* would have quickly unraveled. The Court relied on *Watson* when it decided *Palmore*. It is possible to distinguish the two cases, but the analogy is clear: Melanie's position is comparable to that of innocent white children whose education was disrupted by desegregation. If Florida may deprive parents of custody of a child because people acting out of racial prejudice will ridicule her, causing her psychological damage, then a state can exclude black children from schools on the ground that people (parents and children) acting out of prejudice will disrupt the schools, causing other children's education to be damaged. And if a state can do that, there is little left to *Brown*.

The principle of *Brown*, therefore, required the Supreme Court to reverse the Florida courts' decision in *Palmore*. At the same time, the reversal of the Florida decision was indistinguishable from affirmative action in important respects.

1. The principal argument used in litigation against affirmative action measures is that they violate the rights of innocent white victims.[15] The Court's decision in *Palmore* also created an innocent victim. Both by hypothesis and in fact, Melanie, the child, will suffer psychological harm because of the Supreme Court's decision that she would not have suffered if Judge Buck's decision had been allowed to stand. It will not do to brush this harm aside as speculative or insignificant: nothing in the Court's opinion suggests that it is either.

2. The Supreme Court in *Palmore* rejected an action—Judge Buck's decision—that was, in an important sense, colorblind and race-neutral. To understand why this is so, consider the matter from

---

217, 255–61 (1971) (White, J., dissenting). In Cooper v. Aaron, 358 U.S. 1 (1958), the Court acknowledged the disruptive effects that desegregation was having on the schools of Little Rock (*id.* at 15), but attributed the disruption to the authorities' resistance, not to desegregation itself. Buchanan v. Warley, 245 U.S. 60 (1917), is usually considered to be the first case in this series, but it is unclear whether the constitutional right involved in *Buchanan* was a right not to be subjected to racial discrimination or a right to alienate property. See, *e.g.*, *id.* at 74–75.

[14] See generally Orfield, Must We Bus? (1978); Graglia, Disaster by Decree (1976).

[15] See, *e.g.*, Brief for the United States as amicus curiae at 9–21, Wygant v. Jackson Bd. of Ed., 106 S.Ct. 1842 (1986).

Judge Buck's point of view. It was no part of the Supreme Court's reasoning that he was in any way prejudiced against blacks or interracial couples. The Court assumed that he had applied a race-neutral standard—the best interests of the child criterion—as straightforwardly and conscientiously as he could. In a custody dispute, the fact that a child will suffer psychological damage with one parent but not another is a highly material fact, and a judge would be derelict in his duty if he did not take that fact into account. Judge Buck, acting in a colorblind fashion, treated *Palmore* exactly like every other case: he took into account the prospective psychological damage to the child.

That, the Supreme Court told him, violated the Equal Protection Clause. In *Palmore*, unlike every other case, the Constitution required him to ignore that material fact. Why was he to ignore that fact? One can give a variety of refined and complex answers, but they all derive from one pivotal circumstance—*Palmore* involved a black person. Judge Buck could say, in his own defense, that the import of the Supreme Court's ruling is that he violated the Constitution by treating a case involving a black person in the same way he would have treated every other case.

Obviously, that statement is imprecise. The fact that a black person was involved is only part of the story. But one can make this argument—that Judge Buck acted in a colorblind fashion, and the Supreme Court held that race-conscious action was required— more rigorously and abstractly as well. Suppose we design a thought experiment in which a judge is literally blind to the races of the parties before him. In particular, suppose the only evidence to which a family court judge has access is a crystal ball that reveals nothing whatever about race. It only tells the judge what the future of every child will be under alternative arrangements. In a case like *Palmore*, Judge Buck's crystal ball will tell him that Melanie will be happier with her father than with her mother. The cause of her unhappiness will be related to race, but we are supposing that Judge Buck—being ignorant of everyone's race—does not know that; all his crystal ball allows him to know is that Melanie will be happier with her father.

Suppose further that on the same day that a case like *Palmore* comes before him, Judge Buck must also decide a case in which a divorced father seeks to regain custody of a child from a mother who remarried, say, a notoriously ruthless industrialist who had made many enemies among members of the local community. Judge Buck's crystal ball will look exactly the same in this case as it would have in *Palmore*. In each instance, he will see that allowing the mother to retain custody will be likely to cause the children to be ostracized by her peers and, as a result, to suffer psychological damage. In each case, therefore, Judge Buck will give the father custody of the child. When the mothers seek review in the Supreme Court, the mother who remarried the industrialist has no claim at all. But in a case like *Palmore*, the exact opposite is true: the Court would quickly and unanimously reverse Judge Buck, holding that he misunderstood a fundamental principle of the law of the Equal Protection Clause.

Judge Buck will surely be bewildered by the difference in the treatment of the cases. After all, they appeared absolutely identical to him: the crystal balls looked exactly alike. There is only one way that the Supreme Court will be able to explain its varying results to Judge Buck: the Court will have to introduce race into the picture. It will have to tell him that *Palmore* is different for some reason having to do with race. It will have to tell him that his error was that he did not take race into account. He made the mistake of focusing exclusively on his crystal ball, which revealed nothing about race. In other words, he should have been race-conscious. Judge Buck was colorblind; it was the Supreme Court that was race-conscious, and it held, in an important sense, that race-conscious action was constitutionally required.

3. The Court's justifications for its decision in *Palmore* closely resemble some of the standard justifications of affirmative action. Specifically, the Court seems to have relied on both (1) the unfairness of causing blacks (or those who associate with blacks, such as Linda Sidoti) to suffer disadvantages solely because others in society are prejudiced against them, and (2) the need to strike a blow against racial prejudice. But one common argument for allowing blacks with lesser credentials into universities, for example, is that their deficiencies were caused by racial prejudice—either prejudice against them or prejudice against their ancestors that had an adverse effect on them.

To make the parallel between *Palmore* and affirmative action more precise: In *Palmore* Florida disadvantaged a black on the basis of a race-neutral "best interests of the child" criterion. In the ordinary university admissions process, Florida disadvantages (that is, rejects) many black applicants on the basis of race-neutral admissions criteria. What Florida did in *Palmore* was unconstitutional because it made decisive a black person's disability—Palmore's inability to provide a psychologically healthy upbringing for the child—that was caused by racial prejudice in society as a whole. If blacks' deficiencies in undergraduate grades and standardized test scores are the causal product of racial prejudice in society as a whole, how does denying them admission differ from what Florida did in *Palmore*? Why isn't the application of a race-neutral admissions policy unconstitutional because, like the race-neutral "best interests of the child" criterion, it gives weight to disabilities that blacks genuinely have but that are the product of private prejudice?

The Court said that the Constitution required the result it reached in *Palmore* because "the law cannot, directly or indirectly, give . . . effect" to "[p]rivate biases." Doesn't the law "directly or indirectly give effect" to private prejudice when it allows disabilities caused by private prejudice to keep a person out of a state university? That is, doesn't *Palmore* require states to depart from race-neutral criteria—in other words, to engage in affirmative action—if following those criteria would allow blacks to suffer because of disabilities caused by private prejudice?

There are ways to distinguish the two cases. In one the prejudice is in the past; in the other it is in the future. In one we can be sure the disability results from prejudice; in the other we cannot be certain. In one it may have been prejudice against a person's ancestors, not the person himself, that ultimately affected the person's test scores and the like.[16]

But it is not clear why these distinctions should matter. If a state may not deny a person a benefit (custody of a child) because of a disability caused by prejudice against him, why may it deny him a benefit (admission to the university) because of a disability caused by prejudice against his parents or ancestors? Leaving aside problems of proof, why is that a constitutionally (or morally) relevant distinction? Similarly, why should it matter whether the prejudiced actions creating the disability occur after the government has denied the benefit, as in *Palmore*, or before, as in university admissions?

---

[16]For general discussion, see Schnapper, Perpetuation of Past Discrimination, 96 Harv. L. Rev. 828 (1983).

The problems of proof are greater, of course, in the university admissions case than in *Palmore*, since in *Palmore* prejudice is necessarily the only potential source of the disability. But problems of proof are not enough to place affirmative action in tension with nondiscrimination. Presumably the government should be allowed to defend a claim that affirmative action is constitutionally required in a particular case by showing that the claimant's disabilities are not the result of prejudice, but that is very different from saying that affirmative action is constitutionally suspect. In any event, even if all of these objections are accepted, it appears to follow from the logic of *Palmore* that an unsuccessful black applicant to a state university has a constitutional right to be admitted if he shows that the deficiencies in his credentials were the product of prejudice against him at some point during his life. That is a striking conclusion.

Similar points can be made about the argument that the decision in *Palmore* was necessary in order to combat racism or to keep prejudice from being legitimated. The notion that racists will read Judge Buck's decision and take heart seems a little implausible. It seems far more likely that they would take heart if extremely few graduates of the most renowned professional schools were black—the condition that would exist, according to some advocates of affirmative action,[17] if there were no affirmative action. It is true that decisions such as *Palmore*, and the aggregate visible consequences of such decisions, may have a healthy long-term educative effect. But it seems no more speculative to say, as the proponents of affirmative action do, that affirmative action will have such an educative effect by creating visible groups of successful blacks.

In sum, the Supreme Court's decision in *Palmore* declared that the colorblind application of a race-neutral standard was unacceptable. The Court ruled that benefits had to be given to blacks that would not be given to similarly situated whites (such as the industrialist). Such action was needed in order to prevent people from suffering the consequences of societal racial prejudice and to help bring about better race relations. These objectives warranted

---

[17]See, *e.g.*, Brief for Petitioner 31–32, Regents of the Univ. of California v. Bakke, 438 U.S. 265 (1978), in Kurland & Casper, eds., 99 Landmark Briefs and Oral Arguments of the Supreme Court of the United States: Constitutional Law 140–41 (1978).

inflicting real harm on an innocent victim. This sounds exactly like conventional affirmative action. And the Supreme Court said that the Constitution requires this result.

I am not suggesting that it is impossible to distinguish between affirmative action and what the Court did in *Palmore*. Nor am I claiming to have proved, at this point, that the Constitution requires affirmative action. But *Palmore* does show that affirmative action and nondiscrimination have much in common. Specifically, those aspects of affirmative action that its critics most frequently invoke are characteristics of the prohibition against discrimination as well.

B

Although *Palmore* and *Watson* are especially useful as illustrations, it would be a mistake to think that they are somehow anomalous and can be explained by a special rule. In some respects, the Florida courts' decision in *Palmore* is an example of what might be called "rational discrimination." The dual aspect of the Supreme Court's decision in *Palmore*—it is a necessary corollary of the prohibition against discrimination established by *Brown*, but it also has some of the most prominent characteristics of affirmative action—is generally found in cases involving rational discrimination.

"Rational discrimination," as I am using the term, is a generalization of the economists' notion of "efficient discrimination."[18] Using an explicit racial classification is "rational discrimination" if race is the best available proxy for some other characteristic that the government is unquestionably entitled to use as a basis for classifying people. In such cases, an explicitly racial classification is the best way to accomplish the government's legitimate objective.[19]

Suppose, for example, that as a matter of fact black teenagers between the ages of 17 and 21 are more likely to have automobile accidents than whites.[20] Leave aside for the moment why this is true; there is no reason to rule out the possibility that some such generalization might be true. Suppose further that this generalization continues to be true after every reasonably simple and cheap

---

[18]See, *e.g.*, Arrow, The Theory of Discrimination, in Ashenfelter and Rees, eds., Discrimination in Labor Markets 23–26 (1973).

[19]See Posner, The DeFunis Case and the Constitutionality of Preferential Treatment of Racial Minorities, 1974 Supreme Court Review 1, 10–11.

[20]I am indebted to Geoffrey R. Stone for this hypothetical example.

driver's examination is used to try to identify accident-prone young
drivers. Some very expensive means—perhaps round-the-clock videotape monitoring of all major highways—might enable the state
to identify all the bad drivers, both black and white, and leave on
the road all the good drivers, both black and white. But short of
such extraordinary measures—that is, so long as the categories are
defined in terms of age and the ability to pass examinations of the
conventional sort—a dramatic disparity between the accident rates
of black and white teenagers will remain.

In these circumstances, an unprejudiced legislature could decide
to establish a minimum age of 17 for white drivers and 21 for blacks.
It would reason as follows. Race is obviously a somewhat crude
basis for distinguishing between accident-prone (or "bad") and good
teenage drivers. Consequently, using race as a qualification for a
driver's license entails two kinds of costs: many whites who are bad
drivers will continue to get licenses, and many blacks who are good
drivers will be denied licenses. But, the legislature will reason,
virtually all legislative classifications are somewhat crude in this
way. Race does correlate somewhat with driving skill. And using
race as a basis for classification has one great advantage: it is cheap
and easy to ascertain someone's race. Each of the alternatives to
using race is more costly. Setting the minimum age at 17 causes
too many accidents. Setting the age at 21 prevents too many good
teenage drivers from obtaining licenses. Round-the-clock videotape
monitoring is too expensive.

In this way, it is possible for a legislature to establish an explicit
racial classification even though it is not motivated by anything that
would ordinarily be called racism or prejudice. Of course, it is
possible that the legislature's assessment of the costs and benefits
of classifying on the basis of race will be affected by prejudice or
some other racial element. In particular, the legislature might undervalue the harm done to blacks by denying them licenses until
they are 21 and overvalue the benefits conferred on whites by
allowing them to drive at 17. But this will not necessarily be the
case. The facts might be such that a government decision maker
wholly lacking in any racial bias would rationally choose an explicitly racial criterion as a means of achieving some legitimate
objective.

Indeed, the reasoning process I attributed to the legislature in
connection with race exactly parallels the process legislatures are

supposed to use for any classification. Substitute "age" or "the ability to pass a driver's examination" for race and all the statements might again be true—the proposed basis for classification is crude, but it might be the best one can do. It is possible that, in some instances, race may be as good a proxy as are age and the ability to pass a test in the case of the conventional driver's license statute.

It seems entirely clear, however, that no matter how rational and efficient it were, the overtly racial classification in the driver's license statute would be unconstitutional.[21] That is, it is well established that the prohibition against discrimination established by *Brown* extends to what I have called rational discrimination. A court's decision to strike down rational discrimination would be constitutionally required. But such a decision also has all the important characteristics of affirmative action.

First, there are innocent victims. The explicit racial classification was, by hypothesis, the best way to accomplish the government's legitimate objective—the way that imposed the least cost overall. When that classification is invalidated, the government decision maker will necessarily have to choose a more costly approach. Those additional costs will have to fall on someone. And that someone

---

[21]Since *Brown* the Supreme Court has never been faced with an explicit racial classification disadvantaging minorities that was justified in quite this way. That itself may be a significant datum: even at the height of massive resistance, when some states were trying every tactic to salvage Jim Crow (see, *e.g.*, Powe, The Road to Swann: Mobile County Crawls to the Bus, 51 Tex. L. Rev. 505 (1973)), states apparently did not try to argue that *Brown* would permit racial classification if race were a good proxy for other characteristics. The Court has interpreted the parallel antidiscrimination provision of Title VII of the Civil Rights Act of 1964 to prohibit explicit classifications on the basis of sex even when those classifications were based on indisputably accurate generalizations about male and female mortality rates. Arizona Governing Comm. v. Norris, 464 U.S. 1073 (1984); City of Los Angeles Dept. of Water & Power v. Manhart, 435 U.S. 702 (1978).

It is true that the Court has left open a safety valve; explicit racial classifications may be allowed in truly exigent circumstances. See Lee v. Washington, 390 U.S. 333, 334 (1968) (Black, Harlan, & Stewart, JJ., concurring). Korematsu v. United States, 323 U.S. 214 (1944), if it has not been wholly discredited, may fall in this category. But the Court has not undertaken a general assessment of the extent to which racial classifications are based on accurate generalizations. Only last Term, in Batson v. Kentucky, 106 S.Ct. 1712 (1986), the Court ruled that prosecutors may not exercise peremptory challenges on the basis of a generalization that "black jurors as a group will be unable impartially to consider the State's case against a black defendant" (*id.* at 1719); although the Court did not explicitly say so, its reasoning made clear that the truth of such a generalization would not be a defense. See also *id.* at 1723; *id.* at 1725 (White, J., concurring). See also *id.* at 1737–38 & n.5 (Burger, C.J., dissenting); *id.* at 1743–45 (Rehnquist, J., dissenting).

will have the same complaint as the typical white victim of affirmative action: why am I being sacrificed for the sake of some abstract ideal of racial progress?

In the driver's license hypothetical, the "innocent victims" of the court's decision to invalidate the rational racial classification will be (1) white teenage drivers, if the legislature responds by raising the age to 21 for everyone; (2) accident victims, if it responds by lowering the age for everyone, thereby allowing more accident-prone drivers on the road; or (3) the taxpayers, if the legislature adopts some more costly way of identifying bad drivers. The fact that the victims might be the taxpayers or those injured by accidents, instead of a group of whites who are in some sense in competition with the black beneficiaries, does not distinguish this case from affirmative action. In principle, at least, the burdens imposed by engaging in affirmative action can always be shifted.[22] A state university that sought to increase the percentage of black undergraduates above the level achieved by its customary (race-neutral) standards would have options parallel to those of the legislature. It might follow the familiar course of admitting more blacks and fewer whites, but it might also: (1) in principle, at least, compensate the whites to whom it denied admission for the value of the education of which they were deprived, thus shifting the costs to the taxpayers, or (2) use more lenient race-neutral selection criteria, thus expanding the size of the entering class until the percentage of blacks rose to the desired level.[23] That course would shift the costs to all the students and to society as a whole.

Second, although it sounds paradoxical, there is a sense in which a legislature's decision to adopt the racially explicit driver's license statute would be colorblind, and a court's overturning of that decision would be race-conscious. The legislature's decision is colorblind in the sense that it treats race exactly like any other characteristic. The court's decision is race-conscious because it singles out race as a special characteristic and forces people to become conscious of race in a way they would not otherwise be.

---

[22]See generally Fallon & Weiler, Firefighters v. Stotts: Conflicting Models of Racial Justice, 1984 Supreme Court Review 1, 54–55, 68.

[23]If this approach were used, the percentage of blacks in the class could not exceed the percentage of applicants, but few affirmative action plans are more ambitious than that. In addition, as black applicants' chances of being admitted improved, more would apply. The state could also spend public funds to recruit more.

Suppose we take, as our model for the truly colorblind actor, the proverbial person from Mars to whom racial discrimination is a totally alien concept—as bizarre as, say, discrimination on the basis of eye color, or discrimination on the basis of the day of the week on which one was born, would be to us. If we then showed the visitor from Mars the data about driving records, and the ease with which race can be ascertained, he would wonder why we did not allow the explicit racial classification. He would want to know what it is about race that makes us refuse to use it as a basis for classification even when it is rational to do so.

To put the point another way, suppose we discovered that some arbitrary characteristic, hitherto believed to be as irrelevant as eye color, correlated with an important ability. (Suppose, for example, that skill at certain video games turned out to correlate well with the ability to operate a newly invented computer.) We would consider it perfectly acceptable for the government to begin using that characteristic as a basis for classification. If we were really colorblind, like the visitor from Mars—if we really treated race in the same way as eye color—we would use race as a proxy for another, undoubtedly relevant characteristic whenever the correlation was close enough.

That is precisely what the legislature did when it passed the racially explicit driver's license law. It treated race like eye color, or like the ability to perform a seemingly arbitrary task on an examination. It used that characteristic or ability as the basis for a legislative classification to the extent that the characteristic correlated with an undoubtedly relevant characteristic or ability. When it did so, that legislature acted unconstitutionally. In other words, the legislature was constitutionally required to act in a fashion that did not treat race like eye color, even when doing so resulted in the creation of innocent victims.

Using Martians makes this point sound more artificial than it is. The fact is that the prohibition against racial discrimination makes people intensely race-conscious. That is because when race is involved, people must refrain from acting in the way they would act toward any comparable characteristic. If we are trying to escape "racial thinking," if we are trying to achieve a society in which people really are as unaware of each others' race as they are of eye color, the prohibition against discrimination is not the way to do it. At least, it is not the way to do it in the short run; one must defend it, as affirmative action is defended, as a long-term solution.

Consider the case of an employer engaged in hiring. Assume that all he wants to do is to make money. He has no desire simply to avoid working with the members of any group. On the basis of his experience, he has, more or less consciously, arrived at dozens of generalizations about who will make a good employee. People who look him in the eye during interviews generally do well. People who dress sloppily tend to be creative but not reliable. He has hired three sons from the Jones family and cannot wait to hire the fourth; but the two Smith scions he hired did not work out well and he will not hire another. Children who attended the X Recreation Center seem to be aggressive, competitive, and reliable; children who spent their time at the Y Recreation Center seem to be boastful and lazy. He is aware that all of these are crude overgeneralizations, but they are all he has and they seem to serve pretty well.

Suppose he concludes, on the same impressionistic basis, that people from a certain ethnic group just are not very reliable workers. If it were any other group, he would do what he always does: he would not hire any more of them. But because of the prohibition against discrimination, he cannot do that to this group. He must remind himself that members of this ethnic group are to receive different treatment from—in a sense, better treatment than—Smiths or Joneses or X's or Y's, because those other groups can be subjected to the usual process of generalization. If it were not for the prohibition against discrimination, he would gloss over ethnic background as just another arbitrary but occasionally useful characteristic. Because of that prohibition, he must stop himself short and single out ethnic background for special treatment. The effect of the prohibition against discrimination is to make him focus on ethnic background, not to make him blind to it.

c

The previous section argued that race-consciousness, not color-blindness, is the basis of the prohibition against discrimination. It might be suggested, however, that all I have shown is that rational discrimination should be permitted: since it is the prohibition against rational discrimination that introduces an element of race-consciousness, we can have a colorblind nondiscrimination principle if we just make it clear that rational discrimination is at least sometimes acceptable.

This suggestion is mistaken for at least two reasons. First, we do not have a choice between colorblindness and race-consciousness; we only have a choice between different forms of race-consciousness. Second, it can plausibly be argued that there is no principled way to distinguish between rational discrimination and the hard-core Jim Crow legislation that is unquestionably unconstitutional under *Brown*.

Employers engaged in hiring are not the only ones who generalize. People generalize constantly; that is, they observe that a person has one characteristic, and on that basis they infer that he has another. One cannot survive in the world without doing this.

Race is a very visible characteristic, and it correlates to some extent with other characteristics. Left to their own devices, people will notice the correlations and attribute characteristics to people on the basis of their race.[24] That natural and, under some circumstances, reasonable reaction is one kind of race-consciousness. But if people are precluded from engaging in generalizations of that kind, they will—like my hypothetical employer—be forced to be race-conscious in a different way: they will be aware that racial groups are entitled to different treatment from other groups, because in dealing with them one must alter one's usual patterns of generalizing about people.

The one option that is not open is the ideal of colorblindness— treating race as if it were, like eye color, a wholly irrelevant characteristic. That is because it is not a wholly irrelevant characteristic. Race correlates with other things: that is what forces on us the choice of either generalizing on the basis of race (and thereby being race-conscious in one way) or deliberately refusing to engage in the natural process of generalizing, and thereby being race-conscious in another way. Moreover, it is hardly surprising that race correlates with other things. Whatever the other possible causes of the correlation, centuries of discrimination explicitly based on race have

---

[24]*Cf.* Sandalow, note 4 *supra*, at 664: "The idea that black and white are equal, that race is not a meaningful category, did not begin to gain ascendency until well into the present century."

forced some characteristics on blacks—on all blacks, simply because they are black, since that was the basis of the discrimination.[25] In these circumstances it would be a miracle if a correlation between race and other characteristics did not exist. That correlation makes colorblindness unattainable, no matter what the legal rules.

The second reason that legalizing rational discrimination will not restore colorblindness to the prohibition against discrimination is that all forms of discrimination—including such classic Jim Crow measures as segregated schools and public facilities—can, arguably, be assimilated to rational discrimination. The most notorious forms of racial discrimination were rational in the sense that they were intended to accomplish some objective. Suppose, for example, that segregation were defended on the ground that it promotes peaceful race relations and the mental health of members of both races. No classification other than race, the defenders of segregation would say, can do the job: it is precisely because of the unique historical significance of race that classifying on that basis promotes harmony and stability.[26] It seems likely that any law requiring segregation could have been defended on this ground.[27]

Racial harmony and stability are unquestionably legitimate objectives. And it is difficult to see how a court could second-guess a state legislature's empirical judgment that segregation is the best way to achieve those objectives in its state. Because a court could not have questioned either the legitimacy of the objectives or the efficacy of the means, it would have had to regard any measure requiring segregation as an example of rational discrimination.

This is not just an abstract argument. There may be truly inadvertent legislative classifications,[28] but Jim Crow is not one. Segregation was maintained because those with political power believed that it promoted certain objectives. In some cases people may hon-

---

[25]See Wasserstrom, Racism, Sexism, and Preferential Treatment: An Approach to the Topics, 24 UCLA L. Rev. 581, 586–87 (1977); Fishkin, Justice, Equal Opportunity, and the Family 117 (1983). See also Fiss, Groups and the Equal Protection Clause, 5 Phil. & Pub. Aff. 107 (1976).

[26]See Kurland & Casper, eds., 49A Landmark Briefs and Oral Arguments of the Supreme Court of the United States: Constitutional Law 42–43 (1975) (oral argument of John W. Davis in Briggs v. Elliott, No. 101, O.T. 1953).

[27]*Cf.* Van Alstyne, note 3 *supra*, at 788–98.

[28]*Cf.* Schweiker v. Wilson, 450 U.S. 221 (1981).

estly have believed that it promoted the unquestionably legitimate objectives I mentioned.[29] In any event, it would take little ingenuity to cast the objectives in terms that make them legitimate.[30] Moreover, it is probably true that desegregation was destabilizing. Desegregation may in fact have caused psychological suffering to many people, including many blacks.

It goes without saying that there were many things wrong with segregation, just as there is something unacceptable about my hypothetical racially explicit driver's license statute. Yet there is also no reason to doubt that segregation, like that statute, could have been shown to be the most efficient way of promoting a certain constellation of undoubtedly legitimate state objectives (in the case of segregation, objectives having to do with harmony and stability). If that is true, then all discrimination is rational discrimination, as I have defined it; outlawing discrimination is always similar to affirmative action in the ways I have specified.

II

There remains an evident distinction between nondiscrimination and affirmative action. The prohibition against discrimination forbids what might be called racial generalizations—generalizations that impute a certain characteristic to people on the basis of their race. By contrast, affirmative action seems to involve the use of such generalizations. The true meaning of colorblindness, it might be argued, is not that race is to be treated like eye color or any ordinary characteristic: it is that racial generalizations, whether or not they are accurate, are forbidden.

In *Palmore*, the Florida courts relied on a racial generalization—that children of interracial households suffer psychological damage. My crystal ball hypothetical, the argument would go, does not adequately capture the notion of colorblindness because I allowed the crystal ball to reflect that generalization. My hypothetical driver's license statute obviously relies on a racial generalization, as does classic Jim Crow. And, this argument would continue, affirmative action also involves attributing characteristics to people on the basis of their race. Therefore, the argument would conclude, affirmative

---

[29]See Bickel, The Least Dangerous Branch 61–62 (1962).

[30]See generally Posner, The Economics of Justice 376–77 (1981).

action may or may not be unconstitutional, but it is easy to see why affirmative action is different from, and in tension with, the prohibition against discrimination: affirmative action relies on racial generalizations, but the point of the prohibition against discrimination is precisely to forbid racial generalizations.

There are two principal responses to this argument. First, it forfeits much of the rhetorical appeal of the notion of colorblindness. Second, if one tries to explain why it is that racial generalizations are unacceptable, one finds that no explanation supports the conclusion that affirmative action and nondiscrimination are in tension, and many explanations suggest that they are alike.

A

There is enormous appeal to the ideal of a society in which race is as insignificant a factor as eye color. The proponents of affirmative action must make the unexhilarating argument that we must depart from that ideal for a time in order to reach it ultimately. The advocates of colorblindness respond in effect: we should live our ideals now.[31]

If I am right that the prohibition against discrimination is not an embodiment of this ideal of race-blindness, then this is a fallacious argument. The prohibition against discrimination is itself a measure we have adopted because if we tried to live the ideal—if we tried to treat race like eye color—unacceptable results would occur. It is a race-conscious measure—in the sense that it treats race differently from other characteristics—that we have adopted precisely to get beyond racism. And, as I have argued, it does not suppress the consciousness of race; it may even heighten it.

The prohibition against discrimination reflects a decision to give special treatment to race in order to deal with a serious social problem. It is a matter not of putting the entire problem behind us but of self-consciously maintaining an artificially neutral attitude toward race—an artificial refusal to generalize that we do not maintain with respect to any other characteristic—in order to deal with the problem.[32] Similarly, one cannot attack affirmative action on the

---

[31]See, *e.g.*, Van Alstyne, note 3 *supra*, at 809 ("one gets beyond racism by getting beyond it now").

[32]*Cf.* Bollinger, The Tolerant Society (1986).

ground that it reduces the question to one of "whose ox is gored,"[33] because the prohibition against racial discrimination is itself a matter of whose ox is gored. The Constitution does not require that innocent people suffer in order to combat prejudice against industrialists.

B

The more fundamental answer is that it is not enough simply to assert that racial generalizations are the problem. One has to explain why generalizations based on race are so unacceptable, even if they are accurate, and even though generalizations based on other characteristics—including generalizations based on apparently arbitrary characteristics—would raise no problem whatever.[34] The explanations that have been offered generally fall into familiar categories. Some assert that measures based on racial generalizations are unacceptable because there is an impermissible danger that they are tainted by racial prejudice. Others emphasize the harmful effects that such measures have on certain groups in society or on society as a whole. Each of these theories, however, either does not explain why the prohibition against discrimination exists or does not explain why that prohibition is different from affirmative action.

1. *The danger of racial prejudice.* Different theories emphasize the different ways in which, they assert, prejudice will influence any measure that is based on a racial generalization. Some theories emphasize the danger of inaccurate stereotyping; they assert that the problem with measures based on racial generalizations is that they tend to be based on inaccurate factual premises about the characteristics of different racial groups.[35] Other theories emphasize the danger that prejudice will affect the way in which the decision maker weighs the interests of the various groups. When a decision maker uses a racial generalization, these theories hold, he is likely to undervalue the benefits, and to be insufficiently sympathetic to the burdens, that a measure places on racial groups other than his own.[36] Other theories contend that measures based on explicit racial

---

[33]See Bickel, note 3 *supra*, at 133.

[34]See Lempert, The Force of Irony: On the Morality of Affirmative Action and United Steelworkers v. Weber, 95 J. Ethics 86, 88–89 (1984).

[35]See, *e.g.*, Ely, Democracy and Distrust, 156–60 (1980).

[36]See, *e.g.*, *id.* at 156–62; Brest, note 4 *supra*, at 7–8 (discussing "racially selective sympathy and indifference").

generalizations are too likely to reflect a decision to promote private preferences at the expense of the public interest.[37] Finally, opponents of affirmative action assert more generally that there is a danger of abuse, *i.e.* a danger that any racial generalization will be used as a vehicle of prejudice.[38]

a). To the extent these theories assert that racial generalizations are unacceptable because there is too great a danger that they will be factually inaccurate—for example, because they are based on inaccurate stereotypes—the theories miss the point of the prohibition against discrimination. If the prohibition against discrimination were based on the danger that racial generalizations tend to be overgeneralizations, states would be allowed to defend racial generalizations by showing that they are in fact accurate and are not overgeneralizations. Statements in the Court's opinions suggest that this is the law: that racial classifications are not always unconstitutional and need only be shown to be necessary to the promotion of a compelling state interest.[39]

It is quite clear, however, that this is not the way the prohibition against discrimination operates. Apart from the safety valve that the Supreme Court has left open for truly exigent circumstances, the Court has shown no interest in investigating the accuracy of racial classifications.[40] *Watson* establishes that accuracy is not a defense in that line of cases, and any other conclusion would have reduced *Brown* to a form of words. It is quite clear that accuracy would not be a defense in my driver's license case. And in *Brown* and other cases dealing with classic Jim Crow laws, the Court was not the least bit concerned with the accuracy of the racial generalization—that is, it was not at all concerned with whether the racial classifications actually promoted stability and order or any other state objective.

---

[37]Sunstein, Naked Preferences and the Constitution, 84 Colum. L. Rev. 1689, 1711–13 (1984); Sunstein, Public Values, Private Interests, and the Equal Protection Clause, 1982 Supreme Court Review 127.

[38]See, *e.g.*, sources cited in note 3 *supra.*

[39]See, *e.g.*, Loving v. Virginia, 388 U.S. 1, 11 (1967); McLaughlin v. Florida, 379 U.S. 184, 196 (1964).

[40]See page 110 and note 21 *supra*; Posner, note 19 *supra*, at 21. In *Palmore*, for example, the Court recited that racial classifications may be upheld only if they are necessary to the accomplishment of a compelling purpose (466 U.S. at 432–33), but undertook no inquiry into whether the Florida court's factual conclusions were correct. Indeed, the Court suggested that those conclusions were correct. *Id.* at 433; see page 102 *supra*. And the Court certainly did not suggest that protecting the child's psychological well-being was not a sufficiently important interest.

In addition, it seems irrational to argue that the danger of inaccuracy is so great that we need a broad prophylactic rule prohibiting all racial generalizations. As I have noted, some racial generalizations are likely to be accurate; if nothing else, centuries of racial discrimination have ensured that blacks will tend to have certain characteristics in common. And there is no reason to believe that courts are so unable to determine whether a particular generalization is accurate; courts assess the accuracy of legislative generalizations in other contexts.[41]

Moreover, if accuracy is the only reason for prohibiting explicit racial classifications, it makes no sense to pay the price of discarding every accurate racial generalization solely in order to avoid the inaccurate ones. Whenever an accurate racial generalization is invalidated, the decision maker will, by hypothesis, be forced to use some less accurate ground for classifying people. If the reason for our hostility to racial generalizations is solely the danger that they are inaccurate, then, other things equal, we should view the cost of invalidating an accurate racial generalization as the same as the cost of upholding an inaccurate racial generalization: in both cases, the decision maker will end up using a less accurate generalization than it should. Under these circumstances, it is clearly irrational to make all our mistakes in the direction of invalidating accurate racial generalizations.

What this discussion shows, and what the Court's opinions reveal, is, of course, that accuracy is not the point of the prohibition against discrimination. The cost of upholding an inaccurate racial generalization is something much more than the cost of upholding an inaccurate generalization of some other kind. Something else is wrong with racial generalizations besides the danger that they might be inaccurate. One still has to identify what that something else is and to explain why the same thing is not wrong with, say, a race-neutral admissions policy that excludes almost all blacks from a state university.

b). Theories that condemn explicit classifications on the ground that they are likely to reflect prejudice ultimately fail to explain why affirmative action is in tension with nondiscrimination. Moreover, these theories lead to the conclusion that affirmative action is sometimes constitutionally required. To make this show-

---

[41]See, *e.g.*, Craig v. Boren, 429 U.S. 190, 200–04 (1976).

ing requires two steps. First, the danger that prejudice has affected the decision to adopt a statute is a function not of the language of the statute but of its effects. If, as these theories assert, explicit racial classifications are suspect because of the danger that they reflect prejudice, then any measure with racially disproportionate effects must, for the same reason, also be somewhat suspect. Second, if measures with disproportionate racial effects are suspect for the same reason as explicitly racial classifications, then there is no sharp distinction between nondiscrimination and affirmative action.

i). All of the theories that I am now considering—theories that assert that racial classifications are suspect because of the danger that they reflect prejudice—err in assuming that prejudice emerges only when a legislator uses an explicit racial classification. This assumption is another incarnation of the myth of colorblindness: legislators are innocent of racial prejudice until someone drafts a statute in racial terms. The explicit mention of race precipitates the fall from the paradise of colorblindness.

In fact, the danger of prejudice is a function of the (foreseeable) effects of a measure, not of its explicit language.[42] If a person is prejudiced against black people, his prejudice will manifest itself whenever he deals with a black person. It follows that if a legislator is prejudiced, his prejudice will manifest itself whenever he votes on legislation affecting black people, at least so long as he knows it affects them. If, for example, he has—as one theory holds—a tendency to be insufficiently sympathetic to the burdens placed on blacks, this tendency will manifest itself whenever legislation places burdens on blacks. Whether the explicit terms of the legislation happen to mention blacks is immaterial.[43]

In general, legislators are concerned with the effects of statutes, not their explicit wording. The language is relevant only because it determines the effects; in general, legislators will be indifferent between two statutes with identical effects even if they are worded differently. If a legislator's evaluation of his black constituents' in-

---

[42]Because a decision maker will almost certainly be able to foresee the effects of a measure that has a significant disproportionate impact, I will generally refer only to the effects of a measure without specifying that I mean its foreseeable effects.

[43]*Cf*. Sunstein, note 37 *supra*, at 149–50 (classifications that "target[] a racial problem" present the same concerns that are raised by explicit classifications).

terests is tainted by prejudice, it will be tainted whenever his black constituents are interested. That will happen even when their race is not explicitly mentioned.

One qualification is in order at this point. If a measure affects blacks and whites to the same extent—*i.e.* if it does not have racially disproportionate effects—then there is much less reason to be concerned that it reflects racial prejudice. Such a measure cannot reflect a desire to harm blacks relative to whites, since by hypothesis it harms them both equally. And the political process is likely to deter a legislator from supporting such a measure because of his unfair stereotypes about blacks or insufficient sympathy with their interests. Since such a measure will burden everyone to the same extent that it burdens blacks, everyone will react as if he had been the victim of an unfair stereotype or insufficient sympathy, and the legislator will pay the political price. But when a measure has racially disproportionate effects, this political check does not operate to the same degree. There is accordingly a danger that the measure reflects a desire to harm blacks relative to whites. This will be true whether or not the measure uses an explicitly racial classification.

It might be argued that if there is no explicit racial classification in proposed legislation, it will not occur to legislators to think that some of those affected are black. Only the explicit mention of race, it might be said, will trigger that thought and give rise to prejudice. This argument is incorrect for three reasons. First, it is inconsistent with the premise that legislators tend to be prejudiced. It is precisely the nature of a prejudiced person that he reacts to a person's race whether or not the objective facts invite him to do so. This is especially true in the case of one of the most plausible theories of why legislators' prejudice makes racial generalizations unacceptable, the theory that legislators tend to discount or overlook the burdens placed on racial minorities because those minorities are "invisible."[44] It is sometimes suggested, for example, that legislators do not act to remedy the condition of black ghettos because they tend unconsciously to overlook the problems of blacks in a way that they would not overlook the problems of whites. If this is the kind of prejudice with which we are concerned, it is quite clear that an explicit classification is not needed to trigger it.

---

[44] See, *e.g.*, Brest, note 4 *supra*, at 14–15.

Second, if, as these theories posit, decision makers are susceptible to prejudice, one should expect those who are trying to influence them to appeal, as subtly as necessary, to that prejudice. In any legislative contest, it will be to someone's advantage to trigger the legislator's presumed prejudice by pointing out the racial implications of the proposed measure. For example, if these theories are correct in their assessment of the prevalence of prejudice among legislators, proponents of a measure that has a disproportionately harmful impact on blacks can be expected to use that fact as an argument in favor of the measure. It obviously will not matter whether the measure is explicitly racial. These appeals may be very indirect, but one has to assume that, if they are likely to be effective, they will be made. The premise of these theories is that such appeals are likely to be effective.

Finally, as I argued in showing why colorblindness is a chimera, people will think in racial terms as long as race remains so visibly correlated with other characteristics. As long as so many blacks occupy a distinctive social position, any legislation that calls that position to mind is likely to cause legislators to notice that they are black. The legislators' prejudice, if any, will operate. They will not, as a general matter, need an explicitly racial statute to remind them.

A few commonplace examples help to make the point. According to the theories I am considering, my hypothetical driver's license statute is unconstitutional because of the danger that legislators, acting out of prejudice, undervalued the interests of black teenagers or viewed them as worse drivers than they really are. Suppose the same legislature then considers a bill, making no mention of race, that reduces taxes for the well-to-do, who are disproportionately white, while also reducing levels of welfare payments to a group that is (and is known to be) disproportionately black. If the legislature's reaction to the driver's license statute was prejudiced, then its reaction to this proposal will be prejudiced as well, although perhaps not to the same extent. If the legislators are inclined to undervalue the interests of blacks, they will do so in both cases. If they are inclined to indulge in the stereotype that blacks are irresponsible, that stereotype will affect both decisions. The same will be true of any measure concerning unemployment, or of policy toward inner cities, or of the criminal justice system: the mere fact that the measure is race-neutral on its face provides no assurance that it is not affected by racial prejudice. If the decision of an all-white suburb on a (race-neutral) zoning variance for a mostly black public housing project does not trigger racial prejudice, nothing will.[45]

It is very difficult to say which kind of decision is more likely to be affected by prejudice. The answer depends on empirical speculations about the nature of the prejudice involved. If the "prejudice" takes the form of a conscious desire to harm blacks, then explicit racial classifications should be the most suspect measures, because they are the most efficient way to harm blacks and not whites. But this conclusion that explicit generalizations may be the most suspect measures does not undermine my argument that the danger of prejudice is a function of the effects, not the language, of a statute. Indeed, it follows from that argument: the reason that explicit classifications may be especially suspect is that no other measure has a more starkly or permanently disproportionate effect than an explicit racial classification. For that reason, explicit classifications are an especially effective means of expressing the most blatant form of prejudice.

It can also be argued, however, that explicit racial classifications should be less suspect than other measures that have a disproportionate effect. Today, at least, it seems doubtful that prejudice generally takes the form of a conscious desire to harm blacks. Moreover, in the current climate of opinion, explicit, overt racial statements are not very acceptable. This is a result not just of legal rules but of social mores as well. Consequently, government decision makers, like everyone else, are not likely to make an explicitly racial statement unless they are sure that the statement does not reflect bias. For the conscientious government decision maker, an explicit racial classification will raise a warning flag—he will be aware of the danger of bias, and he will examine the evidence and his own thought processes closely to be sure that they have not been colored by prejudice.[46] No comparable warning flag is raised by, for ex-

---

[45]See Village of Arlington Heights v. Metropolitan Housing Development Corp., 429 U.S. 252 (1977).

[46]*Cf.* Sunstein, note 37 *supra*, at 142–43 (suggesting that an explicit classification raises a warning flag for courts). In addition, if a decision maker is not conscientious but is trying to injure a particular racial group, he has every reason to conceal his intention by not using an explicit classification; so again, it can be argued that explicit classifications are less suspect than other measures with a severely disproportionate impact.

ample, explicitly race-neutral actions that have a severe adverse
effect on blacks. As a result, prejudice may be more likely to play
a role when an explicitly race-neutral measure is adopted than when
a racially explicit measure is adopted and everyone is on guard
against racial bias.

ii). The crucial point is that according to the logic of these theories, disproportionate effects should be what make a measure suspect, because the danger of prejudice is a function of disproportionate effects. Explicit classifications are suspect—arguably, but
not certainly, especially suspect—only because of their dramatically
disproportionate effects. The logical implication of these theories
is that a legislature has an obligation to avoid, or to provide a special
justification for, any measure that has disproportionate effects. The
requirement that it avoid (or provide a special justification for) explicit classifications is a special case of that obligation.

Thus, according to these theories, our hostility to explicit classifications—however strong it is—derives from a more general hostility to measures that have disproportionate effects. It is easy to
see that "hostility to measures with disproportionate effects" is the
same as "hostility to measures that fail to engage in affirmative
action": to the extent that a legislature must ensure that its measures
not only are neutral on their face but have proportionate effects, it
must engage in affirmative action.[47]

It therefore is fair to say that the theories asserting that racial
generalizations are unacceptable because they reflect prejudice treat
explicit classifications and the failure to engage in affirmative action
as different points on the same continuum. Both are suspect and
for the same basic reason. The degree to which they are suspect
may differ. But this is very different from saying that they are in
tension. Moreover, these theories lead to the conclusion that on
some occasions, failing to engage in affirmative action—that is,
enacting a measure with disproportionate effects—will have at least
some of the same constitutional difficulties as an explicit racial
generalization. Since the latter are generally unconstitutional, the
former will at least sometimes be unconstitutional as well.

In sum, it is a necessary implication of these theories that (1)
explicit racial classifications and the failure to engage in affirmative

---

[47]See, *e.g.*, Ely, Legislative and Administrative Motivation in Constitutional Law, 79 Yale
L. J. 1205, 1260 (1970).

action are constitutionally questionable for the same basic reason; and (2) although there may be more reason to be suspicious of explicit classifications, there will be some occasions when the failure to engage in affirmative action will also be constitutionally suspect.

2. *Stigma*. The most frequent explanation of why racial generalizations are unacceptable is that they are stigmatizing. The notion of stigma is obviously amorphous. The idea roughly is that racial classifications brand people as inferior, undermine their self-respect, and exclude them from society.[48]

Since even accurate racial generalizations are unacceptable, this theory must hold that even accurate racial generalizations stigmatize people. (Otherwise, some other theory is needed to explain why accurate racial generalizations are unacceptable.) If accurate racial generalizations stigmatize people, then why does not a race-neutral policy that has the effect of disadvantaging a disproportionate number of black people equally stigmatize them? In both cases, people are being branded as inferior. In both cases, that message is in some sense "true." It is difficult to see why they are not equally stigmatizing.

Compare a driver's license statute that contains, among other things, my hypothetical racial restriction, with a state university's race-neutral admissions policy that has the effect of excluding virtually all black applicants because their scores are too low. Why is the admissions policy any less stigmatizing than the clearly unconstitutional, explicitly racial driver's license statute? Both have the effect of excluding blacks from a social benefit. Both exclude some whites as well, if one takes into account the entire set of driver's license qualifications. Both convey the message that blacks are not good enough to achieve the benefit in question. In both cases the determination that blacks are not "good enough" was made by reference to race-neutral objectives. Under those criteria, the determination in both cases was accurate. The only difference between the two cases is that in the admissions case, it happens that another easily applied, reasonably accurate proxy was available— test scores—so that the decision maker did not have to use race as

---

[48]See, *e.g.*, Black, The Lawfulness of the Segregation Decisions, 69 Yale L. J. 421 (1960); Karst, Foreword: Equal Citizenship under the Fourteenth Amendment, 91 Harv. L. Rev. 1 (1977); Brest, note 4 *supra*, at 8–12.

a proxy. But the fact that there happened to be another proxy more useful than race is only a fortuity. It is unclear why it should have any effect on how stigmatizing the measure is.

It follows that if stigma is the vice that the prohibition against discrimination is intended to combat, a race-neutral admissions policy that excludes (for simplicity's sake) all black applicants from a state university is to be treated in the same way as an accurate racial generalization. Since the Constitution requires a state to refrain from using such generalizations, the Constitution must also require a state to deviate from its race-neutral policy in a way that makes it more favorable to blacks—that is, to engage in affirmative action.

It is certainly counterintuitive to conclude that explicitly neutral policies that exclude blacks are as stigmatizing as explicitly exclusionary policies. But it is not very easy to articulate answers to this argument. Perhaps the explicit use of race has historical connotations that make it especially damaging, even if race is being used as an accurate proxy. There may be some value in having the racial generalization remain officially unspoken, even when a dramatically disproportionate impact betrays the accuracy of the generalization. The use of individual assessments, even where a racial generalization would be valid, increases the incentive of black potential applicants to improve themselves, since an individual can gain admission on merit without waiting for improvement by others to invalidate the generalization. But these arguments establish, at most, only a difference of degree between explicit generalizations and failures to engage in affirmative action. If explicit generalizations are stigmatizing, then some failures to engage in affirmative action must be at least somewhat stigmatizing. Again, there is no reason to conclude that affirmative action and nondiscrimination are in tension, and it is difficult to explain why affirmative action is not, at least sometimes, constitutionally required.

3. *Clarity.* The opponents of affirmative action generally emphasize, in one way or another, the clarity of a rule that forbids all racial generalizations. They often argue, for example, that if we allow any racial generalizations, it will be too difficult to determine which ones we should allow. How can we determine whether a generalization helps or hurts a minority group? Even among the various groups that can claim to be minorities, which should be

allowed to claim the benefits of racial generalizations?[49] They also assert that the prohibition against discrimination will lack moral authority if it is not extended to forbid all racial generalizations.[50] And Judge Posner has argued that a principle that permits some racial generalizations will necessarily allow judges too much discretion.[51]

These arguments have been thoroughly explored by others,[52] and there is no need to recapitulate. I will confine myself to a trying to show that these theories, too, are not inconsistent with my view that affirmative action is akin to, not in tension with, nondiscrimination. The claim that only a principle prohibiting all racial generalizations has the necessary moral authority seems imprecise and problematic. If this means that only such a principle is correct, then it merely states the conclusion. If it means that a principle permitting some affirmative action will be too divisive, then it rests on speculative empirical premises. It seems equally plausible to accept analogous empirical premises suggesting that affirmative action is constitutionally required—for example, that it is divisive and harmful to society to exclude nearly all blacks from important social institutions and benefits, even when the exclusion is the product of race-neutral criteria.

The other arguments generally do not deny that affirmative action has worthwhile objectives, but they assert that once we begin to engage in affirmative action the line-drawing problems become insuperable. They assert, for example, that there is no principled way of distinguishing between affirmative action for blacks and affirmative action for other minorities; between racial classifications that help minorities and those that hurt them; between affirmative action that only helps minorities and that which hurts one minority in the course of helping another; and so on.

Others have suggested that these difficulties have been overstated.[53] One might add that if the objectives of affirmative action are worthwhile and the problem is only one of line-drawing, there

---

[49]See, e.g.,Glazer, Affirmative Discrimination 198–204 (1975); Van Alstyne, note 3 supra, at 797–98, 804–08.

[50]See, e.g., Bickel, note 3 supra, at 133; Wilkinson, From Brown to Bakke 291–94 (1979).

[51]Posner, note 19 supra, at 21–26.

[52]See, e.g., Brest, note 4 supra, at 21–22; Sandalow, note 4 supra, at 663–81.

[53]See sources cited in note 52 supra.

is no reason to believe that drawing the line at a prohibition of all racial generalizations is the best way to proceed. Other lines might serve our purposes better. For example, while it is true that other minorities have been victims of discrimination, it seems clear that discrimination against blacks has played a unique role in our history. If we simply need to draw a reasonable line, why not distinguish affirmative action for blacks from affirmative action for other groups? There is no doubt a danger that some measures purporting to be affirmative action might actually injure blacks, but surely it is significant that every affirmative action case before the Supreme Court has been brought by a white. While certain affirmative action plans may have a disproportionate impact on certain other minorities, it is rare for an affirmative action plan to involve explicit discrimination against other minorities;[54] for the reasons I have noted, the opponents of affirmative action cannot assert that disproportionate impacts alone are troublesome without undermining their entire position.

My principal point, however, is that arguments emphasizing the difficulty of drawing lines are, in a fundamental way, not inconsistent with my suggestion that affirmative action may sometimes be constitutionally required. That is because they concern the difficulties of administration rather than the underlying purposes of the Equal Protection Clause. One can illustrate this point by examining Judge Posner's view. Judge Posner argues that any principle other than a prohibition against all racial generalizations would allow judges to impose "their personal values,"[55] which would be inconsistent with the premises of democratic government. I will assume, for the moment, that this is true.

In order to see why this argument does not implicate the purposes of the Equal Protection Clause, suppose that there were no institution of judicial review. The Constitution would, of course, still limit legislators. Judge Posner's argument about the need to confine judicial discretion would not apply, since it is premised on the concern that courts will usurp the prerogatives of the democratic branches of government. The legislature would have to decide what the Equal Protection Clause required it to do. The Clause clearly prohibits rational discrimination against blacks. If the theories that

---

[54]*Cf.* United Jewish Organizations v. Carey, 430 U.S. 144 (1977).

[55]Posner, note 19 *supra*, at 25.

explain why rational discrimination is unlawful lead to the conclusion that affirmative action is required, then the legislature would be constitutionally obligated to engage in affirmative action. Thus, Judge Posner's theory, like the other theories that assert that only a principle barring all racial generalizations is sufficiently clear to be adopted by a court, is directed toward the difficulties of judicial administration, not toward the underlying purposes of the Equal Protection Clause. It is, at a fundamental level, compatible with my view that those principles may require affirmative action in some instances.

Of course, in a world with judicial review, any affirmative action measure taken by a legislature will not survive unless the courts can apply some standard that upholds it. I suggested above that there are judicially administrable rules that would permit a court to uphold an affirmative action measure that favors blacks. If that suggestion is correct, then there is no barrier to saying that the Constitution requires legislatures to take such measures—although it may be an obligation that the legislature must enforce against itself.

III

A

What this discussion principally demonstrates is the error of thinking that the law governing racial discrimination can be captured in a simple, comforting, easy-to-use term such as "colorblindness." This should not be surprising. Professor Wechsler's famous article on neutral principles argued that no principled foundation for *Brown* could be identified.[56] Others answered him,[57] but the one point he established is that it is not easy to articulate the principle underlying *Brown*. One cannot say that the principle is simply colorblindness. If the answer were that easy, surely Professor Wechsler and those who debated with him would have discovered it.

There are fundamental similarities between nondiscrimination and affirmative action. Moreover, while we have no fully satisfac-

---

[56]Wechsler, Toward Neutral Principles of Constitutional Law, 73 Harv. L. Rev. 1 (1959).

[57]Black, note 48 *supra*; Pollak, Racial Discrimination and Judicial Integrity: A Reply to Professor Wechsler, 108 U. Pa. L. Rev. 1 (1959).

tory theory of why the Constitution forbids racial discrimination, the theories we do have suggest that affirmative action may sometimes be constitutionally required. And despite the theoretical uncertainty, my analysis has several clear implications about the kinds of arguments that can be used in the debate over affirmative action.

1. It is superficial and essentially incorrect to attack affirmative action on the ground that it is a step away from a colorblind society, or that it forces race back before our eyes. For the reasons I have given, race is already before our eyes. The prohibition against discrimination forces us to recognize that race is different from other bases for classifying people and forces us to act differently toward race from the way we act toward other characteristics. There is accordingly no basis for saying that affirmative action increases the consciousness of race.

2. The intense concern with the rights of innocent white victims that often characterizes the affirmative action debate is misplaced. Obviously one should never ignore the burden that any measure places on any person. But there is unquestionably an undertone in the affirmative action debate that affirmative action is different from nondiscrimination because affirmative action causes innocent people to suffer. The assertion that there is a difference in incorrect. Prohibiting discrimination also causes, and has caused, innocent people to suffer. And so far as I am aware, no one has justified the suffering of these victims of nondiscrimination in a way that would not also justify the suffering of victims of affirmative action.

3. There is no basis for asserting that affirmative action is the moral equivalent of discrimination against blacks. This assertion reflects the myth of colorblindness at its worst: it assumes that an ill-defined notion of colorblindness is the correct state of affairs from which any deviation is wrong.[58] I know of no theoretical justification for that view. There is, to be sure, a coherent (if unpersuasive) argument that the only principle that can be judicially administered is a prohibition against all racial generalizations. But as I noted, this argument does not explain why affirmative action is morally equivalent to discrimination against blacks.

The supposed justifications for the view that they are equivalent generally seem to assert that racial generalizations are intrinsically evil. Instrinsically, however, race is just another characteristic. One

---

[58]See generally Sunstein, Lochner's Legacy, 87 Colum. L. Rev. (forthcoming).

must provide some explanation of why racial generalizations are so bad. The explanations that have been given all seem to suggest, if anything, not that racial classifications are always unacceptable but the opposite: that sometimes race-neutral measures are equally bad.

It follows from this that the proponents of affirmative action should not bear the burden of proof. While there is theoretical uncertainty in this area, there is more reason to believe that deviations from race-neutrality are required than that they are forbidden. The proponents of affirmative action should not have to explain why they are not betraying *Brown*'s supposed principle of color-blindness; there is more reason to place the burden on the opponents of affirmative action to explain why maintaining a system in which there are dramatic economic and social disparities between the races is not destructive of the principles underlying *Brown*.

B

The conclusion that affirmative action may sometimes be constitutionally required is less novel than it appears. At one point, the position that the Fourteenth Amendment requires states to eliminate the racially disproportionate effects of at least certain measures was accepted, in one form or another, by several courts of appeals.[59] Indeed, in the late 1960s and early 1970s, the position that de facto school segregation was unconstitutional—or at least, that it was to be treated in the same fashion as de jure segregation—gained considerable support.[60] De facto segregation is segregation—a racially disproportionate effect—that results from racially neutral measures. To say that a school board must eliminate de facto segregation is to say that it must engage in affirmative action. Racial neutrality is not enough. The school board must ensure that the results are at least somewhat proportional.

In this connection, it is a mistake to suppose that constitutionally required affirmative action would mean rigid proportionality in every area. Both the areas in which affirmative action would be required and the extent to which it would be required depend on the underlying theory—that is, the theory of what it is that makes

---

[59]See Washington v. Davis, 426 U.S. 229, 244–45 & n. 12 (1976) (citing cases).

[60]See, *e.g.*, Keyes v. School District No. 1, 413 U.S. 189, 217–53 (1973) (opinion of Powell, J.).

even explicit racial discrimination wrong. If, for example, the point of prohibiting discrimination is to prevent blacks from being branded as inferior, then race-neutral measures need only be abrogated to the extent necessary to prevent that kind of stigmatization. There is no reason to believe that any form of strict proportionality would be necessary.

Finally, the close relationship between affirmative action and non-discrimination tends to reinforce an argument used by opponents of affirmative action: the familiar argument that race-conscious measures intended to aid blacks can stigmatize them as much as old-fashioned segregation did. Perhaps this argument should have little weight in litigation brought by a white person,[61] or in debates over legislation supported by blacks. But the arguments I have made show why it remains a troubling point. Without a full explanation of what is wrong with discrimination, we cannot say with assurance which measures are needed to avoid that wrong, and which measures tend to precipitate the same wrong. Both racial generalizations and race-neutral measures can fall into each category.[62]

Obviously this uncertainty about the explanation of why discrimination is wrong is unsatisfactory.[63] Perhaps its effects can be mitigated by recalling that not all constitutional obligations need be enforced by courts.[64] In view of the difficulty of determining with any degree of certainty when the application of race-neutral criteria is as unacceptable as the use of racial generalizations, there may be something to be said for imposing this obligation on the legislature alone. Courts could continue to enforce the principle that racial generalizations that disadvantage blacks are unlawful. Courts would still face the task of determining which racial generalizations those were, but in view of the infrequency with which

---

[61]*Cf.* Allen v. Wright, 468 U.S. 737, 755–56 (1984) (concluding that even blacks cannot challenge a measure on the ground that it stigmatizes them unless they are also concretely affected).

[62]Moreover, nothing in this analysis suggests that the explicit classifications must always confer concrete benefits on blacks, as most affirmative action measures do. For example, in Otero v. New York City Housing Authority, 484 F.2d 1122 (2d Cir. 1973), the court upheld the use of a racial classification that prevented blacks from obtaining housing units they sought on the ground that it promoted integration.

[63]See generally Ackerman, Beyond Carolene Products, 98 Harv. L. Rev. 713 (1985).

[64]See Sager, Fair Measure: The Legal Status of Underenforced Constitutional Norms, 91 Harv. L. Rev. 1212 (1978).

blacks have challenged measures that arguably aid them, this task does not seem intractable.

It is frequently said that affirmative action is a difficult issue. It is important to be clear about why that is true. By common agreement, few institutions in our history have been as clearly wrong as the regime of racial discrimination against blacks. But it remains annoyingly difficult to articulate why it was wrong. As a result, it is sometimes difficult to identify with precision the objectives that the law in this area should pursue. And when we attempt to pursue those objectives, we will inevitably impose burdens on innocent people.

These difficulties were, however, inherent in the prohibition against discrimination from the start. They did not begin with affirmative action. Only the myth of colorblindness says that they did.

JAMES D. HOLZHAUER

LONGSHOREMEN v. DAVIS
AND THE NATURE
OF LABOR LAW PRE-EMPTION

In the fifty-year history of comprehensive federal regulation of labor relations, no problem has been more vexing and persistent than the pre-emptive effect of federal labor law on state regulation. The Supreme Court has considered pre-emption more often than any other labor law issue; it decided four pre-emption cases during the 1985 Term alone and two the previous Term.[1] Yet the common perception is that pre-emption doctrine remains in a state of considerable confusion.[2]

The most interesting of the 1985 Term pre-emption cases—and the one which generated the most disagreement within the Court—was *International Longshoremen's Association v. Davis*.[3] The issue was whether a union, the defendant in a state tort action, had lost its

James D. Holzhauer is Assistant Professor of Law, University of Chicago Law School.

AUTHOR'S NOTE: I have profited from discussion of pre-emption issues with Douglas Baird, David Currie, Larry Kramer, Bernard Meltzer, and David Strauss. William Levy provided valuable research assistance. Financial assistance was provided by the University of Chicago Law and Economics Program and the Lynde and Harry Bradley Foundation.

[1]Baker v. General Motors Corp., 106 S.Ct. 3129 (1986); International Longshoremen's Association v. Davis, 106 S.Ct. 1904 (1986); Golden State Transit Corp. v. City of Los Angeles, 106 S.Ct. 1395 (1986); Wisconsin Department of Industry, Labor and Human Relations v. Gould, Inc., 106 S.Ct. 1057 (1986); Metropolitan Life Insurance Co. v. Commonwealth of Massachusetts, 105 S.Ct. 2380 (1985); Allis-Chalmers Corp. v. Lueck, 105 S.Ct. 1904 (1985).

[2]See, *e.g.*, Cox, Bok & Gorman, Cases and Materials on Labor Law 895 (10th ed. 1986); Meltzer & Henderson, Labor Law: Cases, Materials and Problems 730–32 (3d ed. 1985).

[3]106 S.Ct. 1904 (1986).

right to raise a pre-emption claim because it failed to do so in a timely fashion under state procedural rules. Is labor law pre-emption a waivable defense? Does the failure to raise a pre-emption claim have the same effect as the failure to raise other federal constitutional claims in state court? Or does pre-emption, by depriving state courts of their "very jurisdiction to adjudicate," preclude state waiver rules?[4] The Court held the latter, and then, reaching the merits of the union's pre-emption claim, held that the tort suit was not pre-empted.

The Court's resolution of the jurisdictional issue—which, in Justice Rehnquist's words, "allows a sophisticated defendant as in the present case to gamble on obtaining a verdict and raise a pre-emption defense only if it loses on the merits"[5]—is counterintuitive. The result also seems likely to confound, rather than to promote, the purposes of pre-emption and the policies underlying the federal labor laws. The Court's decision that, on the facts of the case, Davis's suit was not pre-empted can easily be justified but the Court's analysis—which seems flatly inconsistent with its resolution of the jurisdictional issue and with the Court's previous pre-emption decisions—seems to represent a fundamental and unfortunate revision of the basic operation of labor law pre-emption.

I

The dispute in *International Longshoremen's Association v. Davis* was grounded in the distinction the Act makes between supervisors and other employees. Section 7 of the Act provides: "Employees shall have the right to self-organization, to form, join, or assist labor organizations, to bargain collectively through representatives of their own choosing, and to engage in other concerted activities. . . ."[6] And §8(a) provides that it is unlawful for an employer "to interfere with, restrain, or coerce employees in the exercise of" their §7 rights or to "discriminat[e] in regard to hire or tenure of employment . . . to encourage or discourage membership in any labor organization."[7]

---

[4]*Id.* at 1911.

[5]*Id.* at 1918.

[6]29 U.S.C. §157.

[7]29 U.S.C. §158(a)(1), (3).

The National Labor Relations Board struggled for several years over whether supervisory employees were entitled to the full protection of these provisions, and finally ruled that they were in 1945.[8] The Supreme Court upheld the Board's decision,[9] but Congress disagreed. As part of the Taft-Hartley Act of 1947, the definitional section of the statute was amended to provide that individuals employed as supervisors were not employees within the meaning of the Act and therefore were not entitled to the protections afforded by §7.[10]

The facts of *Davis* are simple. Ben Trione, Larry Davis, and several others employed as ship superintendents or trainee ship superintendents by Ryan-Walsh Stevedoring Co. in Mobile, Alabama, met with representatives of the International Longshoremen's Association in early 1981 to explore the possibility of joining and bargaining through the union. When some of the superintendents expressed concern that they could be discharged for their union membership and activities, a union official assured them that the union would get their jobs restored if they were fired. On the day following the union meeting, Ryan-Walsh fired Trione because of his union organizing. The union picketed the company to protest the discharge and filed an unfair labor practice charge on behalf of Trione.[11] The NLRB Regional Director declined to issue a complaint on the ground that Trione was employed as a supervisor and was therefore not protected by §7 or §8(a). The union did not exercise its right to have this decision reviewed by the NLRB General Counsel. A few days later, in May of 1981, the company fired Davis, apparently because of his continuing union activity. In the light of the Regional Director's decision with regard to Trione, Davis did not file an unfair labor practice charge with the NLRB.

Instead Davis sued the union in the Circuit Court of Mobile County. He alleged that he had relied upon the union's assurances that it would get him his job back were he fired for union activity and claimed that the union's unfulfilled promise constituted fraud

---

[8]*Packard Motor Co.*, 61 N.L.R.B. 4 (1945).

[9]Packard Motor Car Co. v. NLRB, 330 U.S. 485 (1947).

[10]29 U.S.C. §152(3).

[11]The company obtained a temporary restraining order against the picketing. The state court subsequently entered a preliminary injunction based on a finding that Trione was a supervisor.

and misrepresentation under Alabama law. Following more than two years of discovery, the case was tried in November of 1983. The union did not raise any pre-emption issue at the outset of the trial, nor did it introduce any evidence to contest Davis's status as a supervisor. The jury entered a verdict for Davis and awarded damages of $75,000. A month after the jury reached its decision, as the fifteenth of sixteen items in its motion for judgment notwithstanding the verdict, the union for the first time argued that the state tort suit was pre-empted by federal law. The trial court denied the entire motion without opinion. The Alabama Supreme Court affirmed, holding that under state procedural rules the union had waived the pre-emption defense by failing to raise it in a timely manner. In a footnote, the court stated that if it did have to reach that issue, it would hold that the suit was not pre-empted.[12]

The Supreme Court affirmed, but on different grounds. Justice White, writing for the Court, held that the union's failure to raise the pre-emption claim earlier could not work as a waiver of that claim: "A claim of *Garmon* pre-emption is a claim that the state court has no power to adjudicate the subject matter of the case, and when a claim of *Garmon* pre-emption is raised, it must be considered and resolved by the state court."[13] Justice White then looked at whether Davis's suit was pre-empted by the Act, and he concluded that it was not.

Justice Rehnquist, joined by Justices Powell, Stevens, and O'Connor, disagreed with the majority's jurisdictional analysis but concurred with the finding of no pre-emption.[14] Justice Blackmun agreed with the jurisdictional ruling, but disagreed with the pre-emption analysis.[15]

II

The threshold issue in *Davis* was whether a claim of federal labor law pre-emption could be waived if not raised in a timely manner under state procedural rules. The Court equated this issue with whether labor law pre-emption goes to the subject matter

---

[12]470 So.2d. 1215, 1216–1217 n. 2 (1985).

[13]*Id.* at 1913.

[14]*Id.* at 1916–18.

[15]*Id.* at 1918–21.

jurisdiction of the state court. Justice White characterized the issue as "whether *Garmon* pre-emption is in the nature of an affirmative defense that must be asserted in the trial court . . . [or] is in the nature of a challenge to a court's power to adjudicate that may be raised at any time."[16] In holding the latter, Justice White emphasized the "jurisdictional nature" of the previous pre-emption decisions[17] and placed particular reliance on *Construction & General Laborers v. Curry*, in which the Court held that a state court's decision on pre-emption finally resolved the issue of the court's jurisdiction to issue a temporary injunction and was therefore ripe for review before trial.[18]

The Court's emphasis on "subject matter jurisdiction" seems to have deflected it from the essential issue, which was not whether the union's pre-emption claim went to the subject matter jurisdiction of the Court, but whether federal law pre-empts state procedural rules which result in the waiver of claims not properly raised. Even when called upon to resolve federal claims, including federal constitutional claims, state courts are ordinarily free to apply state procedural rules, including rules resulting in waiver.[19] On matters of procedure, and of the consequences of procedural irregularities, "federal law takes the state courts as it finds them."[20] The key question in *Davis* was whether Congress deviated from that general rule and precluded state courts from applying their own procedural rules to labor cases at least to the extent that violation of those rules results in waiver. None of the Court's previous pre-emption decisions dealt with this issue. Although the Court may have referred to pre-emption as jurisdictional in the past, it certainly had not decided or even considered the issue of whether the federal labor laws pre-empt state waiver rules.

One might argue that under Alabama law claims of lack of subject matter jurisdiction were nonwaivable,[21] so the only issue before the state courts was whether *Garmon* pre-emption went to subject mat-

---

[16]106 S.Ct. at 1907.

[17]*Id.* at 1912–13.

[18]371 U.S. 542, 548 (1963).

[19]See Bator *et al.*, Hart and Wechsler's The Federal Courts and the Federal System 531–38 (2d. ed. 1973), and cases cited therein.

[20]Hart, The Relations Between State and Federal Law, 54 Colum. L. Rev. 479, 508 (1954).

[21]470 So.2d at 1216.

ter jurisdiction. But in all respects the interpretation of state procedural rules—including the interpretation of the term "subject
matter jurisdiction" in the context of those rules—is ordinarily a
matter of state law. Moreover, the Supreme Court clearly decided
more than that under Alabama procedural rules *Garmon* pre-emption
claims cannot be waived. It decided that no state waiver rules, even
those that specifically provide for waiver of untimely claims of lack
of subject matter jurisdiction, can be applied to preclude the belated
assertion of a *Garmon* pre-emption claim.

Although lack of subject matter jurisdiction may be raised at any
time in nearly all courts, the rule is not uncontroversial. Allowing
the party who has invoked the court's jurisdiction to challenge it
after the trial has ended unhappily has been called a "fetish" of
federal jurisdiction,[22] and the American Law Institute has advocated
its repeal, pointing out that it "is wholly inconsistent with sound
judicial administration and can only serve to diminish respect for
a system which tolerates it."[23] There is nothing in the Constitution
or other federal law that prohibits waiver of untimely claims of lack
of subject matter jurisdiction. A state or the federal courts could
enact a rule, for example, that if an action is brought and no party
objects to the subject matter jurisdiction of the court before trial
all such objections are waived and the action may proceed.[24] As a
matter of federal law, it is thus altogether possible that a federal
claim in state court could go to the subject matter jurisdiction of
the court, but that any claims of lack of jurisdiction could be waived
if not properly raised. *Davis* precludes any possibility of waiver
Garmon pre-emption claims, and thus further confounds sound judicial administration and diminishes respect for the legal system by
making the "fetish" a matter of federal law even in state courts.
Before it did so, the Court should have made sure that at least some
important federal policy underlying the statute—if not the words
of the statute—required that result.

---

[22]1 Moore, Federal Practice ¶0.60[4] (2d ed. 1948).

[23]American Law Institute, Study of the Division of Jurisdiction Between State and Federal
Courts 366 (1969).

[24]*Id.* at 366–69 (proposing a rule requiring objections to subject matter jurisdiction to be
made prior to trial); Dobbs, Beyond Bootstrap: Foreclosing the Issue of Subject-Matter
Jurisdiction Before Final Judgment, 51 Minn. L. Rev. 491, 520–21 (1967); Restatement 2d
of Judgments §11(d) (1982).

A

There is no statutory language to support the Court's decision that the federal labor laws pre-empt state procedural rules or precludes waiver, and no support can be found in the legislative history of any of the labor laws. Congress could have precluded all state regulation of labor relations in industries affecting commerce when it enacted the National Labor Relations ("Wagner") Act[25] in 1935 or when it amended that law on several occasions thereafter; it could have required that all labor relations disputes be heard by a federal court or by the National Labor Relations Board, and that even-handed state procedural rules could not be applied so as to result in waiver of jurisdictional claims. But neither the language of the federal statutes nor their legislative history even imply that Congress did so.

Unlike other federal statutes, the Wagner Act has no express provision on the pre-emption of state law.[26] It prohibits interference with legitimate union activities by establishing several employer unfair labor practices,[27] but it contains few limitations on union conduct and does not establish any union unfair labor practices. Some members of Congress claimed the bill was one-sided and should be amended to prohibit unfair practices by unions. They expressed a concern that by not prohibiting unfair union tactics, such as coercion, fraud, and violence, the Act could be interpreted as affording affirmative federal protection to those tactics. In response, the bill's supporters pointed out that there already existed an adequate arsenal of local, state, and federal laws regulating—in many cases overly restricting—union conduct.[28] It was clear that the sponsors of the Act did not interpret it as pre-empting all state and local regulation.

---

[25] 49 Stat. 449 (1935).

[26] See, *e.g.*, §514(a) of the Employee Retirement Income Security Act of 1974, 29 U.S.C. §1144(a).

[27] Section 8 of the original Act has been amended and is codified at 29 U.S.C. §158(a).

[28] See Senate Report No. 573, at 16–17, reprinted in II Leg. Hist of the NLRA, 1935, at 2315–16; House Report No. 1147 at 16–17, reprinted in II Leg. Hist. of the NLRA, 1935, at 3064–66; see also United Automobile Workers v. Wisconsin Employment Relations Board, 336 U.S. 245, 257–58 (1949); Magruder, A Half Century of Legal Influence Upon the Development of Collective Bargaining, 50 Harv. L. Rev. 1071, 1107–10 (1937).

Nevertheless, the Act clearly had a substantial pre-emptive effect. The purpose of the Act was to legitimize collective bargaining, which employers had resisted with a variety of tactics—including the use of state tort laws before often anti-union state courts and agencies.[29] The Act's purpose could not be accomplished if employers could continue to use state laws as they had in the past to prevent unions from organizing or, once organized, from using legitimate economic weapons. Because the problem was not simply that state laws were seen as inequitable and anti-union, but that state courts and agencies had used seemingly neutral state laws to defeat legitimate union activities, the Act's purpose could not be accomplished if state courts and agencies continued to be the primary forums for resolving labor disputes, even if they were required to apply federal law. By providing that union activities previously impeded by employers in state courts and agencies were permitted, and protected under a federal law to be enforced by a federal agency, the Act pre-empted any contrary state provision or ruling.

The Wagner Act was amended by the Labor Management Relations ("Taft Hartley") Act of 1947, but the amendment did nothing to clarify the pre-emption issue. In fact, what little there is in the legislative history on this issue casts doubt on the entire labor pre-emption doctrine. Prior to the passage of Taft-Hartley, Wisconsin had been active in regulating labor relations, and several of the early Supreme Court pre-emption cases involved actions of the Wisconsin Employment Relations Board. During the debates on Taft-Hartley, Congressman Kersten of Wisconsin asked one of the bill's sponsors about pre-emption:[30]

> Mr. KERSTEN of Wisconsin: . . . I would like to ask the gentleman about the portion which pertains to the validity of state laws. Wisconsin and other States have their own labor relations laws. We are very anxious that disputes be settled at the State level insofar as it is possible. Can the gentleman give us assurance on that proposition, so that it is a matter of record, that this is the sense of the language and the report?
> Mr. HARTLEY: That is the sense of the language of the bill and the report. That is my interpretation of the bill, that this

---

[29]See Gregory & Katz, Labor and the Law, ch. III–V (3d ed. 1979); Bernstein, The Lean Years, 190–243 (1960); Cox et al., note 2 supra, at 895.

[30]93 Cong. Rec. 6540 (June 4, 1947), reprinted in National Labor Relations Board, I Legislative History of the Labor Management Relations Act 1947, at 883 (1948).

will not interfere with the State of Wisconsin in the administration of its own laws. In other words, this will not interfere
with the validity of the laws within that State.

Mr. KERSTEN of Wisconsin: And it will permit as many
of these disputes to be settled at that State level as possible?

Mr. HARTLEY: Exactly.

The debates over Taft-Hartley are replete with assurances that the
federal labor laws should interfere as little as possible with state
jurisdiction.[31]

Despite the enactment of Taft-Hartley, it thus remained clear
that Congress envisioned a continuing role for the states in regulating labor relations and union activities. Taft-Hartley did not
repeal the basic right of collective bargaining and union organization, however: It reaffirmed that employees were to have the right
to bargain collectively through representatives of their own choosing. This federal policy required that federal labor laws have a
substantial pre-emptive effect on state laws and that the federal law
be enforced primarily by the federal agency, rather than by state
courts and agencies. With the intent of Congress unclear—except
that it rejected both extremes, no pre-emption and complete pre-
emption—the Supreme Court has had to determine the scope of
the federal law's pre-emptive effect, and it has struggled to do so
for the past forty years.

B

The Court's struggle over the years has moved along at least three
distinct paths. The first of these—that involved in *Davis*—is called
Garmon pre-emption, after *San Diego Building Trades Council v. Garmon*
(1959).[32] *Garmon* pre-emption stems from the congressional decision
to grant the National Labor Relations Board exclusive authority to
regulate much of the relationship between employees, employers, and
unions; state laws are said to be pre-empted under *Garmon* when they
require state courts or agencies to resolve matters that are within or
arguably within the realm of the Board. *Garmon* pre-emption is primarily concerned with the forum in which regulation occurs, rather
than with the substance of the regulation; it prohibits not only the en-

---

[31]See Hays, Federalism and Labor Relations in the United States, 102 U. Pa. L. Rev.
959, 965–66 (1954), and sources cited therein.

[32]359 U.S. 236 (1959).

forcement of contrary state law in state courts, but even the enforcement of the federal labor laws in state court.

The second branch of labor pre-emption—called *Machinists* pre-emption, from *Machinists v. Wisconsin Employment Relations Board* in 1976[33]—reflects the federal labor laws' legitimization of collective bargaining and its intention to leave the bargaining parties free, within certain limits, to exercise their economic muscle without interference from the states or the federal government. States are said to be precluded under *Machinists* from regulating labor relations conduct which, to serve the purposes of the federal law, must be left unregulated. *Machinists* pre-emption is thus concerned primarily with the substance of state regulation rather than with the forum in which the regulation takes place; it precludes the applications in state or federal court of state laws that might conflict with federal labor policy.

The third branch of labor pre-emption can be traced to two 1962 cases, *Charles Dowd Box Co. v. Courtney* and *Teamsters v. Lucas Flour Co.*[34] Section 301 of the Labor Management Relations Act provides: "Suits for violation of contracts between an employer and a labor organization representing employees in an industry affecting commerce . . . may be brought in any district court of the United States having jurisdiction of the parties. . . ."[35] The Court first held, in *Dowd Box*, that state courts had concurrent jurisdiction over §301 suits. Then in *Lucas Flour* the Court decided that in exercising that jurisdiction, state court must apply federal law exclusively.[36] So, under §301, there is no pre-emption of state forums, but there is pre-emption of state substantive law.

Davis involved *Garmon* pre-emption, so the Court's inquiry should have focused on whether the interests underlying *Garmon* pre-emption prohibit the application of state procedural rules resulting in waiver of claims not properly brought or preserved. The *Garmon* rule is rather complex and has some substantial exceptions. The Court formulated the basic rule as follows:[37]

---

[33]427 U.S. 132 (1976).

[34]368 U.S. 502 (1962); 369 U.S. 95 (1962).

[35]29 U.S.C. §185.

[36]Previously the Court had held that federal courts must fashion a federal law of labor relations to be applied in §301 suits. Textile Workers v. Lincoln Mills, 353 U.S. 448, 456–47 (1957).

[37]*Id.* at 244, 245.

When it is clear or may fairly be assumed that the activities
which a State purports to regulate are protected by §7 of the
National Labor Relations Act, or constitute an unfair labor
practice under §8, due regard for the federal enactment requires
that state jurisdiction must yield.

    . . . .

When an activity is arguably subject to §7 or §8 of the Act, the
States as well as the federal courts must defer to the exclusive
competence of the National Labor Relations Board if the danger
of state interference with national policy is to be averted.

The first major exception to the rule was announced in *Garmon*
itself: Deference to the NLRB or to federal law would not be
required "where the activity regulated [by the State] was a merely
peripheral concern of the [federal] Act," or "touched interests . . .
deeply rooted in local feeling and responsibility. . . ."[38] This exception has been invoked, for example, in cases involving libel,
picketing violence, and trespassing.[39]

Another major exception was established in 1978 by the Court
in *Sears, Roebuck & Co. v. Carpenters.*[40] *Sears* addressed a problem
inherent in the *Garmon* rule and sharply criticized by Justice White,
among others.[41] Under some circumstances, actions brought in state
forums to enjoin or collect damages resulting from conduct arguably
protected under §7 would be pre-empted under *Garmon*, but the
party seeking state relief—and unable to obtain it because of pre-
emption—could not seek an NLRB determination whether the conduct was in fact protected.[42] For example, in a case involving arguably
protected picketing objected to by an employer as illegal under state
trespass law, the NLRB, and only the NLRB, could determine if
the picketing was actually protected, but there would be no colorable charge of an unfair labor practice that the employer could

---

[38]*Id.* at 243–44.

[39]See, *e.g.*, Linn v. Plant Guard Workers Local 114, 383 U.S. 53 (1966); United Construction Workers v. Laburnum Construction Corp., 347 U.S. 656 (1954); Sears, Roebuck & Co.
v. Carpenters, 436 U.S. 180 (1978).

[40]436 U.S. 180 (1978).

[41]See Amalgamated Association of Street Employees v. Lockridge, 403 U.S. 274, 325
(1971) (White, J., dissenting) and International Longshoremen's Association v. Adriadne
Shipping Co., 397 U.S. 195, 201–02 (1970) (White, J., concurring); Come, Federal Preemption of Labor-Management Relations: Current Problems in the Application of *Garmon*, 56
Va. L. Rev. 1435 (1970).

[42]See, *e.g.*, Taggart v. Weinacker's, Inc., 397 U.S. 223 (1970).

bring against the union to get the Board's attention. The employer could get the Board to decide the case only if it could compel the union to file a charge, perhaps by forcefully evicting the pickets at the risk of further aggravating the dispute. It seems inequitable to prohibit states from regulating conduct that is "arguably" subject to the Act unless there is some reasonable way the complaining party can bring the case before the NLRB and have the possible federal issue resolved.

In *Sears*, the Court held that a state court action might not be pre-empted if the party who could bring the matter before the NLRB had not done so, and the other party (the party invoking the jurisdiction of the state court) had no acceptable way of bringing the matter to the Board.[43] Under such circumstances, the Court held that an exception to *Garmon* might be justified: "Whatever risk of an erroneous state-court adjudication does exist is outweighed by the anomalous consequence of a rule which would deny the employer access to any forum in which to litigate either the trespass issue or the [§7] protection issue. . . ."[44] However, the Court also indicated that even under such circumstances, if the claim of §7 protection is particularly strong, federal policy might require pre-emption of the state suit even though pre-emption might cause a "jurisdictional hiatus."[45]

Sears thus requires state courts not only to consider whether the conduct complained of is arguably protected under §7, but also to consider whether the party invoking the court's jurisdiction can bring the matter before the NLRB and to assess the strength of the §7 argument (*i.e.*, the strength of the argument that the conduct is protected). Keeping in mind the role of the state courts required by *Sears*, the *Garmon* doctrine reflects a curious mix of policies and rules. *Garmon* pre-emption is forum pre-emption, based on the notion that the objectives of the federal labor policy would not be fulfilled if disputes under the federal labor laws were adjudicated as a matter of course in state tribunals. The concern is not with

---

[43]436 U.S. at 202–03.

[44]*Id.* at 206. In his concurring opinion, Justice Blackmun maintained that once the party with the ability to invoke the Board's jurisdiction does so, the state court action must be held in abeyance. *Id.* at 209. This basis for the *Sears, Roebuck* holding was reiterated in *Davis*, 106 S. Ct. at 1913 n. 10.

[45]436 U.S. at 203.

the law to be applied, but with the forum that applies that law. This concern can be traced to two policy considerations which operate in conjunction. The first is that some state tribunals, traditionally hostile to unionization, will not respect the federal policy permitting organization and collective bargaining. The second is that proper development of a consistent body of federal labor law and sound resolution of complex factual disputes requires a specialized federal agency with expertise and experience in labor relations and collective bargaining matters. The latter now seems the more important concern and is emphasized in the Court's decisions; certainly the role of the state courts in §301 suits and their role under *Garmon* and *Sears* is inconsistent with any continuing and overriding federal concern with the evenhandedness of state courts in labor cases.

A state court as a general rule must turn away any dispute subject to §7 or §8 of the federal act, but in every such case that comes before it the state court has a substantial role under federal law. First the court must decide whether the conduct is at least arguably subject to §7 or §8. If it is not, the court must consider whether, under the *Machinists* doctrine, it is conduct that under federal law must be left unregulated. Even if a state suit involves conduct actually or arguably subject to §7 or §8, the state court before dismissing the action must evaluate whether the "activity [is] merely a peripheral concern of the [federal] Act," or whether it "touche[s] interests so deeply rooted in local feeling and responsibility . . ." that the local interests outweigh the federal. Finally, if the suit involves conduct arguably protected under §7, the state court must investigate whether the party invoking its jurisdiction could readily bring the dispute before the NLRB and, if it could not, the court must evaluate the strength of the opposing party's §7 claim in order to determine whether the case fits within the *Sears* exception. In sum, the role of state courts in particular cases raising the *Garmon* issue is neither small nor mechanical.

c

This brings us back to the central issue: whether the concerns underlying the *Garmon* rule, with its exceptions and the role it requires of state courts, requires the pre-emption of state waiver rules. I believe they do not. First, it seems quite anomalous to entrust state courts with considerable responsibility in cases raising *Garmon* pre-emption issues but then to say that those courts cannot apply reasonable procedural rules to govern how those issues must be raised. Moreover, how can it be a great risk to federal labor policy for state courts (because of the operation of fair and even-handed waiver rules) occasionally to regulate conduct that might (arguably) be subject to the federal labor laws, when it is no great risk for state courts to play the important role required by *Garmon* and *Sears?*

It is one thing to say that federal labor policy would be endangered if parties as a general matter had to rely on state courts for the enforcement of their federal labor law rights, but quite another thing to say that federal policy would be harmed in any meaningful way if a party—on rare occasions and through its own neglect, inadvertence or miscalculated guile—found that it had waived its federal statutory rights. First, the latter presents no significant risk to the development of consistent federal labor law. Certainly the NLRB, the federal courts, and the sophisticated parties involved in most labor disputes are not going to consider such judgments to be of any precedential value on issues of federal labor law. State tribunals generally will not even be considering matters of federal law, but will instead be resolving disputes under state law in a way that might, at worst, conflict with how those disputes would be resolved under federal law. The occasional incursion of state courts into a federal realm does not involve the same risk to federalism as does federal encroachment upon state prerogatives. Unlike the state courts, the federal courts, armed with the Supremacy Clause and the power of the Supreme Court to review state judgments, have no difficulty protecting their domain. Any federalism concerns that might support the no-waiver rule in federal courts do not automatically support a similar, federally imposed rule in state courts.[46]

Nor should we be overly concerned that, as a result of waiver, labor disputes will occasionally be resolved by a tribunal lacking the specialized expertise and experience of the NLRB. A state tribunal might at times reach an incorrect result due to lack of labor relations expertise; a party that would have prevailed before the NLRB might lose before the state court. But this is the kind of risk—the risk of losing when one should have won—that litigants

---

[46]See Restatement Judgments 2d §11 (1982).

are regularly subjected to by the operation of fair procedural rules. A defendant with a valid affirmative defense might lose if he fails to raise the defense in a timely manner. A plaintiff with a valid claim might see his suit dismissed if it is not brought within the period prescribed by a statute of limitations or pursued in the manner required by procedural rules. The public interest in the smooth operation of its judicial system, in finality and in putting potential disputes to rest, is ordinarily seen as outweighing the risk of erroneous results. There is no obvious reason why labor law should be an exception. A similar risk was involved in *Sears*, and the Court held that "the risk of an erroneous state court adjudication . . . is outweighed by the anomalous consequence of deny[ing] the employer access to any forum in which to litigate" its claim.[47] If that is the case, it would certainly seem that the same risk is easily outweighed by the important interests served by state waiver rules.

In holding that the union could not waive its pre-emption claim, the Court relied in part on *Kalb v. Feuerstein*,[48] a case involving federal bankruptcy law. As Justice Rehnquist noted, the language of the federal bankruptcy law involved in *Kalb* lent considerable support to the Court's result, and there is no similar language in the federal labor laws. Putting aside the critical difference in statutory language, it is useful to contrast the policy basis underlying *Kalb* with that of *Davis*. A state court had entered a judgment of foreclosure on Kalb's farm and the farm had been sold even though Kalb had previously filed a bankruptcy petition, which at the time of the state judgment and sale was still pending in federal court. Kalb had failed to raise the federal issue in state court and had not directly appealed the state judgment, thus raising the possibility of waiver, but the Court held that federal bankruptcy law precluded the state action.

The Court's language in *Kalb* was imprecise—as in *Davis* it failed to distinguish between jurisdiction and waiver—but its result was correct. Federal bankruptcy law is designed in large part to protect the rights of creditors and to prevent one creditor or group of creditors from getting an unfair advantage over others.[49] Clearly that federal policy would be damaged by allowing the

---

[47]436 U.S. at 206.

[48]308 U.S. 433 (1940).

[49]See Baird & Jackson, Cases, Problems and Materials on Bankruptcy, ch. 1 (1985).

debtor and one creditor, in essence, to waive the federal rights of other creditors in state court. Unlike the situation in *Kalb*, however, in *Davis* the union had waived its own federal rights, not that of others. There is no federal interest in *Davis* comparable to the interest involved in *Kalb* that precludes application of state waiver rules.

Finally, it is far from clear that the *Davis* rule will either keep labor disputes out of state courts or will guarantee that they are considered by the NLRB. Instead, the rule may increase the opportunity for tactical ploys which interfere with proper consideration and resolution of labor disputes. As Justice Rehnquist pointed out in *Davis*, an employer or a union charged in a state suit with conduct arguably prohibited by federal labor law might decide, for tactical reasons, to try first for a favorable verdict in state court, knowing that if it is unsuccessful it can still raise the pre-emption issue after trial, have the verdict set aside, and re-litigate the matter before the NLRB. In many cases, the years of delay and the considerable expense will work in favor of defendants; pre-emption issues often arise in cases such as *Davis* in which individuals sue large institutional entities (*i.e.*, unions and employers) which are better able than individual plaintiffs to sustain the costs and the delays of litigation. Or an employer or union defending such a suit might decide not to raise the pre-emption issue until after the statute of limitations for raising the federal claim has passed.[50] How is the federal labor policy served by allowing a union or an employer to get a second opportunity to litigate—an opportunity it will take only if it loses at trial—or by giving it an opportunity to avoid federal liability altogether by allowing the state suit to continue until it is too late to initiate federal proceedings? If the federal policy is one that seeks to have labor disputes resolved by the specialized federal agency, it is ill-served by a rule that may allow a party to avoid any resolution on the merits or to have the matter fully litigated twice. A preferable rule would be one that forced the party in whose interest it is to assert pre-emption to do so at the outset, thus reducing the delay and the possibility of state court interference in matters that should be left to the NLRB.

---

[50]The statute of limitations for bringing unfair labor practice charges is six months. 29 U.S.C. §160(b).

III

Having decided that labor pre-emption goes to the subject matter jurisdiction of the state court and therefore must be considered whenever raised,[51] the Court turned to the question of whether Davis's suit was pre-empted. The union asserted that Davis was arguably an employee, rather than a supervisor, that his discharge for union activity was therefore arguably prohibited by the Act and that the union's efforts to attract his allegiance were arguably protected by the Act. Supervisory status is not determined by job title, but by factors established and evaluated by the NLRB;[52] if Davis were "arguably" an employee, rather than a supervisor, the determination of his status would have to be left to the Board and his suit would be pre-empted under *Garmon*.

The Court could have resolved this issue quite simply: It could have concluded, in light of the rejection by the NLRB of the similar claim made by Davis's co-worker, Trione, that Davis was not even "arguably" an employee rather than a supervisor. If Davis was not even "arguably" a supervisor, his suit was not pre-empted under *Garmon*. The Court instead resolved the issue by finding that Davis had the burden of establishing a prima facie case for pre-emption and had failed to meet that burden:[53]

> [T]he party claiming pre-emption is required to demonstrate that his case is one that the Board could legally decide in his favor. That is, a party asserting pre-emption must advance an interpretation of the Act that is not plainly contrary to its language and that has not been 'authoritatively rejected' by the courts or the Board. The party must then put forth enough evidence to enable the court to find that the Board reasonably could uphold a claim based on such an interpretation. In this case, therefore, because the pre-emption issue turns on Davis' status, the Union's claim of pre-emption must be supported by a showing sufficient to permit the Board to find that Davis was an employee, not a supervisor. Our examination of the record leads us to conclude that the Union has not carried its burden in this case.

---

[51]As I point out above, the latter does not follow necessarily from the former.

[52]Food Store Employees Union, Local 347 v. NLRB, 422 F. 2d 685, 689–90 (D.C. Cir. 1969); *Winco Petroleum Co.*, 241 NLRB 1118 (1979).

[53]106 S. Ct. at 1914 (citation omitted).

Because the union had not made any evidentiary showing to contest Davis's supervisory status, the Court held that the union's unsupported arguments that its conduct was arguably protected under §7 and that the company's conduct was arguably prohibited under §8 were insufficient to establish pre-emption.

Justice Blackmun argued in dissent that the Court's ruling was contrary to the teachings of *Garmon*:[54]

> The Court today purports to follow *Garmon*, but nonetheless requires that the party 'claiming pre-emption must carry the burden of showing at least an arguable case before the jurisdiction of a state court will be ousted,' and proceeds to require here that the Union make a showing 'sufficient to permit the Board to find that Davis was an employee, not a supervisor.' In transforming the notion that some activities are *arguably* protected or prohibited into a requirement that a party claiming pre-emption make out an 'arguable case,' it seems to me that the Court misses the point of its decision in *Garmon*. As a result of the decision today, a court, under the guise of weighing the sufficiency of the evidence, will be making precisely the determination that *Garmon* makes clear is for the Board, and only the Board, to make.

As Justice Blackmun states, the Court's holding contravenes the policy underlying the pre-emption doctrine. It requires the state court in every case raising an issue of *Garmon* pre-emption to make the very kind of complex determination that *Garmon* declares must be left to the NLRB. In the past the Supreme Court has shown no reluctance to decide pre-emption cases on the basis of the allegations in the pleadings, and has not imposed any affirmative evidentiary burden on parties claiming pre-emption.[55] Of course courts should reject frivolous pre-emption claims; claims of pre-emption must be supported by sufficiently detailed, credible allegations. But to require evidentiary development in the state court and to require that court then to decide whether the dispute is reasonably over §7 or §8 conduct and not outside the Act (" 'authoritatively rejected' by the courts or the Board") is to require the state court to assume the role *Garmon* says belongs exclusively to the Board.

---

[54]106 S. Ct. at 1919 (citations omitted).

[55]See, *e.g.*, Operating Engineers v. Jones, 460 U.S. 669 (1983), with an opinion for the Court by Justice White.

In support of this part of the Court's decision, Justice White cited
Marine Engineers v. Interlake S.S. Co.[56] In that case, a state trial court
had erroneously rejected a union's pre-emption argument, finding
that the union was not a "labor organization" under federal law.
The union had introduced several Board and court decisions holding
that it was in fact a labor organization, but the state court rejected
these decisions and relied on other evidence it believed warranted
a contrary holding. The Supreme Court reversed, and in doing so
criticized the state court for engaging in the kind of evidentiary
inquiry "most wisely entrusted initially to the agency charged with
the day-to-day administration of the Act as a whole."[57] The state
court had heard evidence on the issue whether the union was a
labor organization, and the matter had proceeded to trial after which
a permanent injunction was issued. With that evidence on the record, the Supreme Court reviewed it and found that it demonstrated
not merely that the controversy was arguably subjected to the federal act and therefore pre-empted, but that it was incontrovertibly
subject to the act and pre-empted.[58] But this hardly supports Justice
White's assertion that *Interlake* stands for the proposition that state
courts should engage in such detailed inquiries. The *Interlake* analysis lends greater support to the contrary assertion, that state courts
should not engage in these inquiries but should leave them to the
Board.

The evidentiary burden *Davis* places on the party asserting pre-
emption is difficult to reconcile with the Court's jurisdictional decision. If pre-emption goes to the subject matter jurisdiction of the
state court and can never be waived, under both federal and state
law the court must assure its own jurisdiction and must undertake
the necessary inquiry even if the parties fail to raise the issue.[59] If
anyone bears the burden of establishing jurisdiction, it is the party
invoking it, not the one contesting it.[60]

In *Davis*, the Court is saying on the one hand that pre-emption
goes to the subject matter jurisdiction of the court, can be raised

---

[56]370 U.S. 173 (1962).

[57]*Id.* at 180.

[58]*Id.* at 184.

[59]See, *e.g.*, Rule 12(h), Federal Rules of Civil Procedure; International Longshoremen's
Ass'n v. Davis, 470 So.2d at 1216.

[60]McNutt v. General Motors Acceptance Corp. 298 U.S. 178, 189 (1936).

at any time by either party or at the court's own initiative, and
cannot be waived even under completely fair and reasonable waiver
rules; but, on the other hand, that the jurisdictional defect can, in
effect, be waived if the party asserting pre-emption fails to (or
decides not to) carry its evidentiary burden. Because a party who
might assert pre-emption must support that claim with an evidentiary showing, it can decline to do so, thus—for as long as it is in
that party's interest—waiving the pre-emption claim. But if it later
becomes in that party's interest to assert pre-emption and to present
evidence, it can do so, notwithstanding state procedural rules to
the contrary. The parties thus become the master of the state court's
jurisdiction, and the state courts are blocked from responding by
imposing reasonable procedural rules. This hardly seems to serve
any rational federal policy.

Moreover, the Court's decision says on the one hand that even
an occasional state court involvement in a labor dispute (which
would generally consist only of application of state law to the dispute and not any interpretation or application of federal law) presents such a grave danger to federal labor policy that the right to
avoid state jurisdiction can never be waived; on the other hand, the
Court requires state courts regularly to consider and, at least on a
preliminary basis, to resolve the federal issues in those disputes.
Either the state courts can be entrusted to play a limited role in
labor relations—as *Garmon*, *Sears*, and the history of the labor laws
imply—or they cannot. Either the federal interests involved in *Garmon* pre-emption are of such a nature that the parties can never
intentionally or inadvertently waive pre-emption claims, or they
are not. In *Davis*, the Court seems to want to have it both ways.

CONCLUSION

The actual result in *Davis* is the least objectionable part of
the Court's handling of the case. Had the union raised the pre-
emption claim in a timely fashion, the trial court would have been
justified in rejecting it. The union failed to make any argument that
would distinguish Davis's status from that of Trione, whom the
Board had already deemed a supervisor. Without such an argument,
Davis was not even arguably an employee, and the dispute was not
even arguably subject to §7 or §8. But instead of resting on narrow
grounds, the Court painted with a broad brush, and in doing so

opened new opportunities for wily lawyers to avoid proper resolution of labor disputes. The Court may also have done lasting
damage to the *Garmon* doctrine by requiring state courts to resolve
the very kind of labor law issues *Garmon* said must be left to the
NLRB. Labor law pre-emption is unnecessarily complicated and
mysterious. *Davis* adds considerably to the mystery and introduces
complications that do not serve federal labor policies.

JOHN SHEPARD WILEY JR.

THE BERKELEY RENT
CONTROL CASE:
TREATING VICTIMS
AS VILLAINS

Landlords do not spring to mind when one thinks of society's victims. That fact may explain *Fisher v. City of Berkeley*,[1] a recent and puzzling Supreme Court antitrust decision. The *Fisher* decision treated landlords as if they were the ones who seek rent control—a treatment that will startle landlords everywhere. Maybe the Court's peculiar view of rent control derived from ignorance of the basics of urban politics and a conviction that landlords always are the villains. But I doubt it: the Supreme Court often decides controversially but rarely idiotically. On the hunch that more happened in the *Fisher* opinion than meets the eye, I offer two alternative accounts in support of the Court's reasoning. These accounts would seem to make sense of the Court's apparent nonsense. They also have implications that extend well beyond the context of rent control.

I. The Setting

Rent control came before the Court in *Fisher* wrapped in antitrust packaging. In 1980, voters in the city of Berkeley, California, passed an initiative that froze residential rents. The ini-

John Shepard Wiley Jr. is Acting Professor of Law, UCLA School of Law.

AUTHOR'S NOTE: I thank Stephen Yeazell for helpful comment.

[1]106 S. Ct. 1045 (1986).

tiative gave members of a Rent Stabilization Board the power to permit rent hikes both on a sporadic individualized and on an annual general basis. Some Berkeley landlords challenged the ordinance in state court on a variety of grounds that did not include the Sherman Act. On appeal to the California Supreme Court, *amici* argued for the first time that federal antitrust law preempted the Berkeley law. The California Supreme Court agreed to consider this tardy antitrust argument, and then took the unusual step of trumping it with a test that the Court borrowed—not from federal antitrust precedents—but from federal decisions on the Commerce Clause.

The United States Supreme Court rejected the California Court's transplantation of Commerce Clause rules into the Sherman Act. But the Supreme Court did reach the same result as the state high court: that section one of the Sherman Act, which prohibits any "contract, combination . . . , or conspiracy" in restraint of trade, did not preempt the rent control law.[2] That result is not surprising. An instinctive response to the landlord's argument might be to say that the Sherman Act aims at private contracts, combinations, and conspiracies and so should not apply to a plainly public initiative that city voters had approved directly. That instinct to distinguish between private and public action has precedent that dates back to the first major case to reason about the relationship between antitrust law and state government policy.[3] But significantly, not a single Justice proposed to decide *Fisher* by the simple expedient of ruling that the Sherman Act does not apply to public laws such as municipal initiatives.

Justice Marshall reasoned that Berkeley landlords had never contracted, combined, or conspired to use Berkeley's rent law to restrain rents. He stated that an antitrust conspiracy requires more than "the ordinary relationship between government and those who must obey its regulatory commands."[4] For Marshall and six other

---

[2] Justice Marshall summarily dismissed the landlords' preemption claim regarding section two of the Sherman Act, which outlaws monopolization. He wrote that the landlords had not pressed "with any vigor in [the] Court" their section two argument. 106 S.Ct. at 1051 n.2.

[3] See Parker v. Brown, 317 U.S. 341, 351 (1943).

[4] 106 S.Ct. at 1050. Marshall also noted both that Berkeley's law did not grant to landlords such a degree of private regulatory power as to create a "hybrid" restraint that would be open to further antitrust preemption inquiry, and that no evidence suggested that landlords

Justices, then, that landlords' attempt to use the antitrust rule against agreements in restraint of trade failed because Berkeley landlords had never agreed with each other.

On its face, this reasoning is bizarre. If one is willing to think of public rules setting maximum rents as analogous to a private conspiracy like a cartel, the logical conspiracy to look for would be among tenants, not landlords. No matter how infrequently landlords receive sympathy as the earth's downtrodden, rent control is at least one policy that everyone agrees is aimed at benefiting tenants at the expense of landlords. Yet the opinion only mentions tenants in a single sentence, identifying them as "certainly a group of interested private parties" but making nothing further of this impressive piece of understatement.[5] Ignoring the possibility of concerted tenant action but rejecting antitrust attack on rent control for lack of agreement between landlords is like dismissing a suit against a cartel of oil sellers because motorists have never agreed on gasoline prices. Justice Marshall seems to have treated the victims like villains.

II. THE MYSTERIOUS WISDOM OF FISHER

Yet Justice Marshall's logic may make sense. It has the important virtue of producing a sensible result. Indeed, to the mind untrained in the marvels of recent antitrust federalism law, the most peculiar feature of the *Fisher* case is not the majority's reasoning

---

had corrupted the ordinance's operation to cloak what in reality was their own conspiracy. 106 S.Ct. at 1050–51.

[5]106 S.Ct. at 1051. The entire sentence reads: "While the Ordinance does give tenants—certainly a group of interested private parties—some power to trigger the enforcement of its provisions, it places complete control over maximum rent levels exclusively in the hands of the Rent Stabilization Board." *Ibid*. This aside hardly disposes of the landlords' Sherman Act argument. The Berkeley City Attorney's office informs me that the nine members of the Rent Stabilization Board are elected—by the same city voters who had enacted the rent control law. If organized and successful political action by tenants poses a Sherman Act problem, then the problem is scarcely lessened because tenants choose to elect agents who will administer the scheme rather than choose to fix rents directly by election. In fact, Berkeley tenants had no such implementation choice available to them; the state court had made clear that it would accept Berkeley's rent control law as constitutional only if it provided for a rent control board that "could adjust maximum rents without unreasonable delays . . . ." Birkenfield v. City of Berkeley, 17 C.3d 129, 169, 130 Cal. Rptr. 465, 550 P.2d 1001 (1976).

but rather the proposition that a marketplace law like antitrust should threaten political results like rent control at all.

The lone dissent reveals the pitfalls that await a contrary result in *Fisher*. Justice Brennan argued that Berkeley's pressure on land-lords to set rents at a particular level amounted to per se illegal price fixing. This thinking is spectacularly incomplete on two counts. First, it misleadingly equates price agreements between competing firms with price regulation by public authorities. Justice Brennan said, for instance, that Berkeley's law "has the same effect on the housing market as would a conspiracy by landlords to fix rental prices."[6] The flaw lies in the failure to distinguish between behavior that does and does not harm consumers with great predictability. Simple price agreements between competitors typically are cartel attempts to harm consumers, while public price regulation does not necessarily hurt consumers in the same simple and predictable man-ner. Justice Brennan's statement illustrates this misleading analogy by treating opposites as identical: Berkeley controlled rents at lower levels to help (existing) tenants, while rents set up by a landlord cartel would raise rents to hurt tenants. Not all government price regulation, of course, follows rent control's pattern of setting a price ceiling. Some regulation, as with that by the old Civil Aeronautics Board, aims to raise rather than cut prices. Other regulation may leave overall price levels unchanged, but set different rates for dif-ferent classes of consumers. The simple direction of regulation's effect on prices, moreover, does little to establish whether regulation is good or bad from some particular perspective. The unpredicta-bility of regulation has been just the difficulty that has confronted and defied any general theory of the subject. So it was quite un-supportable for Justice Brennan to argue without particularized analysis that municipal price settings should be condemned on the same summary logic that supports the quite different federal policy against private cartelization.

Apart from its failure to justify the proposed condemnation of rent control, the Brennan dissent contains a related but more serious problem. It logically threatens all government regulation that, in the words of the Sherman Act, "restrain[s]" trade. But much if not

---

[6]106 S.Ct. at 1054. See also *id.* at 1055 n.2: "[T]he price fixing has the same deleterious effect upon the competitive market whether prices are set by an administrative body or by private parties."

most law can be characterized literally as a "restraint" of some market. Justice Brennan offered no principle for distinguishing acceptable from unacceptable regulation, thus implying the fantastic and impossible view that cities, absent state approval, may engage in no market regulation whatsoever. Consequently, Justice Brennan's proposal to decide the *Fisher* case against the city flies into some heavy weather, from which neither he nor anyone else has charted a way out.

Justice Marshall's logic at least had the provisional advantage of avoiding these serious problems. It had another provisional advantage as well. It avoided the embarrassments that attend the alternative and more precedented ground for affirmance proposed by Justice Powell's separate *Fisher* opinion. The law of antitrust federalism that has dominated the opinions of the 1980s employs the rule—first presented in the *Midcal* case—that a market restraint poses no Sherman Act issue if it has been "clearly articulated and affirmatively expressed as state policy."[7] Justice Powell argued in his *Fisher* concurrence that Berkeley's law was acceptable to federal antitrust policy under this *Midcal* standard.

There did exist action by California that offered a basis for saying that the State had "clearly articulated and affirmatively expressed" a policy authorizing municipal rent control. The California legislature in 1972 had ratified the municipal rent control that Berkeley passed that year. The problem for the *Midcal* approach, however, was that the California Supreme Court in 1976 had invalidated the 1972 Berkeley law.[8] And the California legislature had never taken any action at all regarding the replacement law that Berkeley voters enacted in 1980 that was under review in *Fisher*. In fact, reigning state legislation was pointedly agnostic on the wisdom of local rent control. The most that California currently had to say on the subject was a portion of California's Government Code declaring that "nothing in this article shall be construed to be a grant of authority or a repeal of any authority which may exist of a local government to impose rent controls."[9] This neutral language suggests that, after

---

[7]See California Retail Liquor Dealers Ass'n v. Midcal Aluminum, Inc., 445 U.S. 97, 105 (1980).

[8]See Birkenfield v. City of Berkeley, 17 C.3d 129, 130 Cal. Rptr. 465, 550 P.2d 1001 (1976).

[9]Cal. Gov't Code Ann. section 65589(b) (West 1983). See also Cal. Health & Safety Code

1976, the supporters and opponents of rent controls had clashed and deadlocked at the state level. Thus California state policy approved expressly of an earlier and superseded rent control law but took pains to express no view at all on the version actually before the Court.

This State equivocation caused two difficulties for Justice Powell's use of the *Midcal* rule. First, the Supreme Court in an earlier opinion[10] had ruled that State neutrality was not sufficient to insulate local regulation—and neutrality is the best description of California's current stance on local rent control. More seriously, making this ambivalent expression of state policy decisive of the question whether federal judges will review local regulation calls into question with painful sharpness the purpose of the *Midcal* rule in the first place. Why should "clear articulation and affirmative expression" of state policy make a difference to a federal decision to review municipal policy? If the idea is that state officials simply are more competent policymakers than local government—an extremely doubtful premise[11] that perverts the essence of federalism—then the rule should not count state equivocation of the type that California offered in *Fisher*. Indeed, antitrust law is in danger of appearing absurd if it threatens to review city rent control—unless of course the state has announced that it has no clear or currently applicable policy on the topic at all. It does not help to declare further that the state's unclear equivocation sends a "clearly articulated and affirmatively expressed" policy message to federal judges. No one yet has given a satisfactory justification for what increasingly appears to be a pointless search for clear and affirmative state policy that is of little or no significance.

Given the host of hazards lurking in the reasoning of Justices Brennan and Powell, Justice Marshall's logic is worthy of further investigation. Moreover, it is hard to believe that Justice Marshall simply mistook the nature of rent control. The subject contains

---

Ann. section 50202 (West Supp. 1986) ("nothing in this division shall authorize the imposition of rent regulations or controls").

[10]See Community Communications Co. v. Boulder, 455 U.S. 40, 55 (1981).

[11]A typical rationale for this premise—that local governments are less competent than are states to make sound policy—is that local government units are smaller than their state counterparts. See, *e.g.*, Comment, Municipal Antitrust Liability: Beyond Immunity, 73 Calif. L. Rev. 1829, 1846–47 (1985). This rationale has an odd ring in my metropolitan area, which has more inhabitants than the average state.

complexities—but the landlord's opposition to it was plain even from plaintiff Fisher's identity as a landlord. It seems more likely that the Court understood quite clearly that rent control hurts landlords but nonetheless chose to ask whether landlords—not tenants—had acted in concert to achieve it.

The question is why the Court posed the issue in this peculiar manner. The *Fisher* opinion does not answer that question. I offer two alternative interpretations of the *Fisher* Court's reasoning that could complete the sense that the Court believed its reasoning to make. I do not insist that one or the other of these interpretations is "really" what the *Fisher* Court had in mind. My aim is frankly speculative. In particular I seek to justify the *Fisher* Court's silent assumption that, before section one of the Sherman Act could become relevant, it was the landlords rather than the tenants in *Fisher* who must have agreed with each other.

III. ONE POSSIBILITY: FISHER AS ANTITRUST POLICY

One way to support *Fisher*'s reasoning is to interpret the opinion as a significant choice between competing antitrust goals. There is hot dispute over the proper objectives of the Sherman Act. One way to organize this old debate divides the competing objectives into three groups: Jeffersonian; distributivist; and efficiency-oriented. Adherents of the first goal—Jeffersonians—would be quite astonished to learn that landlords were proposing to use a great piece of American populist legislation against tenants. Jeffersonians would see a lawsuit like this as brazenly perverse—like trying to use an antiracketeering law against the FBI. Judges sharing this view of the Sherman Act would be inclined to dismiss the landlord's lawsuit out of hand.

One need not embrace a purely populist view of antitrust to share that reaction. Robert Lande, for example, has argued impressively that the antitrust laws instead represent a fundamental federal distributive judgment in favor of consumers and against producers.[12] Adherents of this pro-consumer distributive antitrust goal also would tend to dismiss the landlords' attack on rent control. This school's reaction is complicated by the tendency of rent control to benefit

---

[12]See Lande, Wealth Transfers as the Original and Primary Concern of Antitrust: The Efficiency Interpretation Challenged, 34 Hastings L.J. 65 (1982).

164 THE SUPREME COURT REVIEW [1986

some consumers—incumbent renters—at the expense of newcomers and others in search of new housing to rent. But ultimately both the Jeffersonian and the pro-consumer distributive views of antitrust probably would reach conclusions about *Fisher* that sound very similar to Justice Marshall's: If there is a Sherman Act conspiracy issue in this case, the only conspiracy of concern to the antitrust law would be a conspiracy of landlords. And because landlords have not conspired, the Sherman Act conspiracy claim must fail.

This populist and distributivist reasoning conflicts with an efficiency analysis of rent control, which typically would reach unfavorable conclusions about rent control's potential to cause economic loss. Standard economic analysis treats rent control as analogous to the problem of monopsony—the centralization of buying power. Economists usually analyze monopsony as a mirror-image counterpart to monopoly's unified selling power. Monopsony thus is thought to create allocative inefficiencies that parallel those caused by monopoly; a market clogged by cooperation between buyers operates as badly as one restrained by cooperation between sellers. Outside the context of antitrust federalism, antitrust law has accepted this parallel analysis and has condemned agreements to monopsonize just as swiftly as it has outlawed agreements to monopolize. In the *Mandeville Island Farms* case, for instance, the Court without elaboration condemned an agreement between sugar refiners to fix the maximum price at which they bought sugar beets.[13]

Consequently one way to understand Justice Marshall's *Fisher* opinion is as an implicit rejection of economic efficiency in favor of alternative antitrust goals like populism or distributive justice for consumers. This interpretation should make headline news throughout antitrust law. Value choices about the proper goals for the field reverberate throughout antitrust's domain. A rejection of the goal of efficiency would be particularly significant. That goal has been the darling of an entire school of economically-oriented antitrust scholars for the last few decades. The Supreme Court has of late seemed quite receptive to the goal—nominally if not always actually.[14]

---

[13]See Mandeville Island Farms v. American Crystal Sugar Co., 334 U.S. 219, 235–36 (1948).

[14]For instance, the Court's recent and unanimous *Aspen Skiing* decision explicitly stressed its willingness to consider any "efficiency justification" for a challenged practice (even though

The efficiency goal frequently conflicts with a populist view of antitrust, which historically sees the productive efficiency of large enterprises as a direct threat to the survival of "small dealers and worthy men."[15] Modern Supreme Court preference for Jeffersonian antitrust attitudes at the expense of an efficiency value would be notable, primarily for its conflict with the antitrust jurisprudence of the Burger Court. That conflict, however, also makes a populist interpretation of *Fisher* implausible as a matter of Supreme Court precedent.

In most instances, however, no such clash occurs between the goals of distributive justice for consumers and economic efficiency. Achieving productive efficiency in a competitive market typically benefits consumers. These two goals conflict only in relatively rare cases, as with practices that increase productive efficiency but that do not pass these improvements on to consumers. For example, a merger between large firms might increase their productive efficiency but also give the merged firm the power to raise product price above its old level. The efficiency goal would approve of this merger unless the increase in prices was so great as to cause an allocative loss that outweighed the productive gain. The distributive goal would condemn the merger if prices to consumers rose at all.

In this light the *Fisher* case is important because it represents another of the relatively rare cases of conflict between the efficiency and the distributive goals. On one analysis, rent control is a distributive policy favoring consumers and harming producers. On a different analysis of rent control, the policy favors current consumers at the expense of both producers and future consumers. But on no analysis does the case implicate the central distributive judgment that outlaws efforts by producers to appropriate wealth to which the Sherman Act entitles consumers. This view of *Fisher* implies that, when it makes a difference, the Court sees antitrust as a means of blocking producer efforts to take from consumers, not as a path to a more abstract goal of economic efficiency independent of distributional concerns. This interpretation suggests similar treatment for other cases, like that of the merger just men-

---

the opinion then failed to explore an efficiency justification concerning free riders suggested by the defendant's "national advertising campaign"). See Aspen Skiing Co. v. Aspen Highlands Skiing Corp., 105 S.Ct. 2847, 2860, 2852 (1985).

[15]United States v. Trans-Missouri Freight Ass'n, 166 U.S. 290, 323 (1897).

tioned, in which concern for guarding consumers' distributive share against producer appropriation conflicts with the goal of efficiency. It would also call for antitrust analysts to take more account of the presently-neglected issue of distributive justice.

This perspective would make sense of Justice Marshall's opinion. It says, in essence, that Berkeley's law does not offend antitrust policy because the Sherman Act is concerned only with preventing producers from exploiting consumers—and no such exploitation could occur in *Fisher* absent a landlord conspiracy.

IV. A SECOND POSSIBILITY: FISHER AS ANTITRUST FEDERALISM

The speculative interpretation of *Fisher* just offered reads the opinion as a case about the merits of federal antitrust policy, a case that delineates forbidden and permitted economic behavior, and, inferentially, the goals of antitrust law. But another interpretation is possible. This reads *Fisher* as a decision expressive, not of the overarching goals of federal antitrust policy, but of the relationship between state and federal regulation of the market. This second view interprets *Fisher* as a statement of antitrust federalism.

Antitrust federalism is a label for the issue whether and how federal antitrust courts should review state and local market regulation. Case law has dealt with this problem by formulating the "state action" or "*Parker v. Brown*" doctrine, which *Midcal* summarized as exempting "clearly articulated and affirmatively expressed" state regulation from federal antitrust review. My second interpretation understands *Fisher* to modify this law by further limiting Sherman Act review to those state and local regulations that have been "captured" by economic producers. This second interpretation, like the first, also perceives the *Fisher* opinion to be significant for reasons different than those on its face. But again this interpretation reaches conclusions about rent control that are identical to Justice Marshall's: Berkeley's ordinance ought to escape Sherman Act scrutiny because this regulation of rental housing did not result from the concerted political activism of Berkeley landlords.

My aim here is to sketch the consistency of the *Fisher* decision with a capture approach to antitrust federalism.[16] To summarize, if judges believe (as I do) that the Sherman Act's language and legislative history are unclear about whether the Act is intended to

---

[16]See Wiley, A Capture Theory of Antitrust Federalism, 99 Harv. L. Rev. 713 (1986).

have a preemptive scope, then those judges face a dilemma. If judges adopt the minimalist position that the Sherman Act has no preemptive scope, they must countenance a considerable threat: that private groups will use state and local government to insulate restraints of trade from Sherman Act attack. For decades scholars have written about the threat of industry capture of government regulations. This capture problem seems like a matter that ought to worry antitrusters. By getting government in the game, industry groups can achieve exactly the outcome for which private cartels strive. In fact, cartels enforced by government usually are thought to be more harmful to consumer interests than their purely private counterparts. Government enforcement is about the only way that price fixers can effectively suppress the routine headaches of cartel cheating, quality competition, and new industry entry. A noninterventionist school of antitrust federalism must look at that threat to competition and say, "I see it, but the difficulty of the problem and the need to defer to state and local decisionmaking puts it out of bounds for antitrust." This interpretive alternative is problematical because it means reading the Sherman Act to disregard a serious threat to the Act's policy of enforced competition.

Alternatively, judges could interpret the law of antitrust federalism as containing some preemptive scope. Since virtually every law that state and local governments pass can be described as a "restraint of trade" in some sense, this law of antitrust federalism, once activated, threatens dramatically to expand federal judicial supervision of the results of state and local democracy. Federal courts need a systematic limitation on their antitrust power to review the integrity of local decisionmaking if they are to avoid relying on one justification for review that has never played very well in this country: a general faith that federal judges are wiser than local voters and officials. Defining a sensible limit on federal antitrust review, however, turns out to be no easy matter.

The Supreme Court by its judgments has rejected a noninterventionist interpretation of antitrust federalism. Just as no Justice in *Fisher* advocated ruling for Berkeley simply on the ground that the city used the undoubtedly public mechanism of initiative to enact rent control, so too the Court on eight different occasions has used the Sherman Act to invalidate state or local market policies.[17]

---

[17]See Schwegmann Bros. v. Calvert Distilling Corp., 341 U.S. 384 (1951); Flood v. Kuhn, 407 U.S. 258 (1972); Goldfarb v. Virginia State Bar, 421 U.S. 773 (1975); Cantor v. Detroit

Those holdings would seem to reflect the impact of critics who have argued for more than twenty years that regulation often poses a serious competitive threat that aids industry at the expense of consumers.

Mancur Olson's modern classic *The Logic of Collective Action* set forth a now-familiar account of how regulation harmful to consumers can arise from a democratic process. Precisely because consumers are more numerous than producers, consumers typically work poorly as a group. The success of joint political action by consumer groups is affected by, and would benefit, each consumer only slightly. In contrast, smaller industry groups are populated by individual firms that consequently have more at stake and know their participation to be relatively critical to group success. According to this line, political fights between the organized firms and the apathetic consumers become an opportunity for the "exploitation of the great by the small."[18] Thus can businesses capture state and local regulatory protection that any industry ought to want: bans on price competition, quality rivalry, new entry, and so forth.

This capture perspective on regulation can offer the law of antitrust federalism what it needs: a preliminary screen to sift those instances of state and local regulation that warrant further federal review from those that do not. The Sherman Act could explicitly incorporate a capture theory of regulation by first asking whether the state or local government enacted its challenged law only as a consequence of decisive producer support. That would lead a court to put just the question that Justice Marshall asked in *Fisher:* was this challenged market regulation the consequence of the concerted political actions of the producers in that market? If so, federal judges would have reason to suspect this regulation. If not, federal judges should drop the matter as properly left to local political resolution. According to this interpretation, the Court in *Fisher* correctly found that the Berkeley law fell in the latter group and thus ended the federal inquiry on that basis.

Imagine a case, however, where landlords had united to obtain a municipal law that fixed rental rates on their terms. In particular,

---

Edison Co., 428 U.S. 579 (1976); Lafayette v. Louisiana Power & Light Co., 435 U.S. 389 (1978); California Retail Liquor Dealers Ass'n v. Midcal Aluminum, 445 U.S. 97 (1980); Community Communications Co. v. City of Boulder, 455 U.S. 40 (1982); and Maryland v. United States, 460 U.S. 1001 (1983) (the AT&T settlement).

[18]Olson, The Logic of Collective Action 29 (1965).

suppose that a "Berkeley Landlords Association" financed lobbying and publicity that plainly had been decisive in legally enacting a high floor for rents. A capture theory of antitrust federalism would find the result of this concerted political activism by landlords to fit the model of producer capture and thus to merit federal review.

Language in the *Fisher* opinion implies the same result. The Court excused Berkeley's law because it had "been unilaterally imposed by government upon landlords to the exclusion of private control," and said that the differences between that case and one involving "concerted action" were "critical."[19] In the rent floor hypothetical, however, a court could hardly say that government "unilaterally" had imposed a high rent floor upon the very landlords who had organized to obtain it. If the difference is "critical," presumably it would lead the Court to an opposite conclusion about the rent floor. In *Fisher* the Court explained, moreover, that unilateral government action created only "[t]he ordinary relationship between government and those who must obey its regulatory commands whether they wish to or not."[20] The relationship between landlords and the government when concerted landlord action causes the very regulation at issue, however, would be one of captor and client—a link that the Supreme Court would be unlikely to describe as "ordinary."[21] That situation would look more like "a state- or municipality-administered price stabilization scheme [that] is really a private price-fixing conspiracy, concealed under a gauzy cloak of state involvement"—a situation that the Court was careful to distinguish in *Fisher*.[22] If I am correct, then *Fisher*'s reasoning implies the same distinction that a capture theory would draw: both would dismiss rent control but would retain rent floors as problems deserving of federal antitrust attention.

Read in this light, *Fisher* has implications for the entire law of antitrust federalism. It suggests three particular questions about a capture model of antitrust federalism. First, does a capture interpretation of *Fisher* conflict with the First Amendment? Second, does

---

[19]106 S.Ct. at 1049.

[20]*Id.* at 1050.

[21]*Cf.* Sunstein, Interest Groups in American Public Law, 38 Stanford L. Rev. 29, 50 (1985) ("In no modern case has the Court recognized the legitimacy of pluralist compromise as the exclusive basis for legislation.").

[22]106 S.Ct. at 1051 (quotation marks omitted).

Fisher imply that no additional analysis is needed to preempt regulations like the rent floor? Third, if not, then what is the character of this additional inquiry?

Do landlords' First Amendment rights bar a federal court from casting a preemptively more hostile eye on regulation that decisively originates from their political advocacy? Antitrust's *Noerr-Pennington* doctrine[23] may seem so to suggest. That doctrine holds that federal courts will not (except in cases of "sham"[24]) use a defendant's initiation of governmental processes—lobbying, petitioning agencies, filing law suits, or the like—to expose that defendant to Sherman Act remedies that would unacceptably chill such political advocacy.

Noerr and *Pennington* should not block a federal test for producer capture in cases like *Fisher*. The plaintiffs in *Noerr* and *Pennington* sued for remedies that the individual defendants probably found quite frightening: treble damages and (in *Noerr*) an injunction against their continued political advocacy. Those prospects do seem potentially chilling. But in *Fisher*, the plaintiffs sued only for an injunction against enforcement of the challenged regulation. This remedy of simply invalidating a sought-after law is too mild to raise serious concerns about chilling producers' decisions to lobby. When deciding whether a state regulation violates the commerce clause, moreover, the Supreme Court has not hesitated to ask whether local producers were mainly responsible for enacting the challenged provision[25]—even if that consideration logically has precisely the same chilling potential as would use of a capture test in *Fisher*. If one really believes that a federal court unacceptably chills by making speech and advocacy relevant to legal decisionmaking, then one must oppose as unconstitutional all proposals to incorporate actual expressions of legislative intent as factors in constitutional adjudication. But does anyone really believe that a legislator's right to advocate racist laws means that federal courts must ignore such advocacy in a legislative history when judging whether the resulting statute transgresses the Equal Protection Clause?

A second relevant question is whether the Court would invalidate a regulation stemming from concerted producer action (like the

---

[23]See Eastern R.R. Presidents Conf. v. Noerr Motor Freight, 365 U.S. 127 (1961); United Mine Workers v. Pennington, 404 U.S. 657 (1972).

[24]See California Motor Trans. Co. v. Trucking Unlimited, 404 U.S. 508, 510–12 (1972).

[25]See Hunt v. Washington State Apple Advertising Comm'n, 432 U.S. 333, 352 (1977).

hypothetical rent floor) without any further analysis. The *Fisher* Court did not directly address the question whether further analysis is a prerequisite to condemnation, preemption, but it did take two steps in that direction. The first was to analyze the Berkeley laws in the rubric of "the *per se* rule against price fixing,"[26] which of course suggests lessened rather than heightened judicial review once the Court finds a regulation to be the product of conspiracy. The second was citation in a related context of the Court's earlier *Professional Engineers* opinion.[27] That opinion, which arose outside the antitrust federalism context, held that antitrust analysis will not explore the fundamental question whether competition is socially desirable in principle. Critics of activist antitrust federalism argue that the *Professional Engineers*' rule dictates peremptory condemnation of regulations that governments justify by the type of arguments that *Professional Engineers* would dismiss: that market failures mean competition produces undesirable results that regulation must counter.[28]

If *Fisher* really does imply that the Court will not further study regulations that stem from producer agreements before condemning them, then this implication of *Fisher* is inconsistent with a capture theory of antitrust federalism—and is unwise. For reasons that spring, ironically, from the weakness of the capture idea itself, a capture interpretation should require significant additional analysis before it preempts captured regulation. The capture notion can explain an observed tendency—that regulation often helps industry at consumer expense—but it fails dramatically as a general theory of regulation. As a general theory, it would imply what obviously is not true: that all industries would be governed by captured regulation. The idea of capture likewise is too simplistic to explain how existing regulation either can injure producers (as with natural gas regulation) or can benefit residential consumers at industry expense (as with the differential rates of return common in regulation of electric utilities).

Some theorists have tried to strengthen the capture idea by adding the notions of focal events or political entrepreneurs who mobilize

---

[26]106 S.Ct. at 1049.

[27]106 S.Ct. at 1049, citing National Society of Professional Engineers v. United States, 435 U.S. 679 (1978).

[28]See, *e.g.*, Community Communications Co. v. City of Boulder, 455 U.S. 40, 66–68 (Rehnquist, J., dissenting).

weak groups' latent political power.[29] These modifications enrich the texture but discard the predictive force of the producer capture model. By explaining all regulation as the product of capture by some coalition, they say that those laws that exist show the power of the groups that supported them—thus rendering the capture idea tautological and useless for purposes of judicial analysis. For this reason, it is correct but pointless to identify rent control as a case of "consumer capture." To expand a capture theory in this manner is simply to abandon any restraint that the limitation might offer.

The simple truth is that we have no comprehensive and satisfying positive theory of regulation. This failure of theory ought not to be surprising. Regulation is in one sense simply a synonym for "government," and few are surprised at our lack of a comprehensive and satisfying positive theory of government. We expect social science (to the extent that it is science at all) to offer only partial and limited insight into the complexities of human affairs. Judicial use of any theory of regulation needs to appreciate the inevitable weaknesses of the theoretical tool. In the case of the theory of producer capture, an admittedly partial and provisional theory helps more than no theory in identifying state and local regulation deserving federal suspicion. But that use should be appropriately modest, by limiting its conclusion to a suspicion triggering further scrutiny rather than a presumption demanding inevitable preemption.

The third question asks what form the needed additional analysis should take. There is a range of possibilities. Current law (as established in *Midcal* and as invoked by Justice Powell) asks whether a state has authorized this form of municipal regulation. I am critical of this "state authorization" test for reasons already suggested. The test burdens state and local government by taxing delegation of responsibility at the same time that it fails to advance any real federal antitrust interest. Those agreeing that the *Midcal* approach is costly and pointless would seek its replacement. If one accepts the Chicagoans' claim that efficiency ought to be the sole goal of the Sherman Act, one replacement candidate would demand that a state or local government offer adequate efficiency justification for its disputed regulation. A critic of the assertedly exclusive antitrust ef-

---

[29]See, *e.g.*, Peltzman, Toward a More General Theory of Regulation, 19 J.L. & Econ. 211 (1976); Wilson, The Politics of Regulation, in The Politics of Regulation 357 (J. Wilson ed. 1980).

ficiency goal might nevertheless ask for precisely the same efficiency justification if that critic sought to apply a goal of distributive justice for consumers. That critic would seek to distinguish those regulations that enlarge the amount of economic pie that consumers receive from regulations that simply widen the producers' slice. Finally, the least desirable choice would mimic the procedural model established by the federal requirement of Environmental Impact Statements. This inquiry would ask whether the local government itself had conducted an adequate efficiency scrutiny to which a federal court could defer. This search for an "Efficiency Impact Statement" by state or local government might be either conjunctive with, disjunctive from, or entirely independent of, a direct federal efficiency or distributive review. Plainly, the law of antitrust federalism could develop in many different directions, each of which would be consistent with a capture approach to the field.

V. Conclusion

Antitrust law is characterized by its common law character. A key feature of common law decisionmaking is its reliance on judicial instinct. Judges change law by relying on their instincts, even when they have a hard time justifying that instinct in a particular case. Doctrinal clarity sometimes emerges only after judges have reacted to facts with responses that can be explained in hindsight, when perspective reveals what proximity obscured.

In hindsight, I have offered two alternative readings of the *Fisher* decision. One interprets the case as a significant statement of antitrust goals, a rejection of the single-minded pursuit of economic efficiency in favor of a determination to prevent producers from taking consumers' just entitlement. The second sees it as an important addition to the law of antitrust federalism, a law of importance to all state and local governments. Both show *Fisher* to be a decision whose rationale conceals the intelligence of its result.

DEAN ALFANGE, JR.

GERRYMANDERING AND THE CONSTITUTION: INTO THE THORNS OF THE THICKET AT LAST

In his dissent in *Baker v. Carr*,[1] decrying the unwisdom of the Court's entry into the "political thicket"[2] of legislative apportionment, Justice Frankfurter warned:[3]

> Apportionment, by its character, is a subject of extraordinary complexity, involving—even after the fundamental theoretical issues concerning what is to be represented in a representative legislature have been fought out or compromised—considerations of geography, demography, electoral convenience, economic and social cohesions or divergencies among particular local groups, communications, the practical effects of political institutions like the lobby and the city machine, ancient traditions and ties of settled usage, respect for proven incumbents of long experience and senior status, mathematical mechanics, censuses compiling relevant data and a host of others. Legislative responses throughout the country to the reapportionment demands of the 1960 Census have glaringly confirmed that these are not factors that lend themselves to evaluations of a nature that are the staple of judicial determinations or for which judges

Dean Alfange, Jr., is Professor of Political Science at the University of Massachusetts at Amherst.

[1] 369 U.S. 186 (1962).

[2] The term originated in Frankfurter's plurality opinion in Colegrove v. Green, 328 U.S. 549, 556 (1946).

[3] 369 U.S. at 323–24.

are equipped to adjudicate by legal training or experience or native wit. And this is the more so true because in every strand of this complicated, intricate web of values meet the contending forces of partisan politics.

When, in *Wesberry v. Sanders*,[4] grounded in Article I, § 2,[5] of the Constitution, and in *Reynolds v. Sims*,[6] based on the Equal Protection Clause of the Fourteenth Amendment,[7] the Court embraced the standard that congressional and legislative districts must be "as nearly of equal population as is practicable"[8] ("one person, one vote"[9]), it neatly skirted all the complexities that Frankfurter identified and settled upon a single objective rule. Districting plans that satisfied the criterion of "one person, one vote" were *ipso facto* constitutional.

The prime virtue of this simple rule is that it defines the constitutional issue in a manner capable of resolution through "judicially discoverable and manageable standards."[10] As John Hart Ely has noted, the rule "is certainly administrable. In fact administrability is its long suit, and the more troublesome question is what else

---

[4]376 U.S. 1 (1964) (congressional districting).

[5]"The House of Representatives shall be composed of Members chosen every second Year by the People of the several States." Justice Harlan wryly commented that the framers were unlikely to have slipped a requirement for equality of population among each state's congressional districts "into the Constitution in the phrase 'by the People,' to be discovered 175 years later like a Shakespearian anagram." 376 U.S. at 27. As recently as Karcher v. Daggett, 462 U.S. 725, 745–46 (1983) (concurring opinion), Justice Stevens recognized that Article I, §2, was inadequate, except for stare decisis, to support a requirement that congressional districts be equally populated. See also Kelly, Clio and the Court: An Illicit Love Affair, 1965 Supreme Court Review 119, 134–36.

[6]377 U.S. 533 (1964) (state legislative districts).

[7]The applicability of the Equal Protection Clause to the right to vote in general and to malapportionment in particular was denied by Justice Harlan in Reynolds v. Sims, 377 U.S. at 590–608. For a critical discussion of Harlan's argument, see Van Alstyne, The Fourteenth Amendment, the "Right" to Vote, and the Understanding of the Thirty-Ninth Congress, 1965 Supreme Court Review 33.

[8]Reynolds v. Sims, 377 U.S. at 577. In Wesberry v. Sanders, the Court had declared that "as nearly as is practicable one man's vote in a congressional election is to be worth as much as another's." 376 U.S. at 7–8.

[9]The Court enunciated the appropriately gender-neutral form of "one person, one vote" in Gray v. Sanders, 372 U.S. 368, 381 (1963).

[10]Baker v. Carr, 369 U.S. at 217. "That standard is 'judicially manageable' because census data are concrete and reasonably reliable and because judges can multiply and divide." Karcher v. Daggett, 462 U.S. at 751 (Stevens J., concurring).

it has to recommend it."[11] The answer may well be precious little else, although the rule clearly encapsulates in a slogan a concept that is so appealing in its expression of the egalitarian assumptions of a democratic society that it attained instant popular acceptance and legislative acquiescence,[12] and enhanced the legitimacy of the Court's constitutional role.[13] By framing the issue exclusively in terms of the numerical aspects of districting, the rule diverts attention from the question of what constitutional objective it is intended to achieve. If the goal is that no person's vote can have a greater political effect than any other person's vote,[14] that cannot be achieved simply by assuring that a citizen lives in a legislative district that is no larger in population than any other district. Some heed must also be paid to insuring that districting plans do not deny representation to, or do not systematically underrepresent, particular social groups or interests or concerns that may be of special importance to some but not necessarily favored by those dominant in the legislature. In short, the rule of "one person, one vote" ignores the problems presented by the practice of gerrymandering.[15] It was understood even at the time of *Wesberry* and *Reynolds* that gerrymandering could still flourish under the standard of "one person, one vote".[16] But with the single exception of racial gerry-

---

[11]Ely, Democracy and Distrust 121 (1980).

[12]See Dixon, Democratic Representation 1–2 (1968).

[13]See, *e.g.*, McKay, Reapportionment: Success Story of the Warren Court, 67 Mich. L. Rev. 223 (1968). Robert Dixon has suggested that "[o]ne man-one vote . . . may turn out to be one of the greatest successes if one of the most Sisyphean ventures of the so-called Warren era." Dixon, The Warren Court Crusade for the Holy Grail of "One Man-One Vote," 1969 Supreme Court Review 219, 224. Martin Shapiro has described it as a "great victory" for the Court as an institution. Shapiro, Gerrymandering, Unfairness, and the Supreme Court, 33 UCLA L. Rev. 227, 252 (1985).

[14]See, *e.g.*, Gray v. Sanders, 372 U.S. at 379–81.

[15]"Gerrymandering is simply discriminatory districting which operates unfairly to inflate the political strength of one group and deflate that of another." Dixon, The Court, the People, and "One Man, One Vote," in Reapportionment in the 1970s 7, 29 (Polsby ed. 1971). For the origin of the term, see Dixon, note 12 *supra*, at 459 n.2; Hardy, Considering the Gerrymander, 4 Pepperdine L. Rev. 243, 245–46 (1977); Luce, Legislative Principles 397–98 (1930).

[16]See, *e.g.*, Baker, The Reapportionment Revolution 82 (1966); Dixon, note 12 *supra*, at 458; Sickels, Dragons, Bacon Strips, and Dumbbells—Who's Afraid of Reapportionment, 75 Yale L.J. 1300, 1307–08 (1966); Elliott, Prometheus, Proteus, Pandora, and Procrustes Unbound: The Political Consequences of Reapportionment, 37 U. Chi. L. Rev. 474, 481–

mandering through multi-member districting,[17] the Court continued to steer clear of the gerrymandering issue—presumably because
of the potential magnitude of the task of dealing with it effectively.[18]

It was not until 1986, in *Davis v. Bandemer*,[19] that the Court
ended two decades of assiduous silence[20] and held that claims of

---

88 (1970); Edwards, The Gerrymander and "One Man, One Vote," 46 NYU L. Rev. 879,
880 (1971). See also Wells v. Rockefeller, 394 U.S. 542, 551 (1969) (Harlan, J., dissenting);
id. at 555 (White, J., dissenting). Indeed, the majority in Reynolds itself noted the danger.
377 U.S. at 578–79.

[17]After consistent deference to legislative decisions to create multi-member legislative
districts, Fortson v. Dorsey, 379 U.S. 433 (1965); Burns v. Richardson, 384 U.S. 73 (1966);
Whitcomb v. Chavis, 403 U.S. 124 (1971), the Court, in White v. Regester, 412 U.S. 755
(1973), affirmed a District Court's ruling that the creation of multi-member districts that
submerged racial and ethnic minorities constituted an unconstitutional abridgment of the
right to vote of the members of the minority groups. But in Mobile v. Bolden, 446 U.S.
55, 61–70 (1980), a plurality ruled that vote dilution through at-large elections could be held
to violate the Constitution only where purposeful discrimination could be shown. In 1982,
Congress amended §2 of the Voting Rights Act of 1965 for the express purpose of extending
the coverage of the Act to reach state actions with regard to voting that had a racially
discriminatory effect even if they lacked a discriminatory purpose. Senate Rept. 97-417
(97th Cong., 2d Sess.) at 15–16; see also Parker, The "Results" Test of Section 2 of the
Voting Rights Act: Abandoning the Intent Standard, 69 Va. L. Rev. 715 (1983); Derfner,
Vote Dilution and the Voting Rights Act Amendments of 1982, in Minority Vote Dilution
145 (Davidson ed. 1984). The Court in Thornburg v. Gingles, 106 S.Ct. 2752 (1986), declined
the Solicitor General's remarkable suggestion that it reject the explicit statement of the
purpose of the amendment to §2 contained in the Report of the Senate Judiciary Committee
because it was the product of compromise. *Id.* at 2763 n.7. It unanimously held invalid
under §2 four multi-member legislative districts in North Carolina, and declared that, to
make out a violation of §2 through multi-member-district gerrymandering, it was necessary
for the minority group to make three showings: (1) "that it is sufficiently large and geographically compact to constitute a majority in a single-member district," *id.* at 2766; (2)
"that it is politically cohesive," *id.* at 2767; and (3) "that the white majority votes sufficiently
as a bloc to enable it . . . usually to defeat the minority's preferred candidate." *Ibid.*

On the issue of racial gerrymandering generally, see, *e.g.*, Parker, Racial Gerrymandering
and Legislative Apportionment, in Minority Vote Dilution 85 (Davidson ed. 1984); Blacksher
& Menefee, At-Large Elections and One Person, One Vote, *id.* at 203; Hartman, Racial
Vote Dilution and Separation of Powers: An Exploration of the Conflict between the Judicial
"Intent" and the Legislative "Results" Standards, 50 Geo. W. L. Rev. 689 (1982); Bonapfel,
Minority Challenges to At-Large Elections: The Dilution Problem, 10 Ga. L. Rev. 353
(1976); Carpeneti, Legislative Apportionment: Multimember Districts and Fair Represen-
tation, 120 U. Pa. L. Rev. 666 (1972); Note, Geometry and Geography: Racial Gerrymandering and the Voting Rights Act, 94 Yale L.J. 189 (1984).

[18]As recently as 1983, the Court noted that "achieving population equality, is far less
ambitious than what would be required to address gerrymandering on a constitutional level."
Karcher, 462 U.S. at 734 n.6.

[19]106 S.Ct. 2797 (1986).

[20]Individual Justices had spoken earlier to the issue of the justiciability of gerrymandering.
Justice Harlan expressed opposition in WMCA v. Lomenzo, 382 U.S. 4, 6 (1965) (concur-

unconstitutional vote dilution through partisan political gerry-mandering were justiciable.[21] By so doing, it implicitly recognized that there was more to the problem of representational equality than could be resolved by the simple expedient of equalizing district populations. At the same time, however, it cut itself loose from the security of an easily administrable standard and created the risk of plunging the judiciary headlong into the process of evaluating the kinds of complex considerations to which Justice Frankfurter had referred, a task that must be carried out in the very center of the arena where "meet the contending forces of partisan politics."

The ultimate success of this newest judicial adventure will be measured by whether the courts will prove able to provide relief from egregious political gerrymandering without exposing vir-tually every districting plan to judicial scrutiny. Judicial inter-vention in the absence of coherent standards for judicial appli-cation, or, worse, the establishment of another simplistic rule equivalent to "one man, one vote"—such as proportional repre-sentation—would require courts and legislatures to go much fur-ther toward the complete disregard of the factors that Justice Frankfurter correctly noted are at the heart of the districting process when properly performed.

---

ring). Declarations of support of justiciability were made by Justices Stevens and Powell. See Mobile v. Bolden, 446 U.S. 55, 86–89 (Stevens, J., concurring); Rogers v. Lodge, 458 U.S. 617, 652 (Stevens, J., dissenting); Karcher v. Daggett, 462 U.S. at 761 (Stevens, J., concurring); *id.* at 787 (Powell, J., dissenting). In 1984, Justice Brennan, for himself and Justices White and Marshall, declared: "We have never concluded, nor in my view should we conclude, that the existence of noncompact or gerrymandered districts is by itself a constitutional violation." Karcher v. Daggett, 466 U.S. 912, 917 (1984) (stay denied) (dis-senting). In light of this categorical statement, it is surprising that these three Justices comprised half of the six-Justice majority holding political gerrymandering claims justiciable in Davis v. Bandemer. See note 285 *infra* and accompanying text.

[21]A number of cases raising the issue of justiciability of partisan political gerrymandering had been brought to the Court earlier, but each had been disposed of without the issue being addressed. In *Davis,* the Court noted four cases in which lower court decisions holding that the issue of political gerrymandering was not justiciable had been summarily affirmed. 106 S.Ct. at 2804. It also noted prior summary affirmances or dismissals of appeals in cases in which the court below had treated political gerrymandering claims to be justiciable. *Ibid.* In Gaffney v. Cummings, 412 U.S. 735 (1973), the Court, without discussing justiciability, rejected a Fourteenth Amendment challenge to a bipartisan political gerrymander in which districts were drawn by a bipartisan commission with the intent of providing each political party with seats in the legislature in proportion to its statewide political support. See text at notes 161–64 *infra.*

I. The Inadequacy of "One Person, One Vote" as an End in Itself

A. "ONE PERSON, ONE VOTE" AS A MEASURE OF FAIRNESS IN DISTRICTING

The decision in *Davis v. Bandemer* brought the Court closer to filling the theoretical void created by the conversion of the salutary general principle of equally populated legislative districts into a rigid rule,[22] still adhered to for congressional districting,[23] if not for state legislative districting,[24] "requir[ing] that a State make a good-faith effort to achieve precise mathematical equality."[25] In its most rigorous application of this standard, the Court in *Karcher v. Daggett* invalidated, for failure to satisfy the requirement of "precise mathematical equality," a New Jersey congressional districting plan in which, using 1980 census figures, the largest district had a population of 527,472, and the smallest a population of 523,798, the largest thus having a population 0.7 percent greater than that of the smallest.[26]

The obvious question raised by *Karcher* is what such an exercise in arithmetical captiousness properly has to do with fairness in districting. What conceivable end is served by requiring a state whose congressional districts have an average population of over half a million persons, and, on the average, deviate from "perfect equality" by about 726 persons, to go through the process again in order to come closer, particularly when the probable deviation of the census data from absolute accuracy is greater than the population deviations between the districts in the state's plan, and when, in any event, the census data have certainly become obsolete in the intervening years since they were compiled? Such insistence on numerical minutiae would not appear to serve any purpose[27] because

---

[22]Reynolds v. Sims, 377 U.S. at 577; Wesberry v. Sanders, 376 U.S. at 18, recognized the impossibility of mathematical precision. That was, of course, before the computer revolution.

[23]See White v. Weiser, 412 U.S. 783 (1973); Karcher v. Daggett, 462 U.S. 725 (1983).

[24]See Mahan v. Howell, 410 U.S. 315 (1973); Gaffney v. Cummings, 412 U.S. 735 (1973); White v. Regester, 412 U.S. 755 (1973). In *Gaffney*, the Court noted that fair and effective representation "does not in any commonsense way depend upon eliminating . . . insignificant population variations." 412 U.S. at 748.

[25]Kirkpatrick v. Preisler, 394 U.S. 526, 530–31 (1969).

[26]462 U.S. at 728.

[27]To be sure, there is language in both Wesberry v. Sanders and Reynolds v. Sims to the

in no way could the elimination of this average deviation of 726 persons in itself have the slightest impact on the weight or effectiveness of anyone's vote.[28] It is heartening that in *Davis* Justice White, writing for a majority that, on this point, included Justices Brennan, Marshall, Powell, and Stevens, noted that, although legislative districts may be equally populated, there may still be a denial to one political group of "the same chance to elect representatives of its choice as any other political group,"[29] and that Justice Powell, writing for himself and Justice Stevens, observed that "one person, one vote" "was not itself to be the only goal of redistricting."[30]

That the Court chose to insist on equality of population purely for its own sake was possibly the result of its misidentification of the rights at stake—employing the language of individual rights to describe equality of representation, which is fundamentally a group right. For example, in *Gray v. Sanders*,[31] the case in which the term "one person, one vote" was first articulated,[32] the Court, striking down the Georgia county-unit system, rested its decision on "[t]he idea that every voter is equal to every other voter in his State."[33] In *Wesberry*, the Court declared that the "Constitution leaves no room for classification of people in a way that unnecessarily abridges this right [to vote]."[34] And in *Reynolds*, Chief Justice Warren, speaking for the majority, referred to the individual's "right to elect legislators in a free and unimpaired fashion."[35] But, even in *Reynolds*, the Court was aware that guaranteeing the individual's right to an

---

effect that the establishment of equally populated districts is in itself the end to be achieved. In *Wesberry*, the Court referred to the "Constitution's plain objective of making equal representation for equal numbers of people the fundamental goal for the House of Representatives," 376 U.S. at 18, and, in *Reynolds*, the Court declared that "*Wesberry* clearly established that the fundamental principle of representative government in this country is one of equal representation for equal numbers of people." 377 U.S. at 560–61. But there is no good reason to believe that the Court did not see the requirement of equally populated districts as instrumental to the achievement of more substantive ends. See text at notes 36–38 *infra*.

[28]"One must suspend credulity to believe that the Court's draconian response to a trifling 0.6984% maximum deviation promotes 'fair and effective representation' for the people of New Jersey." 462 U.S. at 766 (White, J., dissenting).

[29]106 S.Ct. at 2806.

[30]*Id.* at 2829 (dissenting).

[31]372 U.S. 368 (1963).

[32]See note 9 *supra*.

[33]372 U.S. at 380.

[34]376 U.S. at 17–18.

[35]377 U.S. at 562.

equally weighted vote could not be divorced from providing protection for the group rights that were centrally at stake—including
the right to "fair and effective representation" and the right of the
majority to determine the direction of public policy and to govern.
Warren also declared in *Reynolds* that "fair and effective representation for all citizens is concededly the basic aim of legislative apportionment,"[36] and, as Justice Powell correctly observed in *Davis*:
"The concept of 'representation' necessarily applies to groups: groups
of voters elect representatives, individual voters do not."[37] Moreover, with regard to a majority's right to govern, Chief Justice
Warren had this to say:[38]

> Logically, in a society ostensibly grounded on representative
> government, it would seem reasonable that a majority of the
> people of a State could elect a majority of that State's legislators.
> To conclude differently, and to sanction minority control of
> state legislative bodies, would appear to deny majority rights
> in a way that far surpasses any possible denial of minority rights
> that might otherwise be thought to result.

The right to govern and to "elect a majority of [a] State's legislators"
is clearly not an individual right.

This is not to say that individual rights are not adversely affected
by malapportionment. Quite obviously they are. Every individual
has a right to an equal opportunity to influence government policy
through the exercise of the right to vote, and that right is abridged
if the representative for whom one votes, even if elected, is, because
of malapportionment, sure to be outvoted or disregarded in the
legislative assembly.[39] But the opportunity to influence government
policy subsequent to elections is not available to everyone equally.
It is, or should be, principally the prerogative of those whose representatives constitute the legislative majority, and if, through malapportionment, that prerogative is exercised by the minority in

---

[36]*Id.* at 565–66.

[37]106 S.Ct. at 2828 (dissenting).

[38]377 U.S. at 565.

[39]Thus, as early as the 17th century, the Levellers recognized that the elimination of
malapportioned "rotten boroughs" was an essential corollary of the right of universal man-
hood suffrage (servants and alms recipients excepted) that they demanded. See Puritanism
and Liberty 433–44 (Woodhouse ed. 1974); Shaw, The Levellers 59–61 (1968). For an
excellent and thoughtful discussion of apportionment as an issue of equality and individual
rights, see Smith, Liberalism and American Constitutional Law 120–37 (1985).

whose favor the malapportionment works, it is the majority whose right is denied.

Trying to equate guarantees of fair representation and majority rule with the requirement of equally populated legislative districts fails because the "one person, one vote" standard is not consonant with the American geographical districting system for electing legislators. In an effort to make this equation, the Supreme Court initially relied on a measure, the Dauer-Kelsay scale,[40] which simply counted the percentage of the population of the state that resided in the minimum number of the least populous legislative districts necessary to constitute a majority of the legislative houses in question. Thus, in *Reynolds*, it was calculated that, under the then existing districting plan for the Alabama legislature, 25.1 percent of the state's population lived in districts that could elect a majority of the state Senate and 25.7 percent lived in districts that could elect a majority of the lower house.[41] The Dauer-Kelsay scale was both simple and intuitively appealing because, if there is perfect population equality among districts, the legislative districts necessary to comprise a legislative majority must include a majority of the population of the state. But, while it is a useful measure for comparing the relative unrepresentativeness of individual states, it does not measure whether a majority actually controls the legislature. For the Dauer-Kelsay scale to measure that, two absurd assumptions are required: first, that there is a unanimity of view among the residents of a district, and, second, that political issues will divide the state into two camps, with the people residing in the smallest number of districts with the least population necessary to constitute a majority of the legislature squared off against those residing in the largest number of the most populated districts that would just fail to comprise a legislative majority.[42]

But, since the votes in individual districts are never unanimous, it will always be possible for a minority of the people to elect a majority of the legislature even where the districts are perfectly equally pop-

---

[40]Dauer & Kelsay, Unrepresentative States, 44 Nat'l Mun. Rev. 571 (1955).

[41]377 U.S. at 545.

[42]See the dissenting opinion of Justice Stewart in Lucas v. 44th General Assembly of Colorado, 377 U.S. 713, 755 (1964). The Dauer-Kelsay figures can be made even more dramatic by dividing them in half because the votes need not be unanimous in the smallest districts. In theory, a bare majority of the voters in a bare majority of the districts can control the legislature.

ulated. The side winning a minority of the districts with a high percentage of the vote in those districts may well constitute a popular majority, but will not control the legislature. Needless to say, it is precisely the purpose of gerrymandering to make sure that that happens if one's opponents are in the majority.[43] The most extreme case of minority control of a legislature that would be possible in a single-member-district electoral system with perfect population equality would be that a minority of just over 25 percent of the population (one-half plus one of the voters in one-half plus one of the districts) could elect a majority of the legislators.[44] That extreme example requires no more absurd assumptions than those that must be made in using the Dauer-Kelsay scale.

Similarly, either gerrymandering or purely fortuitous considerations of geography and demography can prevent a group, whether racial, ethnic, political, or ideological, from attaining fair and effective representation in a single-member district, and *a fortiori*, in a multi-member district, electoral system, even if all districts are equally populated. If the group is evenly dispersed across the state, constituting a substantial minority everywhere but a majority nowhere, geographical districting will, by its natural operation, insure its underrepresentation. To have an opportunity to achieve significant representation in a districting system, a minority must be sufficiently concentrated in specific geographical areas to constitute a majority in those areas.[45] But gerrymandering can reduce the advantages of population concentration by dividing the group's members among a number of different districts, in each of which they are included among a sufficient number of voters of other groups that they are no longer a majority,[46] or by creating multi-member districts large enough so that the group's population is submerged in a larger constituency in which it is a minority.[47]

Given the districting system, the requirement of equally populated districts can also stand the concept of equally weighted votes for all individuals on its head. If, to comply with the requirement, I am moved

[43]See Hacker, Congressional Districting 50–61 (1964).

[44]See Lucas v. 44th General Assembly of Colorado, 377 U.S. at 750 n. 12 (Stewart, J., dissenting).

[45]See Backstrom, Robins, & Eller, Issues in Gerrymandering: An Exploratory Measure of Partisan Gerrymandering Applied to Minnesota, 62 Minn. L. Rev. 1121, 1127 (1978).

[46]See, *e.g.*, Kirksey v. Board of Supervisors, 554 F.2d 139, 148–51 (5th Cir.), cert. denied, 434 U.S. 968 (1977).

[47]See Thornburg v. Gingles, 106 S.Ct. at 2767.

from an overpopulated competitive district (in which my vote is said to be debased because I share my representative with too many others) into an underpopulated district that is safe for my political opponents (which, from the standpoint of a gerrymanderer, is a perfect move[48]), in what sense has my right to vote been protected or my right to fair and effective representation vindicated? I have been moved from a district where my vote might contribute to the election of a candidate who would represent my views in the legislature to one in which it will have no effect at all. Of course, any redistricting plan may incidentally disadvantage me in this way, but there is an enormous irony if it is done under judicial compulsion to protect my right to an equally weighted vote. In the district that is safe for my opponents, not only am I denied representation for my own interests and concerns, but my person is being used (by counting me in the district's population total) to increase the representation to which my opponents are due. If my constitutional rights are violated when I am compelled to contribute my money for the purpose of propagating ideas with which I do not agree,[49] is it not also a violation of my constitutional rights if I am compelled to contribute my person to augment the representation in the legislature of ideas with which I do not agree? It is small wonder that the Court's efforts to insure "fair and effective representation" through an ever more rigorous enforcement of the requirement of equality of district populations have been characterized by terms such as "silly,"[50] "naive,"[51] "ridiculous,"[52] "absurd,"[53] "make[s] no sense,"[54] "counterproductive,"[55] "sterile,"[56] or "inan[e]."[57]

---

[48]See Cain, The Reapportionment Puzzle 178–80 (1984).

[49]See *e.g.*, Abood v. Board of Education, 431 U.S. 209 (1977).

[50]Shapiro, note 13 *supra*, at 233.

[51]*Id.* at 234.

[52]Backstrom, Problems of Implementing Redistricting, in Representation and Redistricting Issues 43, 46 (Grofman, Lijphart, McKay & Scarrow eds. 1982).

[53]Grofman, Criteria for Districting: A Social Science Perspective, 33 UCLA L. Rev. 77, 113 n.161 (1985).

[54]Howard & Howard, The Dilemma of the Voting Rights Act—Recognizing the Emerging Political Equality Norm, 83 Colum L. Rev. 1615, 1650 (1983).

[55]Dixon, note 13 *supra*, at 243.

[56]Baker, Whatever Happened to the Reapportionment Revolution in the United States? in Electoral Laws and Their Political Consequences 257, 274 (Grofman & Lijphart eds. 1986).

[57]Bickel, The Supreme Court and Reapportionment, in Reapportionment in the 1970s 57, 74 (Polsby ed. 1971).

If the "one person, one vote" standard is a mismatch with a system of geographical districting, there are two electoral systems with which it is perfectly compatible. The fact that these two systems would lead to strikingly different results indicates that "one person, one vote" can mean different things depending on which of the two basic functions of the legislature—representation or law-making—one is concerned with. These two functions are, in critical respects, contradictory, and any improvement in the legislature's capacity to perform one is likely to lead to a diminution of its capacity to perform the other.[58]

The first of the two systems with which "one person, one vote" would be consistent is proportional representation, under which each political party would be awarded seats in the legislature in proportion to the percentage of the votes it receives in the legislative election. Proportional representation would maximize the representativeness of the legislature because each group with sufficient strength to obtain at least one seat would be assured of representation for its interests and concerns, and thus assured that those interests and concerns will be articulated and considered in the course of the legislature's deliberations.[59] Experience with proportional representation, however, demonstrates that it has a fractionalizing effect on the political party system, tending to defeat the creation of an effective legislative majority.[60] Because small parties do not need to coalesce with other groups or parties to create an electoral majority in individual districts in order to be represented in the legislature, there is no incentive for them to do so. Consequently, while single-member-district electoral systems with plurality winners tend to support the maintenance of two-party regimes, legislatures under proportional representation tend to be made up of a larger number of splinter parties,[61] none of which

[58]See Dixon, Representation Values and Reapportionment Practice: The Eschatology of "One-Man, One-Vote," in Representation 167, 173–75 (Pennock & Chapman eds. 1968).

[59]For a discussion of the seemingly inexorable linkage between the standard of "one person, one vote" and proportional representation, see Rogowski, Representation in Political Theory and Law, 91 Ethics 395, 411 (1981); Note, The Constitutional Imperative of Proportional Representation, 94 Yale L.J. 163, 182–88 (1984).

[60]See Rae, The Political Consequences of Electoral Laws 98–99 (1971).

[61]See Duverger, Political Parties 217, 239 (1963); Sartori, The Influence of Electoral Systems: Faulty Laws or Faulty Method? in Electoral Laws and Their Political Consequences 43, 64 (Grofman & Lijphart eds. 1986).

commands a majority. Under such circumstances, the legislature's ability to enact a coherent legislative program is necessarily impaired.

On the other hand, "one person, one vote" would also be consistent with a system under which all legislators would be elected at large. Under such a system, no person's vote would be worth more than another's, but the statewide majority could overwhelm all opposition. An at-large system would have the obvious defect of calling upon every voter to vote for as many candidates as there are legislative seats, but that is not the principal problem it presents. A legislature elected entirely at large could be expected to be single-minded and purposeful and capable of enacting its legislative program in the name of the majority. But it would be seriously unrepresentative.[62] Only one voice would be heard, and the interests and values not shared by the majority might be excluded altogether from consideration in whatever deliberations the legislature might choose to engage in. Even sizable minorities could be denied any representation at all, let alone "fair and effective representation."[63]

Although proportional representation and at-large elections are diametric opposites in terms of the nature of the legislative assembly that would be elected under them, both are compatible with the principle of "one person, one vote," because they have one critical aspect in common: the elections are held in statewide constituencies, and "one person, one vote," as employed by the Court, is intended as measure of the effectiveness of an individual's vote, not in the district in which it is cast, but statewide. Beyond doubt, "one person, one vote" is the proper standard for evaluating the effectiveness of an individual's vote within a given constituency, but it

---

[62]Although the problem of at-large elections for city and county governing bodies is not as severe because of the generally much smaller number of places to be filled, it is nevertheless an effective device for denying representation to racial minorities of significant size. See Engstrom & McDonald, The Effect of At-Large Versus District Elections on Racial Representation in U.S. Municipalities, id. at 203.

[63]In Colegrove v. Green, 328 U.S. at 553, Frankfurter warned of the dangers of at-large elections for state delegations to the House of Representatives—an objection that would apply even more emphatically to at-large elections for state legislatures—and cited the observation of Chancellor Kent, who spoke of "the wisdom and justice of giving, as far as possible, to the local subdivisions of the people of each state, a due influence in the choice of representatives, so as not to leave the aggregate minority of the people in a state, though approaching perhaps to a majority, to be wholly overpowered by the combined action of the numerical majority, without any voice whatever in the national councils." 1 Kent, Commentaries on American Law 230 n.c (1848).

is another matter when it is used to assess the effectiveness of a vote beyond the boundaries of that constituency. The fact is that, as long as the United States remains committed to the election of legislators in individual (geographically defined) districts, the requirement of "equal representation for equal numbers of people"[64] cannot insure either "that a majority of the people of a State [will be able to] elect a majority of that State's legislators"[65] or that "fair and effective representation for all citizens"[66] will be provided. To insure their provision, attention must be paid to the results of the districting process and to the possibilities of gerrymandering.

B. "ONE PERSON, ONE VOTE" AS AN ANTIGERRYMANDERING
   STANDARD

A persuasive case can be made for the proposition that the malapportionment problem with which the Court set out to do battle in *Baker v. Carr,* and for which it established the standard of "one person, one vote," was never really a problem of numbers at all, but was, from the outset, simply a gerrymandering problem. Robert Dixon suggested "that the central goal of the *Baker* plaintiffs, and plaintiffs in reapportionment cases generally, is a *political representation* goal."[67] Population equality was not demanded as a matter of abstract fairness, but as a matter of partisan equity or of equity in the representation of interests. The Court in *Reynolds* nevertheless chose, misleadingly, to emphasize abstract fairness, declaring that "[t]o the extent that a citizen's right to vote is debased [by having its effectiveness depend on place of residence] he is that much less a citizen."[68]

If that is so, the method established in the Constitution for the election of members of the United States Congress denies equality of citizenship. In the Senate, the state of Alaska, with a population, according to the 1980 census, of 402,000, has the same representation as California, with a 1980 census population of 23,668,000, despite the population variance of just under 59 to 1.[69] Moreover,

[64]Wesberry v. Sanders, 376 U.S. at 18.

[65]Reynolds v. Sims, 377 U.S. at 565.

[66]*Id.* at 565–66.

[67]Dixon, note 12 *supra,* at 458.

[68]377 U.S. at 567.

[69]See Lucas v. 44th General Assembly of Colorado, 377 U.S. at 746 (Stewart, J., dissenting).

even in the House of Representatives population variances between states, as opposed to those within states, are considerable. One may wonder how much less a citizen a resident of South Dakota feels when he realizes that a member of the House of Representatives from Montana represents only some 393,000 persons, while his congressman represents 691,000, or three-quarters again as many.

Why, then, given the public willingness to tolerate a malapportioned Congress,[70] was there so much agitation for remedying the malapportionment of state legislatures and state congressional delegations prior to 1962?[71] It is hardly the case that the public is more resigned today to the existence of unfairness. Nor is it true that the population variances among state legislative districts and congressional districts that existed at that time, as large as they were,[72] were consistently larger and more dramatic than the 59–1 variance that exists today between Alaska's and California's per capita representation in the Senate. The difference is that it was clear with regard to those malapportionments, as it is not clear with regard to the current congressional malapportionment,[73] that the discrepancies were all in the same direction—that one set of interests, rural and agrarian, were consistently overrepresented at the expense of urban, and later suburban, interests. Writing in 1958, Anthony Lewis identified the problem: "Malapportionment has an almost universal rural bias. One estimate is that in 1947 residents of urban areas made up 59 per cent of the United States population but elected only about 25 per cent of the state legislators in the country."[74] The situation was similar with regard to state congres-

---

[70]See Press, Commentary, in Reapportionment in the 1970s 142, 144 (Polsby ed. 1971).

[71]For a description of the apportionment problem as it existed prior to Baker v. Carr, see McKay, Reapportionment 35–58 (1965).

[72]*E.g.*, the Tennessee legislative apportionment that was challenged in Baker v. Carr gave the same representation to counties whose populations differed by more than 10 to 1. See 369 U.S. at 255 (Clark, J., concurring). The Illinois congressional districts challenged in Colegrove v. Green varied in population from 112,000 to 914,000. See 328 U.S. at 566–67 (Black, J., dissenting). In Florida, the populations of state legislative districts varied by over 100 to 1. In California, the use of counties as an apportionment base led to the allocation of one state senator to Los Angeles, whose population exceeded six million, and one state senator to a group of rural counties whose combined population was less than 15,000, a variance of over 400 to 1. See Dixon, note 12 *supra*, at 8–9.

[73]The situation could change if it begins to be perceived that congressional malapportionment significantly favors one set of interests at the expense of another. See Press, note 70 *supra*, at 144.

[74]Lewis, Legislative Apportionment and the Federal Courts, 71 Harv. L. Rev. 1057, 1064 (1958). See also Baker, Rural Versus Urban Political Power 16–17 (1955).

sional delegations. Andrew Hacker calculated at the time of the *Wesberry* decision that "[d]istricts with predominantly rural populations had 102 congressmen, whereas their actual numbers would have entitled them to only 86,"[75] and concluded that "[t]he problem of rural overrepresentation . . . is very real."[76]

The population disparities that existed in state legislative and congressional districts when *Baker v. Carr* was announced had developed in part through inertia, a simple failure to respond to the changes in population patterns that occurred as the United States became an urbanized and industrialized nation, as immigration swelled the population of cities still further, and as suburban areas underwent explosive growth.[77] In part, the disparities resulted from an understandable desire on the part of legislators to escape the onerous task of redrawing district lines and to maintain stable constituencies, both to allow the development of a feeling of mutual confidence between the legislator and the voters in a particular location[78] and to avoid the confusion among voters that could be created by repeatedly shifting them from one district to another.[79] In very large part, they resulted from the fact that legislators were well aware that observing the duty to redistrict would likely mean the end of their own legislative careers and their replacement by new representatives from metropolitan areas.[80] Finally, there was a strong Jeffersonian feeling that rural America represented virtue and wholesomeness whereas cities were centers of sin and corruption, and that the transfer of political power from rural to urban areas would be morally wrong.[81]

Whatever the reasons, the fact that the existing malapportionments consistently favored the interests of the dominant political

---

[75] Hacker, note 43 *supra*, at 95.

[76] *Ibid.*

[77] Neither the Tennessee legislature at the time of Baker v. Carr, 369 U.S. at 191, nor the Illinois delegation at the time of Colegrove v. Green, 328 U.S. at 567 (Black, J., dissenting), had been reapportioned since 1901. The Alabama legislature whose apportionment was challenged in Reynolds v. Sims had been reapportioned in 1901, but not again until after *Baker* was decided. See 377 U.S. at 540–45.

[78] See DeGrazia, Apportionment and Representative Government 145–46 (1963).

[79] See Press, note 70 *supra*, at 145.

[80] See Baker, note 16 *supra*, at 28–29.

[81] See Hacker, note 43 *supra*, at 114–18; Baker, note 16 *supra*, at 21–22; McKay, note 71 *supra*, at 50–51.

group brought them squarely within the definition of a gerrymander. As Justice Stevens noted while a member of the Court of
Appeals for the Seventh Circuit, in wiping away these malapportionments, the Court, "without analysis of the term 'gerrymander,'
. . . decisively invalidated the means by which the 'ins' maximized
their ability to exclude the 'outs.' "[82] Pre-*Baker* malapportionment
has been described as a "silent gerrymander"[83] because it was accomplished by simple inaction, but, in effect, it was as much a
gerrymander as if the lines had been drawn with a conscious design
to achieve a political purpose. Indeed, the effects of the malapportionments were clearly understood, and the determination not to
change was grounded in the desire to preserve and perpetuate those
effects. Urban and suburban voters appealed to the courts for relief
because, under the existing system of malapportionment, they were
politically impotent. Although Justice Frankfurter called on them
to obtain relief by "sear[ing] the consciences of the people's representatives,"[84] the self-interest of those representatives in the maintenance of the status quo assured the futility of such efforts. The
Court, thus faced with a situation involving both the denial of fair
representation and the frustration of majority rule through the
maintenance of legislative districts of unequal size in a context in
which no political remedy was available, responded by accepting
jurisdiction and establishing the constitutional standard of "one
person, one vote."

But it was the gerrymander that led the Court to respond, not
the population discrepancies in and of themselves. Had those discrepancies been random, operating to the detriment of rural interests and to the advantage of urban interests as often as the other
way around, it is unlikely that these discrepancies would have generated sufficient concern to have induced the Court to enter the
political thicket. Robert Dixon observed that once population disparities no longer constituted a form of gerrymandering, litigants
ceased to "care a hoot about numbers," and their arguments for
strict application of the population equality standard became "simply ploys for arguing in favor of [their] own politically preferred

---

[82]Cousins v. City Council of Chicago, 466 F.2d 830, 847 (7th Cir. 1972) (dissenting).

[83]Baker, Gerrymandering: Privileged Sanctuary or Next Judicial Target? in Reapportionment in the 1970s 121, 122 (Polsby ed. 1971).

[84]*Baker*, 369 U.S. at 270.

plan."[85] The standard of "one person, one vote" is thus best understood as a rule to combat gross political gerrymandering, and *Baker*
as standing for the proposition that political gerrymandering claims
are justiciable. The Court's formal acceptance of this proposition
in *Davis v. Bandemer* merely made explicit what was implicit in the
reapportionment decisions from the beginning.

II. The Reapportionment Cases as Antigerrymandering Cases

If "one person, one vote" is properly understood as an antigerrymandering standard, the cases applying that standard should
be looked upon as antigerrymandering decisions, and it is useful to
evaluate them as such. To what extent do they inhibit the practice
of manipulating district boundaries for the purpose of disadvantaging groups with inadequate power in the political process effectively to protect themselves; to what extent do they actually encourage gerrymandering; and to what extent are they simply
irrelevant to the issue. If they did nothing else, *Reynolds v. Sims* and
Wesberry v. Sanders required the states to give up the tempting practice of ignoring the obligation to engage in periodic redistricting,
thus insuring decennial reapportionment and ending the silent gerrymander—which even the Court's sternest detractors in this area
concede was a healthy development.[86] Moreover, the establishment
of the requirement that legislative districts be equally populated
made the future task of gerrymandering considerably more difficult.
As Andrew Hacker put it:[87]

> Gerrymandering is [still] possible when districts are equal in
> size. . . . Indeed, the artistry of the political cartographer is put
> to its highest test when he must work with constituencies of
> equal population. At such times, his skills can be compared to
> those of a surgeon, for both work under fixed and arduous rules.
> However, if the mapmaker is free to allocate varying populations
> to different districts, then the butcher's cleaver replaces the

---

[85]Dixon, Computers and Redistricting, A Plea for Realism, 2 Rut. J. Computers & Law
15, 19 (1971).

[86]See Bickel, note 57 *supra*, at 61. Of course, even healthy developments may have a cost.
The requirement for periodic redistricting creates opportunities to engage in the traditional
forms of gerrymandering in place of the "silent gerrymander." See Dixon, note 12 *supra*, at
457.

[87]Hacker, note 43 *supra*, at 59.

scalpel; and the results reflect sharply the difference in the method of operation.

Throughout the *Reynolds* opinion there are inchoate suggestions that the Court is aware that to strive too hard for population equality among districts could be costly in terms of protecting political fairness, and, at one point, it was conceded that "[i]ndiscriminate districting, without any regard for political subdivision or natural or historical boundary lines, may be little more than an open invitation to partisan gerrymandering."[88]

Justice Harlan complained in dissent that, although the Court warned against the dangers of "indiscriminate districting," it "nevertheless exclude[d] virtually every basis for the formation of electoral districts other than 'indiscriminate districting.' "[89] He cogently observed that "people are not ciphers and . . . legislators can represent their electors only by speaking for their interests—economic, social, political."[90] The Court's failure to allow some deviation from the rule of population equality to provide for the representation of interests, was perhaps due to a concern that an exception for interest representation might prove to be sufficiently open-ended to undermine the effectiveness of the rule. Nevertheless, if the Court's intent was to discourage gerrymandering, its reasoning was seriously deficient. For to imply that the legislature need not be concerned with insuring that interests are properly represented, at least to the extent that meeting that concern might require deviation from the principle of population equality, is to suggest that it also need not be concerned if interests are poorly represented. But for the Court to instruct legislatures that insuring the fair representation of interests is not a crucial factor in districting is to inform those seeking to gerrymander that they may achieve their goal without any concern for adequate representation as long as they have satisfied the standard of "one person, one vote."[91]

On the day *Reynolds* was decided, the Court, in *Lucas v. 44th General Assembly of Colorado*,[92] voided a districting plan adopted through statewide initiative and referendum by an overwhelming

---

[88]377 U.S. at 578–79.

[89]*Id.* at 622 (dissenting).

[90]*Id.* at 623–24.

[91]See Dixon, note 12 *supra*, at 272–73. But see Auerbach, The Reapportionment Cases: One Person, One Vote—One Vote, One Value, 1964 Supreme Court Review 1, 55.

[92]377 U.S. 713 (1964).

margin (including a majority in every county) over a competing equal-population plan.[93] The plan approved by the voters was invalidated for failure to adhere to the principle of population equality in the establishment of districts for the state Senate. The Court regarded as irrelevant the fact that the plan was favored by the voters in every part of the state and was subject to repeal or modification through the same process by which it was adopted should the majority have become dissatisfied with it, declaring that "[a]n individual's constitutionally protected right to cast an equally weighted vote cannot be denied even by vote of a majority of a State's electorate."[94] The Court's reaction was a clear indication that, despite the language to the contrary in the *Reynolds* opinion,[95] it perceived the issue as a simple matter of protecting the individual's right to vote, and that the rights of groups to "fair and effective representation" and the right of the majority to govern were distinctly subordinate. There was no evidence that the districting plan approved by the voters was designed to limit the political power of groups with disfavored interests or that it was an attempt by an entrenched minority to avoid yielding its political dominance to the majority.[96] Indeed, there was no indication of anything other than an attempt to provide, in a state with extraordinary geographical characteristics and diverse and distinct economic interests, for adequate representation of groups and areas whose needs and concerns might be overlooked if the principle of population equality were rigidly followed. The fact that the plan was approved even by the voters in the cities demonstrated that it did not result from a rural stranglehold on the political process that could be broken only by judicial intervention.

In *Lucas* the principle of population equality was vindicated purely for its own sake. There was no examination of the nature of the individual and group rights that were actually at stake or of the purpose for which the individual's right was to be protected. If this

---

[93]*Id.* at 717–18.

[94]*Id.* at 736. The Court justified its position by reliance on Justice Jackson's famous declaration for the Court in the second flag-salute case: "One's right to life, liberty, and property . . . and other fundamental rights may not be submitted to vote; they depend on the outcome of no elections." West Virginia State Board of Education v. Barnette, 319 U.S. 624, 638 (1943).

[95]See 377 U.S. at 565–66, 577–79.

[96]377 U.S. at 753–54, 759 (Stewart, J., dissenting).

had been an instance of the denial to an individual of the right to cast a vote, or to have it counted, or otherwise to participate in the political process, no extrinsic justification for its protection would be needed. But the right asserted here was of a different nature. The individual litigants were not seeking to vindicate something personal to themselves, but to vindicate the right of the majority (of which they presumably saw themselves as part) to govern. But if it is a majority right, the majority should be able to waive it in the interest of fairness to the minority. To allow an individual to frustrate the majority's decision on an issue as fundamental as how the state legislature should be organized, in the absence of any evidence of denial to anyone of fair representation, "would appear to deny majority rights in a way that far surpasses any possible denial of [individual] rights that might otherwise be thought to result."[97] The effect of *Lucas* was to undercut the contribution of *Reynolds* to the development of antigerrymandering standards. Instead, it emphasized, as *Reynolds* ultimately had done, that issues of representational fairness were of no moment so long as population equality was preserved.

Five years later, in *Kirkpatrick v Preisler*,[98] the Court eliminated all doubt that the ambiguities in the *Reynolds* opinion were to be resolved in favor of the most rigorous application of the "one person, one vote" standard, and that the hints dropped in that opinion that there might be some room for pragmatic flexibility were to be disregarded. Now it was to be required "that the State make a good-faith effort to achieve precise mathematical equality."[99] There was no longer any question but that "one person, one vote" had taken on a life of its own. There was not even any pretense that the strict demands of the standard were needed to guarantee fair representation or majority rule. The rule had no function as a brake on gerrymandering. It was a rule whose sole purpose was to insure population equality among legislative districts, the tacit assumption being that that was all that was necessary to protect the individual's right to an equally weighted vote.[100]

---

[97]377 U.S. at 565.

[98]394 U.S. 526 (1969).

[99]*Id.* at 530–31.

[100]As Robert Dixon despairingly commented, "the Court majority apparently forgot that

Kirkpatrick involved the issue of the validity of a districting plan for the Missouri congressional delegation. A companion case, *Wells v. Rockefeller*,[101] involved the validity of a New York congressional districting plan. In Missouri, the legislature had created districts the largest of which had a population of 445,523 (according to the 1960 census) and the smallest a population of 419,721. The ideal district size was approximately 432,000.[102] There can be no doubt that any state whose districts were this close to perfect population equality before 1962 would have been held up as a shining model, but by 1969, these minuscule differences made the plan unconstitutional.[103]

Viewed even on its own terms, the *Kirkpatrick* decision makes little sense because there can be absolutely no difference—other factors relating to the representativeness of the districts being equal (as was assumed here)—between the effective weight of the vote of an individual who resides in a district of 445,523 and one who resides in a district of 419,721. Moreover, by 1969, when *Kirkpatrick* was handed down, the 1960 census figures that were to be used to measure district population were obsolete, and voters in other states resided in districts that varied by perhaps hundreds of thousands from the population of any of the Missouri districts. Viewed in terms of its effectiveness as a deterrent to gerrymandering, it was an utter disaster. It invited, encouraged, and rewarded gerrymandering.

Missouri sought to justify the trivial population variances between its districts, as *Reynolds* had declared it could do, by showing that they were "based on legitimate considerations incident to the effectuation of a rational state policy."[104] It claimed that the variances

---

the problem was political and that the issue was political representation, not numbers." Dixon, note 13 *supra*, at 219.

[101] 394 U.S. 542 (1969).

[102] 394 U.S. at 529 n.1.

[103] In Wells v. Rockefeller, 394 U.S. 542, the Court struck down the New York congressional districting plan. The population variances in the New York districts were somewhat larger than in Missouri because the New York legislature had divided the state into regions for congressional districting purposes, and had sought only to equalize the population of districts within each region. The resulting 41 districts varied in population from 382,277 to 435,880. The legislature had employed this scheme "as a means to keep regions with distinct interests intact." 377 U.S. at 546. From the standpoint of assuring fair and effective representation, there was much to be said for the legislature's idea, but the Court was not interested.

[104] Reynolds v. Sims, 377 U.S. at 579.

resulted from efforts to accomplish such ends as (1) preventing the fractionalization of communities of interest among different districts in order to provide them with effective representation, (2) arriving at a compromise districting plan acceptable to the legislative leaders of both parties, (3) preventing the fragmentation of political subdivisions by not violating their boundaries, and (4) ensuring the geographical compactness of each district. The Court rejected these justifications out of hand. Insuring adequate representation for interests was impermissible because interests don't vote; population variances cannot be used to resolve partisan political disputes; and concern for protecting the integrity of political boundaries or for establishing compact districts cannot warrant any deviation from population equality.[105]

Kirkpatrick's message to the gerrymanderer was clear: there is absolutely no reason to be hesitant about splitting communities among various districts or to be concerned about bipartisan fairness (unless the other party's votes are needed for the plan's adoption). Lines that cross and recross political boundaries may be drawn with impunity, and so may lines that wind districts around the state in whatever grotesque shapes are politically, if not aesthetically, pleasing. Chief Justice Warren's warnings of the dangers of "[i]ndiscriminate districting" were forgotten.[106] The dissenters, Justices White, Harlan, and Stewart, pointed out the magnitude of the opening the Court was leaving for gerrymandering,[107] but the majority paid no heed. Repercussions did not take long in coming. The relatively politically fair New York plan struck down in *Wells v. Rockefeller* was replaced, after the Republicans gained control of both houses of the state legislature, by a plan that carefully conformed to the principle of population equality but ignored political boundaries and considerations of compactness, and was clearly intended to enhance Republican fortunes.[108] This plan was sustained by the Court.[109]

---

[105] 394 U.S. at 533–36.

[106] See 377 U.S. at 578–79.

[107] See Wells v. Rockefeller, 394 U.S. at 551 (Harlan, J., dissenting); *id.* at 554–55 (White, J., dissenting).

[108] See Edwards, note 16 *supra*, at 884–87; Baker, One Man, One Vote, and "Political Fairness"—Or, How the Burger Court Found Happiness by Rediscovering Reynolds v. Sims, 23 Emory L.J. 701, 712–13 (1974).

[109] Wells v. Rockefeller, 398 U.S. 901 (1970). See Dixon, "One Man, One Vote"—What Next? 60 Nat'l Civic Rev. 259, 265 (1971).

In 1971, the Court began a retreat from the extreme rigidity of its 1969 position, but it continued to refuse to recognize a gerrymander when confronted with it. In 1968, the Court had extended the applicability of the equal population requirement to include elections to local governmental bodies with lawmaking authority where the members of those bodies are elected from individual districts,[110] and in 1970, in *Hadley v. Junior College District*,[111] it struck down, for failure to satisfy this requirement, a Missouri law providing for the apportionment of the trustees of junior college districts among the component school districts. The law was a pure apportionment law rather than a districting law (since trustees were being distributed among preexisting districts);[112] there was thus no possibility of gerrymandering. The Court nevertheless held the plan invalid as a "built-in discrimination against voters in large districts" because, under the terms of the apportionment, the largest district would always have been somewhat underrepresented.[113]

In 1971, in *Abate v. Mundt*,[114] the Court upheld a plan for apportionment of the members of a county board of supervisors among the county's towns under which the smallest town was allocated one supervisor and the others allocated a number of supervisors in proportion to the population of each relative to that of the smallest town, but rounded to the nearest integer. The Court upheld the plan despite the fact that some towns would be overrepresented and some underrepresented depending on whether they were rounded up or rounded down. It recognized the appropriateness of representing towns as towns on the county board, thus accepting respect for the integrity of political boundaries as a justification for population variances. It distinguished this apportionment plan from the one struck down in *Hadley* in part because, under the Missouri law, the most heavily populated district would always be underrepresented, whereas, under this plan, the identity of the towns to be overrepresented or underrepresented would be entirely ran-

---

[110]Avery v. Midland County, 390 U.S. 474 (1968).

[111]397 U.S. 50 (1970).

[112]*Id.* at 56–57.

[113]For criticism of the Court's approach in *Hadley*, see Leventhal, Courts and Political Thickets, 77 Colum. L. Rev. 345, 351 (1977).

[114]403 U.S. 182 (1971).

dom,[115] thus giving express recognition to the fact that randomly distributed malapportionment has far different implications from that which will always favor one set of interests or one geographical area over others.

Also in 1971 the Court, in *Whitcomb v. Chavis*,[116] considered an Indiana state legislative districting plan that contained what was, in effect if not by intent, a racial gerrymander. Under this plan, Marion County, which includes Indianapolis and surrounding townships, was established as a single legislative district for both House and Senate elections. It was to be an extremely large multi-member district, from which eight Senators and fifteen House members were to be elected at large. Black residents of the county challenged this arrangement as unconstitutionally diluting their voting strength by submerging them in a predominantly white district, thus denying representation for their unique needs and interests. A unanimous three-judge District Court found that, if the county had been divided into single-member districts, the population of the black ghetto in Indianapolis was sufficiently large to elect two House members and one Senator,[117] and, in the light of this and other evidence of dilution of the effectiveness of the voting strength of blacks in the county,[118] held that the use of these multi-member districts violated the Equal Protection Clause.[119]

The Supreme Court did not accept this argument. In an opinion by Justice White, who had strongly dissented in *Kirkpatrick* and *Wells*, it continued the deference to the use of multi-member districts for state legislatures that it had demonstrated in *Fortson v. Dorsey*[120] in 1965 and *Burns v. Richardson*[121] in 1966. In *Fortson*, the Court sustained the use of such districts against the claim that they were facially invalid,[122] but added that the question would be different

---

[115]*Id.* at 185–86.

[116]403 U.S. 124 (1971). See Carpeneti, note 17 *supra*, at 67–85; Clinton, Further Explorations in the Political Thicket: The Gerrymander and the Constitution, 59 Iowa L. Rev. 1, 17–23 (1973).

[117]Chavis v. Whitcomb, 305 F.Supp. 1364, 1385 (S.D. Ind. 1969).

[118]*Id.* at 1381–85.

[119]*Id.* at 1385–86.

[120]379 U.S. 433 (1965).

[121]384 U.S. 73 (1966).

[122]379 U.S. at 435–39. The Court noted that *Reynolds* had identified multi-member districting as one of the valid alternatives open to the legislature. *Id.* at 436.

if "designedly or otherwise" their use "operate[d] to minimize or cancel out the voting strength of racial or political elements of the voting population."[123] In *Burns*, the Court reiterated that position,[124] and suggested factors that would make the validity of these districts dubious: if the districts "are large in relation to the total number of legislators," or "are not appropriately subdistricted to assure distribution of legislators that are resident over the entire district," or if they "characterize both houses of a bicameral legislature rather than one."[125] The District Court in *Chavis* found all three of the *Burns* factors clearly present in the Indiana plan.[126] The Supreme Court, although forced to concede their presence, was not disposed to give them any weight because it was not satisfied that any vote dilution had been proved. It noted that no purposeful discrimination had been alleged, and declared that a holding that unconstitutional vote dilution had occurred had to be based on "evidence and findings that ghetto residents had less opportunity than did other Marion County residents to participate in the political processes and to elect legislators of their choice."[127] Ghetto residents, it held, were underrepresented, not because they had less opportunity to participate in the political process, but because they voted overwhelmingly for Democratic candidates in a county that was carried by the Republicans in four out of five elections in the 1960s.[128] Thus blacks were underrepresented not because of discrimination but because their party lost.[129] The Court simply rejected as unproved the claim that blacks in the inner-city ghetto had unique needs and were without an effective voice in the legislature to express those needs.[130] The Court did affirm the District Court's invalidation of the overall

---

[123]*Id.* at 439.

[124]384 U.S. at 88–89.

[125]*Id.* at 88.

[126]305 F.Supp. at 1386–87.

[127]403 U.S. at 149.

[128]*Id.* at 149–52.

[129]One can scarcely imagine a greater boon to the gerrymanderer than the Court's suggestion that if the group victimized by a gerrymander loses the election, the fact that the election was lost insulates the gerrymander from constitutional review. See Engstrom, The Supreme Court and Equipopulous Gerrymandering: A Remaining Obstacle in the Quest for Fair and Effective Representation, 1976 Ariz. St. L. Rev. 277, 307; Clinton, note 116 *supra*, at 20–21.

[130]403 U.S. at 155.

plan, but on the ground that the population variances were too great to satisfy the requirement of "one person, one vote".[131] Although *Kirkpatrick* and *Wells* were cited,[132] the population disparities were much greater in *Chavis* and the rigidity of those cases unnecessary to the decision.

Whitcomb v. Chavis is of particular interest because it shows the Court, when faced with a gerrymandering claim the validity of which was supported by its own dicta, scurrying back to the security and comfort of the "one person, one vote" standard. It is particularly instructive that the Court rejected a claim of racial gerrymandering by noting that blacks were Democrats while the multi-member district in which they lived was predominantly Republican. This is tantamount to arguing that not only is political gerrymandering not unconstitutional, but its use can legitimate any racial gerrymandering that it may coincidentally bring about. For it seems plain that the use of multi-member districting in Marion County was a political gerrymander. Except for the aberration brought about by the 1964 Democratic landslide, the Democrats, with a sizable minority of the vote in the county, were essentially precluded from winning *any* of the county's eight Senatorial and fifteen House seats because the county as a whole was Republican.

Justice Harlan, in an opinion dripping with sarcasm,[133] declared that the Court's approach "should be recognized for what it is: a manifestation of frustration by a Court that has become trapped in the 'political thicket' and is looking for the way out."[134] Justice Douglas, joined by Justices Brennan and Marshall, saw the issue as simply "whether a gerrymander can be 'constitutionally impermissible.' "[135] For them, "[t]he question of the gerrymander is the other half of *Reynolds v. Sims*," and it involves the guarantee of "fair representation."[136] This recognition of the validity of the constitutional claim to fair representation is particularly remarkable in light

---

[131]*Id.* at 161–62.

[132]*Id.* at 162 n.41.

[133]See the discussion of this opinion in Kurland, 1970 Term: Notes on the Emergence of the Burger Court, 1971 Supreme Court Review 265, 281–83.

[134]403 U.S. at 170 (separate opinion).

[135]*Id.* at 176 (concurring and dissenting opinion).

[136]*Ibid.* Justice Douglas's concern was limited to the prevention of racial gerrymandering. *Id.* at 180.

of the abandonment of all apparent concern for fairness of representation in favor of pure arithmetic in *Kirkpatrick* and *Wells*, which Brennan wrote for the Court and the other two joined. Apparently they had now arrived at the realization that, in the context of race, equalizing the population of legislative districts was not enough to insure fairness of representation. The majority, however, saw that to recognize a claim of entitlement to fair representation by a racial minority would open the door to such claims by political groups, an eventuality for which it was not yet prepared.[137]

By 1973, Richard Nixon's four appointees had taken their places on the Court. Issues of redistricting and representation were thenceforth to be considered by a Court far different in its orientation and outlook from the Court that had enunciated the doctrine of "one person, one vote" and had defined that standard in *Kirkpatrick* and *Wells* as requiring "a good-faith effort to achieve precise mathematical equality." The new Justices, however, respected *stare decisis*. In *White v. Weiser*,[138] the Court unanimously adhered to the *Kirkpatrick* and *Wells* standard, refusing to accept even the smallest avoidable deviations from "precise mathematical equality." Three of the new Justices—Powell, Burger, and Rehnquist—concurred specially to note that they believed *Kirkpatrick* and *Wells* to have been wrongly decided, but that they would agree to follow the standard of those cases "unless and until" they were reconsidered by the Court.[139]

From the point of view of the gerrymander, however, the most important aspect of *White v. Weiser* had to do with the choice of which of the alternative plans to implement. The District Court had ordered the implementation of a plan whose population variances were slightly larger than those of an alternate plan, because the former plan was free of the taint of infection by political considerations. It had been drawn without regard to such factors as protecting the districts of incumbent congressmen or providing representation for social, cultural, or economic interests, and its districts were more compact.[140] The Court, however, reversed on

---

[137]*Id.* at 156–57. The Court expressed concern that "affirmance of the District Court would spawn endless litigation concerning the multi-member district systems now widely employed in this country." *Id.* at 157.

[138]412 U.S. 783 (1973).

[139]*Id.* at 798 (concurring opinion).

[140]See *id.* at 794.

this point.[141] It could have done so, as Justice Marshall urged,[142] simply on the ground that the alternate plan's population variances were smaller, but it went further and held that it was to be preferred because it "most clearly approximated the reapportionment plan of the state legislature, while satisfying constitutional requirements."[143] Because "[d]istricting inevitably has sharp political impact and inevitably political decisions must be made by those charged with the task,"[144] courts should defer to those political decisions insofar as they can do so within constitutional limitations. Courts should seek to adopt a plan as close to the legislature's as possible, making only the minimum number of modifications necessary to equalize the district populations. The legislature's political choices should not be set aside because of a judicial preference for more compact districts or because of a sense that it is improper that districts be drawn "so as to preserve the constituencies of congressional incumbents."[145] The legislature is entitled to attain legitimate political goals. Clearly, the Court did not want federal judges to be scrutinizing districting plans to insure compliance with neutral criteria, the observance of which has been seen by some commentators as necessary to control gerrymandering and to promote fairness of representation,[146] but the enforcement of which would convert districting from a legislative to a judicial function. As long as the standard of population equality was observed, the political choices should be made by the legislature.

If the newly formed Burger Court felt itself bound by *stare decisis* with regard to congressional districting, it did not deem itself so bound with regard to state legislative districting. There were no precedents dealing with state legislative districting which had actually held that *Kirkpatrick's* requirement of "a good-faith effort to achieve precise mathematical equality" was applicable. Thus, in *Mahan v. Howell*,[147] decided four months before *White v. Weiser*, the

---

[141]*Id.* at 794–97.

[142]*Id.* at 798–99 (concurring opinion).

[143]*Id.* at 796.

[144]*Id.* at 795–96.

[145]*Id.* at 797.

[146]See, *e.g.*, Edwards, note 16 *supra*, at 893–95 (compactness); Common Cause, Toward a System of Fair and Effective Representation 29–30 (1977) (no consideration of incumbency).

[147]410 U.S. 315 (1973).

Court applied a different standard, despite the objections of Justices Brennan, Marshall, and Douglas, who insisted that *Kirkpatrick* applied to both types of districting.[148]

Resuscitating the language of *Reynolds v. Sims*, the Court, in an opinion by Justice Rehnquist, declared in *Mahan* that, for state legislatures, "some deviations from the equal-population principle are constitutionally permissible" if "based on legitimate considerations incident to the effectuation of a rational state policy."[149] The use of a different standard was justified by the recognition in *Reynolds* that "[s]omewhat more flexibility may . . . be constitutionally permissible with respect to state legislative apportionment than in congressional districting."[150] And, finally, in deciding whether the state of Virginia had relied on "legitimate considerations" in establishing a districting plan for the lower house of its legislature that had a maximum percentage deviation of 16.4 percent,[151] the Court recalled *Reynolds's* concession that "a State can rationally consider according political subdivisions some independent representation in at least one body of the state legislature," and that its interest in doing so is "more than insubstantial."[152] Applying these criteria, the Court concluded that the deviation of 16.4 percent was acceptable;[153] it was justified by the valid state policy of according counties independent representation in the lower house where feasible.[154]

Four months later, in *Gaffney v. Cummings*[155] and *White v. Regester*,[156] both decided on the same day as *White v. Weiser*, the Court carried *Mahan's* distinction between state legislative districting and congressional districting one step further. Again over the dissent of Justices Brennan, Marshall, and Douglas, it held that *Kirkpatrick's* rejection of a *de minimis* approach and its insistence that "the State must justify each variance, no matter how small,"[157] were not ap-

---

[148]*Id.* at 334 (dissenting opinion).

[149]*Id.* at 325, quoting Reynolds v. Sims, 377 U.S. at 579.

[150]*Id.* at 578.

[151]See 410 U.S. at 319.

[152]*Id.* at 321, quoting Reynolds v. Sims, 377 U.S. at 580.

[153]410 U.S. at 328–29.

[154]*Id.* at 325–27.

[155]412 U.S. 735 (1973).

[156]412 U.S. 755 (1973).

[157]394 U.S. at 531.

plicable in determining the constitutionality of state legislative districting plans, and that "minor deviations from mathematical equality among state legislative districts are insufficient to make out a prima facie case of invidious discrimination under the Fourteenth Amendment" even if the deviations are avoidable and even if the state offers no justification for them.[158] By "minor deviations," the Court evidently meant a maximum percentage deviation that does not exceed 10 percent. (In *White v. Regester*, the Court sustained, without requiring justification, a districting plan with a maximum percentage deviation of 9.9 percent, but added that "[v]ery likely, larger differences between districts would not be tolerable without justification.")[159]

The Court in *Gaffney* explicitly conceded that the single-minded focus of *Kirkpatrick* and *Wells* on "precise mathematical equality" to the exclusion of all other considerations opens the way for the denial of "fair and effective representation" by other means.[160] The reference to gerrymandering was clear, but no suggestion was offered as to how to combat that problem other than to relax the *Kirkpatrick* standard to enable states to respect the integrity of political subdivision boundaries. Implicit in *Gaffney*, as in *Weiser*, was the view that political gerrymandering was beyond the control of the courts, and that, while they should avoid the adoption of constitutional standards that would encourage it, they could do little to prevent it.

Moreover, in *Gaffney*, the Court reviewed and upheld a districting plan for the Connecticut legislature that deliberately eschewed neutral factors such as compactness, respect for political boundaries, disregard for incumbents, etc., and, instead, established districts that wandered across the state in virtually total disregard of political boundary lines, that displayed the greatest concern for the welfare of incumbents, and employed as its basic criterion for determining where to place the district lines, a political judgment as to what effect a particular configuration would have on the political welfare of the Democratic and Republican parties.[161] The plan was drawn by a bipartisan apportionment board, and ostensibly sought to insure that each party's strength in the legislature was roughly pro-

---

[158]412 U.S. at 745.

[159]*Id.* at 764.

[160]*Id.* at 749.

[161]*Id.* at 752.

portional to its statewide voting strength. To accomplish this end required the board "to 'wiggle and joggle' boundary lines to ferret out pockets of each party's strength."[162]

In practice, the plan favored the Republicans. Because of the heavy concentration of Republican voters in suburban Fairfield County, no randomly drawn districting plan would have given them seats in the legislature in proportion to their statewide voting strength. The Democrats were aware that they would fare better (*i.e.*, win a disproportionate share of legislative seats) under a plan that employed neutral districting criteria, and thus contended that the board's plan was "nothing less than a gigantic political gerrymander."[163] But the Court found no difficulty in upholding the plan. It rejected the idea that it was either possible or desirable to exclude politics from the districting process. A "politically mindless approach may produce, whether intended or not, the most grossly gerrymandered results; and, in any event, it is most unlikely that the political impact of such a plan would remain undiscovered by the time it was proposed or adopted, in which event, the results would be both known and, if not changed, intended."[164] The fact that plans are drawn with close attention to their political consequences is not a basis for their invalidation, particularly if the purpose of the plan is not to deny a party its equitable share of representation, but to insure that both are treated fairly.[165]

However, at the same time that the Court was offering little prospect for judicial protection from the political gerrymander, it acted to invalidate a racial gerrymander. Although only two years earlier, the Court in *Whitcomb v. Chavis* had refused to sustain the District Court's conclusion that the use of multi-member districts in Marion County, Indiana, invidiously discriminated against blacks living in the inner-city ghetto in Indianapolis, in *White v. Regester*

---

[162]*Id.* at 752 n.18.

[163]*Id.* at 752. See Engstrom, note 129 *supra*, at 301–04; Wells, Con Affirmative Gerrymandering, 9 Policy Studies J. 863, 863–64 (1980-81).

[164]412 U.S. at 753. Robert Dixon, who successfully defended the Connecticut plan before the Supreme Court, noted that the plan for districting the legislature drawn by a Special Master without reference to political data so favored the Democrats that the Special Master, Robert Bork, was sent congratulations by the Democratic state chairman. See Dixon, Fair Criteria and Procedures for Establishing Legislative Districts, in Representation and Redistricting Issues 7, 18–19 (Grofman, Lijphart, McKay & Scarrow eds. 1982).

[165]412 U.S. at 753–54.

it unanimously sustained the holdings of a three-judge District Court in Texas[166] that the use of multi-member districts in Dallas and Bexar Counties operated invidiously to dilute the effectiveness of the votes of blacks and Mexican-Americans, respectively. This time the Court agreed that the requisite evidence of reduced opportunity for political participation was to be found in the history of official discrimination against blacks and Mexican-Americans in Texas, the disproportionally low percentage of members of these groups elected to the state legislature from these counties, their long exclusion from effective involvement in political affairs, the failure of the elected representatives from these counties to provide adequate representation for minority concerns, etc.[167] Under those circumstances, the submergence of blacks and Mexican-Americans within multi-member legislative districts constituted an unconstitutional abridgment of their right to fair representation.

White v. Regester was a milestone. For the first time, the Court declared a legislative districting plan unconstitutional despite the fact that districts were equally populated. To be sure, the Court continued to insist that districting was a political responsibility. But, once it was recognized that the rule of "one person, one vote" was not enough to protect the right to fair representation, the next step—to equate the political gerrymander with the racial gerrymander—was not a big one. Indeed, the step was logically easier to take than to avoid.[168] After all, when the Court first recognized in 1965 that the discriminatory use of multi-member districting could create a constitutional violation, it declared that a violation could occur where the districts "operate[d] to minimize or cancel out the voting strength of racial or political elements of the voting population."[169]

By the end of 1973, the Court's basic criteria for assessing the constitutionality of districting plans and, by indirection, the constitutionality of gerrymandering activities, were in place. They were:

1. The "basic constitutional standard" is that both state legislative and congressional districts "must be apportioned on a population

---

[166]Graves v. Barnes, 343 F.Supp. 704 (W.D. Tex. 1972).

[167]See 412 U.S. at 767, 769–70.

[168]See Shapiro, note 13 *supra*, at 232.

[169]Fortson v. Dorsey, 379 U.S. at 439.

basis,"[170] and the districts must be "as nearly of equal population as is practicable."[171] The latter requirement makes impossible the kind of "butcher's cleaver" gerrymandering[172] that could be accomplished through the construction of districts with gross population inequalities.

2. What is meant by "as nearly equal as is practicable" is not the same for congressional districting as for state legislative districting.

a. For congressional districting, this standard requires "a good-faith effort to achieve precise mathematical equality."[173] None of the neutral factors that might inhibit gerrymandering may be taken into account if the result of doing so is the creation of districts that have greater population disparities than those of an alternative plan that does not heed them. The gerrymanderer is thus given a free hand as long as he complies with the requirement that districts be of equal population.

b. For state legislative districting, more leeway is possible. If the sum of the percentage deviations from the ideal of the largest and smallest districts in a plan does not exceed 10 percent, no justification for, or explanation of, whatever deviations it contains will be necessary. This allows, but does not require, a state to preserve the integrity of political subdivision boundaries or to avoid the fragmentation of communities of interest, even if slight deviations from "precise mathematical equality" result. The task of the gerrymanderer, however, is made a little easier because, if he keeps within a maximum deviation of 10 percent, he is free to build in some slight population inequalities without a corresponding need to heed boundary lines or to respect other neutral criteria. Maximum deviations that exceed 10 percent (up to at least 16.4 percent)[174] may also be upheld if adequate justification can be provided. The requirement of justification places constraints on the gerrymanderer because deviations from population equality must be explainable in terms of neutral, rational, and legitimate considerations. One basis for deviation that has been

---

[170]Reynolds v. Sims, 377 U.S. at 568.

[171]*Id.* at 577. See also Wesberry v. Sanders, 376 U.S. at 7–8.

[172]The term is from Hacker, note 43 *supra*, at 59. See text at note 87 *supra*.

[173]Kirkpatrick v. Preisler, 394 U.S. at 530–31.

[174]Mahan v. Howell, 410 U.S. at 329. But *cf.* Brown v. Thomson, 462 U.S. 835 (1983); *id.* at 850 (concurring opinion).

expressly approved is the provision of representation for political
subdivisions as political subdivisions[175]—at least as long as the
formula on which the deviation is based does not systematically
favor certain communities or areas over others.[176]

3. The task of drawing district lines is political, and courts should
not interfere with the outcome of this political process unless there
is a constitutional violation to be remedied. A plan devised by a
legislature or an apportionment commission is not rendered unconstitutional because political considerations were consciously and
overtly taken into account in its design. "Politics and political considerations are inseparable from districting and apportionment."[177]
Nevertheless, racial gerrymandering through the use of multi-member districts is constitutionally impermissible where it can be shown
that its victims have "less opportunity than [other residents of the
district] to participate in the political processes and to elect legislators of their choice."[178]

After 1973, the Court altered those principles only to recognize
the legitimacy of justifying minor deviations from "precise mathematical equality" in congressional districting by such considerations as respecting the integrity of political subdivision boundaries
or preserving the compactness of districts. Whereas in *Kirkpatrick
v. Preisler* it had categorically rejected the legitimacy of these considerations,[179] in *Karcher v. Daggett*, without acknowledging the contradiction, it declared that these factors could validly be relied on
to justify population variances.[180]

Despite the logical ease with which the step from reviewing racial
gerrymandering to reviewing political gerrymandering could be
taken, the Court continued to refrain from taking it. Thus, when,
in *Karcher v. Daggett*[181] in 1983 it was faced with a districting plan
for the New Jersey congressional delegation that had all the ear-

---

[175]Abate v. Mundt, 403 U.S. at 185; Mahan v. Howell, 410 U.S. at 325–26 (municipalities);
Brown v. Thomson, 462 U.S. 835 (counties).

[176]Compare Abate v. Mundt, 403 U.S. at 185–87, with Hadley v. Junior College District,
397 U.S. at 56–58.

[177]Gaffney v. Cummings, 412 U.S. at 753.

[178]Whitcomb v. Chavis, 403 U.S. at 149.

[179]394 U.S. at 533–36.

[180]462 U.S. 725, 740 (1983). See the comments of the dissenters "welcom[ing] this change
in the law." *Id.* at 785 n. 1 (Powell, J., dissenting); *id.* at 778–80 (White, J., dissenting).

[181]See text at notes 26–28 *supra*.

marks of a political gerrymander,[182] a bare majority of the Court was content to treat it as an equal population case, and to void the plan for failure to conform to the standard of "one person, one vote," despite the fact that the largest district was only 0.7 percent more populous than the smallest. It was clear, however, that at least one of the five Justices comprising the majority subscribed to the opinion of the Court only as an exercise in the "backdoor invalidation of gerrymandering"[183]—seizing upon other reasons to strike down a plan as a camouflage for the real reason that it is perceived to be a gerrymander. Justice Stevens candidly conceded that he was "convinced that judicial preoccupation with the goal of perfect population equality is an inadequate method of judging the constitutionality of an apportionment plan," and went on to contend, as he had done earlier, that political gerrymandering should be held to violate the Constitution,[184] a view with which Justice Powell, dissenting in *Karcher*, expressed agreement.[185] If racial gerrymanders are unconstitutional, Stevens argued, then political gerrymandering must also be unconstitutional: "Since the [Equal Protection] Clause does not make some groups of citizens more equal than others, . . . its protection against vote dilution cannot be confined to racial groups. As long as it proscribes gerrymandering against such groups, its proscription must provide comparable protection for other cognizable groups of voters as well."[186] It remained for *Davis v. Bandemer* to confirm the validity of that proposition.

III. Political Gerrymandering: The Problem of Standards

The troublesome question presented by political gerrymandering claims is not whether discrimination against political groups constitutes a violation of the Equal Protection Clause, but whether

---

[182]The Congressional Quarterly described the plan as a "four-star gerrymander that boasts some of the most bizarrely shaped districts to be found in the nation." 40 Cong. Q. Weekly Rept. 1190 (1982), quoted by Justice Stevens, 462 U.S. at 762 n.30 (concurring opinion).

[183]See Dixon, note 12 *supra*, at 493–96.

[184]462 U.S. at 750 (concurring).

[185]*Id*. at 787–88 (dissenting).

[186]*Id*. at 749. To be sure, the Court has found the prohibition against population disparities in congressional districts in Art. I, §2, of the Constitution, rather than the Equal Protection Clause, but Justice Stevens would rely on the Equal Protection Clause. See 462 U.S. at 745–47.

the enforcement of a prohibition against gerrymandering is within the scope of judicial capacity. Is it possible to concede the justiciability of this issue "without spawning more dilution litigation than the judiciary can manage," and without "deny[ing] legislatures the right to perform the districting function"?[187] Can judicially manageable standards be devised that would not only provide judges with a means of objectively ascertaining whether a districting plan is constitutional, but would provide legislatures with fair notice of what they must do to stay within constitutional bounds? As has been frequently suggested, any judicial standard for identifying a political gerrymander is likely to be as amorphous as Justice Stewart's statement regarding his ability to define obscenity—"perhaps I could never succeed in intelligibly doing so. But I know it when I see it."[188]

Every line drawn on a map to define a legislative district has a political significance—whether the person (or computer) drawing the line knows it or not. And, since the legislators who will generally be called upon to draw the lines (or to provide the program for the computer that will do so) are professional politicians, it is hardly likely that they will be unaware of that significance or that they will be able to resist the urge to draw the line in a place that will be more advantageous to them or to their party than if it were drawn somewhere else. If all district boundary lines that are knowingly put in a particular place for partisan political purposes are unconstitutional, then it is hopeless to continue to treat districting as a legislative function. Moreover, the possibilities for litigation are boundless. Although, as Justice White has observed, districting plans are open to challenge under the "one person, one vote" standard "by anyone with a complaint and a calculator,"[189] the possibilities are not quite infinite. The closer the legislature can come to "precise mathematical equality," the less likely it is that its plan will be subject to successful attack. Similarly, racial gerrymandering claims are limited by the fact that only a few districts in a state will have a sufficiently sizable minority population to create a gerrymandering opportunity. But with political gerrymandering claims

---

[187]Mobile v. Bolden, 446 U.S. at 90, 92 (Stevens, J., concurring).

[188]Jacobellis v. Ohio, 378 U.S. 184, 197 (1964) (concurring opinion), cited, *e.g.*, by Justice Stevens in Karcher v. Daggett, 462 U.S. at 755 (concurring).

[189]*Id.* at 778 (dissenting).

there are no limits. A line, wherever it is drawn, will be open to challenge because it can be perceived to have political significance. Even if all but a few districting plans ultimately survive judicial scrutiny, the fact that virtually all can be tied up in court while their probable effects are debated can make a shambles of the districting process. Although the holding in *Davis* that political gerrymandering claims are justiciable flows ineluctably from the premises on which the justiciability of equal population and racial gerrymandering claims are based, it should not be forgotten that, as Justice White, speaking for the Court, admonished in *White v. Weiser*: "Districting inevitably has sharp political impact and inevitably political decisions must be made by those charged with the task."[190] To cast doubt on the legitimacy of a districting plan because partisan considerations played a role in the process by which it was arrived at would be to try to remove politics from politics. No more quixotic effort can be imagined.

A. COMPACTNESS

There has long been a sense that the hallmark of a gerrymander is the oddly shaped district. After all, the term was derived from the perception that a district was shaped like a salamander. Under that view, there is no difficulty in identifying a gerrymander—one simply looks for a districting plan in which the boundaries take peculiar twists and turns, and there it is.[191] It is not surprising, therefore, that compactness of districts is, for many observers, the critical standard for determining whether a gerrymander exists. The Common Cause monograph on apportionment states that gerrymandering "is usually, but not exclusively, manifested in the manipulation of the shape of legislative districts,"[192] and James Edwards has declared that "[c]ompactness and contiguity are almost universally recognized as appropriate antigerrymandering standards."[193]

---

[190]412 U.S. at 795–96.

[191]See, *e.g.*, 40 Cong. Q. Weekly Rept. 1190, 1193–95, describing the New Jersey districting plan challenged in Karcher v. Daggett; Common Cause, note 146 *supra*, at 16, 20, 29.

[192]*Id.* at 12.

[193]Edwards, note 16 *supra*, at 893. Contiguity has not been a problem because it is not much of a restraint on gerrymandering, although sometimes it may be necessary to stretch the point by running a very thin strip across the map to connect two otherwise noncontiguous

Justice Stevens has suggested that lack of compactness is one of the most important ways in which a plaintiff in a political gerrymandering case can make a prima facie showing of discriminatory districting.[194]

One possible objection to the use of compactness as a standard for identifying a political gerrymander is that, since not all districts can be squares, and even fewer can be circles, there is the difficulty of defining what constitutes improper twists and turns, and of determining how many of them would be needed to invalidate a plan. But that is not a formidable problem because compactness can be quantified and a permissible limit determined that could be objectively applied by the courts. For example, Common Cause suggests that "the aggregate length of the boundaries of all districts [should not] exceed by more than five percent the shortest possible aggregate length of all the districts under any other plan."[195] The principal objection to the establishment of a compactness requirement is that the construction of oddly shaped districts may serve beneficent as well as devious purposes. Gordon Baker has perceptively observed that "compactness can readily cloak a genuine gerrymander, while districts that look untidy and suspect may merely reflect the irregular geography of natural political communities."[196] Similarly, Justice Stevens has conceded that it would be an error to define a gerrymander by district shapes,[197] and argues only that odd shapes should be looked upon as "a signal that something may be amiss."[198]

Irregular district shapes may legitimately be used to prevent fragmentation of cohesive communities of interest that are not conveniently concentrated in a compact geographical location but are scattered across a wider area in an eccentric pattern. For example,

---

areas. In the New Jersey congressional districting plan challenged in Karcher v. Daggett, Judge Gibbons noted the legislature included one district "which is contiguous only for yachtsmen." 535 F.Supp. at 984, quoted by Justice Stevens, 462 U.S. at 764, n.33.

[194]Karcher v. Daggett, 462 U.S. at 755–58 (concurring).

[195]Common Cause, note 146 *supra*, at 54. Other generally less drastic formulas for quantification have been proposed. A compendium of these proposals may be found in Justice Stevens's concurring opinion in Karcher v. Daggett, 462 U.S. at 756–58 n. 19.

[196]Baker, note 83 *supra*, at 139.

[197]Karcher v. Daggett, 462 U.S. at 755 n.15 (concurring opinion).

[198]*Id.* at 758. See Niemi, The Relationship Between Votes and Seats: The Ultimate Question in Political Gerrymandering, 33 UCLA L. Rev. 185, 190.

because Mexican-American communities tend to be dispersed, any attempt to draw district lines to avoid fragmentation of these communities is likely to have to rely on odd shapes.[199] As Bruce Cain has noted: "Those who argue for the importance of compactness must be willing to accept limitations on the achievement of equity for minorities."[200] A compactness requirement may also obstruct the provision of adequate representation for persons with shared interests derived from common residence in a geographical area that is not compact. The lack of compactness may be artificial—as in the case of a political subdivision that is not compactly shaped—or natural—as in the case of a region, such as a coastal area or a river valley, whose topographical features do not fit a compact pattern.[201]

The manner in which the strength of a group or a political party is distributed in a state will determine whether its interest in fair representation will be served by compact or noncompact districts.[202] If it is a substantial minority whose strength is more or less evenly distributed throughout the state, compact districts may substantially disadvantage it because it will be in the minority in most districts—or even all the districts—and, under the single-member district system, it will simply lose the elections in those districts. In that case, the creation of some irregular districts to bring that party's representation in the legislature up to a level more closely approximating its actual statewide voting strength would not appear to be an unworthy goal. Similarly, if a party's strength is overwhelmingly concentrated in a small geographical area, compact districts will disserve its interests since, while it will carry the districts in that area by heavy majorities, its excess votes will be wasted in those districts, and thus, although it may be the majority party statewide, it may be unable to win a majority of the seats in the legislature. The plan upheld by the Supreme Court in *Gaffney v. Cummings* was an attempt by the Republicans who dominated

[199] See Cain, note 48 *supra*, at 46–48.

[200] *Id.* at 51.

[201] *Id.* at 38–43.

[202] For this reason, Daniel Lowenstein and Jonathan Steinberg argue strongly against a compactness criterion on the ground that it is not neutral. Because Democratic strength tends to be concentrated in urban areas, a requirement of compactness would force the "wasting" of far more Democratic than Republican votes. See Lowenstein & Steinberg, The Quest for Legislative Districting in the Public Interest, 33 UCLA L. Rev. 1, 23–27 (1985).

the apportionment board that devised it to lessen the number of
Republican votes wasted in Fairfield County, Connecticut, by the
creation of noncompact districts with Republican majorities, each
of which comprised part of Fairfield County but were stretched out
to include non-Republican areas to bring their populations up to
the level required by the "one person, one vote" standard. If this
had been done by the majority party to protect itself against an
effective challenge in the future or to crush its opposition, such
line-drawing would be indefensible. As an effort to provide a minority party with legislative representation more in proportion to
its statewide voting strength, it would seem less objectionable.[203]
Before courts rely on odd shapes to invalidate a districting plan,
they should assure themselves both that the legislature's purpose
was invidiously discriminatory and that that purpose has been successfully achieved.

B. MAINTAINING THE INTEGRITY OF POLITICAL SUBDIVISION
   BOUNDARIES

It cannot be argued that respect for the integrity of political
subdivision boundaries is a constitutional requirement. Nevertheless, there is much to be said for preserving the integrity of these
boundary lines as a means of discouraging gerrymandering, and
constitutional districting standards, while they cannot forbid such
line crossing, should not be designed to encourage it. Its denigration
of the concern for keeping political subdivisions intact was one of
the reasons that *Kirkpatrick v. Preisler* has been seen as an invitation
to gerrymander.[204] The Common Cause proposal calls for district
lines to follow political boundaries whenever this can be done consistently with the equal population requirement, not only because
it "places limits on the reapportionment authority's discretion to
gerrymander," but also because it enhances "the ability of constituencies to organize in an effective manner" and "minimizes voter
confusion."[205] These concerns have been belittled because "boundaries of racial, social, and economic communities may be sharp or

---

[203]See Dixon, note 12 *supra*, at 461. The plan upheld in Gaffney v. Cummings may not
have been benevolently motivated. See Engstrom, note 129 *supra*, at 301–05.

[204]The Court reversed itself on this point in *Karcher*. 462 U.S. at 740. See text at notes
179–80 *supra*.

[205]Common Cause, note 146 *supra*, at 53.

barely perceptible, but in either event, there is no evidence that they conveniently coincide with municipal boundaries."[206] But arguments against treating political boundaries as meaningless lines are not so easily downed.[207]

Voters do identify with the place in which they live, and do have a feeling of sharing concerns with others who live in that place regarding the administration of public affairs.[208] Division of a county or municipality among a variety of districts so that voters may find themselves together with only a small number of fellow residents of their city, town, or county in a district overwhelmingly made up of persons from other places is disorienting, deterring both political interest and political organization. It is not necessary to argue for representation of political units as such in the legislature—although there are strong arguments as to why it may be desirable to do so in a more intimate body, such as a county board of supervisors—or that subdivisions larger in population than would be appropriate for a single district should not be divided into separate districts, in order to argue that "counties and cities smaller in population than a district should be divided only if it is unavoidable."[209] In this context, "unavoidable" should be understood to mean when it is not desirable to do so for other valid but conflicting reasons, such as preventing the dilution of minority representation, avoiding the fragmentation of racial, social, or economic communities whose boundaries do not coincide with those of political subdivisions, or, in some cases, bringing a political party that would otherwise be underrepresented closer to its proportional share of seats in the legislature. The heaviest pressure to ignore political subdivision boundaries comes, of course, from the rule of equal population, and, while too great a deviation from the requirements of that rule would be inadvisable, there is little reason why deviations on the order of the 16.4 percent recognized as acceptable in *Mahan v. Howell* should not be allowed both to discourage gerrymandering and to encourage political participation.

---

[206]Lowenstein & Steinberg, note 202 *supra*, at 34.

[207]See, *e.g.*, Morrill, Political Redistricting and Geographic Theory 23 (1982); Backstrom, note 52 *supra*, at 47.

[208]A recent study has documented that where political units are not fragmented, there is enhanced recognition of congressional candidates by voters. See Niemi, Powell, & Bicknell, The Effect of Community-Congressional Districting Congruity on Knowledge of Congressional Candidates, 11 Legis. Studies Q. 187, 190–93 (1986).

[209]Morrill, note 207 *supra*, at 25.

C. MULTI-MEMBER DISTRICTING

The Court has repeatedly refused to rule that multi-member districting is facially invalid. The high-water mark of its willingness to tolerate such districting came in *Whitcomb v. Chavis* in 1971, when it ignored the consequences of enveloping the city of Indianapolis within surrounding townships in a single multi-member district. *Chavis* involved a claim of racial gerrymandering, but the fact that blacks in Indianapolis were, by this arrangement, denied any legislative representation despite their sizable numbers—numbers which only served to swell the number of Republicans that the district was entitled to return to the legislature—was dismissed by the Court with the simplistic comment that "one candidate wins, the others lose," and that losers have no claim to representation.[210] In the course of its opinion, the Court made clear that one reason for its lack of sympathy with the racial gerrymandering claim was its concern that the same claim could be made in a political gerrymandering case, and thus "spawn endless litigation."[211]

The Court declared itself "not insensitive to the objections long voiced to multi-member district plans,"[212] and cited among those objections "their winner-take-all aspects, their tendency to submerge minorities and to overrepresent the winning party as compared with the party's statewide electoral position,"[213] but refused to examine the implications of those objections or to scrutinize with any seriousness the discriminatory effects of the system. Out of an expressed concern to avoid "spawn[ing] endless litigation," the Court effectively immunized multi-member districting from constitutional challenge except where it could be proved that those disadvantaged by it "had less opportunity . . . to participate in the political process and to elect legislators of their choice."[214] This exception was subsequently to prove adequate to sustain challenges to multi-member districting as racial gerrymandering, but, as the Court noted in *Davis v. Bandemer*, it "is not helpful where the claim is that such districts discriminate against [a major political party], for it could hardly be said that Democrats, any more than Republicans,

---

[210]403 U.S. at 153.

[211]*Id.* at 156–57.

[212]*Id.* at 157.

[213]*Id.* at 158–59. The Court has also noted other drawbacks. See Chapman v. Meier, 420 U.S. 1, 15–16 (1975).

[214]403 U.S. at 149.

are excluded from participating in the affairs of their own party or from the processes by which candidates are nominated and elected."[215]

But why should multi-member districting be immune from challenge as a political, as opposed to a racial, gerrymander? Its virtues are debatable[216] and its discriminatory potential manifest. Although not every use of multi-member districting will operate to disadvantage the minority party, and, indeed, it has recently been demonstrated that, overall, such districting does not have a discriminatory partisan effect,[217] particular uses may constitute the grossest form of gerrymandering. It may be that, as the Court noted in *Chavis*, multi-member districting has "been with us since colonial times,"[218] but so has political gerrymandering, and its venerability is not an adequate reason for shielding its effects from judicial scrutiny. The fact that it is "widely employed," although now less widely than earlier,[219] should be no more determinative of its validity. In 1965, the Court suggested that such districting would raise constitutional questions if used as a means of discriminating against "racial or political elements of the voting population,"[220] and there is no reason to limit the scope of review to instances of racial discrimination. The Court has sensibly held that redistricting plans drawn up by courts must not employ multi-member districts except in unique circumstances,[221] and it is not clear why there should be

---

[215] 106 S.Ct. at 2813.

[216] The principal theoretical advantage of multi-member districting is that, by providing for a widening of the electorate, better and less parochial candidates will be chosen. See Klain, A New Look at the Constituencies: The Need for a Recount and a Reappraisal, 49 Am. Pol. Sci. Rev. 1105, 1118 (1955). The development of at-large elections (of which multi-member districts are a variety) was the result of the efforts of reformers in cities who wished to break the hold of the political bosses who controlled the election of the candidates from their wards. Grofman, Alternatives to Single-Member Plurality Districts: Legal and Empirical Issues, in Representation and Redistricting Issues 107, 108–09 (Grofman, Lijphart, McKay & Scarrow eds. 1982). It is unlikely that either of these considerations would be given much weight today.

[217] Niemi, Hill, & Grofman, The Impact of Multimember Districts on Party Representation in U.S. State Legislatures, 10 Legis. Studies Q. 441 (1985).

[218] 403 U.S. at 157–58.

[219] Multi-member districting for state legislative elections reached a peak in the early 1960s. Its use has declined somewhat since then. As of 1984, it continued to be used in 16 states. Niemi, Hill, and Grofman, note 217 *supra*, at 443.

[220] Fortson v. Dorsey, 379 U.S. at 439.

[221] See Connor v. Johnson, 402 U.S. 690, 692 (1971); Chapman v. Meier, 420 U.S. at 19.

greater tolerance for legislative decisions to employ them in situations where they can be shown to interfere with the ability of the minority party to attain fair representation. It is difficult to believe that the Court would allow the majority party to adopt an at-large electoral system for choosing state legislators, and thereby to extinguish the minority party's representation altogether, even though such a system would perfectly fit the requirements of "one person, one vote." But if a statewide at-large election would be impermissible, why should it be possible for a state to approximate, or, indeed, to achieve, the same result by a system of mini-at-large elections (which is what multi-member districts provide) that either cover the entire state or else encase the areas where the minority party's voting strength is concentrated within a shell of majority party strength sufficient to extinguish or diminish the minority party's representation?

A rule against multi-member districting in situations where its use would be discriminatory could eliminate an important tool of political gerrymandering. Such districting is neither necessary nor useful for gerrymandering purposes where the voting strength of the parties is fairly evenly dispersed, but can be extraordinarily effective where the minority party's strength is concentrated in specific areas—which is why both blacks and Democrats in cities are ready victims. Thus, the Court need not lay down a *per se* rule against multi-member districting, but should prohibit it in areas in which its use leads to the denial to the minority party of the representation that it can demonstrate it could be expected to receive in a system of single-member-district elections.[222] Such a rule would appear to pose no serious problems in terms of judicial administrability.

D. THE "VOTES/SEATS" RATIO

The effective political gerrymander is one in which district lines are drawn in a way that maximizes the efficiency of the votes of the gerrymandering party and minimizes the efficiency of the votes of the opposing party. If there are two candidates in an individual

---

For an example of an exception created by unique circumstances, see Mahan v. Howell, 410 U.S. at 330–33.

[222]See, *e.g.*, Blacksher & Menefee, From Reynolds v. Sims to City of Mobile v. Bolden, 34 Hastings L.J. 1, 55–56 (1982), cited in Thornburg v. Gingles, 106 S.Ct. at 2767 n.17.

election, one more than 50 percent of the vote is all that is needed
to elect the winner. All votes cast for the winning candidate in
excess of that 50 percent plus one, and all votes cast for the losing
candidate, are "wasted," in the sense that they have no effect on
the outcome of the election, either within the district or statewide.
The unfairness of this arrangement is built in to the single-member-
district electoral system and is the price to be paid for enjoying the
political advantages of that system over a system of proportional
representation. The astute gerrymanderer will want to make the
most of the votes for the candidates of his party by "wasting" as
few of them as possible while seeing to it that as many as possible
of the opposing party's votes are wasted. This may be done either
by "stacking" opposition voters—putting as many of them as possible in a particular district to maximize the number of votes cast
for the opposition candidate that will be in excess of the number
necessary for election—or by "cracking" them—fragmenting concentrations of opposition voters and distributing them among different districts, in each of which they would constitute a sizable
minority, but not enough to carry the election.

In any election in which there are only two candidates, the number of wasted votes will necessarily be 50 percent of the total number
of votes cast minus one—the sum of all of the votes for the losing
candidate and the excess votes (those above 50 percent plus one of
the total vote) cast for the winning candidate—and the perfect gerrymander would be one in which the opposition party is required
to absorb all of the wasted votes. That would be done, at least in
theory, by distributing all of the supporters of the gerrymandering
party among the districts that the party can carry in such a way as
to create a majority of 50 percent plus one in those districts, while
distributing the supporters of the opposition party in such a way
as to insure that they would waste the maximum of 50 percent
minus one in every district—either because that number of votes
would be cast for the party's losing candidate or because the opposition's winning candidate would receive 100 percent of the vote.
Obviously, for reasons ranging from the fact that a party cannot
know, from election to election, who its supporters are to the fact
that a substantial margin for error must be allowed in every district
that the party intends to carry, nothing coming anywhere near to
the perfect gerrymander is realistically possible, but that is the goal
to be approximated.

   Since maximizing the wasted votes of the opposing party while
minimizing the wasted votes of one's own party is the way that
partisan political gerrymandering works, the judiciary's capacity
to review political gerrymandering claims will necessarily be of
limited effectiveness unless a standard can be devised for measuring the invidiousness of a districting plan that leads one party
to waste a higher percentage of its vote than the other party. No
adequate formula has yet been established for distinguishing between a vote that is wasted due to natural causes and one that is
wasted because of the discriminatory effect of a partisan gerrymander. Once the Court begins to grapple with the question,
Bruce Cain has noted, "it will quickly discover that there are as
many versions of what constitutes a fair result as there are quantitative political scientists."[223]
Because the percentage of votes for a party's legislative candidates that are wasted statewide determines the success that
the party will have in winning seats in the legislature with a
given percentage of the statewide vote, attempts to measure the
unfairness of a districting plan have most commonly relied on
the "votes/seats" ratio, which simply compares the percentage
of the statewide vote cast for a party's legislative candidates
with the percentage of seats in the legislature won by those
candidates. Like the compactness criterion, the "votes/seats" ratio appears to offer an easy means by which individuals can
know a gerrymander when they see it. Despite its superficial
appeal, however, the "votes/seats" ratio is no more determinative
of the existence of a gerrymander than the compactness standard.
   The hidden assumption of the "votes/seats" ratio is that it is only
fair and proper that the percentage of seats that a party wins in the
legislature should be proportional to the percentage of the total vote
that its legislative candidates receive—in other words, that there
should be proportional representation. The electoral system for
choosing legislators in the United States is not, however, a proportional representation system but a single-member-district, plu-
rality-winner, system. Although anyone is "free to pursue the goal
of attempting to convert our electoral system to proportional rep-

---

[223]Cain, Simple vs. Complex Criteria for Partisan Gerrymandering: A Comment on Niemi
and Grofman, 33 UCLA L. Rev. 213, 216 (1985).

resentation through our normal political processes,"[224] as long as the system remains unchanged, it should not be expected to yield proportional results. To begin with, the results of individual single-member-district elections are wildly disproportional. The party whose candidate wins 50 percent plus one of the votes in a particular district (or perhaps an even smaller percentage if there are more than two candidates) will win 100 percent of the seats in that district (one out of one). What possible reason is there to assume that the sum of all these individual elections with utterly disproportional results will yield a neat proportional outcome, or that, if such an outcome is not attained, the electoral system must have been gerrymandered?

The extent to which a party's votes will be naturally wasted, leading to disproportional results, depends on how the parties' statewide voting strength is distributed.[225] If the parties' supporters are perfectly evenly distributed across the state so that the minority party will be a sizable minority everywhere but a majority nowhere, all of its legislative votes will be naturally wasted, and, without any gerrymandering at all, it will win no legislative seats.[226] On the other hand, if a party's strength is concentrated in particular geographical areas so that it will normally win by very large majorities in those areas, it can expect to win a substantially smaller percentage of the seats in the legislature than its proportional share of the statewide legislative vote because so many of its votes will be wasted as in excess of its needs.[227] However unfair these results may be, they are not brought about by gerrymandering except in the sense that "all districting is gerrymandering."[228] A districting system will

---

[224]"Declaration of Nelson W. Polsby in Badham v. Eu," in Political Gerrymandering: Badham v. Eu, Political Science Goes to Court, 18 PS 537, 570 (1985).

[225]See, e.g., Engstrom, Post-Census Representational Districting: The Supreme Court, "One Person, One Vote," and the Gerrymandering Issue, 7 Southern U. L. Rev. 173, 214–17 (1981).

[226]The fact that the majority party will, when there is anything resembling homogeneity in the distribution of the statewide population, tend to win a larger percentage of legislative seats than its overall percentage of the statewide vote has been characterized as the "balloon effect." Backstrom, Robins, & Eller, note 45 supra, at 1134. See also Tufte, The Relationship Between Seats and Votes in Two-Party Systems, 67 Am. Pol. Sci. Rev. 540, 540 (1973); Grofman, For Single-Member Districts Random is Not Equal, in Representation and Redistricting Issues 55, 55–58 (Grofman, Lijphart, McKay & Scarrow eds. 1982).

[227]See Backstrom, Robins, & Eller, note 45 supra, at 1127.

[228]Dixon, note 12 supra, at 461.

skew the results away from the proportional unless, by sheer co-incidence, the majority party happens to be in the majority in precisely the same percentage of legislative districts as its percentage of the statewide legislative vote. To achieve proportional representation in a districting system, it would probably be necessary to engage in a process of reverse gerrymandering, creating meandering districts that violate the compactness criterion, as in the Connecticut plan sustained in *Gaffney v. Cummings*.

There are additional reasons why the "votes/seats" ratio is an inadequate measure of the fairness of a districting plan.[229] Among other things, it is in tension with the "one person, one vote" standard, under which it is generally understood that districts should be drawn so as to equalize the number of census persons in each. But census persons are not necessarily voters. In a district with a low percentage of eligible voters relative to total population or where there is low voter turnout—which is to be expected in areas marked by poverty or a high concentration of racial minorities—the winning candidate should receive a smaller number of votes than the winning candidate of the other party in another district where there is a high percentage of eligible voters among the total population, and a high percentage of these actually vote. Each of the parties in this example will win one seat, as is proper, but the candidate of one party will have received significantly more votes, and thus the ratio of votes to seats will appear to be out of balance.

Moreover, the "votes/seats" ratio does not take into account un-contested races in which the unopposed candidate of one party will pile up a large number of votes (and win only one seat) while no votes will be cast for the nonexistent candidate of the other party even though many persons who voted for the unopposed candidate may have voted for the opposition candidate had there been one. Obviously, when the results of such races are added into the state-wide totals, a severe skewing of the "votes/seats" ratio is inevitable.[230]

Finally, and not least important, the use of the "votes/seats" ratio to measure the fairness of the statewide outcome of a legislative election is grounded in an assumption which need have no basis in reality—that a person who votes for a candidate of one party in

---

[229]For a thorough review of the flaws, see Lowenstein & Steinberg, note 202 *supra*, at 49–64.

[230]See Backstrom, Robins, & Eller, note 45 *supra*, at 1128.

one district would vote for the candidate of the same party in another district and would want that party to be in the majority in the legislature. Individual legislative elections are often intensely personal matters, turning not in the slightest degree on which party the voter wants to control the legislature, but on local issues or on the voters' perceptions as to the individual merits of the opposing candidates.[231] It just cannot be assumed that a vote for a particular candidate in a particular district is a vote for that candidate's party statewide.

Reliance on the "votes/seats" ratio as an indicator of gerrymandering is not merely erroneous; it is actually pernicious in that it has both enormous superficial appeal and an apparent quantitative objectivity that suggests that it may be as easily administrable by the courts as the standard of "one person, one vote." In combination, as Martin Shapiro has warned, these falsely attractive features of this standard could ultimately lead the courts to adopt the catastrophic course of requiring proportional representation,[232] thus "fundamentally chang[ing] the most successful democratic political system the world has ever known without having any idea what they have done or whether the system can survive it."[233] Professor Shapiro's warning appears to have had effect. In *Davis v. Bandemer*, Justice O'Connor specifically cited his argument as a reason why the Court should treat political gerrymandering claims as nonjusticiable,[234] while Justice White, for the plurality, emphasized that the Court's precedents "clearly foreclose any claim that the Constitution requires proportional representation or that legislatures in reapportioning must draw district lines to come as near as possible to allocating seats to the contending parties in proportion to what their anticipated statewide vote will be."[235]

E. PROTECTION OF INCUMBENTS

Popular perceptions of gerrymandering frequently include an image of members of the legislature sitting down to draw districts

---

[231]*Id.* at 1127–28. See also Lowenstein & Steinberg, note 202 *supra*, at 60.

[232]Shapiro, note 13 *supra*, at 252–56.

[233]*Id.* at 255–56.

[234]106 S.Ct. at 2823–24 (concurring).

[235]*Id.* at 2809.

that will allow each of them to be returned at the next election. All forms of political activity in which each actor conspires to maximize his or her individual self-interest are generally regarded as unsavory, and this form of self-protection by incumbents is no exception. It is to eliminate this unsavoriness that the Common Cause proposal on legislative districting would take this responsibility from the legislature and assign it to "an independent, nonpartisan reapportionment commission" which would not be "allowed to take into account the addresses of incumbent legislators."[236]

Indignation at the prospect of politicians feathering their nests is appropriate, but it still needs to be asked whether the current practice is inconsistent with the public interest. It is ironic that the more widespread the conspiracy, the less likely it is to be contrary to the public interest in providing fair and effective representation. For if all legislators are allowed to participate, partisan political gerrymandering will not be the result, whatever else may occur.[237] If the legislature is already seriously unrepresentative, incumbency protection for its own sake may be a major barrier to reform, but it should not make matters worse. What a bipartisan gerrymander (which this would be) will do is to lessen the competitiveness of individual districts and protect incumbents against challenges from the opposition party,[238] neither of which is an unmitigated evil. Common Cause sets forth three reasons for seeking to maximize competitive elections: (1) safe districts lessen individual interest in political participation and dampen debate on issues because the outcome of the election is foreordained; (2) they lessen the responsiveness of legislators to their constituencies because such responsiveness is not necessary for reelection; and (3) they allow parties to put forward weak candidates since there is no need to seek out superior nominees.[239] But given the fact that legislatures have representational as well as law-making functions to perform, and that safe districts enhance the legislators' ability to fulfill the representational function, the

---

[236]Common Cause, note 146 *supra*, at 27, 29–30.

[237]See Cain, note 48 *supra*, at 159.

[238]See *id.* at 160–61.

[239]Common Cause, note 146 *supra*, at 23–24.

argument for competitive elections is much weaker with regard to legislatures than executive offices.[240]

Safe districts provide assurance that particular points of view will always be represented in the legislature even when swings of public sentiment create a strong trend for one party or the other. If all districts were made competitive (which would, of course, require some form of reverse gerrymandering), the party against which such a trend runs might be denied any effective representation, and swings back and forth as one party succeeds the other in becoming overwhelmingly dominant would make it very difficult for any stable and coherent public policy to be established.[241] With regard to the claim that representatives from safe districts are less responsive to their constituencies, there is another side to the coin. Representatives who anticipate close competition in their bid for re-election tend to "devote disproportionately more time and energy to 'tending their districts' and less to the drudgery of legislation and oversight."[242] In addition, "[t]he more competitive the election, the more the candidates will feel the need to spend and, therefore, to raise large amounts of campaign money, with all the attendant problems, including the enhanced influence of special interests."[243] Finally, the claim that competitive elections will produce stronger candidates is almost certainly false. The prospect of a close election may, indeed, cause a party to seek a strong candidate, but strong candidates are far less likely to be interested in seeking election to the legislature if they are aware that every election will be a struggle and that they cannot look forward to a long legislative career because they will be vulnerable to defeat with every partisan swing. Moreover, strong candidates will find service in the legislature far more attractive if, once elected, they were able to devote themselves principally to the substantive affairs of government without the need constantly to give priority to local constituency relations.

In any event, the notion that the reelection of incumbents is intrinsically undesirable is an odd one. Certainly some accumulation of experience and seniority is highly desirable in a deliberative

---

[240]Mayhew, Congressional Representation: Theory and Practice in Drawing the Districts, in Reapportionment in the 1970s 249, 256–59 (Polsby ed. 1971).

[241]See Lowenstein & Steinberg, note 202 *supra*, at 39–40.

[242]Mayhew, note 240 *supra*, at 258. See also Lowenstein & Steinberg, note 202 *supra*, at 43–44.

[243]*Id.* at 43. See also Cain, note 48 *supra*, at 68.

body, and it would be irresponsible for a legislature not to protect the leaders and most effective legislators of both parties by insuring that they are not placed in an unwinnable, or even uncertain, district by an apportionment commission that is forbidden to take into account the addresses of incumbents.

The issue, however, is academic as a matter of constitutional law. As long as the protection of incumbents is done on a bipartisan basis, it cannot be said to discriminate against any political group, and, therefore, it is hardly likely that courts would be moved to call it into question.[244] Such dicta as appear in Supreme Court opinions suggest that the practice of protecting incumbents is not only legitimate, but constitutes an end of such importance that its attainment would be a valid justification for some deviation in equality of district population.[245]

But if bipartisan protection of incumbents presents no constitutional issue, incumbent protection as an aspect of partisan gerrymandering is a different matter. Bernard Grofman has listed twelve aspects of single-member-district plans that provide prima facie evidence of partisan gerrymandering, and three of the twelve involve differential treatment of the parties' incumbents.[246] (He regards "incumbent-centered partisan bias as one of the most pernicious forms of sophisticated partisan gerrymandering, and perhaps [the] single strongest indicator of probable partisan gerrymandering."[247]) Given the importance to a party of maintaining continuity of membership in the legislature, and given the increased electability of incumbents in districts at least approximating those from which they were most recently elected, it is a powerful gerrymandering technique for the dominant party to dismantle the districts of the opposing party's incumbents while keeping those of its own incumbents intact. If a districting plan, while preserving the seats of the majority party's incumbents, collapses those of the minority party's incumbents,[248] or combines the districts of two minority party incumbents, or moves the core of the constituency of minority

---

[244]Mayhew, note 240 *supra*, at 256, suggests that it is "surpassingly unlikely."

[245]See Karcher v. Daggett, 462 U.S. at 740.

[246]Grofman, note 53 *supra*, at 117–18.

[247]*Id.* at 157.

[248]Collapsing a seat takes place where a state or a region within a state must give up a district. The district "collapsed" is eliminated, and surrounding districts absorb its territory. See Cain, note 48 *supra*, at 27–30.

party incumbents into different districts, that is a reasonably unequivocal sign of a partisan political gerrymander, and courts may
justifiably rely on evidence of such disparate treatment to hold the
plan invalid.

F. DUE PROCESS OF DISTRICTING

The "independent, nonpartisan commission" proposed by Common Cause to effectuate legislative districting would be denied
information relating to the addresses of incumbent legislators and
be forbidden to "use the political affiliations of registered voters,
previous election results, or other demographic information for the
purpose of favoring any political party, incumbent legislator, or
other person or group."[249] To enforce this prohibition, the commission would have to be denied access to all relevant political or
demographic data. If the commission has such information and uses
it, it will necessarily know who will be favored by the choice of
one line rather than another; thus, inevitably, whatever decision it
makes, it will have used the information to favor one person or
group over another. Those responsible for performing an act with
enormous political consequence are to be denied any way of knowing what those consequences will be.

That may well be the worst possible way to draw a districting
plan. Fear that decision makers may use relevant information to
arrive at judgments beneficial to themselves or their friends is not
a justification for requiring them to make decisions without relevant
information. Blindly drawn plans will have political consequences
no less than those drawn to achieve political ends, and, given the
fact that the population of a state is never evenly distributed by
race, economic interest, or partisan leanings, so that the achievement of fairness may require a certain degree of imaginative car-
tography, it is possible that a blindly drawn plan could produce
districts more unfair than a political party would dare to produce
on its own.[250]

Just as every line drawn in a districting plan has political consequences, every line involves a compromise among competing
principles of fair representation such as preventing the fragmen-

---

[249]Common Cause, note 146 *supra*, at 30–31.

[250]See note 164 *supra*. See also Cain, note 48 *supra*, at 13–14.

tation of racial groups, communities of economic interest, or political subdivisions, maintaining population equality among districts, insuring compactness, or protecting incumbents.[251] While
these choices may sometimes be made with partisan vindictive-
ness, it is better that they be made consciously. At least in that
way, responsibility can be affixed for the decisions made. Although Common Cause asserts that its proposal would have the
support of scholars such as Gordon Baker and Robert Dixon,[252]
what Professors Dixon and Baker have seen merit in is bipartisan,
as opposed to nonpartisan, districting, in which the responsibility
for drawing up a plan would be assigned to a board or commission,
made up of members of both political parties, that would be
charged with the responsibility of arriving at a compromise arrangement fair to all.[253] Arriving at such a compromise is easier
said than done, but the board should be expected to carry out
its task in much the same way that it would be carried out by a
legislature not controlled by either party.[254] Like the legislature,
but unlike the nonpartisan commission, the bipartisan board would
not be prohibited from considering and utilizing any piece of
information relevant to the accomplishment of its political responsibilities; it would not be required to perform what the Supreme Court has described as "the impossible task of extirpating
politics from what are the essentially political processes of the
sovereign States."[255]

Whatever one's views of the desirability of arriving at a districting
plan through political trade-offs, the process should not yield a
result that discriminates against either party, and thus should not
be subject to constitutional attack, either substantively or proce-
durally. A different issue arises, however, if, as in the New Jersey
congressional plan challenged in *Karcher v. Daggett* or the Indiana
state legislative plan challenged in *Davis v. Bandemer*, the state political process is controlled by one party which draws up a plan
through a process from which the other party is effectively excluded, particularly where, as in both of these cases, the legislative

---

[251]*Id.* at 68–74.

[252]Common Cause, note 146 *supra*, at 31.

[253]See Dixon, note 12 *supra*, at 380–84; Baker, note 56 *supra*, at 274.

[254]See Cain, note 48 *supra*, at 160–61.

[255]Gaffney v. Cummings, 412 U.S. at 754.

leadership of the dominant party is perfectly candid about its intention to take the fullest partisan advantage of the opportunity.

Gross procedural unfairness of this sort should be regarded as violating basic principles of due process of districting, but it is not clear what kind of judicial remedy could be provided. The availability of a remedy cannot be made to depend on the frank admission of a partisan purpose by the legislative leadership, for frankness would simply cease. If the remedy were to be available when, as in Indiana, the minority party is denied access to the relevant demographic data used by the majority to develop its plan, and not allowed to participate in the deliberations leading to the plan's construction, the process can readily be modified to allow such access and such participation in the future, even though the outcome would be no different since the majority would approve whatever plan it desired. It would not matter that the plan would pass on a straight party-line vote for there is no constitutional requirement that a law—even a districting law—have bipartisan support. Judicial pressure on the legislature in the first instance would be, if anything, counterproductive, since more would be known about a plan if the leadership can express its intentions frankly instead of being required to dissemble. Judicial pressure on the legislature in the second case, however, would be healthy. Even if it would be politically futile for the minority party to devise alternative districting plans based on the more complete demographic data used by the majority, the consequent availability of alternate plans would be helpful in identifying the questionable aspects of the majority's plan. Except as a means of confirming a court's conclusion that a challenged plan should be struck down as a gerrymander, however, the shortcomings of the procedure by which a plan was drawn up, debated, and approved do not seem to offer a promising avenue for effective judicial review.

It may perhaps be that the best hopes for controlling or ameliorating the effects of most partisan gerrymanders are practical rather than constitutional.[256] Partisan gerrymanders are possible only when a party controls both houses of a state legislature and the Governor is of the same party. If the Governor is of the opposing party or if state law requires that a districting plan be adopted by an extraordinary majority, the gerrymandering party must have enough votes to override a veto or to achieve the extraordinary majority unless it can attract the votes of members of the opposing party who have been given very safe seats. In addition, there is a tension between the interests of the gerrymandering party as a whole

---

[256]See Cain, note 48 *supra*, at 148–57.

and those of the individual legislators of that party. Since a gerrymander is effective to the extent that it requires the opposition party to absorb as many as possible of the 50 percent minus one "wasted" votes that are cast in every legislative district, the party would like to cut its margin of victory in each district it plans to carry to the smallest amount compatible with a reasonable degree of safety. On the other hand, the individual legislator is primarily interested in his or her own election, and desires to have the district as safe as possible. For the legislator, the wasted votes of supporters are a great source of comfort. Since the districting bill cannot be enacted unless the individual legislators of the gerrymandering party are willing to vote for it, the party will be obliged to limit the scope of its aspirations by wasting sufficient votes in its legislators' districts to induce them to vote for its passage.[257] And then what seems like an ideal gerrymander when enacted may prove far less so if unforeseen demographic changes occur or if a strong trend in favor of the minority party sweeps the candidates of that party into the legislative seats for which an insufficient margin of safety was provided.

It was for these reasons that Justice O'Connor argued in *Davis* that "political gerrymandering is a self-limiting enterprise" that "simply does not cause intolerable harm to the ability of major political groups to advance their interests,"[258] and that, therefore, the Supreme Court should decline to enter this thorniest part of the political thicket. But the zeal with which the gerrymandering enterprise is undertaken by those who are in a position to control the process of districting and the insistence with which political groups who feel themselves victimized by gerrymandering demand judicial relief suggest that, although the enterprise may be self-limiting, a great deal of political good or ill (depending on your perspective) can be accomplished before that limit is reached.

IV. DAVIS V. BANDEMER

A. POLITICS IN INDIANA

Davis v. Bandemer arose following the redistricting of the two houses of the Indiana state legislature in 1981.[259] The Republicans

---

[257]See *id.* at 154–55.

[258]106 S.Ct. at 2820–21 (concurring).

[259]For a description of the contents of the districting bill, the process by which it was enacted, and its impact, see the District Court opinion in Bandemer v. Davis, 603 F.Supp. 1479, 1482–89 (S.D. Ind. 1984).

had won a majority of both houses in the 1980 Reagan landslide, and Robert Orr, a Republican, had been elected Governor. The districting plan was drafted by a conference committee of both houses, all of whose members were Republicans. Four Democrats were appointed as "advisers" to the committee, but they were allowed neither to vote nor to have access to the computer-generated data on the basis of which the district lines were to be drawn. The District Court characterized the committee's proceedings as "fiercely competitive and unashamedly partisan," and it noted that the leadership of both houses had conceded that the principal aim of the districting process was to favor the Republican party.[260] The plan it produced was approved by both houses of the legislature on party-line votes after time was allowed for only cursory debate. Under the plan, all 50 members of the state Senate were to be elected from single-member districts, while the 100 members of the House were to be elected from 61 single-member districts and 16 multi-member districts, nine of which had two representatives and seven of which had three.[261] Great care was taken to insure that the plan would not be vulnerable to challenge on the ground of population disparity or of retrogression with regard to minority representation. The reported deviations between district populations was 1.05 percent in the House and 1.15 percent in the Senate, and there was no diminution in the number of districts with black voting majorities as compared with the previous districting plan.[262]

Two suits were promptly filed to challenge the constitutionality of the plan. Individual members of the Democratic Party alleged that the plan was a partisan gerrymander which discriminated against Democrats;[263] the state NAACP, various of its branches, and eight

---

[260]*Id.* at 1484.

[261]This Indiana districting plan made much less use of multi-member districts than the plan challenged inWhitcomb v. Chavis. In that plan there were only 14 single-member House districts and 23 single-member Senate districts. The other 86 House members and 27 Senate members were elected from multi-member districts, which were as large as 15-member districts in the House and 8-member districts in the Senate. See 403 U.S. at 127–28.

[262]*Id.* at 1485. The fact that the plan had as many districts with black voting majorities as its predecessor insured compliance with the "no retrogression" standard applied by the Court in cases involving redistricting for which preclearance is required under §5 of the Voting Rights Act of 1965, 42 U.S.C. §1973c. See Beer v. United States 425 U.S. 130 (1976).

[263]The plan was also challenged as being in violation of the Indiana Constitution. 603 F.Supp. at 1482. The District Court majority did not reach the state constitutional claims. *Id.* at 1495. The dissenting judge found the state claims meritless. *Id.* at 1504—05.

individual members alleged that the plan unconstitutionally diluted the voting power of blacks by splitting up concentrations of black voters.[264] The two suits were consolidated and tried together by a three-judge District Court. All three judges agreed that the plan did not discriminate against blacks as blacks,[265] but the majority held that blacks had been discriminated against as Democrats, and granted them relief to that extent. The NAACP did not appeal. On the claim of the Democratic Party, the District Court divided 2–1. The majority, Judges Noland and Brooks, sustained the Democrats' claim that they had been the victim of an unconstitutional gerrymander.[266] Judge Pell dissented.

The majority refused to evaluate the merits of the competing statistical arguments, stating that it did "not wish to choose which statistician is more credible or less credible."[267] It relied instead on the data which it deemed most relevant for assessing the charge of gerrymandering. Most conspicuous among these data was the fact that there was a discrepancy in the "votes/seats" ratio. Specifically, in the 1982 elections, Democratic candidates for the Indiana House of Representatives received 51.9 percent of the overall statewide vote, but won only 43 of the 100 seats. In the state senatorial elections, Democratic candidates received 53.1 percent of the statewide vote, but won only 52 percent of the seats (13 of the 25 seats that were up for election in 1982).[268] (The fact that the "votes/seats" ratio in the Senate was as close to perfect as possible was not acknowledged.) In addition, the majority noted that many of the legislative districts had shapes which were "contorted," which failed to meet "any remote definition of compactness,"[269] and whose lines were drawn without regard to political subdivision boundaries (except for township boundaries, which were generally respected), and without "any *consistent* application of 'community of interest' principles."[270] The use of multi-member districts in the House plan was cited as having been employed as a "particularly effective"

---

[264]*Id.* at 1482.

[265]*Id.* at 1489–90; 1496–97 (dissenting opinion).

[266]The majority, *id.* at 1490, declared that it was "persuaded" that political gerrymandering was violative of the Equal Protection Clause by Justice Stevens's analysis of the issue in *Karcher.* See 462 U.S. at 749.

[267]603 F.Supp. at 1485.

[268]*Id.* at 1486.

[269]*Id.* at 1488.

[270]*Id.* at 1486–87 (emphasis is in original).

device for submerging concentrations of Democratic voters—especially blacks—in districts large enough to render their votes ineffective.[271] For example, by employing multi-member districts in Marion and Allen Counties, the Republicans were able to win 18 of the 21 House seats from those districts, despite the fact that 46.6 percent of the population of those districts were found by the majority to be "Democrats, or at least have Democratic voting tendencies."[272] They concluded that "such a disparity speaks for itself."[273] The majority conceded that a finding of intentional discrimination was necessary,[274] but concluded that the requisite discriminatory intent could be inferred from the characteristics of the plan.[275] Since the state had not rebutted this prima facie showing of discrimination by demonstrating that the district lines were supported by rational and legitimate considerations, it ruled that the plan was invalid as a partisan gerrymander.[276]

Two aspects of the District Court's opinion are quite puzzling. First, although great emphasis was placed on the discrepancies in the "votes/seats" ratio in summarizing the statistical evidence of gerrymandering, no mention was made of these discrepancies in the course of arriving at the conclusion that a prima facie showing of intentional discrimination against the Democrats had been made. Second, the majority never explained the reasons for the invalidation of the Senate plan. All the cited evidence of gerrymandering related to the House plan, and no apparent discrepancy in the "votes/seats" ratio occurred in the 1982 Senate elections.[277]

Judge Pell, on the other hand, contended that the Democrats had failed to prove that the districting plan had in any way adversely affected their voting strength.[278] He noted that there was no discrepancy in the "votes/seats" ratio in the Senate election,[279] and he

---

[271]*Id.* at 1488–89. The majority noted that 81.2 percent of blacks in Indiana, but only 35 percent of whites, resided in multi-member districts under the House plan. *Id.* at 1488.

[272]*Id.* at 1489.

[273]*Ibid.*

[274]See Mobile v. Bolden, 446 U.S. at 66.

[275]603 F.Supp. at 1493–95.

[276]*Id.* at 1495.

[277]See Grofman, note 53 *supra*, at 121.

[278]603 F.Supp. at 1501.

[279]*Ibid.* In the Supreme Court, Justice Powell noted that the reason that the Democrats appeared to fare well in the 1982 Senate elections was that the half of the Senate that was

suggested that the fairness of the House election should be determined by using a different base than the percentage of the statewide
vote won by Democratic House candidates. Instead he would use
as the base for determining actual Democratic statewide voting
strength the percentage of the vote won by the party's candidates
for statewide offices with low visibility because, unlike voting for
one's legislator, voting for the candidates for such offices is usually
simply a matter of selecting the party.[280] Averaging the percentage
of votes cast for the Democratic candidate for Auditor in 1982 and
the Democratic candidate for Clerk of the Supreme Court in 1980
and 1982, he concluded that the statewide voting strength of the
Democrats was 46.8 percent. While this figure was still higher than
the 43 percent of the House seats won by Democrats in 1982, he
believed that the discrepancy was compensated for by the opposite
discrepancy in the Senate election, where the Democrats won 52
percent of the seats, or more than 5 percent more than their base
strength suggests would be appropriate.[281]

B. IN THE SUPREME COURT

The question how the Supreme Court would address the political gerrymandering issue generated a great deal of interest in
political circles. *Amicus curiae* briefs were filed on behalf of the
Indiana Democrats not only by the plaintiffs in the NAACP
litigation, Common Cause, and the American Civil Liberties
Union, but also by the Republican National Committee, the
latter no doubt moved less by an overriding sense of fair play
than by a belief that, with state legislatures more often to be
found in the control of Democrats,[282] Republicans would, in the

---

up for reelection in that year included a high percentage of safe Democratic seats. When
the other half of the Senate was elected in 1984, the Democratic senatorial candidates won
42.3 percent of the statewide vote but only 7 out of the 25 seats. See 106 S.Ct. at 2837.

[280]603 F.Supp. at 1501. Judge Pell's method of analysis was suggested by Backstrom,
Robins, & Eller, note 45 *supra*, at 1131.

[281]603 F.Supp. at 1501–02. But see Niemi, note 198 *supra*, at 205–6.

[282]As of January, 1985, of the 49 states with bicameral legislatures and partisan elections
(Nebraska being the exception in both categories), Democrats held majorities in both houses
in 26 states, and Republicans held majorities in both houses in 11. In 9 states, each party
held a majority in one house, and, in the remaining 3 states, the Democrats held a majority
in one house, and neither party held a majority in the other. 26 The Book of the States,
1986–87 87.

long run, more frequently be the victims than the perpetrators of gerrymandering. The Republicans in all likelihood perceived California's 45-seat delegation in the United States House of Representatives as of more substantial political significance than any outcome to be anticipated in Indiana, and were looking beyond the Indiana litigation to the resolution of a pending suit challenging the districting plan for the California congressional delegation as a partisan gerrymander favoring the Democrats. The California litigation[283] had become bogged down over certain technical issues of state law that have since been compromised, and the trial of the federal constitutional question was postponed to await the Supreme Court's decision in the Indiana case.[284] On the other side, the Indiana Republicans were supported in *amicus curiae* briefs filed by the Mexican-American Legal Defense Fund and by the California Democratic congressional delegation. It may be assumed that neither of these two groups was overly concerned with the welfare of the Republican Party in Indiana, but both were well aware that they had critical interests that would be jeopardized if California's congressional districts were opened to judicial scrutiny.

The Court heard oral argument on the very first day of the Term, October 7, 1985, but did not hand down its decision until June 30, 1986. Three of the six Justices who joined in the majority's conclusion that claims of vote dilution through partisan political gerrymandering were justiciable—including Justice White, the author of the prevailing opinion—had to be brought around to that position since, only a year and a half prior to oral argument, they had declared flatly that the Court should not rule "that the existence of noncompact or gerrymandered districts is by itself a constitutional violation."[285] But, when the decision was

---

[283]See Badham v. Eu, 568 F.Supp. 156 (N.D. Cal.), aff'd *sub nom.* Badham v. United States District Court, 721 F.2d 1170 (9th Cir. 1983), 749 F.2d 36 (9th Cir. 1984), cert. denied *sub nom.* Badham v. Secretary of State of California, 105 S.Ct. 1844 (1985).

[284]See Grofman, note 53 *supra*, at 102.

[285]Karcher v. Daggett, stay denied, 466 U.S. 910, 917 (1984) (Brennan, J., dissenting). Brennan, joined by White and Marshall, added that the principal factors which might form the basis for a gerrymandering claim, such as compactness, respect for political subdivision boundaries, respect for the boundaries of previous districts, and protecting incumbents, were not "necessarily . . . relevant to the constitutionality of a State's congressional reapportionment plan in the absence of numerical inequalities that themselves violate the Constitution." *Id.* at 917 n.2.

finally announced, tnese three Justices—White, Brennan, and Marshall—had joined Justices Stevens, Powell, and Blackmun, the first
two of whom had already urged the Court to recognize that political
gerrymandering could violate the Constitution,[286] to form a majority
for the holding that political gerrymandering claims were justiciable.[287] Justices Powell and Stevens would have gone further and
affirmed the decision of the District Court that the Indiana districting plan was an unconstitutional gerrymander, and they thus
dissented from the judgment of the Court (there was no majority
opinion on this point) reversing the District Court on the merits.[288]
Justice O'Connor, joined by Chief Justice Burger and Justice Rehnquist, would have dismissed the suit on the ground that the issues
presented were nonjusticiable.[289]

1. Justiciability. In light of the fact that the Court had hesitated
to take the step for nearly a quarter of a century after *Baker v.
Carr,* and that half of the members of the majority had expressed
an unwillingness to take it scarcely more than two years earlier,
the Court resolved the issue of the justiciability of political gerrymandering claims with an extraordinary economy of argument.
Indeed, in the majority's view, the justiciability question essentially resolved itself once it was recognized that the issue did not
fall within any of the categories of political questions identified
in *Baker v. Carr,*[290] and that, in *Reynolds v. Sims,* the Court had
held that "the achieving of fair and effective representation for all
citizens is concededly the basic aim of legislative apportionment."[291] The importance of this essentially offhand reaffirmation
of the principle stated in *Reynolds* that the requirement that legislative districts be equally populated was intended to further a
goal—"fair and effective representation"—cannot be overstated.
By conceding that equal population among legislative districts was
mandated for representational purposes—that is, as a bar to districting that denies fair representation, or, in other words, as a
bar to gerrymandering—it necessarily acknowledged the inescap-

---

[286]See note 20 *supra.*

[287]106 S.Ct. at 2803–07.

[288]*Id.* at 2825–38.

[289]*Id.* at 2816–25 (concurring).

[290]*Id.* at 2804–05, citing 369 U.S. at 217.

[291]106 S.Ct. at 2806, citing 377 U.S. at 565–66.

able fact that it had obscured for so long, that "one person, one vote" is, at bottom, an antigerrymandering rule.

Speaking for the majority, Justice White declared that the essential similarity between political gerrymandering claims and equal population claims dictates the conclusion that if the latter are justiciable because they do not involve a political question, the former must be justiciable also.[292] He confidently asserted that, even though "we may not now . . . perceive a likely arithmetic presumption" for the resolution of such claims, such as the "one person, one vote" rule, "we are not persuaded that there are no judicially discernible and manageable standards by which political gerrymandering cases are to be decided."[293] Moreover, he asserted, since claims of racial minorities challenging denial of fair representation through discriminatory districting were recognized as justiciable,[294] the entitlement of political groups to raise the same claim before the courts should be no less.[295]

For the majority, it was just as simple as that. Justice O'Connor's argument that political gerrymandering issues should be deemed nonjusticiable was not based on disagreement with the majority's logic, but rested on practical concerns. She expressed grave doubts regarding the majority's easy assumption that standards for the resolution of political gerrymandering claims will prove to be "judicially discernible and manageable." She saw these claims as presenting political questions for two reasons—the absence of such standards and the need for "an initial policy determination of a kind clearly for nonjudicial discretion."[296] Manageable judicial standards proved to be discoverable in malapportionment cases only because the Court, treating malapportionment as an abridgment of the individual's right to vote, was able to employ a simple arithmetical standard.[297] The rights asserted in political gerrymandering cases are, in contrast, group

---

[292] 106 S.Ct. at 2805.

[293] *Ibid.*, paraphrasing Baker v. Carr, 369 U.S. at 226.

[294] See note 17 *supra* and the cases discussed therein.

[295] 106 S.Ct. at 2806. The Court here adopted the position expressed in Justice Stevens's concurring opinion in Karcher v. Daggett, 462 U.S. at 749.

[296] 106 S.Ct. at 2818, quoting Baker v. Carr, 369 U.S. at 217.

[297] 106 S.Ct. at 2819.

rights—"the right to be free from discriminatory impairment of
. . . group voting strength,"[298] and standards for the resolution of
the necessarily complex claims of that nature cannot coherently
be reduced to rules of simple application. The majority, however,
was confident of its ability to cross that bridge when it came to
it. Justice White pointed out that the Court had not yet devised
the "one person, one vote" standard when it declined in *Baker* to
conclude that standards could not be found for the resolution of
apportionment disputes. Standards need not be discovered before
they may be adjudged to be discoverable.[299]

More likely, Justice O'Connor's principal concern was not that
the Court would be unable to fashion a simple standard for the
adjudication of political gerrymandering claims, but that it would
ultimately yield to the temptation to fashion one that would be all
too simple—proportional representation. That is, that the Equal
Protection Clause would be held to require that legislative districts
be drawn in such a way as to approximate equivalence under the
"votes/seats" ratio—each party having the same percentage of seats
in the legislature as the percentage of votes it receives in the legislative election statewide:[300]

> Of course, in one sense a requirement of proportional rep-
> resentation, whether loose or absolute, is judicially manageable.
> If this Court were to declare that the Equal Protection Clause
> required proportional representation within fixed tolerances, I
> have no doubt that district courts would be able to apply this
> edict. The flaw in such a pronouncement, however, would be
> the use of the Equal Protection Clause as the vehicle for making
> a fundamental policy choice that is contrary to the intent of its
> Framers and to the traditions of this republic. The political
> question doctrine as articulated in *Baker v. Carr* rightly requires
> that we refrain from making such policy choices in order to
> evade what would otherwise be a lack of judicially manageable
> standards.

The majority, of course, denied "a preference for proportionality *per se*," and spoke instead merely of "a preference for a level
of parity between votes and representation sufficient to insure that

---

[298]*Id.* at 2820.

[299]*Id.* at 2805.

[300]*Id.* at 2823–24. Here Justice O'Connor was specifically echoing the grim prediction of
Martin Shapiro. See text at notes 232–35 *supra*.

significant minority voices are heard and that majorities are not consigned to minority status"[301]—that is, in other words, sufficient to insure "fair and effective representation" and the ability of the majority to control the legislature, the purposes adduced in *Reynolds v. Sims* for the establishment of the standard of "one person, one vote." Moreover, in speaking for the plurality, Justice White categorically rejected any easy equation between disproportionality and a violation of Equal Protection.[302] Nevertheless, Justice O'Connor's fear that any judicial commitment to avoid proportional representation may not "be enduring in the face of the tremendous political pressures that courts will confront when called on to decide political gerrymandering claims"[303] is not groundless. As she noted, "[c]ourts will be forced to look for some form of 'undue' disproportionality with respect to electoral success if political gerrymandering claims are justiciable, because otherwise they will find their decisions turning on imponderables such as whether the legislators of one party have fairly represented the voters of the other."[304] If these fears become reality, opening this issue to judicial scrutiny will prove to have been a mischievous undertaking. To demand such proportionality as a matter of constitutional law would be to impose a rule that would unfairly penalize the majority party, which, in a single-member-district electoral system, tends naturally to win a higher percentage of legislative seats than its percentage of the total votes cast in the legislative election,[305] and thus hamper its ability to govern as a majority and to enact its legislative program.[306] Such a result would bring the Court full circle because it would have adopted an antigerrymandering standard whose effect would be to thwart majority control of the legislature, the protection of which was one of the two principal underlying purposes justifying its imposition of constitutional limitations on legislative districting in the first place.[307]

---

[301]106 S.Ct. at 2807 n.9.

[302]*Id.* at 2810.

[303]*Id.* at 2823.

[304]*Ibid.*

[305]See, *e.g.*, Backstrom, Robins, & Eller, note 45 *supra*, at 1134–35.

[306]See *id.* at 1135 n.47.

[307]Reynolds v. Sims, 377 U.S. at 565–66.

Justice O'Connor saw no justification for the Court's conclusion that because racial gerrymandering claims are justiciable, political gerrymandering claims must also be. Legislative districting which undercuts the political effectiveness of racial minorities, she argued, is appropriately subject to judicial scrutiny because the principal purpose of the Fourteenth and Fifteenth Amendments was to protect blacks against discriminatory state action,[308] and because, "as a matter of past history and present reality, there is a direct and immediate relationship between the racial minority's group voting strength in a particular community and the individual rights of its members to vote and to participate in the political process,"[309] a relationship that does not exist between the voting strength of a political party and the individual rights of its members to political participation. Thus, in the former case, but not in the latter, she saw the gap as being bridged between justiciable issues of individual voting rights and nonjusticiable issues of group rights.[310] Neither Democrats nor Republicans "are a discrete and insular group," and they are plainly not "incapable of fending for themselves through the political process."[311] While there are no inherent limits to the degree to which a racial minority's voting power can be rendered ineffective through a gerrymander, she noted that because individual legislators of a gerrymandering party would want to maximize the safeness of their individual seats and because leaving too fine a margin of error could backfire,[312] "there is good reason to think that political gerrymandering is a self-limiting enterprise."[313]

---

[308]106 S.Ct. at 2820, citing Justice Frankfurter's explanation in Baker v. Carr of why judicial intervention into the functioning of state political processes to protect the voting rights of blacks was consistent with the general rule against judicial decision of political questions. 369 U.S. at 285–86.

[309]106 S.Ct. at 2820.

[310]As Justice O'Connor also commented, "while membership in a racial group is an immutable characteristic, voters can—and often do—move from one party to the other or support candidates from both parties. Consequently, the difficulty of measuring voting strength is heightened in the case of a major political party." *Id.* at 2823.

[311]*Id.* at 2820. Justice O'Connor's insight that the Republican and Democratic parties "*are* the dominant group" in the American political process, *ibid.*, and thus not in need of judicial protection for their interests was plainly ignored in Buckley v. Valeo, 424 U.S. 1 (1976).

[312]106 S.Ct. at 2820–21, citing Cain, note 48 *supra*, at 152, 154–55.

[313]106 S.Ct. at 2820, citing Cain, note 48 *supra*, at 151–59.

The majority gave Justice O'Connor's distinctions between racial and political gerrymandering short shrift, declaring that the fact "[t]hat the characteristics of the complaining group are not immutable or that the group has not been subject to the same historical stigma may be relevant to the manner in which the case is adjudicated, but these differences do not justify a refusal to entertain such a case."[314] It insisted that the answer to the question whether an issue presents a nonjusticiable political question depends entirely on whether it fits into one of the categories described in *Baker v. Carr.* To insert considerations of the desirability of, or need for, judicial intervention into the process of categorization would mean that the decision as to whether an issue presents a political question would turn on *ad hoc* and subjective judgments as to the wisdom of having a particular dispute decided by the courts.[315] Justice White also expressed doubt that political gerrymandering actually was "a self-limiting enterprise,"[316] a doubt that seems warranted in the light of the concern displayed by political groups over the outcome of the case. It would appear that if the enterprise were self-limiting, the participants do not perceive it to be so.

As the majority correctly perceived, the decision that political gerrymandering claims are justiciable flows ineluctably from the Court's earlier judgments that cases raising claims of population inequality among districts and of racial gerrymandering are justiciable. Justice O'Connor's argument that they should be regarded as political questions does not fundamentally challenge this logic. Her distinction was based on practical considerations: an arithmetic solution is available for the population inequality cases; racial minorities cannot defend themselves as effectively as a major political party. The Court would be imprudent not to heed her warnings about the dangers of careless or simplistic adjudication in this area, and it appears to be fully cognizant of this. Indeed, the fact that the decision was not handed down for almost nine months after oral argument suggests that it was striving diligently to avoid carelessness or oversimplicity. But it is a happy event that the Court recognized the identity of the constitutional issues of "one person, one vote" and of gerrymandering. That identity requires that po-

---

[314]106 S.Ct. at 2806.

[315]*Id.* at 2807.

[316]*Ibid.*

litical gerrymandering issues be deemed justiciable; how the courts can deal with these issues is the remaining and urgent question.

2. *The plurality's test.* The majority that coalesced on the issue of justiciability disintegrated on the merits. Only the six Justices who agreed that the issue was justiciable addressed the merits, and Justice White's opinion concluding that no constitutional violation had been proved was subscribed to by only a plurality of four Justices— White, Brennan, Marshall, and Blackmun. Justice Powell, joined by Justice Stevens, strongly dissented. They agreed with the District Court that the Indiana districting plan was clearly invalid as a partisan gerrymander.

The plurality's opinion on the merits seemed to render nugatory much of the hope that the Court offered the victims of gerrymandering by conceding justiciability. It would appear that the four Justices of the plurality were strongly affected by a concern for the possible dire consequences of treating the gerrymandering issue as justiciable: a flood of litigation leading to arbitrary decisions because of the impossibility of articulating standards that would allow a judicially administrable line to be drawn between valid partisan districting and invalid political gerrymandering, perhaps culminating in the adoption of a simple but politically disastrous requirement of proportional representation for the political parties in the legislature. If, indeed, they had such a concern, they sought to allay it by adopting a standard for establishing an unconstitutional gerrymander that would be virtually incapable of being satisfied except in the most extreme circumstances.

The plurality agreed with the District Court that proof of discriminatory intent was essential to make out a violation of the Equal Protection Clause in a gerrymandering case[317] and conceded that "if the law challenged here had discriminatory effects on Democrats," the District Court's conclusion that those effects were intended would be supported by the record.[318] In fact, it went so far as to concede—recognizing that politicians drawing district lines will be fully aware of the political meaning of what they are doing— that "[a]s long as redistricting is done by a legislature, it should not be very difficult to prove that the likely political consequences of

---

[317]*Id.* at 2808.
[318]*Ibid.*

the reapportionment were intended."[319] But it refused to accept the suggestion implicit in the District Court's opinion that an imbalance in the "votes/seats" ratio in a given legislative election represents proof of an unconstitutional gerrymander. It correctly noted that, to the extent that the parties' support is evenly distributed throughout the state, "even a narrow statewide preference for either party would produce an overwhelming majority for the winning party in the state legislature";[320] it saw no reason why the majority party should be required, as a matter of constitutional law, to draw district lines in such a way as selflessly to dispense with this natural advantage.[321] "Our cases clearly foreclose any claim that the Constitution requires proportional representation or that legislatures in reapportioning must draw district lines to come as near as possible to allocating seats to the contending parties in proportion to what their anticipated statewide vote will be."[322]

The plurality not only rejected proportionality as a basis for challenging the constitutionality of statewide districting plans, it also drew the parallel conclusion that the constitutionality of a specific multi-member district does not turn on whether the district returns representatives to the legislature in proportion to the voting strengths of the parties within the district.[323] This equation of statewide results with results within an individual multi-member district is a fundamental *non sequitur* that substantially undercuts the plurality's reasoning—for the two represent entirely different types of electoral systems. The statewide legislative election is a sum of individual district elections; a multi-member-district election is an at-large election. To be sure, both are different from proportional

---

[319]*Id.* at 2809. The plurality added, however, that the fact "[t]hat discriminatory intent may not be difficult to prove in this context does not . . . mean that it need not be proved at all." *Id.* at n.11.

[320]*Id.* at 2809.

[321]*Ibid.* See Backstrom, Robins & Eller, note 45 *supra*, at 1134–37. As was held in Gaffney v. Cummings, 412 U.S. at 752–54, however, the fact that a plan is drawn up for the purpose of overcoming these natural advantages and obtaining a more proportional result would not render it unconstitutional. It should be noted that any plan that seeks to attain this end will very likely have to have districts of fairly distorted shapes. Salamander-like configurations may be expected to be as necessary in the quest to obtain proportional representation of the major parties as in the quest to maximize disproportionality. See Lowenstein & Steinberg, note 202 *supra*, at 23 n.62.

[322]106 S.Ct. at 2809.

[323]*Id.* at 2810.

representation systems, and, therefore, neither should be expected
to yield proportional results, but the consequences of their failure
to do so are not the same and are not equally justified. The single-
member-district electoral system is maintained despite its failure to
yield proportional results because it supports the preservation of a
two-party system and prevents party fragmentation. The disproportionality of the results it produces is an unfortunate but ines-
capably necessary by-product of the system. On the other hand,
the at-large electoral system—either statewide or as conducted within
multi-member districts—maximizes the disadvantages of disproportionality with little by way of compensating benefits. It completely submerges the interest in fair representation and normally
produces totally unrepresentative results. It is thus much more
serious, and much less justified, when disproportionality of representation occurs because a multi-member district returns a delegation that is virtually all of one party despite the fact that there
is a sizable percentage of members of the other party within the
district, than when disproportionality occurs because of the natural
effects of cumulating, statewide, the results of individual single-
member-district elections.

The plurality's assumption that proportionality of results is irrelevant both statewide and within individual legislative districts
leads the plurality to the startling conclusion that whether the disadvantaged party is able to win any elections at all simply is not
the issue in either context.[324] The issue with regard to a specific
legislative district is whether the voters who supported the losing
candidate retain the opportunity effectively to influence the behavior of the winner, and, with regard to the statewide legislative
election, it is whether the members of the group or party whose
candidates are disproportionally defeated retain the opportunity to
exert effective influence in the state's political processes.[325]

One can imagine that it came as something of a surprise to the
Republican National Committee to be told that whether their candidates are able to win elections is not essentially relevant to the

---

[324]For the plurality, because "the power to influence the political process is not limited to
winning elections," *ibid.*, "a group's electoral power is not unconstitutionally diminished by
the simple fact of an apportionment scheme that makes winning elections more difficult."
Ibid.

[325]   *Ibid.*

question whether they have been victims of a gerrymander. It is, of course, not without relevance to individuals whether the person elected to represent their district in the legislature regards them as enemies to be overcome or as constituents to be wooed in anticipation of the next election. Therefore, in cases involving racial gerrymandering through multi-member districting or at-large elections in areas where there is racial bloc voting—which are the cases principally cited by the plurality here—the fact that the elected representatives may have little or no incentive to be sensitive to the concerns of racial minorities is obviously of considerable significance in measuring the discriminatory impact of the challenged districting. But it requires an enormous leap to move from that valid insight to the conclusion that being able to be heard by your representative is what really matters, and that having a reasonable opportunity to win elections—and, *a fortiori*, to win enough elections statewide or nationwide to be able to attain a legislative majority—is not a critical measure of whether "fair and effective representation" has been afforded or whether effective majority rule has been frustrated.

It is one thing to say, as the plurality does, that it is unlikely "that the candidate elected will entirely ignore the interests of those voters [who supported the candidate of the opposing party],"[326] but it is quite another thing to imply that there is not a critical difference between having a representative who will listen sympathetically to one's concerns and who will be careful not to disregard them unnecessarily, and having a representative who will actively seek to promote them. And if the issue becomes whether the majority in the legislature will be made up of persons like the former or like the latter, the difference becomes all the more significant. As Justice Powell observed in his dissent, "it defies political reality to suppose that members of a losing party have as much influence over state government as do members of the victorious party. . . . I cannot accept the plurality's apparent conclusion that loss of this 'crucial' position is constitutionally insignificant as long as the losers are not 'entirely ignored' by the winners."[327] If the plurality has lost sight of the truth of that, it has lost sight of a fundamental aim of the

---

[326]*Id.* at 2810.

[327]*Id.* at 2830.

rule of "one person, one vote"—to enable a majority of the people to elect (not merely to be listened to by) a majority of the legislature.[328]

If electoral results are not the proper measure of whether a districting plan is an unconstitutional gerrymander, what is? The plurality set down as its test that "unconstitutional discrimination occurs only when the electoral system is arranged in a manner that will consistently degrade a voter's or a group of voters' influence on the political process as a whole."[329] "[A] finding of unconstitutionality must be supported by evidence of continued frustration of the will of a majority of the voters or effective denial to a minority of voters of a fair chance to influence the political process."[330] Reference to "the political process as a whole" clearly suggests that more must be shown than the inability to convert voting strength into electoral victory, and the requirements of consistent degradation and of "continued frustration" suggest that the discriminatory effects must be shown to be likely to persist over a very long period of time. Moreover, the plurality explicitly emphasized that the level of discriminatory effect that must be shown to support a finding of unconstitutionality must be above a certain threshold, even though discriminatory intent is proved. They rejected the position that "*any* interference with an opportunity to elect a representative of one's choice would be sufficient to allege or make out an equal protection violation, unless justified by some acceptable state interest."[331] Not to require such a threshold would "invite attack on all or almost all reapportionment statutes," and "would too much embroil the judiciary in second-guessing what has consistently been referred to as a political task for the legislature."[332]

The principal source for this standard, as the plurality makes clear,[333] was the constitutional law developed in cases of minority

---

[328]See Reynolds v. Sims, 377 U.S. at 565.

[329]106 S.Ct. at 2810.

[330]*Id.* at 2811.

[331]*Ibid.*

[332] *Ibid.* The plurality noted that the requirement that a threshold level of discriminatory effect must be exceeded before an Equal Protection violation can be found—even where there is discriminatory intent—was adopted in light of "the peculiar characteristics of these political gerrymandering claims," and took care to point out that no "similar requirement would apply to our Equal Protection cases outside of this particular context." *Id.* at n.14.

[333]*Id.* at 2810 n.12.

vote dilution through multi-member districting. But as Justice Powell pointed out, the issue involved in recent minority vote dilution cases has concerned the level of proof of discriminatory effect that was needed to establish discriminatory intent.[334] Effects above a threshold level had to be demonstrated before discriminatory intent could be inferred.[335] But, as the plurality acknowledged, demonstrating discriminatory intent is not the problem in political gerrymandering cases because it will not commonly "be very difficult to prove."[336] What will need to be proved is that the districting plan has a discriminatory effect. While it may be appropriate to require a showing that the discriminatory effects of a plan are above a threshold level in order to prove intent by inference from the existence of those effects, one cannot derive from that requirement an analogous requirement that a showing of more than a certain threshold effect is necessary to prove the existence of an unconstitutional effect in a situation in which discriminatory intent has been proved. Justice Powell was therefore correct in denying "that a standard requiring proof of 'heightened effect,' where invidious intent has been established directly, has support in any of our cases."[337] Surely it is true, as he notes, that "[i]f a racial minority established that the legislature adopted a redistricting law for no purpose other than to disadvantage that group," there would be no justification for a requirement that the discriminatory effect of the law would have to be shown to be above a threshold level before it could be struck down as a violation of Equal Protection.[338] It was undoubtedly for this reason that the plurality was careful to admonish that the standard it was employing here was not "intended in any way to suggest an alteration of the standards developed in [racial gerrymandering] cases for evaluating such claims."[339]

---

[334]*Id.* at 2831 n.10.

[335]For example, the plurality cited language from Rogers v. Lodge, 458 U.S. 613 (1982), for the purpose of showing that "a finding of unconstitutional vote dilution" requires "evidence that excluded groups have 'less opportunity to participate in the political processes and to elect candidates of their choice.' " 106 S.Ct. at 2809–10, quoting from 458 U.S. at 624. But the quoted passage concerns proof of discriminatory intent, not discriminatory effect.

[336]106 S.Ct. at 2809.

[337]106 S.Ct. at 2831 n.10.

[338]*Ibid.*

[339] *Id.* at 2810 n.13.

3. The constitutionality of the Indiana districting plan. The plurality concluded that the findings of the District Court were insufficient to justify its conclusion that the Indiana districting plan was unconstitutional. In arriving at this conclusion, it accepted without challenge all of the facts found by the District Court majority regarding the plan's characteristics and the discriminatory purpose with which it was enacted.[340] It thereby conceded that the plan was drawn up entirely by Republican members of the legislature, while the Democrats were denied access to the demographic data employed to construct it and all effective voice in the process by which the lines were drawn. It also conceded that the primary motivation of the plan's drafters was to maximize Republican strength in the legislature at the expense of the Democrats,[341] and that, to achieve this maximization of Republican advantage, they drew districts which were "contorted, with little apparent emphasis on 'community of interest,' [which did] not adhere to any remote definition of compactness,"[342] which ignored the constraints imposed by municipal and county boundaries, and for which no justification had been offered in terms of a legitimate state interest.[343] Moreover, it conceded that the plan "through the use of multi-member districts stacked or split concentrations of black Democratic voters so that their elective power would be minimized."[344] It recognized that, in the 1982 legislative elections, Democratic candidates statewide had received 51.9 percent of the total vote in elections to the state House of Representatives yet had won only 43 percent of the seats,[345] and that, in the multi-member House districts in Marion and Allen Counties, the Democrats, with 46.6 percent of the voters in those districts, had been able to win only three of the 21 seats.[346]

The plurality accepted all that and held that those "findings do not satisfy [the] threshold condition to stating and proving a cause of action."[347] The evidence drawn from the 1982 election results

---

[340]*Id.* at 2815 n.20.

[341]See 603 F.Supp. at 1483–84, 1488, 1492, 1495.

[342]*Id.* at 1488.

[343]*Id.* at 1486–88, 1493.

[344]*Id.* at 1494.

[345]*Id.* at 1486.

[346]*Id.* at 1489.

[347]106 S.Ct. at 2811.

was dismissed because "[r]elying on a single election to prove un-constitutional discrimination is unsatisfactory"[348]—in another election, the results could be different. In fact, the plurality commented, the results could have been different in the 1982 election, for if the Democrats had been able to win "an additional few percentage points of the votes cast statewide, they would have obtained a majority of the seats in both houses."[349] The relevance of that observation is hardly clear. Obviously, it will always be true that if the disadvantaged party could manage to win "an additional few percentage points of the votes cast statewide," they would be able to defeat even the most grossly manipulated gerrymander. The plurality was impressed by the absence of any finding by the District Court of the effects the districting plan would have in future elections. Specifically, they noted the absence of a finding that the plan "would consign the Democrats to a minority status in the Assembly throughout the 1980's or that the Democrats would have no hope of doing any better in the reapportionment that would occur after the 1990 census."[350] "Without findings of this nature," it added portentously, "the District Court erred in concluding that the 1981 Act violated the Equal Protection Clause."[351]

It is possible to glean from these observations some sense of what the plurality intended the terms it employed in articulating its constitutional standard to mean. Because the results of one election can never suffice to prove a gerrymander, and findings with regard to the possible outcome of future elections or even future reapportionments are essential, the requirement of "evidence of continued frustration of the will of a majority of the voters" would appear to mean that, before a districting plan can be held to be unconstitutional, it must be demonstrated that even if the disadvantaged party can consistently command the majority of the votes in a legislative election, it can never, because of the plan's discriminatory characteristics, reasonably expect to win a majority of the legislative seats. Under those circumstances, of course, it will be powerless to protect its interests politically or to bring about an alteration of its situation following the next decennial redistricting, and then,

---

[348] *Id.* at 2812.

[349] *Ibid.*

[350] *Ibid.*

[351] *Ibid.*

and only then, can it obtain judicial relief. "[E]ffective denial to a
minority of voters of a fair chance to influence the political process"
would appear to mean that even if the candidates of a minority
party receive as many votes, statewide, as they can reasonably
expect, the party cannot, given the effects of the gerrymander, hope
to attain sufficient strength to be able to exert an influence—either
in the legislature as a whole or with individual representatives of
the dominant party—over issues of the establishment or implementation of public policy. In either case, the electoral system can
be said to be "arranged in a manner that will consistently degrade
a voter's or a group of voters' influence on the political process as
a whole."

If this is the meaning of the plurality's test, judicial relief would
be available from a political gerrymander only when the situation
is as politically irremediable as that of the malapportioned districts
prior to *Baker v. Carr*. Only if the disadvantaged party can show
both that it has been subjected to flagrant discrimination and that
the discrimination makes it impossible to obtain relief except through
litigation, will courts be allowed to invalidate districting plans drawn
up through the political processes. Robert Dixon has written that,
in *Baker v. Carr*, "[t]he Supreme Court finally concluded that some
judicial participation in the politics of the people—to an undeter-
mined degree—was a precondition to there *being* any effective politics."[352] The plurality here appears to have agreed that political
gerrymandering claims should be justiciable in order to leave open
the possibility of judicial relief where a gerrymander has prevented
"there *being* any effective politics" in a state or district, but, at the
same time, has sought to limit "judicial participation in the politics
of the people" only to those most extreme contexts.

Of course, the plurality did not provide lower courts with the
remotest help in devising the methodology by which to ascertain
whether a discriminatory effect above the critical threshold level
had been demonstrated. The lower courts are left entirely on their
own both to select the particular statistical techniques or other
methods to be used to make this determination and to decide how
they know when they have found that the threshold level has been
passed. All that they are given by the plurality are words of encouragement, the effectiveness of which, however, is likely to be

---

[352]Dixon, note 12 *supra*, at 188.

diminished by the fact that a majority of the Justices do not disguise their belief that the task is essentially hopeless. Justice O'Connor expressed the view that the plurality's test "will over time either prove unmanageable and arbitrary or else evolve towards some loose form of proportionality,"[353] and Powell flatly declared that the plurality had simply "fail[ed] to enunciate any standard that affords guidance to legislatures and courts."[354] There is great force in Powell's observation that, in conjunction, the recognition of justiciability and the establishment of an all but insurmountable standard of proof may have the anomalous effect of "inviting further litigation even as it appears to signal the 'constitutional green light' to would-be gerrymanderers."[355]

Justice Powell agreed that there should be "a heavy burden of proof" on those challenging the constitutionality of a districting plan, both out of respect for the doctrines of separation of powers and federalism and because "federal judges are ill-equipped generally to review legislative decisions respecting redistricting."[356] Nevertheless, he considered this case "a paradigm example of unconstitutional gerrymandering."[357] He based that judgment on the findings of the District Court regarding the disproportional results of the 1982 House elections, the exclusion of the Democrats from participation in the drafting and discussion of the plan, the statements of the Republican legislative leadership openly declaring the partisan purposes of the plan, the fact that the plan was characterized by strangely shaped districts that bore no apparent relation either to recognizable communities of interest or to municipal and county boundaries, that the House plan employed multi-member districts as a device for diluting Democratic voting strength, and that the state had been unable to provide neutral explanations for any of these factors.[358] For Justice Powell, a plan exhibiting all these characteristics is clearly a partisan gerrymander, but he made no effort precisely to describe how to distinguish between an uncon-

---

[353] 106 S.Ct. at 2822.

[354] *Id.* S.Ct. at 2831. Justice Powell underscored the fact that "there is no 'Court' " for the plurality's standard since five Justices reject it. *Id.* at 2838 n.25.

[355] *Id.* at 2831. The internal quote is from Edwards, note 16 *supra*, at 880.

[356] 106 S.Ct. at 2838.

[357] *Ibid.*

[358] *Id.* at 2831–38.

stitutional gerrymander and a plan—which he would regard as
valid—that was adopted by the majority party because it "gives it
an advantage at the polls."[359]

If the majority party may choose a plan that "gives it an advantage
at the polls," but may not gerrymander, the line between the constitutional and the unconstitutional in this area is very fine, indeed,
and locating that line most certainly will require a "sensitive and
searching inquiry."[360] Powell provides the lower courts no more
concrete advice than does the plurality on how to make that critical
distinction. It is well enough to catalogue the warning signs of
gerrymandering, but it is precisely the fact that there are so many
considerations that need to be examined and weighed that has led
those who have urged against judicial involvement to argue that the
task of identifying a gerrymander coherently and reliably, instead
of purely arbitrarily, is beyond judicial capacity. It is in this area
that Justice Frankfurter's warning in *Baker v. Carr* takes on special
relevance:[361]

> Room continues to be allowed for weighting. This of course
> implies that geography, economics, urban-rural conflict, and all
> the other non-legal factors which have throughout our history
> entered into political districting are to some extent not to be
> ruled out in the undefined vista now opened by review in the
> federal courts of state reapportionments. To some extent—aye,
> there's the rub.

The plurality, however, made it clear—and here its instructions
to the lower courts were unequivocal—that factors such as strangely
shaped districts, disregard of political subdivision boundaries, fragmentation of communities of interest, the adoption of the plan
through unfair and one-sided procedures, and the use of multi-
member districts to dilute the voting power of the minority party,
were all irrelevant to the issue whether the threshold level of discrimination had been reached insofar as they provided evidence of
discriminatory intent.[362] The plurality had conceded from the very
outset that discriminatory intent, while necessary to prove, was not

---

[359]*Id.* at 2827.
[360]*Ibid.*
[361]369 U.S. at 269 (dissenting opinion).
[362]106 S.Ct. at 2813–15.

likely to be difficult to prove.[363] Thus, if discriminatory intent is essentially a given, it is a waste of effort to accumulate evidence of intent, for the plurality has put the focus elsewhere. No matter how discriminatory the legislature's intent in drawing a districting plan, the plurality declared, a party's constitutional rights are not violated "unless the redistricting does in fact disadvantage it at the polls."[364] In the plurality's view, questions of the legislature's purpose take on relevance once it is established that the discriminatory effect of a plan exceeds the requisite threshold level for then they are important in determining whether the plan could be justified by legitimate state interests.[365]

At least one of the District Court's findings, however, was relevant to the question of discriminatory effect as well as discriminatory intent. The use of multi-member districts in Marion and Allen Counties limited the Democrats to three of 21 seats from those counties despite the fact that they had over 46 percent of the voting strength there. Although the District Court's statistics were based on the results of a single election, and thus could have been set aside on that ground alone according to the plurality's reasoning, their significance was dismissed primarily on the basis of *Whitcomb v. Chavis*, in which it had been held that multi-member districts can be held unconstitutional only if the group claiming discrimination can prove that it "had less opportunity . . . to participate in the political processes and to elect legislators of their choice."[366] Because that standard is "not helpful" where the claim is brought by a major political party,[367] the parties cannot challenge that kind of districting. This approach totally ignores the capacity of multi-member districting to decimate the representation of the party that is in the minority in such a district. Particularly where it can be shown that the district in question was drawn with discriminatory intent, this practice should not be tolerated.

In *Thornburg v. Gingles*,[368] decided the same day as *Davis v. Bandemer*, the Court held that multi-member districting that dilutes the

[363]*Id.* at 2809.

[364]*Id.* at 2813–14.

[365]*Id.* at 2815.

[366]403 U.S. at 149.

[367]106 S.Ct. at 2813.

[368]106 S.Ct. 2752 (1986).

voting power of a racial minority violates §2 of the Voting Rights Act where (1) the minority "is sufficiently large and geographically compact to constitute a majority in a single-member district"; (2) the minority "is politically cohesive"; and (3) the majority "votes sufficiently as a bloc to enable it . . . usually to defeat the minority's preferred candidate."[369] There is no reason why this standard could not be applied equally effectively to resolve the constitutional questions raised by political gerrymandering by multi-member districting. The fact that the *Thornburg* test is solely a measure of discriminatory effect should not diminish its applicability to instances of multi-member districting for partisan political purposes, because, in those cases, discriminatory intent is essentially conceded. Such a rule could be administered by the courts without undue difficulty, would require nothing more of the states than to subdivide the affected districts into single-member districts, and would not, in itself, require judicial efforts to resolve the difficult political and statistical problems involved in assessing the constitutionality of a districting plan in its entirety. It would not halt gerrymandering, but it would provide the opportunity to halt one of its grosser manifestations.

Because it could have been dealt with as a separate, simple, and straightforward matter, it is regrettable that the plurality chose to maintain a rule that leaves such multi-member districting beyond the pale of judicial scrutiny. Whatever the difficulties of assessing the fairness of a statewide legislative election where persons in different constituencies are voting for different candidates for different reasons, the same difficulties do not obtain in measuring the impact of an at-large election in a multi-member district, where the same persons are voting for the same candidates. In that context, as the District Court stated, where "the Republicans enjoy approximately 86 percent of the House seats apportioned to the populations of Marion and Allen counties, of which 46.6 percent are identifiable as Democratic voters . . . such a disparity speaks for itself."[370]

There are otherwise significant virtues in the plurality's approach. It was extremely wise in failing to give weight to the imbalance in the statewide "votes/seats" ratio, particularly in a single

---

[369]*Id.* at 2766–67.

[370]603 F.Supp. at 1489.

election, both because of the difficulty of establishing what, if anything, such an imbalance signifies, and because to have done so would have been a major step down the dangerous and undesirable path toward proportional representation. Its concession that discriminatory intent will be readily provable in political gerrymandering cases, thus obviating the need to examine district shapes to determine whether they are suspiciously noncompact or to search for the reasons why a particular line was placed here rather than there, was impressively ingenious. It will allow courts to concentrate on evidence of discriminatory effects in seeking to decide political gerrymandering cases without the distraction of having to assess the propriety of the legislature's purpose for every line-drawing decision.

Beyond this, the plurality's opinion stops being instructive and leaves the lower courts on their own. However, it is at least clear that the plurality rejects the easy arithmetical route to a quick remedy that characterized, and marred, the "one person, one vote" decisions. No political party can go to court, point to some oddly shaped districts and an imbalance in the "votes/seats" ratio, and have an easy win. That is not only salutary but essential if legislatures are to be allowed to continue to carry out the fundamentally political task of districting. It is fully appropriate that litigation in political gerrymandering cases be successful only in cases of egregious discrimination. But the task of challenging the constitutionality of districting plans as political gerrymanders should only be difficult, not impossible. Gerrymandering claims ought not to be justiciable but without prospect of judicial relief. The necessary first step to avoiding that end is to recognize, as the plurality fails to do, that winning elections is what politics is about, and that neither the achievement of fair and effective representation nor majority control of the legislature can be assured if a party is consistently artificially barred from a fair chance to win. The opportunity to obtain a hearing from the elected representatives of the opposing party is not an acceptable compensation for being deprived of a fair chance to have a representative of one's own party elected.

V. Conclusion

Davis v. Bandemer may mark an important turning point in the development of the constitutional law of legislative districting.

By reviving the identity of "fair and effective representation" as the constitutional goal in this area, a goal which applies (together with the goal of preserving effective majority rule) both to the issue of "one person, one vote" and to the issue of political gerrymandering, the Court has taken an important step toward the formal recognition that the prohibition of gerrymandering has properly been its purpose in legislative districting cases from the outset. This recognition would provide a basis for the Court to cease its simplistic fascination with numbers for the sake of numbers as a means of resolving constitutional questions of fair districting, and to address the concerns that actually motivate the litigants who, as Robert Dixon noted, have "not care[d] a hoot about numbers"[371] since the enormous population disparities of the 1960s have been eliminated. The litigants are now, and have always been, concerned with gerrymandering. The constitutional problem is now, and has always been, one of gerrymandering. The fact that it has taken the Court over two decades to recognize and acknowledge that does not lessen the importance of the acknowledgement.

The value of *Davis v. Bandemer* will be determined by future litigation. The test will be whether courts will be able to identify and invalidate the most egregious and politically irremediable gerrymanders without such a profound intrusion into the districting process as to make it impossible for legislatures to carry out this function, and without yielding to the fatal temptation to bring stability and objectivity to this area of constitutional law by imposing an arithmetical standard of proportional representation analogous to the standard of "one person, one vote." In a brief concurrence in which he expressed agreement with Justice O'Connor's view that political gerrymandering claims should be treated as nonjusticiable, Chief Justice Burger recalled Justice Frankfurter's stern suggestion in *Baker v. Carr* that the Court's acceptance of the apportionment issue was "to indulge in merely empty rhetoric, sounding a word of promise to the ear, sure to be disappointing to the hope."[372] The Chief Justice made an odd choice of passages to quote, for Frankfurter's was surely one of the worst predictions in the history of American constitutional law. It will be interesting to see if it proves to be any better in this context.

---

[371]Dixon, note 85 *supra*, at 19.

[372]106 S.Ct. at 2816, quoting 369 U.S. at 270 (dissenting opinion).

JAMES LINDGREN
WILLIAM P. MARSHALL

THE SUPREME COURT'S EXTRAORDINARY POWER TO GRANT CERTIORARI BEFORE JUDGMENT IN THE COURT OF APPEALS

The Supreme Court may review a case before decision in the court of appeals under the little known procedure of certiorari before judgment.[1] The Court's standards for using this procedure are obscure. In part this is because the Supreme Court Rule on the subject inaccurately explains the cases where the writ has been granted; in part this is because the cases themselves only vaguely imply the actual standards used. The writ, nonetheless, has been granted in some of the most important cases in this century.

James Lindgren is Visiting Professor of Law, University of Virginia, and William P. Marshall is Associate Professor of Law, Case-Western Reserve School of Law.

AUTHORS' NOTE: We thank the many people who have read earlier drafts or made research suggestions: Peter Low, John Jeffries, Daniel Ortiz, Randy Block, Lori Andrews, Ray Solomon, Mark Janis, Hugh Macgill, Norval Morris, Spencer Kimball, Geoffrey Stone, David Currie, Franklin Zimring, Martin Redish, Karen Moore, Elizabeth Michelman, David Jones, Jordan Gruber, Elizabeth Arnold, and Alice Lenick. This article is dedicated to the friend who brought the authors together, Randy Block.

In June 1942, eight German agents left their submarines and stepped onto the beaches of Long Island and Florida, thus beginning the events that culminated in *Ex Parte Quirin, The Nazi Saboteurs Case.*[2] Some were arrested shortly after landing, others were apprehended later. On July 2, 1942, President Roosevelt ordered a military commission to try them,[3] instead of the civil courts. Undoubtedly, Roosevelt's purpose in part was to make possible the death penalty, a punishment that would have been unavailable in the civil courts. Seven days after the order setting up the commission, the trial began.[4] The defendants, at least one of whom was an American citizen,[5] sought to challenge the jurisdiction of the military tribunal by asking the Supreme Court for an original writ of habeas corpus.[6] On July 29, the Court returned from its summer recess for a special session to hear the case.[7] The Court heard oral arguments, deliberated, wrote a short per curiam opinion, and announced its decision—all within three days.

At oral arguments, the Assistant Attorney General threatened that if the Court held the military commission illegal, the President might defy its order.[8] Also, Justice Frankfurter—ever the law professor—questioned the Court's power to issue an original writ of habeas corpus.[9] The defendants' attorneys were made aware that they should instead ask for a writ of certiorari before a judgment of the court of appeals. Before doing this, the defendants had to

---

[2]317 U.S. 1 (1942). The *Washington Post* called it "the most portentous emergency session in the history of the Republic." Washington Post, July 29, 1942, at 1. See generally, Oaks, "Original" Writ of Habeas Corpus in the Supreme Court, 1962 Supreme Court Review 153; Note, Federal Military Commissions: Procedure and "Wartime Base" of Jurisdiction, 56 Harv. L. Rev. 631 (1943); Comment, Saboteurs and the Jurisdiction of Military Commissions, 41 Mich. L. Rev. 481 (1942).

[3]7 Fed. Reg. 5103 (1942).

[4]317 U.S. at 22–23. Public opinion against the defendants ran high. Washington Post, July 29, 1942, at 9; New York Times, July 28, 1942, at 10.

[5]See New York Times, July 28, 1942, at 10; *id.*, July 30, 1942, at 4.

[6]317 U.S. at 5, 18–20. They petitioned the Court for leave to file petitions for habeas corpus. This surprised the press covering the military trial, which had speculated that the defendants would approach the lower courts first. New York Times, July 28, 1942, at 10.

[7]317 U.S. at 19.

[8]Washington Post, July 31, 1942, at 1, 5; *id.*, August 1, 1942, at 4; New York Times, July 31, 1942, at 4.

[9]New York Times, July 30, 1942, at 4; *id.*, August 1, 1942, at 3; Washington Post, July 30, 1942, at 1, 12. See also New York Times, July 29, 1942, at 1; *id.*, July 31, 1942, at 1; Washington Post, August 1, 1942, at 1.

go back to the lower courts to perfect an appeal from the district
court to the court of appeals, which they did.[10] Just before noon on
July 31, the third day of the Court's special session, the defendants'
attorneys filed with the Supreme Court a petition for certiorari
before judgment.[11] Within a few minutes, the Court not only granted
certiorari but issued a brief per curiam opinion on the merits,[12] an
opinion obviously written before the Justices had received the petition for certiorari. They upheld the legality of the military tribunal. The Court brushed aside the classic 1867 precedent of *Ex
parte Milligan*,[13] which had held that Milligan, an Indiana lawyer,
should not have been tried by a military tribunal during the Civil
War. Milligan was not a soldier, Indiana was not a battlefield, and
the civilian courts were functioning normally in Indiana at that
time.[14] The Nazi saboteurs did not fare as well, because, as the
Court later explained,[15] the defendants were belligerents not civilians.

The military trial ended quickly.[16] Two defendants were given
long prison sentences.[17] And less than two weeks after the Supreme
Court announced its decision, the other six defendants were
executed.[18]

Three decades later, the Court was faced with another challenge
to Presidential authority.[19] President Nixon was withholding sixty-
four tape recordings that had been subpoenaed by Special Prose-

---

[10]On the eve of the Supreme Court arguments, July 28, the defendants sought habeas
corpus from a district court, which was immediately denied. New York Times, July 30,
1942, at 4. The Court opinion is misleading on this point, implying that the application to
the district court preceded the habeas corpus application to the Supreme Court.

[11]The papers supporting habeas corpus, by stipulation of the parties, were treated as a
petition for certiorari before judgment; the petitions for an original writ of habeas corpus
were abandoned. 317 U.S. at 18–20.

[12]*Id.* at 18–19.

[13]4 Wall. 2 (1866).

[14]4 Wall. 2, 29 (1866). The Court stated, "Martial rule can never exist where the courts
are open, and in the proper and unobstructed exercise of their jurisdiction." *Id.* at 127.

[15]At the end of the Special Term on July 31, 1942, the Court issued a short per curiam
opinion. The full opinion was filed on October 29, 1942.

[16]New York Times, Aug. 4, 1942, at 1.

[17]Dasch, who had not sought Supreme Court review, was sentenced to 30 years. Burger
was sentenced to life in prison. New York Times, August 9, 1942, at 1.

[18]New York Times, Aug. 10, 1942, at 3.

[19]United States v. Nixon, 418 U.S. 683, 714 (1974). See generally the symposium on the
case, 22 UCLA L. Rev. 4 (1974); The Supreme Court, 1973 Term, 88 Harv. L. Rev. 43,
50–61 (1974).

cutor Leon Jaworski for use in the criminal trial of six of Nixon's former aides.[20] District Judge John Sirica ordered Nixon to produce the tapes. Nixon's attorneys appealed this decision to the circuit court of appeals.[21] But before the case could be heard by the Court of Appeals,[22] Jaworski, who had prevailed below, petitioned the Supreme Court for certiorari before judgment. The Supreme Court granted certiorari, expedited the briefing schedule, and extended the normal term of the Court until the decision was announced.[23]

In the wake of the Court's unanimous decision on July 24, 1974, Nixon's dilatory strategy dissolved.[24] The decision resulted in the release of the "smoking gun" tape of a conversation showing that Nixon had tried to use the CIA to interfere with the FBI's Watergate investigation.[25] After hearing the tape, Nixon's staff decided that resignation was the only option.[26] The Judiciary Committee of the House of Representatives voted three articles of impeachment[27] in the week following the Supreme Court decision, the tapes were released on August 5, and Nixon himself was finally convinced to resign by the public reaction to the tape. Gerald Ford took the oath of office as President on August 9, 1974, sixteen days after the Court's decision.

In both the *Nazi Saboteurs* and *Nixon* cases, the Supreme Court used its "extraordinary power"[28] to grant certiorari before a judg-

---

[20]United States v. Mitchell (D.C. Crim. No. 74–110). Seven aides had been indicted on March 1, 1974 (Mitchell, Haldeman, Ehrlichman, Colson, Mardian, Parkinson, and Strachan), but one defendant (Colson) plead guilty before the Supreme Court decision. United States v. Nixon, 418 U.S. at 686–87, 687 n.3.

[21]418 U.S. at 689–90.

[22]The District Court stayed its subpoena order on condition that review be sought before 4 P.M., May 24, 1974. On May 24, 1974, the President appealed to the Court of Appeals for the D.C. Circuit, 418 U.S. at 689–90, after which the Special Prosecutor filed a petition for a writ of certiorari before judgment. 418 U.S. at 690. The petition was granted May 31, 1974. 417 U.S. 927. Nixon filed a cross-petition for certiorari before judgment on June 6, 1974, 418 U.S. 690, which was first granted on June 15, 1974, 417 U.S. 960, and then dismissed as improvidently granted on July 24, 1974. 418 U.S. at 687 n.2. Nixon's petition for certiorari before judgment challenged the propriety of naming Nixon as an unindicted co-conspirator.

[23]The case was argued on July 8, 1974, and decided on July 24, 1974. 418 U.S. at 683.

[24]See Woodward & Bernstein, The Final Days 266–383 (1976) (hereinafter cited as Final Days).

[25]The conversation is summarized in Final Days at 267–72.

[26]See note 24 *supra*.

[27]See Final Days at 461.

[28]Ohio v. Price, 360 U.S. 246, 247 (1959).

ment of the court of appeals. Either party may apply for it at any time after an appeal has been filed in the court of appeals. Such writs have been granted relatively infrequently since the intermediate appellate courts were created in 1891.[29]

Certiorari before judgment has been used in highly charged political cases. In *Dames & Moore*,[30] the Court upheld the Iran hostages agreement before the deadline set in that document. The writ was also used several times by the Nine Old Men to strike down important New Deal legislation.[31] The Vinson Court took the *Steel Seizure* case,[32] just as five years before it had granted the writ to decide another major labor dispute, *United States v. United Mine Workers*.[33] In the celebrated cases of *Wilson v. Girard*[34] and *Reid v. Covert*,[35] the Warren Court considered who may try American servicemen and their dependents for crimes committed in foreign coun-

---

[29]There are, of course, other ways to control the speed of litigation and other ways to bypass the intermediate appellate courts. See generally, *e.g.*, Wright, Miller, & Cooper, Federal Practice and Procedure 4037–40. See also notes 161–67 *infra* and accompanying text.

[30]Dames & Moore v. Regan, 453 U.S. 654 (1981). See generally, The Supreme Court, The 1980 Term, 95 Harv. L. Rev. 93, 191–201 (1981); Note, Claims Settlement: Executive Action Limiting Suits against Iran, 22 Harv. Int'l L.J. 661 (1981); Comment, Dames & Moore v. Regan—Rights in Conflict:The Fifth Amendment Held Hostage, 31 Am. U.L. Rev. 345 (1982).

[31]*E.g.*, Carter v. Carter Coal Co., 298 U.S. 238 (1936); Rickert Rice Mills v. Fontenot, 297 U.S. 110 (1936); Railroad Retirement Board v. Alton Railroad, 295 U.S. 330 (1935); United States v. Bankers' Trust Co., 294 U.S. 240 (1935), 293 U.S. 548 (1934). See Frankfurter & Fisher, The Business of the Supreme Court at the October Terms, 1935 and 1936, 51 Harv. L. Rev. 577, 615–18 & 616 n.69 (1938); Dahl, Decision-Making in a Democracy: The Supreme Court as a National Policy-Maker, 1959 J. Pub. L. 279.

[32]Youngstown Sheet & Tube Co. v. Sawyer, 343 U.S. 579 (1952).

[33]330 U.S. 258 (1947). See generally, Watt, The Divine Right of Government by Judiciary, 14 U. Chi. L. Rev. 409 (1947); Note, Judicial Considerations in United States v. United Mine Workers, 47 Colum. L. Rev. 505 (1947); Note, Jurisdiction to Determine Jurisdiction: United States v. United Mine Workers, 60 Harv. L. Rev. 811 (1947); Note, Substantial Doubt Doctrine of the Lewis Case and the Norris–LaGuardia Act, 42 Ill. L. Rev. 372 (1947); Comment, 45 Mich. L. Rev. 469 (1947); Note, 22 N.Y.U.L.Q. Rev. 337 (1947); Note, Recent Applications of the Civil-Criminal Contempt Distinctions, 15 U. Chi. L. Rev. 202 (1947); Note, 33 Va. L. Rev. 266 (1947).

[34]354 U.S. 524 (1957). See generally Note, 71 Harv. L. Rev. 140 (1957); Note, The Treaty Making Power and the Extraterritorial Effect of the Constitution: Reid v. Covert and the Girard Case, 42 Minn. L. Rev. 825 (1958); Note, 43 Va. L. Rev. 939 (1957); Note, Foreign Jurisdiction and the American Soldier, 1958 Wis. L. Rev. 52 (1958).

[35]354 U.S. 1 (1957), reversing 351 U.S. 487 (1956), decided with Kinsella v. Krueger, 351 U.S. 470 (1956). See generally, Note, Courts-Martial Jurisdiction and Civilian Dependents: Constitutional Restrictions, 7 Duke L.J. 155 (1958); Note, 71 Harv. L. Rev. 136, 712 (1958); Comment, 56 Mich. L. Rev. 287 (1957); Note, 32 NYU L. Rev. 594 (1957).

tries. When the extension of the Equal Rights Amendment was held unconstitutional by a federal district court,[36] the Supreme Court again granted certiorari before judgment—though it later dismissed the case as moot.[37] Certiorari before judgment also figured (if only tangentially) in *Brown v. Board of Education*[38] and *Roe v. Wade*.[39]

The use of certiorari before judgment has been criticized for unduly rushing the Court's deliberations or for foreshortening efforts at political resolution. In the *Steel Seizure* case,[40] a secret deal settling the strike had been almost worked out under pressure from President Truman, but the deal fell apart when prejudgment certiorari was granted.[41] Justices Burton and Frankfurter broke a long-standing tradition by filing a dissent from a grant of certiorari.[42] Paul Freund was also skeptical of the Court's action.[43] And in the *Nixon* case, the early certiorari prompted criticism by three prominent Supreme Court scholars—Alexander Bickel,[44] Gerald Gunther,[45] and Philip

---

[36]Idaho v. NOW, 529 F. Supp. 1107 (D.C. Id. 1982).

[37]NOW v. Idaho, 455 U.S. 918, dismissed as moot, 459 U.S. 809 (1982).

[38]The Court brought up Bolling v. Sharpe on certiorari before judgment to hear it along with *Brown*. 347 U.S. 483 (1954); Brown v. Board of Education, 344 U.S. 1, 3 (1952); Bolling v. Sharpe, 347 U.S. 497 (1954). In *Bolling* the Court ordered desegregation of the District of Columbia schools at the same time as the state schools.

[39]410 U.S. 113 (1973). See notes 258–60 *infra* and accompanying text.

[40]343 U.S. 579 (1952). See generally, Freund, The Supreme Court, 1951 Term, Foreword: The Year of the Steel Case, 66 Harv. L. Rev. 89 (1952); Kamper, The Steel Seizure Case: Congress, the President and the Supreme Court, 51 Mich. L. Rev. 141 (1952); Note, 53 Colum. L. Rev. 53 (1953); Note, The Steel Seizure Cases, 41 Geo. L.J. 45 (1952).

[41]See Marcus, Truman and the Steel Seizure Case: The Limits of Presidential Power 146–48 (1977).

[42]It is allegedly the first recorded dissent from the grant of certiorari, whether before or after judgment. Ohio v. Price, 360 U.S. 246, 247 (1959).

[43]Freund, The Supreme Court, 1951 Term, Foreword: The Year of The Steel Case, 66 Harv. L. Rev. 89, 89–94 (1952).

[44]New York Times, June 1, 1974, at 12.

[45]Professor Gunther concluded his 1974 article discussing the Nixon decision: "I wish that the Court had delayed speaking; and that, if it had to speak, it had chosen its words more carefully." Gunther, Judicial Hegemony and Legislative Autonomy: The Nixon Case and the Impeachment Process, 22 U.C.L.A. L. Rev. 30, 31–33, 39 (1974).

It is interesting that Gunther joined Bickel in questioning the grant in the Nixon case. In Gunther, The Subtle Vices of the "Passive Virtues"—A Comment on Principle and Expediency in Judicial Review, 64 Colum. L. Rev. 1 (1964), Gunther criticizes Bickel's emphasis on expediency in certiorari practice. Gunther argued that expediency in choosing cases can undercut the principled development of doctrine. See also A. Bickel, The Least Dangerous Branch (1962).

Kurland.[46] When Benno Schmidt recently reviewed the legacy of the Burger Court, he pointed to two actions of almost unprecedented judicial activism—*Roe v. Wade*[47] and the early grant of certiorari in the *Nixon* case.[48]

These and other debates[49] over individual grants or denials are brief and impoverished because there are no general principles against which to evaluate any particular grant. Moreover, much of what has been written about the writ is misleading or just plain wrong.[50] The practice manuals and treatises mention the writ in a few sentences or paragraphs, but usually describe the standards so broadly that a litigant is encouraged to think that his case really qualifies for early review.

Supreme Court Rule 18,[51] the rule governing certiorari before judgment, is of little help. The standard it describes, a case of "imperative public importance,"[52] is only one of the four classes of cases where the Court has granted the writ. The others are: (1) cases raising issues similar or identical to those in a case already before the court,[53] (2) cases coming back to the Court a second time,[54] and (3) where the litigants have erroneously taken a direct appeal.[55]

---

[46]Professor Kurland's comments were even stronger than Gunther's: "The decision of the Supreme Court in this case was a political decision not a judicial one. Relying primarily on slogans, nonsequiturs, and a recognition of the fact that public opinion was in its corner and not in that of the executive, the Court proudly proclaimed the supremacy of the judiciary. Jefferson's fears had been realized, once again. The judgment may well have been the right one. But it is difficult, if not impossible to find its justification in the unanimous opinion authored by the Chief Justice." Kurland, Who Killed Cock Robin?, 22 U.C.L.A. L. Rev. 68, 70–73 (1974). See also New York Times, June 1, 1974, at 12.

[47]410 U.S. 113 (1973).

[48]New York Times, June 22, 1986, §IV, at 27.

[49]See, *e.g.*, San Antonio Conservation Soc'y v. Texas Highway Dept., 400 U.S. 968 (1970) (Black, J., dissenting); Stainback v. Mo Hock Ke Lok Po., 336 U.S. 368, 384–86 (1949).

[50]It is a common misconception that the writ has been granted only seven or eight times. See, *e.g.*, The Final Days; New York Times, May 25, 1974, at 1.

There is a fairly substantial literature on certiorari generally. Some sources are collected in Stern & Gressman, Supreme Court Practice §§4.1–4.26 4 (6th ed. 1986).

[51]445 U.S. 983, 1003–04 (1980).

[52]445 U.S. at 1004. See notes 159–87 *infra* and accompanying text.

[53]See notes 188–234 *infra* and accompanying text.

[54]See notes 235–53 *infra* and accompanying text.

[55]See notes 254–65 *infra* and accompanying text.

This article's analysis of certiorari before judgment assumes that standards can be applied to this aspect of Supreme Court procedure—or at least that the wisdom of particular grants is open to question. The main purpose of the Supreme Court Rules, presumably including Rule 18 governing certiorari before judgment, is to disclose the Court's standards to litigants. Rule 18 does this poorly, if at all. Moreover, to gain its wide discretionary jurisdiction, the Court promised Congress that it would exercise its certiorari power according to "recognized principles."[56] As to certiorari before judgment, the Court has never made a serious effort to enunciate these principles. Thus to discover and analyze the principles for certiorari before judgment should be consistent with the Court's own stated goals.

I. Statutes, Rules, and History

A. FROM 1891 TO 1922—THE FIRST USES OF CERTIORARI BEFORE JUDGMENT

1. *An implied power.* In 1891, to relieve the burden that the rise of big business had placed on the Supreme Court's docket,[57] Congress passed the Evarts Act, creating the circuit courts of appeals[58] and interposing them between the Supreme Court and the lower federal courts. This change allowed for two appeals in some cases,[59] while in others it made the decision of the court of appeals final unless reviewed by certiorari or extraordinary writ.[60] To give the Supreme Court the power to tailor much of its own business, the Evarts Act created a discretionary statutory writ of certiorari,[61] allowing the Court to consider any issue normally raised on appeal.

---

[56]Procedure in Federal Courts: Hearing on S.2060 & 2061 Before a Subcommittee of the Senate Committee on the Judiciary, 68th Cong., 1st Sess., 46–47 (1924) (hereinafter cited as 1924 Hearing). See also note 85 *infra* and accompanying text.

[57]See Forsyth v. Hammond, 166 U.S. 506, 512 (1897).

[58]See Act of March 3, 1891, 26 Stat. 826; Robertson & Kirkham, The Jurisdiction of the Supreme Court of the United States 247 (Wolfson & Kurland ed. 1951); Wright, Federal Courts 6 (4th ed. 1983). See generally, Stookey, Creating an Intermediate Court of Appeals, in The Analysis of Judicial Reform 153 (Dubois ed. 1982).

[59]The Supreme Court during the 1916–1925 terms decided an average of forty cases each term that came from the courts of appeals by appeals of right. See Frankfurter & Landis at 261, 295.

[60]Act of March 3, 1891, ch. 517, §6, 26 Stat. 826, 828.

[61]See Robertson & Kirkham at 205.

Sadly, the Evarts Act was poorly written. In particular, the section governing certiorari was ambiguous. It provided:[62]

> [I]n any such case as is hereinbefore made final in the Circuit Court of Appeals it shall be competent for the Supreme Court to require, by certiorari or otherwise, any such case to be certified to the Supreme Court for its review and determination with the same power and authority in the case as if it had been carried by appeal or writ of error to the Supreme Court.

The phrase "in any such case as is hereinbefore made final in the Circuit Court of Appeals" was ambiguous. Did it mean that the Supreme Court could bring up a case on certiorari only after it became final in the court of appeals? Or did it mean that, if the case was of the type that would eventually become final in the court of appeals, the Supreme Court could bring up the case at any time? Only under the second reading would certiorari before judgment be possible.

In 1893 the Court first addressed this ambiguity in *American Construction Company v. Jacksonville Railway.*[63] That case involved an application for certiorari seeking to review an interlocutory order of a court of appeals.[64] Thus, unlike a true case of certiorari before judgment, the *American Construction* case did not bypass the court of appeals. The Supreme Court was simply reviewing an issue that did not dispose of the merits of the case and therefore was not in this sense a final judgment.

The Supreme Court resolved the statute's ambiguity by adopting the second alternative construction: if the case was of the type that could be decided by the court of appeals, the Supreme Court could bring it up early.[65] It asserted its jurisdiction to review the interlocutory (nonfinal) orders of a court of appeals:[66]

The common law writ of certiorari allowed a higher court to command the record of a lower court to review jurisdictional issues. See Jenks, The Prerogative Writs in English Law, 32 Yale L.J. 523, 528–29 (1923); Weintraub, English Origins of Judicial Review by Preregative Writ: Certiorari and Mandamus, 9 N.Y.L.F. 478, 503–16 (1963). Statutory certiorari became, not a writ limited to jurisdiction, but a form of discretionary review of the merits. See Robertson & Kirkham at 260.

[62] Act of March 3, 1891, ch. 517, §6, 26 Stat. 826, 828.

[63] 148 U.S. 372, 385 (1893).

[64] The case involved an appeal from a circuit court to a Circuit Court of Appeals. *Ibid.*

[65] 148 U.S. at 385. Every time the Supreme Court has construed §6, it has reached the same conclusion. See, *e.g.*, Forsyth v. Hammond, 166 U.S. 506, 513 (1897).

[66] 148 U.S. at 385.

> Doubtless this power [to grant certiorari] would seldom be exercised before final judgment in the Circuit Court of Appeals, and very rarely indeed before the case was ready for decision upon the merits in that court. But the question at what stage of the proceedings, and under what circumstances, the case should be required, by certiorari or otherwise, to be sent up for review, is left to the discretion of this court, as the exigencies of each case may require.

The Court did not enunciate standards for certiorari in cases in intermediate stages, stating that it would proceed case by case.

2. *Imperative public importance: The Three Friends.* After the Court established its power to grant certiorari before a final judgment of the court of appeals, it was only a matter of time before the Court considered whether to grant certiorari before any intermediate court judgment.[67] In 1897, four years after *American Construction* and six years after Congress set up the courts of appeals, the Supreme Court for the first time in *The Three Friends* decided to use certiorari to bypass those intermediate courts.

During the Cuban revolution that preceded the Spanish-American War, the collector of customs for St. John's, Florida, seized a ship, the Three Friends, and sought to have it forfeited by filing a libel.[68] The government claimed that equipping the steamer to aid the revolutionaries violated a century-old federal law that prohibited outfitting a ship for a "foreign colony, district or people."[69] The ship's owner and its master excepted to the government's libel, arguing that Cuban revolutionaries were not distinct enough to qualify as a "foreign colony, district or people." The federal district court agreed and dismissed the libel. Five days after this decree, the government appealed to the court of appeals. Nine days later, the government petitioned the Supreme Court for a writ of certiorari before a judgment of the circuit court of appeals. The writ was immediately granted.[70]

---

[67]A search of the meager literature on certiorari before judgment yielded no case before 1897 in which certiorari before judgment was denied.

[68]The Three Friends, 166 U.S. 1 (1897).

[69]See 166 U.S. at 53. The Act was based on an old statute, recommended in 1793 by President Washington, drafted by Alexander Hamilton, and passed on June 5, 1794, 1 Stat. 381. *Id.* at 52–53.

[70]Application for certiorari before judgment was made on February 1, 1897, the case was argued before the Supreme Court on February 15, 1897, and the decision was rendered on March 1, 1897.

Although the grant of certiorari before judgment was the first ever, Chief Justice Fuller (writing for the Court) gave it short shrift. Adopting the *American Construction* Court's interpretation of the Circuit Courts of Appeals Act, Fuller stated:[71] "[T]he writ of certiorari may be issued . . . to the Circuit Court of Appeals, pending action by that court, and although this is a power not ordinarily to be exercised, we were of the opinion that the circumstances justified the allowance of the writ in this instance, and the case is properly before us." Beyond this reassertion of jurisdictional power, the Court's decision remained silent on certiorari. No standards were stated.

In *Forsyth v. Hammond* later in the Term the Court explained its earlier grant of certiorari:[72] "[We granted certiorari before judgment in *The Three Friends* because] the question involved was one affecting the relations of this country to foreign nations, and therefore one whose prompt decision by this court was of importance, not merely for the guidance of the Executive Department of Government but also to disclose to each citizen the limits beyond which he might not go in interfering in the affairs of another nation without violating the laws of this." The rationale for the grant of certiorari before judgment in *The Three Friends* is the earliest recognition of one category of cases that today justifies such a grant—that a prompt Supreme Court opinion is important to the public. This was the ground, for example, in the *Nixon* case[73] and in *Dames & Moore*.[74]

Indeed, if a goal of the writ is to allow the Supreme Court to respond quickly, that purpose was well served in *The Three Friends*. Only one month passed from the application for certiorari until final judgment in the Supreme Court.

3. *Taking cases again and wrongly taken appeals:* St. Louis Railroad. The need for prompt Supreme Court review cannot explain the grant of certiorari before judgment in *St. Louis, Kansas City & Colorado Railroad v. Wabash Railroad*.[75] This was the only case other than *The Three Friends* in which the Court granted certiorari before judgment before the jurisdictional statute was amended to give the

---

[71]166 U.S. at 49.

[72]Forsyth v. Hammond, 166 U.S. 506, 514 (1897).

[73]418 U.S. 683.

[74]453 U.S. 654.

[75]217 U.S. 247 (1910).

Court the explicit authority to do so. Rather than promptness, the circumstances of *St. Louis Railroad* suggest that it might fit two other categories of early certiorari—cases that have been before the Court earlier and cases where a direct appeal was erroneously taken.

In 1891, five years after foreclosure against the Wabash Railroad, the Supreme Court in *Joy v. St. Louis*[76] ordered that the St. Louis Railroad could use of some of Wabash's tracks and right-of-way. Eleven years later in 1902, a dispute arose about the rights granted by the Supreme Court in 1891. After six more years of litigation, the St. Louis Railroad in 1908 sought certiorari to review a district court judgment.[77] The Supreme Court explained its grant of certiorari before judgment:[78]

> That question involves the construction of a prior decree of a United States Circuit Court, affirmed by this Court. It is not a question of the payment of money, but of the extent of the use belonging to one railroad company in the tracks, right of way and terminal facilities of another, as well as the rights of access by the one company to industries established along the line of the other. This, in view of the increasing number of industries in a great and growing city like St. Louis, is of constantly enlarging importance, and ought, so far as possible, to be settled. It seems to us that both the private interests of the railroad companies, and of the separate industries and the greater interests of the public call for the granting of the writ of certiorari, and it is, therefore, so ordered.

Even so, the proceedings remained protracted. The case was not decided until 1910, seventeen months after certiorari was sought. By this time over twenty-four years had passed since the litigation began.

St. Louis Railroad may also have foreshadowed a third category of certiorari before judgment. The St. Louis Railroad took two appeals from the 1908 district court decision, one directly to the Supreme Court and the other to the court of appeals. Apparently concerned that the jurisdictional basis of the direct appeal was deficient, the St. Louis Railroad petitioned for certiorari before judgment. The Supreme Court dismissed the direct appeal for lack of jurisdiction, but granted early certiorari. Like the first two cat-

---

[76]138 U.S. 1 (1891).

[77]217 U.S. at 249.

[78]*Id.* at 251.

egories of certiorari before judgment, this one has also been used by the Court in later cases.[79]

B. FROM 1924 TO 1953—CREATING STATUTES AND RULES TO GOVERN CERTIORARI BEFORE JUDGMENT

In 1925 Congress and the Supreme Court finally put certiorari before judgment on a sound jurisdictional basis. A committee of Supreme Court justices, led by Justice Van Devanter, drafted the Judges' Bill of 1925.[80] Its purpose was to reduce the backlog of cases on the docket by decreasing the Court's mandatory jurisdiction, thus allowing the Court to choose most of its cases by certiorari. The Justices not only drafted the Bill, they testified for it before Congress and even lobbied Congress with letters.

The Judges' Bill explicitly rejected the view of the Supreme Court as "the vindicator of all federal rights."[81] Although several Senators expressed concern over the loss of the right to a Supreme Court hearing,[82] Senator Cummins asserted that fairness to litigants was well served by hearings in two courts, a district court and a court of appeals, and that "any further review ought to be in the discretion of the Supreme Court."[83] Justice Sutherland testified "that when a litigant has had a trial before a trial judge, and has gone to a court of appeals of as high a rank as the Circuit Court of Appeals of the United States, he ought to stop there."[84] Justice Van Devanter sought to reasssure the Senate about the Court's certiorari practice. He told Congress that in deciding whether to grant certiorari, the Court uses sound judicial discretion, choosing cases according to recognized principles.[85]

---

[79]See notes 253–65 *infra* and accompanying text.

[80]Act of February 13, 1925, ch. 229, 43 Stat. 936, 938. See generally, Wright, *Federal Courts* 7 (4th ed. 1983).

[81]Frankfurter & Landis at 260–61.

[82]*Id.* at 251 n.19.

[83]66 Cong. Rec. 2750, 2752 (Jan. 31, 1925).

[84]1924 Hearing, note 56 *supra*, at 46–47.

[85]Justice Van Devanter argued: "When I speak of discretionary jurisdiction on certiorari I do not mean, of course, that the Supreme Court merely exercises a choice or will in granting or refusing the writ, but that it exercises a sound judicial discretion, gives careful thought to the matter in the light of the supporting and opposing briefs, and resolves it according to recognized principles." *Ibid.*

Besides reducing the Court's obligatory appellate jurisdiction and enlarging its discretionary jurisdiction, the Bill was designed to consolidate the various statutes dealing with the appellate jurisdiction of the Supreme Court and to "restate the law on the subject,"[86] including the law of certiorari before judgment. Although the Supreme Court had never indicated that it doubted whether it had the power to grant the writ, the legislative history of the Judges' Bill reveals otherwise. In their Senate testimony, Justices McReynolds and Van Devanter made the following remarks:[87]

> MR. JUSTICE McREYNOLDS: You might also say that this bill very much enlarges the power of the Supreme Court to review before final judgment in the Circuit courts of appeals, so that in cases of importance the matter does not have to await an adjudication there but may be brought up in advance.

> MR. JUSTICE VAN DEVANTER: Yes.

Lest these words of the authors of the Bill be dismissed as loose talk, the Report accompanying the Bill said:[88]

> The insertion of the words, "either before or after a judgment or decree by such lower court," was for the purpose of expressly conferring jurisdiction upon the Supreme Court to review on certiorari any case in the circuit courts of appeals at any stage of the proceedings, some question having arisen as to the power of the Supreme Court to do this under section 240 as it now stands.

Probably the Justices realized that the timbers supporting certiorari before judgment needed shoring up.

Thus when enacted in 1925, the Judges' Bill specifically provided for certiorari "before or after a judgment or decree."[89] The present statutory bases for certiorari before judgment are 28 U.S.C. §2101(e) and 28 U.S.C. §1254(1), enacted in 1948 and 1949 in forms only slightly different from the text of the provisions in the 1925 Judges' Bill. Section 2101(e) allows a litigant to apply for certiorari "at any time before judgment." Section 1254(1) permits the Supreme Court to review by certiorari "before or after rendition of judgment or

---

[86]Act of February 13, 1925, ch. 229, 43 Stat. 936.

[87]1924 Hearing, note 84 *supra*, at 40.

[88]*Id.* at 13.

[89]43 Stat. 936, 938–39, 950.

decree." None of the statutes identify what standards the Court should use to evaluate petitions for early certiorari. The Supreme Court Rules governing certiorari before judgment were little better. The first was promulgated shortly after the Judges' Bill was passed.[90] After being renumbered and slightly revised in 1928, it read:[91]

> Rule 39 . . . Proceedings to bring up to this court on writ of certiorari in a case pending in the circuit court of appeals or the Court of Appeals of the District of Columbia, before judgment is given in such court, should conform, as near as may be, to the provisions of Rule 38 [concerning certiorari]; and similar reasons for granting or refusing the application will be applied; that the public interest will be promoted by prompt settlement in this court of the questions involved may constitute a sufficient reason.

As to standards, Rule 39 said two things. First, the Court would apply similar standards for certiorari before or after judgment.[92] In fact, the Court has never used similar standards; certiorari before judgment has always been available only in a much more limited class of cases than certiorari after judgment. Second, Rule 39 weakly

[90]Supreme Court Rule 36, 266 U.S. 682 (adopted June 8, 1925, effective July 1, 1925).

[91]Supreme Court Rule 39, 275 U.S. 625–26 (adopted June 5, 1928, effective July 1, 1928).

[92]The 1925 certiorari rule was Rule 35. 266 U.S. at 680–82 (adopted June 8, 1925, effective July 1, 1925). The 1928 certiorari rule was Rule 38. 275 U.S. at 622–25 (adopted June 5, 1928, effective July 1, 1928). The relevant portion of Rule 38 is as follows:

5. A review on writ of certiorari is not a matter of right, but of sound judicial discretion, and will be granted only where there are special and important reasons therefor. The following, while neither controlling nor fully measuring the court's discretion, indicate the character of reasons which will be considered:

(a) Where a state court has decided a federal question of substance not theretofore determined by this court, or has decided it in a way probably not in accord with applicable decisions of this court.

(b) Where a circuit court of appeals has rendered a decision in conflict with the decision of another circuit court of appeals on the same matter; or has decided an important question of local law in a way probably in conflict with applicable local decisions; or has decided an important question of general law in a way probably untenable or in conflict with the weight of authority; or has decided an important question of federal law which has not been, but should be, settled by this court; or has decided a federal question in a way probably in conflict with applicable decisions of this court; or has so far departed from the accepted and usual course of judicial proceedings, or so far sanctioned such a departure by a lower court, as to call for an exercise of this court's power of supervision.

(c) Where the Court of Appeals of the district of Columbia has decided a question of general importance, or a question of substance relating to the construction or application of the Constitution, or a treaty or statute, of the United States, which has not been, but should be, settled by this court; or where that court has not given proper effect to an applicable decision of this court. *Id.* at 624–25.

embraced the need for a prompt decision that was the standard in
The Three Friends, providing that the public's interest in prompt
settlement "may constitute a sufficient reason." The language of
Rule 39 covers a class of cases considerably broader than that in
which the Court has ever granted certiorari before judgment.

The first case of certiorari before judgment under the new rule
was *Hicks v. Merchantile Trust Company.*[93] It established a new category: cases raising issues similar to those already pending before
the Court.[94] The Court brought up *Hicks,* a Missouri federal district
court case, to consolidate it with several cases on appeal from the
D.C. Court of Appeals. Also, *Hicks* itself was already consolidated
with other district court cases. Justice Holmes explained that the
Court granted the writ because "the questions raised had been
presented to it by the above mentioned appeals"[95] pending before
the Court. The cases were based on notes issued by the Imperial
German Government. The Supreme Court affirmed the lower court
decrees allowing the claimants to recover funds seized by the United
States Government.[96] What the need for precipitate review in *Hicks*
might have been is not clear.

C. FROM 1954 THROUGH 1985—RULE 18

Not only were the Supreme Court Rules of the early 1950s of
little help to practitioners, but also "they were obsolete and misleading, on occasion fatally so."[97] In their first edition of *Supreme
Court Practice,* Robert Stern and Eugene Gressman suggested that
practitioners with questions simply "ask the Clerk's office."[98] During
the 1952 Term, Chief Justice Vinson appointed a committee of
Justices to revise the rules. The Court solicited suggestions from
experienced practitioners, law professors, and most helpfully, the
Clerk of the Court.[99] Later, Chief Justice Warren concluded: "We
found out that there was little criticism of our practice and that if

---

[93]Reported *sub nom.* White v. Mechanics Securities Corp., 269 U.S. 283 (1925).

[94]See notes 188–234 *infra* and accompanying text.

[95]269 U.S. at 299.

[96]269 U.S. 283 (1925).

[97]Weiner, The Supreme Court's New Rules, 68 Harv. L. Rev. 20, 38 (1954) (hereinafter
Weiner).

[98]Stern & Gressman, Supreme Court Practice 6 (1st ed. 1950), quoted in Weiner, at 38.

[99]Weiner at 38.

our rules were made to conform the bar would have no complaint.
And with some minor improvement, that is what has been done."[100]

Out of the revision came a new rule governing certiorari before
judgment.[101] In 1980 it was renumbered and slightly revised. Rule
18 now reads:[102]

> A petition for writ of certiorari to review a case pending in
> a federal court of appeals, before judgment is given in such
> court, will be granted only upon a showing that the case is of
> such imperative public importance as to justify the deviation
> from normal appellate practice and to require immediate set-
> tlement in this Court. See 28 U.S.C. § 2101(e); see also, *United
> States v. Bankers Trust Co.*, 294 U.S. 240 (1935); *Railroad Retire-
> ment Board v. Alton R. Co.*, 295 U.S. 330 (1935); *Rickert Rice
> Mills v. Fontenot*, 297 U.S. 110 (1936); *Carter v. Carter Coal Co.*,
> 298 U.S. 238 (1936); *Ex parte Quirin*, 317 U.S. 1 (1942); *United
> States v. Mine Workers*, 330 U.S. 258 (1947); *Youngstown Sheet &
> Tube Co. v. Sawyer*, 343 U.S. 579 (1952); *Wilson v. Girard*, 354
> U.S. 524 (1957); *United States v. Nixon*, 418 U.S. 683 (1974).

Supreme Court Rule 18 makes it appear as if there were only one
category of cases—those of "imperative public importance" requiring prompt Supreme Court action. The rule entirely fails to mention
any of the other categories in which the writ has been granted.

This is one of only two Supreme Court Rules containing a case
citation in its text. Why did the Court decide to use a string citation,
and why did it choose these particular cases?

As first adopted in 1954, the rule cited seven cases. Two cases
decided since then were added in the 1980 amendment. The cases
themselves are important; all nine are *causes celebres*. Four were constitutional attacks on major New Deal programs.[103] Two cases,
United Mine Workers[104] and the *Steel Seizure* case,[105] involved national
strikes in basic industries during a war or its immediate aftermath.
Ex parte Quirin was the infamous Nazi Saboteurs case.[106] *Wilson v.*

---

[100]*Id.* at 39.

[101]Supreme Court Rule 20, 346 U.S. 968 (adopted April 12, 1954, effective July 1, 1954).

[102]Supreme Court Rule 18, 445 U.S. 983, 1003–04 (1980).

[103]United States v. Bankers Trust Co., 294 U.S. 240 (1935); Railroad Retirement Board
v. Alton Railroad, 295 U.S. 330 (1935); Rickert Rice Mills v. Fontenot, 297 U.S. 110 (1936);
Carter v. Carter Coal Co., 298 U.S. 238 (1936).

[104]330 U.S. 258.

[105]Youngstown Sheet & Tube Co. v. Sawyer, 343 U.S. 579.

[106]317 U.S. 1 (1942).

Girard decided Japan's right to try an American citizen for killing a Japanese woman.[107] And the last case, *United States v. Nixon*, helped bring down a President.[108]

The Rule does not explain why these particular cases are singled out for citation. Since the Court granted certiorari in all of them, it might be saying to litigants: Don't bother applying if your case isn't as important as these. The closer these citations are examined, however, the odder they appear. They make poor models for litigants. The Court cannot really be suggesting that litigants follow the procedure in the *Nazi Saboteurs* case. There the litigants did not apply for certiorari before judgment until after the Court had already heard the case and written a per curiam opinion. *Rickert Mills* and *Bankers Trust* were not good examples of imperative public importance. These two cases, though important, are better categorized as instances where certiorari was granted because other cases raising similar issues were already before the Court. Finally, the citations to *Carter* and *Alton* are anachronistic. If they were to come before the Court today, they would come on direct appeal.

The original citations seem to have been selected from the 1951 edition of Robertson and Kirkham's *Jurisdiction of the Supreme Court of the United States*,[109] which cites six cases for the proposition: "Questions of great importance, requiring prompt settlement in the interests of the public, were involved in the remaining cases in which certiorari before judgment has issued."[110] This passage in the treatise is similar to the 1954 version of the Rule.[111] It cited the same six cases (plus the newly decided *Steel Seizure* case), also in order from the oldest case to the newest, also without the year of decision. The 1980 amendment to the Rule in large part followed this tradition. The Court changed the Rule's number from Rule 20 to Rule 18, added the *Nixon* and *Girard* citations, and at last included the years of decisions for all cases cited.

Discovering the source of the Rule only opens up another question. If the Supreme Court based its rule on the Robertson and

---

[107]354 U.S. 524.

[108]418 U.S. 683 (1974).

[109]Robertson & Kirkham, The Jurisdiction of the Supreme Court of the United States (Wolfson & Kurland ed. 1951) (hereinafter Robertson & Kirkham).

[110]*Id.* at 235 n.2.

[111]The treatise itself derives some of this language from Forsyth v. Hammond, 166 U.S. 506, 514 (1897), quoted at note 72 *supra* and accompanying text, and Supreme Court Rule 39, quoted at note 91 *supra* and accompanying text.

Kirkham treatise, why did the Rule fail to mention other categories in which the writ is used? The Rule embraces only imperative public importance cases. Yet the treatise had recognized two other categories: (1) cases that had been previously before the Court and (2) cases raising questions similar to those currently before the Court in a pending case.[112] By excluding these two classes obviously known to the drafters, they may have intended to abandon these two types of certiorari grants. Yet the Supreme Court has continued to grant certiorari before judgment in similar cases. Sadly, therefore, Rule 18 is an unclear guide for practitioners—still less does it control the procedure it purports to govern.

II. CERTIORARI BEFORE JUDGMENT—GENERAL CONSIDERATIONS

Certiorari before judgment is designed to permit the Court to accomplish two overlapping objectives: increasing the speed of the litigation and bypassing the court of appeals. Ironically, these advantages may at the same time be major disadvantages for promoting good decision making. Moreover, certiorari before judgment cannot be fully understood without evaluating why the intermediate appellate courts were created and why the Supreme Court was given such an expanded certiorari power.

A. DOCKET REDUCTION

Congress created the federal courts of appeals in 1891 to reduce the Supreme Court's docket.[113] But the problem did not stay fixed. By the 1920s, Congress had to give the Court the power to choose most of its cases.[114] Certiorari before judgment appears to run counter to this policy of docket reduction, since it provides the direct access

---

[112]Robertson & Kirkham at 234–36.

[113]*Id.* at 251–74. This concern, of course, is even more important today. See, *e.g.*, Posner, The Federal Courts (1984); Black, National Court of Appeals: An Unwise Proposal, 83 Yale L.J. 883 (1974); Brennan, National Court of Appeals, 40 U. Chi. L. Rev. 473 (1973); Casper & Posner, Caseload of the Supreme Court: 1975 and 1976 Terms, 1977 Supreme Court Review 87; Casper & Posner, A Study of the Supreme Court's Caseload, 3 J. Legal Stud. 339 (1974); Freund, National Court of Appeals, 25 Hastings L.J. 1301 (1974); Hruska, Commission Recommends New National Court of Appeals, 61 ABA J. 819 (1975); Hruska, National Court of Appeals: An Analysis of Viewpoints, 9 Creighton L. Rev. 286 (1975); Kurland, Jurisdiction of the United States Supreme Court: Time for Change?, 59 Cornell L. Rev. 616 (1974).

[114]1924 Hearing, note 56 *supra*, at 6–7.

to the Supreme Court that Congress intended to limit. Some might argue, however, that there is no increase in cases heard by the Court. Certiorari before judgment is supposed to be granted only in cases where sooner or later a Supreme Court decision is necessary. Cases that would eventually reach the Court are simply presented at an earlier time. This argument would suggest that by granting certiorari early, the Court may actually promote judicial efficiency, since it saves work in the court of appeals.

This reasoning, however, is faulty. First, it ignores the principal purpose behind the Supreme Court's control over certiorari. Efficiencies gained by the courts of appeals are largely irrelevant. More fundamentally, even if a case may be considered likely for Supreme Court review, this does not mean that it will continue to be so after a decision in the court of appeals. A clear ruling by the court of appeals or by the Supreme Court in another case may lessen the import of the legal issues presented. Or the applicable statutory law may change. Or the parties may settle or otherwise change their circumstances.

Here the Court's experience in stay petitions is telling. As with early certiorari, a stay is appropriate only if it is likely that the Court will later undertake to decide the case.[115] Yet even a cursory examination of stays reveals that many cases where stays are granted never reach the Supreme Court on the merits. To illustrate, during the 1980 Term, only four of the eleven stay cases where stays were granted remained important enough to merit a full hearing. Another two were decided summarily by the Court without a full hearing; both were sent back to be decided in light of a recent Supreme Court opinion or a recent statutory change. Nearly half, for one reason or another, fell by the wayside. Thus an early prediction is often not borne out by later review. Only in a few cases of certiorari before judgment will eventual review be obvious.

Moreover, the costs of ignoring docket reduction are not expended solely on those cases the Court decides to hear. The Court must also use resources in denying petitions for certiorari. A rule that invites litigants to file more petitions necessarily increases the

---

[115]*E.g.*, Rostker v. Goldberg, 448 U.S. 1306 (1980) (Brennan, J., as Circuit Justice); New York Times v. Jascalevich, 439 U.S. 1301 (1978) (White, J., as Circuit Justice). The Court has characterized this standard as whether four Justices would be likely to vote for certiorari. 439 U.S. at 1301–02.

Supreme Court's workload, even if on occasion granting the writ would promote the overall efficiency of the federal judicial system.

B. INCREASING THE SPEED OF LITIGATION

1. *Haste.* In rare cases granting certiorari before judgment is a useful tool, a device to shorten litigation when time is particularly crucial. But haste has its inherent problems. Rushed deliberations may cause the Supreme Court to reach a wrong result or to write a poorly reasoned opinion. At times, the Court itself has admitted this problem. In *O'Brien v. Brown*,[116] the Court was faced with a challenge to the credentials process of the 1972 Democratic National Convention. The McGovern forces were unseating some elected and appointed delegations and replacing them with delegations with more blacks, more women—and perhaps more to the point—more McGovern loyalists. The case was presented to the Court less than four days before the convention was to open.[117] The Court refused to decide the case on the merits, asserting that it would not be rushed to judgment in a case of such obvious import. As the Court explained:[118]

> This Court is now asked to review . . . novel and important questions. . . . The Court concludes it cannot in this limited time give to these issues the consideration warranted for final decision on the merits; we therefore take no action on the petitions for certiorari at this time.

The Court in *O'Brien* issued a stay of the lower court's opinion, rather than reach a potentially faulty decision.[119]

O'Brien is not a certiorari before judgment case, since it had been heard by the court of appeals. Yet the concern with hasty decisions shows up as well in certiorari before judgment cases. Notable in this respect is *Dames & Moore v. Regan*,[120] the case challenging the Iranian hostage agreement. Here the majority opinion implies that, because the case was decided under extreme time pressures, it

---

[116] 409 U.S. 1 (1972).

[117] The court held a special July 1972 Term to consider the case, although there was no oral argument and the Court apparently acted without convening. Stern, Gressman & Shapiro, Supreme Court Practice 9, 10 (6th ed. 1986).

[118] 409 U.S. at 3.

[119] 409 U.S. at 5.

[120] 453 U.S. 654.

should probably not be used as precedent in later cases.[121] The message is clear. If a case is really of imperative public importance, it is important that it be decided correctly.

Haste has probably contributed to deficiencies in several questionable opinions, some involving certiorari before judgment and some involving an expedited hearing in both the court of appeals and the Supreme Court. For example, the *Nixon* opinion has been sharply criticized for its weak reasoning and for potentially setting unwise (and possibly unintended) precedents. In the *Pentagon Papers* case,[122] the dissenters vigorously argued that they lacked the time to consider the merits of the case adequately.[123]

An excellent example of where haste was later admitted by the Court as leading to incorrect results was in the civilian court-martial cases, *Kinsella v. Krueger* and *Reid v. Covert*. Both cases were presented to the Court without the benefit of an intermediate court decision. *Reid* was before the Court on direct appeal under 28 U.S.C. §1252. *Kinsella* was before the Court on certiorari before judgment because it presented issues similar to those in *Reid*. *Reid* and *Kinsella* involved the power of a military court-martial to try the wife of an American serviceman overseas for murdering her husband. The two cases were originally argued on May 3, 1956, in the waning days of the October 1955 Term of the Court.[124] On June 11, 1956, the Court ruled for the first of two times in the case, holding that the courts-martial indeed could try these wives of servicemen.

In both cases, Justices Warren, Black, and Douglas joined in a brief dissent, arguing that more time was needed "than is available in these closing days of the Term in which to write our dissenting views."[125] They promised to file their dissents at the next term. Justice Frankfurter went further, reserving his judgment for a later date:[126]

---

[121]"[W]e stress that the expeditious treatment of the issues involved by all of the courts . . . makes us acutely aware of the necessity to rest decision on the narrowest possible grounds in deciding the case. . . . We attempt to lay down no general 'guidelines' covering other situations not involved here." 453 U.S. at 660–61.

[122]New York Times v. United States, 403 U.S. 713 (1971).

[123]*Id.* at 752–63.

[124]351 U.S. at 487.

[125]*Id.* at 486.

[126]*Id.* at 485.

Time is required not only for the primary task of analyzing in detail the materials on which the Court relies. It is equally required for adequate reflection upon the meaning of these materials and their bearing on the issues now before the Court. Reflection is a slow process. Wisdom, like good wine, requires maturing.

Frankfurter went on to point out that the "judgments of this Court presuppose full consideration and reconsideration by all [Justices] of the reasoned views of each."[127] Frankfurter argued that in *Kinsella* and *Reid* this interchange of ideas was lacking.

When the Supreme Court reconvened in the fall of 1956, things looked different. It granted petitions for rehearing in both *Reid* and *Kinsella*,[128] held rearguments, and reversed itself by a six to two margin.[129] Justice Harlan, whose changed views contributed to turning a minority into a majority, explained that rehearing "afforded an opportunity for a greater degree of reflection" than was possible in the closing days of the previous term.[130] Thus, not only did the Court reverse itself in a certiorari before judgment case, but undue haste was blamed.

2. *Expedited hearing, stays, and other ways to control the speed of appellate litigation.* The drawbacks of rushing a decision are clear.

---

[127]*Ibid.* Frankfurter explained his position as follows: "Grave issues affecting the status of American civilians throughout the world are raised by these cases; they are made graver by the arguments on which the Court finds it necessary to rely in searching its result. Doubtless because of the pressure under which the Court works during its closing weeks, these arguments have been merely adumbrated in its opinion. To deal adequately with them, however, demands of those to whom they are not persuasive more than has been available to examine and to analyze in detail the historical underpinning and implication of the cases relied upon by the Court, as a preliminary to a searching critique of their relevance to the problems now before the Court. . . . Moreover, the judgments of this Court are collective judgments. They are neither solo performance nor debates between two sides, each of which has its mind quickly made up and then closed. The judgments of this Court presuppose full consideration and reconsideration by all of the reasoned views of each. Without adequate study there cannot be adequate reflection. Without adequate reflection there cannot be adequate deliberation and discussion. And without these, there cannot be that full interchange of minds which is indispensable to wise decision and its persuasive formulation." *Id.* at 483–85.

[128]352 U.S. 901 (1956).

[129]Reid v. Covert, 354 U.S. 1 (1957).

[130]*Id.* at 65. Although haste was blamed for the reversal, this haste did not result directly from the grant of certiorari before judgment in the *Kinsella* case. The *Reid* case was already before the Court on appeal, so it would likely have decided the legal issue raised—the legality of a court-martial of a civilian for a capital offense—with as much haste as it did, regardless of the grant of certiorari before judgment in the *Kinsella* case.

What is less clear is that the benefits of certiorari before judgment in shortening litigation may be overstated. In the *Pentagon Papers* case,[131] for example, the parties through the mechanism of expedited appeal were able to obtain Supreme Court review without significant delay. The entire process from filing in the district court through decision in the court of appeals to final judgment in the Supreme Court took less than three weeks.[132] Arguably, then, the time-saving benefits of certiorari before judgment may be gained without losing an intermediate court decision.

Expedited appeal, however, raises problems of its own. A rushed schedule in two appellate courts may not produce a more considered opinion than a somewhat longer deliberation in one court. Moreover, the lower appellate court may not expedite its scheduling. Thus, even if it is possible that a litigant may be able to obtain expedited review in the court of appeals, there may be good reasons to avoid the risk that such relief may not be granted. The better alternative, at least for the litigant, may be to proceed directly to the Supreme Court.

A more elusive problem is determining why time considerations require the use of certiorari before judgment at all. Supreme Court Rule 44[133] authorizes the Court to issue provisional relief such as stays and injunctions. Since the Rule is frequently used when the litigation requires immediate relief, it stands as an obvious alternative to early certiorari. This is particularly true since, like certiorari before judgment, Rule 44 demands that any case where a stay is issued be both important to the public and likely to be heard by the Court on the merits.[134]

Why might a stay or injunction be better than certiorari before judgment? First, a stay or injunction can avoid the problems inherent in a rushed deliberation. Second, such provisional relief will secure the advantage of an intermediate review—and the possibility that the court of appeals will resolve the case before the Supreme Court hears it.[135]

---

[131]New York Times v. United States, 403 U.S. 713 (1971).

[132]403 U.S. at 753–55 (Harlan, J., dissenting).

[133]Supreme Court Rule 44, 445 U.S. 1038 (1980).

[134]*Ibid*.

[135]See United States Parole Commission v. Geraghty, 445 U.S. 388, 400 (1980); Sosna v.

One line of authorities suggests that a stay rather than certiorari before judgment is the favored procedure.[136] In cases involving ballot access and election law generally—for example, the *O'Brien* case—the Court has ordered stays or affirmative injunctions.[137] On the other hand, in *Anderson v. Celebreeze*,[138] another ballot access case, the Court denied an application for early certiorari, even though the Court eventually heard the case on the merits.[139] Indeed, in its later opinion in *Anderson*, the Court noted that the party seeking early certiorari had not requested a stay—perhaps suggesting that, if requested, a stay would have been granted.[140]

It might seem that early certiorari should be restricted to cases where a stay or injunction would be inadequate. Whatever the merits of such a proposal, it is not the way the Supreme Court does business. On the one hand, the Court has never made a litigant show the inadequacy of provisional relief as a prerequisite to obtaining early certiorari. For example, the writ was granted in two cases that were good candidates for stays or injunctions, *Rickert Rice*

Iowa, 419 U.S. 393, 398–403 (1975). Lest there be concern that the circumstances giving rise to the litigation will evaporate before definitive judicial pronouncement, the Court's flexible approach to mootness assures that those issues that are capable of repetition yet evading review can be eventually adjudicated on the merits should that be appropriate.

[136]Resort to stays or injunctions, however, is not without its drawbacks. First, as with any provisional relief, the initial decision may be at odds with the final decision on the merits. If the party against whom the provisional relief has been maintained has suffered substantial harm, an eventual decision for that party on the merits may be of little solace. This, of course, is a problem endemic to injunctions and certainly not peculiar to Supreme Court relief. On the other hand, to protect its prestige the Supreme Court may be particularly wary of granting relief that it may later disavow, relief that may in itself cause harm to a litigant who is later vindicated. There is an easy answer. When the Court acts provisionally, it usually does so by a single Justice. It does not speak as a whole. In this sense, a provisional decision does not implicate the Court as an institution. But this is not without its difficulties. First, in deciding whether to issue a stay, sometimes the Court does act as a whole. See Note, The Powers of the Supreme Court Justice Acting in an Individual Capacity, 112 U. Pa. L. Rev. 981 (1964). Second, even when it does not, the quest for stays has often led to the unseemly practice of "Justice shopping" by those seeking to evoke the sympathies of particular Justices. It has also led to another problem: single Justices being asked to overrule the decision of one of their colleagues. See generally Holtzman v. Schlesinger, 414 U.S. 1316 (1973).

[137]*E.g.*, Fishman v. Schaffer, 429 U.S. 1325 (1976) (Marshall, J., as Circuit Justice); McCarthy v. Briscoe, 429 U.S. 1317 (1976) (Powell, J., as Circuit Justice).

[138]See Celebreeze v. Anderson, 448 U.S. 918 (1980).

[139]460 U.S. 780 (1983).

[140]*Id.* at 784.

Mills[141] and *Alton Railroad.*[142] *Rickert* was an attack on a federal agricultural processing tax; *Alton* an attack on a statute mandating railroad pensions. In both cases, if the litigants were suffering irreparable harm, the Court could have enjoined the legislative programs and waited for a ruling by the court of appeals. Conversely, if no irreparable harm is present, there may not be need for either provisional relief or early certiorari.

On the other hand, the Court has refused certiorari before judgment even where provisional relief would not protect the litigants. Examples of this are the ballot access cases. If a candidate is thrown off a ballot, he obviously suffers irreparable harm. If, however, a candidate is included on a ballot to which he is not entitled, the other candidates may suffer irreparable harm. In *Anderson v. Celebreeze*, for example, including John Anderson on the ballot undoubtedly affected the vote totals for Jimmy Carter and Ronald Reagan.[143] If the inadequacy of provisional relief were the touchstone of certiorari before judgment, the writ should have been granted in this case.

C. BYPASSING THE COURT OF APPEALS

1. *The advantages of an intermediate appellate court opinion.* Sometimes a tool designed for one purpose becomes useful for others. A good example is the circuit court of appeals. Although originally designed to reduce the Supreme Court's docket, the court of appeals has become an increasingly important aid to Supreme Court decision making. Justice Burton explained this role in his dissent from the grant of certiorari before judgment in the *Steel Seizure* case:[144]

> The Constitutional issue which is the subject of the appeal deserves for its solution all of the wisdom that our judicial process makes available. The need for soundness in the result outweighs the need for speed in reaching it. The Nation is

---

[141]See generally, Note, Recent Developments in Federal Tax Injunctions—the Rice Millers Cases, 21 St. Louis L. Rev. 140 (1936); Note, 13 NYU L.Q. Rev. 474 (1936).

[142]See generally, Comment, 33 Mich. L. Rev. 1214 (1935); Note, 35 Colum. L. Rev. 932 (1935); Note, 25 Geo. L.J. 161 (1936).

[143]As it turned out, Jimmy Carter would have lost the election even if he had received every one of Anderson's votes. Of course, the Court could not have known this. See Information Please Almanac 1982 595 (1981). In Ohio, where the case arose, Carter lost by 454,131 votes, while Anderson received 254,472 votes. *Ibid.*

[144]343 U.S. at 938. Justice Frankfurter joined Justice Burton in dissent.

entitled to the substantial value inherent in an intermediate
consideration of the issue by the Court of Appeals. Little time
will be lost and none will be wasted in seeking it. The time
taken will be available also for constructive consideration by the
parties of their own positions and responsibilities. Accordingly,
I would deny the petitions for certiorari and thus allow the case
to be heard by the Court of Appeals.

Burton's thesis implies two separate justifications. First, an intermediate appeal allows the litigants to sharpen their own positions.
Second, a decision of the court of appeals filters the issues and gives
the Court important legal insights into the case. As the United
States successfully argued while opposing certiorari before judgment in *Radio Television News Directors Association v. United States*,[145]
an appellate court decision sifts and refines the record and the issues
so that the bases for decision are clearer, just as it clarifies the issues
that need not be reached at all. To this we add that the court of
appeals is much like the Supreme Court—a federal appellate court,
detached, nonpartisan, and staffed by the judges with backgrounds
similar to the Supreme Court's. Thus it should be the single most
useful aid in deciding cases.

The importance of an intermediate court opinion is pervasive.
Its effect on Supreme Court practice extends beyond certiorari
before judgment. The Court has adopted a rule that, absent extraordinary circumstances, it will refuse to consider issues not decided by the court of appeals—even when the case itself is properly
before the Court.[146] Indeed, the policy is so strong that the Court
has criticized those jurisdictional statutes where Congress has provided a direct appeal from the district court, since they "deprive
[the Court] of the valuable assistance of the Court of Appeals."[147]
This assistance should not be sacrificed lightly.

2. *Where an appellate court decision may not be necessary.* It is sometimes claimed that an intermediate appellate opinion would not help
the Supreme Court. This contention is most plausible where for
some reason there is an existing appellate opinion for guidance.
This can occur where the case has previously been before the Court
on the same issue. Here the Supreme Court can look to the earlier

---

[145]Respondent's Brief in Opposition to Certiorari, Radio Tel. News Directors Ass'n v.
United States, 390 U.S. 922 (1968).

[146]*E.g.*, Adickes v. S.H. Kress & Co., 398 U.S. 144, 147 n.2 (1970).

[147]See United States v. Singer Mfg. Co., 374 U.S. 174, 175 n.1 (1963).

Supreme Court opinion and to the appellate court opinion that preceded the first Supreme Court decision. Also, if the Court is bringing up a case to consolidate it with another case already before the Court raising the same issue, the Supreme Court will usually have the benefit of an appellate court opinion from the pending case.

Less plausible arguments that an appellate court opinion would be of no benefit are occasionally raised. Supposedly, either the facts or the legal issues are so clear that there would be little value in a hearing before the court of appeals. In *Carter Coal Company*,[148] the petitioner argued that an intermediate appellate decision was not needed because "[a]ll essential questions of jurisdiction and procedure were fully explored in the tribunal of first instance."[149] In the *Nixon* case, the Special Prosecutor argued that early certiorari "would not sacrifice any benefits of intermediate appellate review," because the D.C. Circuit had "considered and ruled at length [in *Nixon v. Sirica*] on the principal constitutional issues presented for review."[150] In *Alton Railroad*, the Court itself stated that it was

---

[148]298 U.S. 238. See generally, Comment, 34 Mich. L. Rev. 1167 (1936); Note, Production and Commerce among the States: Carter v. Carter Coal Co., 50 Harv. L. Rev. 307 (1936); Note, 23 Va. L. Rev. 79 (1936).

[149]Petition for Certiorari, Carter v. Carter Coal Co., 298 U.S. 238 (1936).

Support for this argument may be gained from a dissent in Lurk v. United States, 366 U.S. 712 (1961). In *Lurk* the Supreme Court remanded to the court of appeals the jurisdictional issue whether a criminal defendant could constitutionally be tried by a judge of the Court of Customs and Patent Appeals. The circuit court had not reached this issue earlier because it had disposed of the case on other grounds. Dissenting from the remand, however, was none other than Justice Frankfurter. In other contexts, of course, he has been a staunch opponent of short-circuiting the appellate process. Frankfurter's dissent is notable: "Solution of this [jurisdictional issue] will call into consideration a number of subsidiary questions. What are the characteristics of an Article III court? Is the Court of Customs and Patent Appeals an Article III court? If so, when did it become such a court? Assuming arguendo that the Court of Customs and Patent Appeals has been an Article III court only since 1958 (when Congress enacted legislation conferring that status), what is the bearing of this fact on the status of a judge who retired from the court prior to that time? These are not questions on which, with all due respect, a lower court can be of effective assistance to this Court. They do not involve the valuation of evidence or the application of rules of local law or special familiarity and experience with the materials and the underlying considerations on which judgment must be based. On the contrary, the constitutional history and the cases upon which the decision ultimately must turn are the special concern of this Court." Lurk v. United States, 366 U.S. 712, 712–13 (Frankfurter, J., dissenting).

[150]Petition for Certiorari, United States v. Nixon, 418 U.S. 683 (1974). Nixon's attorneys countered by asserting, "[I]t will be illuminating to see how the court that devised the *Sirica* standard thinks it applies to the present set of facts." Respondent's Brief in Opposition to Certiorari.

bypassing the court of appeals because the facts were clear.[151]

Ultimately, these arguments for bypassing the court of appeals are unpersuasive. By analyzing the legal issues and the facts, the court of appeals should be of some help to the Supreme Court. When a litigant points to only the law as being clear, he is ignoring the appellate court's aid in interpreting the record and the facts. Likewise, a litigant who focuses only on the facts ignores the appellate court's assistance on the legal issues.[152] In certiorari before judgment cases, the litigants do not go so far as to argue that both the facts and the law are clear—perhaps because, if this were true, there would be little need to go before the Supreme Court. Moreover, in every case review by an intermediate appellate court will give the litigants the opportunity to refine their own positions, and the longer proceedings may cause the case to settle or become moot.

3. *Where a court of appeals decision may be harmful.* Different considerations, however, apply when a hearing before the court of appeals may actually be harmful. One reason for avoiding the court of appeals is to protect the intermediate court's authority. In some circumstances, there may be a legitimate concern that a court of appeals decision will be ignored by a party who asserts that a lower court decision is not authoritative. This, for example, is what the White House announced in *United States v. Nixon*.[153] Similarly, in the *Nazi Saboteurs* case, the lawyer for the government warned that President Roosevelt might defy the Supreme Court. Here an intermediate court opinion would have carried little weight. In such

---

[151]In *Alton Railroad*, a case cited in Rule 20, the Supreme Court granted a certiorari petition challenging the constitutionality of a major piece of New Deal legislation. Suit was filed shortly after the Railroad Act of June 27, 1934 (ch. 868, 48 Stat. 1283) took effect. The trial court, the Supreme Court of the District of Columbia, held the statute unconstitutional. The government appealed to the Court of Appeals and then applied for certiorari before judgment, which was granted by the Supreme Court. 293 U.S. 552. The only comment the Court made about its grant of certiorari before judgment was, "[T]he petitioners applied for a writ of certiorari, representing that no serious or difficult questions of fact were involved, and urging the importance of an early and final decision of the controversy. In the exercise of power conferred by statute we issued the writ." 295 U.S. at 344. See also Frankfurter & Fisher, The Business of the Supreme Court at the October Terms, 1935 and 1936, 51 Harv. L. Rev. 577, 616 n.69 (1938).

[152]*Lurk*, 366 U.S. at 713 (Frankfurter, J., dissenting). After remand, the case was eventually heard by the Court and decided *sub nom.* Glidden v. Zdanok, 370 U.S. 530 (1962).

[153]The Final Days at 264, 272–78. *Cf.* Henkin, Executive Privilege: Mr. Nixon Loses But the Presidency Largely Prevails, 22 UCLA L. Rev. 40, 44–45 (1974).

circumstances, it may be better to save the court of appeals from the embarrassment of issuing ultimately unenforceable decisions.

In *Ex Parte Peru*,[154] the Supreme Court may have recognized another situation where a hearing before the court of appeals could be considered harmful. At issue in *Peru* was whether the Court should issue a mandamus to prevent the lower federal courts from continuing to litigate a libel against a Peruvian ship.[155] The Court held that mandamus was appropriate, resting its decision mainly on foreign policy concerns. The Court also suggested that the "dignity" of the foreign sovereign might suffer if forced to pursue litigation in the lower courts.[156]

Similar concerns must have also been present in *Wilson v. Girard*.[157] Here President Eisenhower had promised to turn over to Japanese authorities a soldier accused of murdering a Japanese woman. When the soldier tried to block this move by resorting to the federal courts, the Supreme Court granted certiorari before judgment. It was probably hesitant to subject Japan to protracted lower court proceedings after the President had already spoken. Preserving the dignity of particularly important defendants may also in part explain the *Nixon* and *Steel Seizure* cases. There is a legitimate interest in protecting presidents and foreign sovereigns from lengthy litigation in the lower courts.

III. Where Certiorari before Judgment Is Justified— Analyzing the Cases

A. CASES OF IMPERATIVE PUBLIC IMPORTANCE

Concerns for reducing the docket, avoiding undue haste, and securing the benefits of an intermediate court opinion all point in the same direction—to a strong presumption against the use of certiorari before judgment. To identify what extraordinary circumstances justify issuing the writ, we begin with the only category explicitly recognized in the Supreme Court rule—cases of "imperative public importance." At first glance, this is a messy class with

---

[154]318 U.S. 578 (1983).

[155]*Id.* at 585–87.

[156]*Id.* at 587.

[157]354 U.S. 524 (1957).

few obvious standards. But on closer examination, all the public importance cases fall into three subcategories—cases challenging the constitutionality of Congressional statutes, foreign policy cases, and cases needing the institutional authority of the Court.[158] Certiorari before judgment has been denied in cases—even very important ones—that do not fit into these subcategories.[159]

1. *Cases challenging the constitutionality of Acts of Congress.* One source of direction about what kinds of cases are important may be Congress. In what circumstances has Congress indicated that it is appropriate to bypass the intermediate courts? Currently, the major statute authorizing direct appeals from the district court to the Supreme Court is 28 U.S.C. §1252.[160] It authorizes direct appeals from the district court in cases where the United States is a party and an Act of Congress has been found unconstitutional.

The writ of certiorari before judgment and §1252 have more than simply a casual relationship. Section 1252 was originally enacted in 1937. Almost immediately preceding this enactment, the Court granted early certiorari in two cases where direct appeal would have been allowed had the statute existed. History is not alone in establishing the close connection between §1252 and certiorari before

---

[158]Cases in which certiorari before judgment has been granted exclusively for imperative public importance are: Dames & Moore v. Regan, 453 U.S. 654 (1981); United States v. Nixon, 418 U.S. 683 (1974); Wilson v. Girard, 354 U.S. 524 (1957); Youngstown Sheet & Tube Co. v. Sawyer, 343 U.S. 579 (1952); United States v. United Mine Workers, 330 U.S. 258 (1947); Ex parte Quirin, 317 U.S. 1 (1942); Cincinnati Soap v. United States, 301 U.S. 308 (1937); Carter v. Carter Coal, 298 U.S. 238 (1936); Railroad Retirement Bd. v. Alton R.R., 295 U.S. 330 (1935); The Three Friends, 166 U.S. 1 (1897).

[159]See, *e.g.*, Celebreeze v. Anderson, 448 U.S. 918 (1980), subsequently decided *sub nom.* Anderson v. Celebreeze, 460 U.S. 780 (1983). In addition to *Anderson*, the Court, after denying certiorari before judgment, eventually accepted several cases for argument after a decision in the circuit court. Guam v. Olsen, 431 U.S. 195 (1977); cert. before judgment denied, 425 U.S. 960 (1976); Saxe v. Anderson, cert. denied, 305 U.S. 589 (1938) dismissed on motion of petitioner, 305 U.S. 665 (1939), cert. before judgment denied, 302 U.S. 688 (1937); Electric Bond & Share Co. v. S.E.C., 303 U.S. 419 (1938), cert. before judgment denied, 301 U.S. 709 (1937); United States Navigation Co. v. Cunard S.S. Co., 284 U.S. 474 (1932), cert. before judgment denied, 281 U.S. 759 (1930); Blackmer v. United States, 284 U.S. 421 (1932), cert. before judgment denied, 281 U.S. 746, 747 (1920). In United States v. Montgomery Ward & Co., 324 U.S. 858 (1945), the Court originally denied certiorari before judgment. After a decision in the Court of Appeals and a subsequent petition, the Court granted certiorari and remanded the case to the district court with instructions to dismiss it as moot. 326 U.S. 690 (1945).

[160]The statute was originally promulgated as a part of President Roosevelt's court packing bill. See Moore's Federal Practice ¶411.01.

judgment. The two cases, *Carter Coal Co.*[161] *and Alton,*[162] are cited in Supreme Court Rule 18, apparently as models for using the writ.[163] Yet, if they were to come up again, direct appeal would now be available. Indeed, the writ and the statute are almost symbiotic. Where the constitutionality of a federal statute is challenged, whether the writ or direct appeal is appropriate depends solely on whether the government won or lost in the district court.[164]

The two are also closely related by policy. The obvious rationale behind §1252 is to allow the United States to protect its interest in the validity of its statutes.[165] Section 1252 presumes that the government's interest is sufficiently protected when the United States prevails in the district court. Early certiorari may be needed, however, if, despite the government's victory, the litigation raises a cloud over the statute. Thus in several cases the Court granted early certiorari on the petition of the government, even though the government won in the district court.[166]

Yet there is a caveat. The policies of §1252 appear to be furthered only when the United States seeks relief.[167] As noted, §1252 is

---

[161]298 U.S. 238 (1936).

[162]295 U.S. 330 (1935).

[163]See Sup. Ct. Rule 18, 445 U.S. 983, 1003–04 (1980).

[164]Compare *Reid*, 351 U.S. 487 (government lost) with *Kinsella*, 351 U.S. 470 (government won).

[165]See Moore's Federal Practice ¶411.01. The statute does not express an absolute concern for the respect of Congressional enactments since it does not apply unless the United States is a party, an option that the Attorney General has in any case where a Congressional act is threatened. See 28 U.S.C. §2403(a).

[166]Kinsella v. Krueger, decided *sub nom.* Reid v. Covert, 354 U.S. 1 (1957); United States v. Bankers' Trust Co., 294 U.S. 240 (1935), 293 U.S. 548 (1934). In Dames & Moore v. Regan, 453 U.S. 654, the United States, while not itself a petitioner, supported the petition for certiorari before judgment brought by its opponent. In this respect it is also significant that the government did not oppose the grant of certiorari before judgment in Cincinnati Soap Co. v. United States, 301 U.S. 308 (1937).

In *Nixon*, 418 U.S. 683, and United States v. United Mine Workers, 330 U.S. 258, where the constitutionality of an Act of Congress was not at stake, the United States as a winning party applied for certiorari before judgment, which was granted. In *The Steel Seizure Case*, 343 U.S. 579, the government as losing party prepared and filed a petition for certiorari before judgment only to discover that the steel industry as winner had already filed a petition. The Court granted both petitions, 343 U.S. 937 (1952). The steel industry's apparent purpose in filing its own petition was to ensure the right to open and close at oral argument. See Marcus, Truman and the Steel Seizure Case 143–44.

[167]For example, the government's support for the petition in *Dames & Moore* was undeniably critical. This is evidenced by the Court's denial of an application in a similar case, after the

designed only to further the United States's interest in protecting
its own laws, rather than to promote a general interest in the constitutionality of Acts of Congress. Thus, as a practical matter, a
private litigant may not be able to argue that early certiorari would
further the policies of §1252 unless the United States is a party and
acquiesces in the petition.[168]

2. *Foreign policy cases.* A second kind of "imperative public importance" case is one affecting foreign policy. As the Court stated
in *McCulloch v. Sociedad Nacional:* "the presence of public questions
particularly high in the scale of our national interest because of
their international complexion is a uniquely compelling justification
for prompt judicial resolution of the controversy."[169]

The cases strongly support this position. Certiorari before judgment was granted in *The Three Friends* to prevent citizens from
interfering with the neutrality of the United States by aiding Cuban
revolutionaries. *Dames & Moore v. Regan* challenged President Carter's deal to end the Iranian hostage crisis. The infamous *Nazi
Saboteurs* case stood as a warning to enemy agents that they would
be severely dealt with by the United States military. *Cincinnati Soap
v. United States* challenged the constitutionality of a tax to assist the
Philippine Government. In the *Steel Seizure* case, President Truman
took over the steel mills because he feared that a strike and lockout
would paralyze our conduct of the Korean War. Even some non-
foreign policy cases, such as *United States v. United Mine Workers*
and *United States v. Nixon*, have foreign policy components. The
first involved a national strike in a basic industry that potentially

---

government expressed opposition to granting the writ. See Electronic Data Corp. v. Iran,
452 U.S. 931 (1981). The support of the United States, however, does not guarantee a grant
of certiorari before judgment. See United States v. Montgomery Ward & Co., 324 U.S. 858
(1945).

The social science literature suggests that cases where the United States is a party are
more likely to be selected on certiorari. See Provine, Case Selection in the United States
Supreme Court 83 (1980) (United States as a petitioner or respondent); Tanenhaus, Schick,
Muraskin, & Rosen, The Supreme Court's Certiorari Jurisdiction: Cue Theory, in Schubert,
ed., Judicial Decision-Making 111, 119–22 (1963) (United States as a petitioner).

[168]An argument that granting certiorari before judgment will further the policies of a
statute providing direct appeal will not always succeed. In American Tel. & Tel. Co. v.
United States, 429 U.S. 1071 (1977), the petitioners argued that the granting of the writ in
that case, was "entirely consistent, and indeed furthered the policies of the Expediting Act."
Petitioner's Brief, cert. denied, 429 U.S. 1071 (1977). Nonetheless, the Court denied the
petition for early certiorari.

[169]372 U.S. 10, 17 (1963).

hindered the United States in its efforts immediately after World War II. Similarly, in *Nixon* the government had nearly ground to a halt,[170] and Secretary of State Kissinger worried that other nations were taking advantage of our weakness.[171]

Sound reasons support the use of certiorari before judgment in foreign policy cases. An example is *Wilson v. Girard.* In *Girard,* a serviceman charged with killing a Japanese woman challenged his trial by Japanese authorities. Although the Secretary of Defense waived any jurisdiction the United States might have had over the killing and agreed to turn over the serviceman to Japan,[172] the District Court for the District of Columbia granted declaratory relief and enjoined the serviceman's delivery to Japanese authorities.[173] At the same time it denied his petition for habeas corpus. The Secretary of Defense appealed and then filed for certiorari before judgment, which was granted, as was the serviceman's cross-petition to review the denial of habeas corpus.

The Supreme Court gave no explanation for granting early certiorari. Yet it is clear from the promptness of the Court's decision (coming only three days after argument)[174] that the Court felt a need to decide the case as quickly as possible. The reasons for this are not discussed in the opinion. Both the killing of the Japanese civilian and the dispute over whose court should govern had created severely strained relations between the United States and Japan. The issue had become so charged that the Supreme Court's decision merely to grant certiorari before judgment was itself a front page story in the United States.[175] It must have been an even greater concern in Japan. Thus time was pressing. Moreover, the Court may have been worried about other factors. A foreign nation may deserve a definitive ruling from our nation's highest legal authority; in any event, the Japanese may not have understood a lengthy court pro-

---

[170]During a visit to the University of Virginia School of Law in October 1985, Chief Justice Warren Burger stated that early certiorari was granted because the government had ground to a halt. Somewhat inconsistently, though, Burger stated that he gave no thought to the political effect of the case on the impending impeachment, and that there was no discussion of it among the Justices.

[171]*Cf.* Final Days, at 422.

[172]See Joint Statement of Secretary of State & Secretary of Defense, 354 U.S. at 544–48.

[173]Girard v. Wilson, 152 F.Supp. 21 (D.D.C. 1957).

[174]The case was argued on July 8, 1957, and decided on July 11, 1958. 354 U.S. at 524.

[175]See New York Times, June 22, 1957, at 1.

ceeding. Also, the appellate process may lead to conflicting results at each stage of review. Effective foreign policy, on the other hand, requires consistent signals.

In *Ex Parte Peru*, the Court granted expedited review under the Extraordinary Writs Act, not certiorari before judgment; yet it explicitly recognized similar foreign policy concerns. *Peru* involved a libel issued against a foreign vessel by a private party. The district court upheld its jurisdiction over the case.[176] Peru objected by filing a writ of mandamus in the Supreme Court. The Supreme Court granted the writ, holding that the district court had no jurisdiction over Peru.[177] Although the case was not a certiorari before judgment case, the result in using an extraordinary writ was the same—the court of appeals was bypassed. The Court's reason for granting the writ is revealing:[178]

> We conclude that we have jurisdiction to issue the writ as prayed. And we think that—unless the sovereign immunity has been waived—the case is one of such public importance and exceptional character as to call for the exercise of our discretion to issue the writ rather than to relegate the Republic of Peru to the circuit court of appeals, from which it might be necessary to bring the case to this Court again by certiorari. The case involves the dignity and rights of a friendly sovereign state, claims against which are normally presented and settled in the course of the conduct of foreign affairs by the President and by the Department of State. When the Secretary elects, as he may and as he appears to have done in this case, to settle claims against the vessel by diplomatic negotiations between the two countries rather than by continued litigation in the courts, it is of public importance that the action of the political arm of the government taken within its appropriate sphere be promptly recognized, and that the delay and inconvenience of a prolonged litigation be avoided by prompt termination of the proceedings in the district court.

The Court continued this theme in its decision on the merits of the case. It emphasized that its own power in foreign policy issues was secondary: "Our national interest will be better served in such cases if the wrongs to suitors, involving our relations with a friendly

---

[176]See 318 U.S. at 581–82.

[177]*Id.* at 585–88.

[178]*Id.* at 586–87.

foreign power, are righted through diplomatic negotiations rather than by the compulsions of judicial proceedings."[179]

Thus foreign policy cases appear to be appropriate candidates for certiorari before judgment. Effective foreign policy may require a pronouncement from the Supreme Court as the representative of the judicial branch of government, a branch that has taken on itself the right to review most of the decisions of the other two branches. And as the *Peru* litigation indicates, it is important that the judicial branch remove itself from foreign policy as quickly and as authoritatively as possible. Moreover, as we have suggested before, subjecting foreign states to the court of appeals may be seen as affirmatively harmful. The foreign states may feel that continued litigation in the lower courts is demeaning. Also, they may not understand that the legal system could subject them at various points to conflicting orders.

3. *Institutional authority cases.* The last subcategory of "imperative public importance" cases raises the Court's institutional authority. Theorists of judicial review sometimes speak of the Court's prestige or political capital as a limited resource that should be saved for those cases that require it.[180] In the institutional authority cases, this special power is needed to stand up to a challenge to the federal courts or the laws of the nation from someone who will not be effectively bound by the lower courts.[181]

The most obvious instances where this authority is needed are cases where a party to be bound is the president. If a president is suggesting, as in *Nixon*, that he may not be subject to the judicial power of the United States,[182] it will take the political prestige of the Supreme Court to make enforcement possible. This may be true even when the Court or the judiciary is not the direct target of presidential action. In the *Steel Seizure* case,[183] it was apparent

[179]*Id.* at 589.

[180]"As some have suggested, the Court has or perceives itself as having, a limited amount of 'political capital'." Stone, Seidman, Sunstein, & Tushnet, Constitutional Law 68 (1986). See also, e.g., Dahl, Decision-Making in a Democracy: The Supreme Court as a National Policy-Maker, 1959 J. Pub. L. 279, 280 ("much of the legitimacy of the Court's decisions rests upon the fiction that it is not a political institution but exclusively a legal one"); Choper, Judicial Review and the National Political Process (1981).

[181]Obviously, the Court's expenditure of its political capital is not limited to certiorari before judgment cases. See, *e.g.*, United States v. New York Times, 403 U.S. 713 (1971).

[182]See Final Days at 264, 272–78. *Cf.* Henkin, Executive Privilege: Mr. Nixon Loses But the Presidency Largely Prevails, 22 UCLA L. Rev. 40, 45 (1974).

[183]An attack on judicial and executive authority from a source other than the President

(as in *Nixon*) that an appellate court opinion would have little effect on a determined president.

The difficulty with using the writ in these circumstances is that it requires judicial statesmanship of the most delicate kind. The Court must protect the republic and its own judicial power against unwarranted encroachments. And yet it must not spend its political capital too freely. But when the authority of the federal courts or the federal government is under public attack, the Court may have little choice but to act forcefully. Even so, there is a final problem: in some cases, a dramatic response by the Court may be counter-productive. By taking seriously an unprincipled attack on the Court's authority, the Court may seem to legitimize the challenge.[184]

4. *Important cases where the Court has not granted certiorari before judgment: state cases.* Apparently there is an additional limit on imperative public importance cases that the Court itself recognizes, though this limit is difficult to justify. The Court has not granted certiorari before judgment when the issue was the legality of state government action. *Cooper v. Aaron*[185] and *Anderson v. Celebreeze* are dramatic examples of denials of certiorari in important state cases. *Cooper* involved the desegregation of the Arkansas schools, an action that was vehemently opposed by the state and its governor.[186] *An-*

---

explains the grant of certiorari before judgment in United States v. United Mine Workers, 330 U.S. 25 (1946). There it was a union that was defying judicial authority, a restraining order. And it was clear that the defiance would continue until the Supreme Court itself spoke. Given the threat to the president's authority to continue wage controls and the lower court's inability to ensure that the law was enforced, the Court probably considered quick action to be necessary.

The case grew out of a strike by the United Mine Workers (UMW) led by John L. Lewis against the coal industry, which was then being run by the Department of Interior under a post–World War II executive order. Exec. Order. No. 9728, 11 Fed. Reg. 5593 (1946). Lewis notified the Department that their contract was terminated and the UMW struck. Lewis and the UMW ignored a restraining order and were found guilty of both criminal and civil contempt. 330 U.S. at 269. After the defendants appealed, the government filed a petition for certiorari before judgment, which was granted. *Id.* at 708. The defendants' subsequent applications for certiorari before judgment were also granted. *Id.* at 709–10 (1946).

[184]Cooper v. Aaron, 358 U.S. 1 (1958), cert. before judgment denied *sub nom.* Aaron v. Cooper, 357 U.S. 566 (1958). See note 239. See also United States v. Nixon, 418 U.S. 683 (1974).

[185]See generally The Supreme Court, The 1958 Term, 73 Harv. L. Rev. 163 (1959); Note, 37 N.C. L. Rev. 177 (1959).

[186]In Cooper v. Aaron, the Court delivered a short per curiam opinion denying an application for certiorari before judgment. 357 U.S. at 567. The district court had entered an order authorizing the suspension for two and a half years of a plan of integration for the Little Rock schools. Although the Supreme Court recognized the need for promptness, it

derson, which we have discussed, involved the constitutionality of denying a third party candidate his place on the ballot.

Obviously, both of these cases raised serious national concerns. In *Cooper* Governor Orville Faubus was publicly challenging the power of the federal courts to integrate Arkansas schools. As in the *Nixon* and *Steel Seizure* cases, it appeared likely that the full prestige of the Supreme Court would be necessary to enforce the law. In *Anderson*, not only did the underlying issue involve a presidential election, but also (as we have seen) the case could not have been effectively resolved by a stay. In denying the writ in these and other cases involving state government action, perhaps the Court is trying to establish an absolute rule to promote certainty and to limit expenditures of its political capital. As laudible as these desires may be, it would still be unwise to adopt a rule categorically excluding early certiorari for institutional authority cases involving state government action. As *Cooper v. Aaron* illustrates, cases challenging the Court's authority may transcend state boundaries.[187]

Within the class of imperative public importance, then, there are three subcategories. The first is constitutional cases that complement the direct appeal statute. The second is foreign policy cases. And the last is institutional authority cases. Other important cases

---

noted that the court of appeals had previously considered the plan of integration three times and saw no reason that it would not handle the case properly and promptly: "We have no doubt that the court of appeals will recognize the vital importance of the time element in this litigation, and that it will act upon the application for a stay or the appeal in ample time to permit arrangements to be made for the next school year." *Ibid.* Of course, the Court implied that this is a case in which an opinion of the court of appeals will suffice, an implication that is notably absent from some of the other cases.

The later history of the *Cooper* case does not bear out the Supreme Court's professed faith in the court of appeals. The Eighth Circuit Court of Appeals convened a special session on August 4, 1958, heard the case, and on August 18, 1958, reversed the district court decision. 257 F.2d 33 (1958). Three days after a prompt decision ordering integration was rendered by the court of appeals, however, it stayed its mandate "to permit the School Board to petition [the Supreme] Court for certiorari." The Supreme Court had to act quickly, if arrangements were to be made before the beginning of the next school year. 358 U.S. at 14. The Supreme Court came back in special session to grant certiorari, 358 U.S. 29 (1958), to hear the case, and to decide it only three days before school was scheduled to begin on September 15, 1958. 358 U.S. at 4–5. The case was argued on September 11, 1958, and decided with a short per curiam decision on the next day. 358 U.S. at 5.

[187]In *Cooper*, it is a close question whether the Court's denial of certiorari before judgment was appropriate. Certainly the attack on Supreme Court authority by Governor Faubus was one of the most serious in our nation's history. On the other hand, the Supreme Court may have been attempting to minimize the legitimacy of the state's position by consigning the state to the court of appeals and thus treating the challenge as routine legal business.

are not likely to gain review unless there is something special about their procedural posture that would bring them within the other categories discussed in the following sections.

B. CONSOLIDATION WITH ANOTHER CASE ALREADY BEFORE THE SUPREME COURT

1. *Overview.* The text of Supreme Court Rule 18 recognizes only one class of certiorari before judgment, the "imperative public importance" case. But the writ is more often granted to consolidate a case with another case pending before the Court. The Rule's failure to note this category is strange. First, two of the cases cited in the Rule are actually examples of consolidation, rather than imperative public importance.[188] Second, two other consolidation cases involve the Court taking the unusual step of inviting the litigants to file a petition for certiorari before judgment.[189] Thus, the Court has not only tolerated, but encouraged consolidation cases. Yet Rule 18 does not mention this class.

The consolidation cases arise where the legal issues are identical or similar to those raised by a case already pending before the Court.[190] When we call this category consolidation cases, we are using the term loosely. Sometimes the cases are formally consolidated for briefing, hearing, and decision in the Supreme Court. Other times they are kept formally separate, yet heard at the same time and decided on the same day in separate opinions. More rarely, they are heard at roughly the same time and decided in separate opinions, a week or two apart.

The Court first granted early certiorari for consolidation in 1925 in *Hicks v. Merchantile Trust Company.*[191] *Hicks* foreshadowed the

---

[188]Rickert Rice Mills v. Fontenot, 297 U.S. 110 (1936), decided with United States v. Butler, 297 U.S. 1 (1936); United States v. Bankers Trust Co., decided with and reported *sub nom.* Norman v. Baltimore & Ohio Ry Co. 294 U.S. 240 (1935).

[189]United States v. Thomas, 362 U.S. 58, 361 U.S. 950 (1960), decided with United v. Raines, 362 U.S. 17 (1960); Bolling v. Sharpe, 347 U.S. 497 (1954), decided with Brown v. Board of Education, 347 U.S. 483 (1954).

[190]In some cases, the litigants in the two actions are exactly the same. Either the parties originally filed two concurrent lawsuits or one lawsuit has been severed into bifurcated appeals. See, *e.g.*, Gions v. Railway Executive Assoc., 455 U.S. 999 (1982); Republican National Committee v. Federal Election Commission, 445 U.S. 965 (1980), The New Haven Inclusion Cases, 399 U.S. 392 (1970).

[191]Another early case granting certiorari before judgment is Royal Insurance Co. v. United

Court's later approach in consolidation cases. Usually the Court has not commented on the grant of certiorari before judgment, except occasionally to note the pendency of the related litigation.[192] Often, as in *Hicks*, the extra case does not appear to have benefited the Court's final decision. Sometimes, though, the extra case has helped the pending appeal in some way—and it is around these cases that we build our rationale in this category.

Because practice manuals mention the category of similar cases, many litigants think that a similarity of issues is enough. Indeed, consolidation is the most common reason that litigants seek certiorari before judgment. Yet examining the consolidation cases more closely reveals two patterns beyond a mere similarity of issues. In all grants for consolidation, one or both of two factors were present. First, at least one party in the case where certiorari before judgment was sought was identical to at least one party in the similar case already before the Court (or were officers of the same government). Or second, two or more similar cases were already before the Court.

Neither situation suggests a compelling reason to bypass the intermediate court. The first factor—a partial identity of parties— might be based on concerns for the litigant's convenience. Perhaps the Supreme Court has accepted the questionable notion that, if it is already hearing one of a litigant's cases, it should hear the other.[193] The second factor—the pendency of more than one case—suggests that it may be less taxing to the Court to add a third or fourth case than it is to add a second.[194] If neither of these two factors is present, the chances are slim that the Court will grant early certiorari for consolidation. Even if one of these two factors is present, certiorari

States Shipping Board Fleet Corp., 280 U.S. 320 (1930), an admiralty case that raised a question similar to three other cases already before the court: "whether the Suits in Admiralty Act excludes the remedy invoked by the plaintiffs." 280 U.S. at 325. The Court held that it did, without discussing its grant of certiorari before judgment.

[192]See Taylor v. McElroy, 360 U.S. 709, 710 (1959), noting pendency of Greene v. McElroy, 360 U.S. 474 (1959); Porter v. Dicken, 328 U.S. 252 (1946), noting pendency of Porter v. Lee, 328 U.S. 246 (1946). "[Certiorari was granted] by reason of the close relationship of the important question raised to the question presented in *Porter v. Lee.*" Porter v. Dicken, 328 U.S. 252, 254 (1946).

[193]This may appeal to one's sense of fairness, but usually the other case can be stayed and later decided by a court of appeals. The administrative savings accrue to the litigants and the court of appeals and not the Supreme Court.

[194]Undoubtedly, it is less taxing to add another case once the Court is already in a "multiple-decision making mode." But the same concerns are brought into play. What good reason is there for taking the case?

before judgment is far from certain. What additional criteria the Court uses are not clear.

One matter is clear. Many of the drawbacks of early certiorari in imperative public importance cases are lessened in consolidation cases—but then so are the benefits. The first harm that is reduced is that of a rushed decision. The Court is not really using the writ to expedite the deliberation of the legal issues, because there is another pending case that the Court would have to decide anyway. And indeed, consolidation cases are decided at a more leisurely pace than imperative public importance cases. On average, consolidation cases take more than five months from the grant of certiorari to decision, while public importance cases take less than two months.[195] Second, there is less risk that the Court will unnecessarily spend its political capital. The case is not singled out for its importance, nor is the case being brought up by itself. The public pressure on the Court is not appreciably increased since, once again, the issue would be decided anyway in the pending related case. Third, since another case is already before the Court, in most instances, there will be an appellate court opinion to help the Court in its deliberations. Admittedly, this will not always be true. Sometimes the pending case is before the Court on direct appeal;[196] even here, however, there are two cases before the Court on the same issue and thus two lower court opinions for guidance.

The disadvantages of expedited review in consolidation cases are thus minimized. As we shall see, docket control problems still persist. But it can be fairly stated that, while the policies favoring the writ in consolidation cases may not be as pressing, neither are the concerns that oppose the writ.

2. *Cases that do not benefit the pending litigation.* As *Hicks* illustrates, sometimes certiorari before judgment for consolidation does not help the Court resolve the issue raised in the already pending case. Rather, consolidation is simply a way to dispose of the additional case seeking certiorari. In these circumstances, granting the writ is not appropriate.

---

[195] The mean number of days from grant of certiorari before judgment to argument is 46 days in all cases, 32 in public importance cases, and 72 in consolidation cases. From argument to decision, it is 52 days in all cases, 26 days in public importance cases, and 62 days in consolidation cases. From the grant or argument to decision, whichever is longer, it is 108 days in all cases, 59 days in public importance cases, and 159 days in consolidation cases.

[196] The New Haven Inclusion Cases, 399 U.S. 392 (1970).

Of the fifteen consolidation cases, no fewer than ten fit within this subcategory.[197] Typical of these cases is *Eastern Equities v. United States*,[198] which was consolidated with eight other cases. The Court issued its eventual opinion for all nine cases under the name *Graham and Foster v. Goodcell*,[199] a case brought up after judgment in the circuit court of appeals. The opinion discusses only the facts of the title case, stating that it was "typical of this group of cases."[200] Adding *Eastern Equities* appeared to add nothing to the Court's analysis.

A rationale that may be offered for cases such as *Hicks* or *Eastern Equities* is that granting the writ promotes judicial efficiency. First, the Supreme Court can avoid a duplication of effort by simultaneously hearing and deciding several cases raising the same or similar issues. Second, the court of appeals is saved from the needless exercise of deciding an issue when a definitive ruling by the Supreme Court in the similar case will become the governing principle. But even if efficiency in the court of appeals has some value, this savings could be gained without certiorari before judgment. The court of appeals could simply stay its hand until the Supreme Court decides the similar case.

This efficiency rationale makes less sense here than in cases of public importance. Any administrative savings accrues entirely to the benefit of the court of appeals, which is relieved of the obligation to decide the particular case. The burden falls on the Supreme Court, both to decide the case itself and to review the additional petitions that other litigants may bring under this rationale. This undercuts the policy basis of certiorari, which is designed to reduce

---

[197]*E.g.*, Belgarde v. Squamish Indian Tribe, reported *sub nom.* Oliphant v. Squamish Indian Tribe, 435 U.S. 191 (1978); Hannah v. Slawson, reported *sub nom.* Hannah v. Larche, 363 U.S. 420 (1960); United States v. Thomas, 362 U.S. 58 (1960); Kinsella v. Krueger, 352 U.S. 487 (1956), rev'd on rehearing *sub nom.* Reid v. Covert, 354 U.S. 1 (1957); United States v. Bankers Trust Co., reported *sub nom.* Norman v. Baltimore & Ohio Ry Co. 294 U.S. 249 (1935); Eastern Equities Corp. v. United States, reported *sub nom.* Graham & Foster v. Goodcell, 282 U.S. 409 (1931); Royal Ins. Co. Ltd. v. U.S. Shipping Board Merchant Fleet Corp., reported *sub nom.* Johnson v. U.S. Shipping Board Emergency Fleet Corp., 280 U.S. 320 (1931); and Hicks v. Merchantile Trust Co., reported *sub nom.* White v. Mechanics Securities Corp., 269 U.S. 283 (1925).

[198]282 U.S. 409 (1931).

[199]282 U.S. 409 (1931), affirming, 35 Fed.2d 586 (9th Cir. 1930). See generally Note, 5 Tul. L. Rev. 654 (1931).

[200]282 U.S. at 414.

the Supreme Court's docket.[201] Where judicial efficiency is concerned, the crucial question is not whether granting early certiorari will promote overall efficiency, but whether granting early certiorari will reduce the workload of the Supreme Court. Here it does not.

Efficiency aside, a second rationale that may be offered in consolidation cases is fairness to litigants, that is, allowing a party to "have his day in court." It appeals to one's sense of fairness to let a litigant go before the Court that will decide the legal issues raised by his case. Many petitions for certiorari before judgment raise this argument. In *Keller v. Mixon*,[202] for example, the state of Florida unsuccessfully argued that it had "an obligation to its citizens to request a hearing by this Court so that its arguments and conclusions may be presented prior to this Court reaching a decision which will bind the State of Florida."[203] The petitioners in *Hawaiian Telephone Company v. Hawaii Department of Labor*[204] argued that the Court should grant certiorari because "organized labor, as well as the

---

[201]One close case for certiorari before judgment arises when the purpose is to consolidate on appeal cases that were consolidated in the trial court. An example is Hannah v. Larche and Hannah v. Slawson, 363 U.S. 420 (1960). Combined pre-trial proceedings were heard by a single district court judge. Because the *Larche* complaint attacked the constitutionality of the Civil Rights Act, a three-judge court was convened to hear the matter. The two cases continued to be heard together, however, since the single judge assigned to *Slawson* was also a member of the three-judge panel assigned to *Larche*. The district court held for the plaintiffs in both cases on the grounds that Congress had not authorized the Commission to adopt the rules in question. The Commission appealed, but was faced with different appellate requirements in the two cases.

The Commission had a direct appeal to the Supreme Court in the three-judge case (*Larche*) but only an appeal to the court of appeals in the single-judge case (*Slawson*). To consolidate the cases, the Commission therefore sought certiorari before judgment in *Slawson*. The Court granted the petition.

Slawson is a sympathetic case for early certiorari. It was brought and tried with *Larche* and raised the identical issue on appeal. A refusal to consolidate the case might force the litigants to go through the tedious and potentially inconsistent process of bifurcated appeals. But of course, the court of appeals could stay its hand to wait for the Supreme Court. To avoid inconsistent results, the grant of certiorari before judgment in such a case may be appropriate. But see Gross v. National Association of Securities Dealers, cert. denied, 419 U.S. 843 (1974) (denying certiorari before judgment on somewhat similar facts).

Where lower courts are working at cross purposes—issuing inconsistent rulings and refusing to stay their own proceedings—the Supreme Court may want to grant early certiorari for consolidation. The New Haven Inclusion Cases, 399 U.S. 392, 418 (1970), may be an example of such a grant.

[202]Cert. denied, 419 U.S. 880 (1974).

[203]Petition for Certiorari at 8, cert. denied, Keller v. Nixon, 419 U.S. 880 (1974).

[204]Cert. denied, 435 U.S. 943 (1978).

Chamber of Commerce of the United States, would be afforded an opportunity to participate as parties in the resolution of these important issues."[205] The Supreme Court again denied certiorari. A slightly more sympathetic petition, where the Court nevertheless denied certiorari, was *California Department of Human Resources v. Crow*.[206] There the petitioner argued that the other case already before the Court had been rushed through the lower courts in an attempt to thwart the petitioner from receiving Supreme Court review.

The Court was clearly correct in denying certiorari before judgment in *Crow* and these other cases. Not every litigant has a right to a Supreme Court hearing. The advocates for the Judges' Bill explicitly recognized that a Supreme Court hearing would rarely be granted, and then primarily when the case was important to the public, rather than to the litigants.[207] Moreover, the judicial system assumes (perhaps naively) that legal issues are adequately presented and that the law will be decided uniformly by the Supreme Court regardless of the identity of the parties or the quality of their presentation. But more important, where the litigants do not fully brief and argue the legal issues, the Court itself may request additional briefing, dismiss certiorari as improvidently granted, or conduct its own research. Finally, those seeking access to the deliberations may request leave to file as an amicus curiae. Fairness does not require being a party to a Supreme Court case.

Since neither administrative efficiency nor fairness justify consolidation by certiorari before judgment, the harsh conclusion is that the writ should not be granted when it serves no benefit to the pending litigation.

---

[205] Joint Petition for Certiorari at 12, cert. denied, Hawaiian Telephone Co. v. Hawaii Dep't of Labor, 435 U.S. 943.

[206] Petition for Certiorari, California Dep't of Human Resources Development v. Crow, 408 U.S. 924 (1972).

[207] In Congressional debates on the 1925 Judges' Bill, Senator Cummins, a proponent of the bill, stated: "It will be remembered that any case that reaches the circuit court of appeals has already been tried in the district court of the United States, and when it is decided by the circuit court of appeals the litigant has had a second trial in the circuit court of appeals. These courts of appeals, as you all know, are composed of from three to five judges; and it is believed, I think, by most people who have examined the subject that when a litigant has had an opportunity to try his case in two courts, one of them being a court of appeals composed of lawyers of the highest standing and ability in the country, any further appeal or review of the case ought to be in the discretion of the Supreme Court of the United States, and not a matter of right with the litigant." 66 Cong. Rec. 2752 (1925).

3. *Cases of inadequate benefit to the pending litigation.* It is obviously more justifiable to grant certiorari where the additional case would aid the Court in the case already pending before the Court. But this rationale, too, is not free from difficulty. One problem is practical. To gain consolidation, a petitioner must argue that his case raises issues identical or similar to those in a pending case. Yet if the case is really the same, then why should the Supreme Court take it? So a petitioner must also argue that his case adds something to the pending case. This puts the litigant in the anomalous position of arguing that his case is both the same as the case already before the Court and yet significantly different from it.

Litigants must also tread lightly in suggesting that the Court should look at several variations of the same issue at once. What they suggest is contrary to the implications of case-by-case adjudication.[208] It is primarily a legislative function to consider simultaneously the various factual applications of a particular rule of law.[209] Courts resolve particular disputes presented to them by litigants.[210] Litigants misapprehend the Court's role if they think that

---

[208]See, *e.g.*, Levi, An Introduction to Legal Reasoning (1949); Weiler, Two Models of Judicial Decision-Making, 46 Canadian B. Rev. 406, 410–16 (1968); Hart & Sacks, The Legal Process: Basic Problems in the Making and Application of Law 139 (tentative ed. 1958): "While the statute and the decisional doctrine may operate in similar or even identical fashion in particular cases, however, they have a different form and a different basis of authority and these differences may make for important differences in effect over a period of time and in special situations. The statute owes its authority to the settling power of the legislature, which gave that particular set of words the force of law. The decisional doctrine finds its justification as an original matter in the power and obligation of the court to decide the case which announced it on reasoned grounds fairly reflective of general community understanding."

We do not mean to be too doctrinaire. After all, the primary role of the Supreme Court is to declare the law, not to resolve particular disputes. Yet it still decides real cases. And there are benefits to incremental decision making.

[209]The Court "makes law" in a different sense than a legislature makes law: "To the extent that the court assigns generalized grounds for its decision and to the extent that those ground[s] are respected in the disposition of similar controversies thereafter, the determination will serve also to guide the future. In some cases 'law' will have been 'made.' " Hart & Sacks, *id.* at 185. Professor Levi has argued that "what a court says is dicta" and that a decision is the result of a case based on its facts, and little else. Levi, An Introduction to Legal Reasoning 6. Levi has also stated that a legislature may have many different, even conflicting, examples in mind: "Matters are not decided until they have to be. For a legislature perhaps the pressures are such that a bill has to be passed dealing with a certain subject. The precise effect of the bill is not something upon which the members have to reach agreement. If the legislature were a court, it would not decide the precise effect until a specific fact situation arose demanding an answer." *Id.* at 30.

[210]See, *e.g.*, Gordon, 'Administrative' Tribunals and the Courts, 193 L. Q. Rev. 94, 100 (1933); Weiler, note 208 *supra*, at 410–16.

that it must resolve all applications of a particular rule of law while deciding one case. More important, however, it is seldom necessary to take on an additional case just to resolve an already existing one.

Nonetheless, petitioners have argued that their cases complemented a case already before the Court:

> (*a*) by providing better facts or a better court record,[211]

> (*b*) by raising new issues,[212]

> (*c*) by placing "all major facets of the question . . . before the Court,"[213] or

> (*d*) by allowing the "[c]onsideration of the full implications of the question, rather than the piecemeal and incomplete adjudication [otherwise] possible."[214]

These and similar assertions[215] are suspect. All principally argue that the pending case may not be the best vehicle for deciding the legal issues. Even if this were so, the litigants in the case already before the Court could easily present these additional factors to the Court by using hypotheticals or simply referring to the other cases. Appellate argument, in short, is adequate to make the Court aware of the implications and breadth of the legal principles sought. The

---

[211]See Petition for Certiorari at 3, cert. denied, Shields v. Franklin, 423 U.S. 1037 (1975) (better record); Petition for Certiorari at 13, cert. denied, Radio Tel. News Directors Ass'n v. United States, 390 U.S. 922 (1968) (same); Petition for Certiorari at 19, cert. denied, California Dep't of Human Resources Development v. Crow, 408 U.S. 924 (1972) (record not "sparse and incomplete"); Petition for Certiorari at 2, Taylor v. McElroy, 360 U.S. 709 (1959), 358 U.S. 918 (1958) (a record that amplifies and illuminates the issues); Petition for Certiorari at 7, cert. denied, Liberty Mutual Ins. Co. v. Wetzel, 429 U.S. 1000 (1976) ("a factual context of sufficient breadth to resolve the critical commonplace issues"); Petition for Certiorari at 2, Taylor v. McElroy, 360 U.S. 709 (1959), 358 U.S. 918 (1958) ("a broader factual basis").

[212]Petition for Certiorari at 6, cert. denied, Taylor v. Roberts, 423 U.S. 878 (1975).

[213]Petition for Certiorari at 13, cert. denied, Radio Tel. News Directors Ass'n v. United States, 390 U.S. 922 (1968).

[214]Petition for Certiorari at 11, cert. denied, Tidee Products, Inc. v. NLRB, 417 U.S. 921 (1974).

[215]Others have asserted that a second case will benefit the pending litigation: Petition for Certiorari at 19, cert. denied, Coe v. Califano, 431 U.S. 953 (1977) (additional party); Petition for Certiorari at 17, cert. denied, California Highway Comm. v. LaRaza Unida, 409 U.S. 890 (1972) (revealing "ramifications"); Petition for Certiorari at 7, Liberty Mutual Ins. Co. v. Wetzel, 429 U.S. 1000 (1976) (better for clarifying the law); Petition for Certiorari at 8, Ferguson v. United States, 408 U.S. 915 (1972) (better defined and documented).

Court need not have a particular context on its docket to know it exists.

Although these contentions of petitioners are weak, the Court endorsed them in *McCulloch v. Sociedad Nacional*.[216] There the Court said it was taking a second case because it put the issues in a "better perspective" than a pending case.[217]

Sociedad Nacional challenged the jurisdiction of the National Labor Relations Board over the maritime operations of foreign ships employing alien seamen.[218] The Labor Board had held that its jurisdiction extended to a Honduran vessel. This determination was attacked in two separate proceedings. In the case where certiorari before judgment was sought, a Honduran union representing the alien seaman brought an action in the District of Columbia against the board members of the NLRB. The petitioners sought to consolidate their action with one from a New York district court brought by the ship's owner against the Regional Director of the NLRB.

Announcing that the District of Columbia case "presents the question in better perspective, [the Supreme Court chose] it as the vehicle for the adjudication on the merits."[219] The Court promptly decided both cases under the name of the District of Columbia case. This is the only instance where it has assigned top billing to the case brought before it by certiorari before judgment when that case and a pending one were decided in a combined opinion.

Nonetheless, *Sociedad Nacional* is not really a "better perspective" case. The Court proceeded as it did because there were jurisdictional issues that may have barred a review of the decision on the merits in the New York case. These were not present in the District of Columbia case. Certiorari before judgment was used, in effect, to avoid this jurisdictional problem.

Using certiorari before judgment to avoid legitimate issues of federal jurisdiction seems a dubious proposition. Perhaps *Sociedad Nacional* is explicable as an "imperative public importance" case, since it involved foreign policy. There are some indications in the

---

[216]372 U.S. 10 (1963). See generally, Note, 1963 Duke L.J. 578 (1963); Note, 32 Ford. L. Rev. 167 (1963); The Supreme Court, The 1962 Term, 77 Harv. L. Rev. 183 (1963).

[217]372 U.S. at 16.

[218]*Id.* at 10–11.

[219]*Id.* at 16.

opinion that would support this theory.[220] For present purposes, however, it is enough that the case does not stand as a general proposition in favor of granting certiorari before judgment simply to provide the Court with better facts on which to decide a case.

4. *Cases that benefit the pending litigation: a second case provides something missing from the first.* Some situations do merit certiorari before judgment for consolidation. But they do not reflect the rationales presented in the petitions of the litigants. Rather, in rare cases early certiorari is needed to give adequate relief to the litigants in the case already before the Court. Here the underlying facts or law affects the litigants already before the Court in an important way not raised in the pending case. Early certiorari is granted, not to help the petitioners, but to give relief to the other litigants.

A good example of this is *Rickert Rice Mills v. Fontenot.*[221] The Court brought up *Rickert* to decide it along with similar cases already before the Supreme Court, eventually decided under the title *United States v. Butler.*[222] Butler challenged the constitutionality of the Agricultural Adjustment Act of 1933.[223] In 1935, after the Butler case was filed, Congress amended the Agricultural Adjustment Act in an attempt to remove some of the alleged defects of the 1933 Act.[224] Since the controversy in *Butler* was not mooted by the 1935 amendments, *Butler* remained justiciable. But if the *Butler* taxpayers prevailed on the unconstitutionality of the 1933 Act, their right to relief could not be resolved until the effect of the 1935 amendment was decided.

Rickert challenged both the 1933 Act and its 1935 amendment. Thus, considering the *Rickert* case along with the *Butler* case ensured that the litigant in Butler would have his rights fully adjudicated. The *Butler* decision preceded the *Rickert* decision by one week. The *Butler* case covered eighty-eight pages in the U.S. Reports—the *Rickert* case, just four. The only case cited in *Rickert* is *Butler* and the extent of the *Rickert* holding is that the 1935 Amendment does not cure the infirmities of the 1933 Act.[225]

---

[220]See 372 U.S. at 17, 19, and 21.

[221]297 U.S. 110.

[222]297 U.S. 1 (1936).

[223]48 Stat. 31 (1933).

[224]49 Stat. 750 (1935).

[225]297 U.S. at 113.

Another example of this use of certiorari before judgment is *Porter v. Dicken*.[226] The issue pending before the Court in *Porter v. Lee*[227] was whether under the Emergency Price Control Act a federal district court had jurisdiction to enjoin a landlord from evicting a tenant in a state court proceeding.[228] *Dicken* raised a complementary issue whether, even if there was jurisdiction under the Price Control Act, the anti-injunction statute still prohibited a federal court from enjoining a state eviction proceeding. In its decision, the Court held that neither the Price Control Act nor the anti-injunction statute prevented injunctive relief.

The advantage in hearing the cases together is obvious. If *Lee* had been heard by itself, the litigants would still not know whether an injunction could issue. Certiorari before judgment was necessary to give complete relief.

The second type of case appropriate for consolidation is illustrated by *Bolling v. Sharpe*.[229] There, certiorari before judgment was used less to aid the litigants than to aid the Court. *Bolling*,[230] a companion case to *Brown v. Board of Education*,[231] held that the desegregation requirements applicable to the states under the Fourteenth Amendment also applied to the District of Columbia under the Fifth Amendment.[232]

Bolling is notable in several respects. First, the Court took judicial notice of the case and took the unprecedented step of inviting the litigants to petition for early certiorari.[233] Second, unlike the usual

---

[226]328 U.S. 252 (1946).

[227]328 U.S. 246 (1946).

[228]*Id.* at 247–52.

[229]347 U.S. 497 (1954).

[230]Bolling v. Sharpe, 347 U.S. 497 (1954).

[231]347 U.S. 483.

[232]347 U.S. at 498–500.

[233]See *Brown*, 344 U.S. at 3. *Brown* was continued on the docket during the 1952 term so that Bolling could be heard with it. 344 U.S. at 3. Justice Douglas dissented from the postponement to wait for *Bolling*. 344 U.S. at 3.

Since *Bolling* the Court has actively sought certiorari before judgment in two cases, United States v. Thomas, 362 U.S. 58 (1960), 361 U.S. 950 (1960) (inviting a petition for certiorari before judgment), and Barefoot v. Estelle, 459 U.S. 1169 (1983) (treating a request for a stay as a petition for certiorari before judgment).

In some respects, cases heard on the Court's own motion might be said to form their own eclectic category. Obviously, it is not a category of interest to litigants, since by definition

consolidation case, resolving the major issue in the pending case would not have direct precedential effect on the *Bolling* litigation. A holding that the Fourteenth Amendment required the states to integrate their schools did not necessarily imply that the Fifth Amendment imposed similar obligations on the United States. Third, although it involved an obvious question of public importance, *Bolling* is not properly understood as a public importance case. If *Brown* had not been before the Court, certiorari before judgment in *Bolling* would not have been granted.[234] It was the pendency of *Brown* that made an early resolution of Bolling critical. Had the cases not been consolidated an embarrassing anomaly could have resulted.

If the Court had decided *Brown* without *Bolling*, it would have opened itself up to a serious political attack, forcing the states to integrate while leaving the District of Columbia alone. By hearing the cases together, the Court both protected itself and helped legitimize its decision in *Brown*. In any event, the unique circumstances in *Bolling* should give little hope to petitioners in other cases. *Brown* has few if any parallels.

Consolidation cases comprise the largest class of certiorari before judgment cases. Moreover, most recent petitions raise consolidation as a reason for seeking certiorari before judgment. Perhaps enunciating a more limited rule for consolidation would reduce the petitions requesting the writ. Even if the Court continues to grant certiorari before judgment on more expansive grounds than suggested here, it should openly state what it is doing and why. Such a clarification would at least make it easier for litigants to argue sensibly. Now they are in the difficult position of arguing that their cases are both the same as another case before the court and yet significantly different from it.

C. CASES THAT HAVE PREVIOUSLY BEEN BEFORE THE COURT

A third category of cases where certiorari before judgment has been granted are those that are coming before the Court a second time. As with consolidation cases, many of the disadvantages associated with certiorari before judgment are absent when a case is heard a second time. A hasty decision is not a danger since pre-

---

litigants have no part in the Court's certiorari decision. Nevertheless, the Court should not deviate from normal appellate processes without a good reason.

[234]344 U.S. at 3.

sumably the Court has reviewed the issue before and is not rushing to judgment. Likewise, since the case has already been before the Court, it has already sifted through the factual and legal issues. A lower court opinion is less help to the Court than it would be if the case had not already been before the Court.

The mere absence of strong countervailing considerations, however, does not justify granting the writ. The Court needs a good reason to deviate from normal appellate processes. One such rationale is efficiency, a policy dramatically demonstrated in *Fetters v. United States.*[235] The *Fetters* litigation came before the Court a first time when a federal marshal sought certiorari to review a court of appeals decision ordering the discharge of a prisoner. While the case was pending, however, the marshal left office without a substitution taking place. The Court granted certiorari and immediately vacated the judgment, remanding with directions to dismiss the proceeding on the gorund that there was no remaining respondent to the habeas petition.[236] Subsequently, the defendant surrendered himself to a new marshal and reinstituted habeas corpus proceedings. The district court, holding itself bound by the first decision of the court of appeals, ordered discharge. The marshal then sought certiorari bypassing the court of appeals. His petition was granted.[237]

The reasons for the grant in *Fetters* are not hard to discern. The only difference between the first case and the second was the identity of the federal marshal. Since the court of appeals had already issued its judgment in the first case, a second decision would be redundant.[238] The Supreme Court already had all the advantages of an intermediate appellate opinion. Similarly, the chance of settling or otherwise mooting the case during litigation before the circuit court was virtually nil. Also, the Supreme Court was familiar with the case, having reviewed it the previous term. In short, nothing would have been gained by returning to the court of appeals. Thus granting the writ was sensible.[239]

---

[235]283 U.S. 638. 812 (1931).

[236]Matheus v. United States, 282 U.S. 802 (1930).

[237]Fetters v. United States, 283 U.S. 812 (1931).

[238]See Robertson & Kirkham, Jurisdiction of the Supreme Court of the United States 235, 625 (1936).

[239]Robertson & Kirkham also suggest that the importance of the issue in *Fetters* may have been part of the Court's decision to grant the writ. *Ibid.* The issue in *Fetters*, however, which

Fetters, however, is undoubtedly a rare case.[240] In almost every other circumstance, there will be at least some value in a hearing before the court of appeals. When this is so, some reason other than judicial efficiency in the court of appeals should be required for granting the writ.

One such additional concern is reflected in the cases—certiorari implementing the Court's previous decisions. This can arise where the Court has issued a decision and the lower courts have been either dilatory or wrong in applying the Supreme Court mandate.

When the Court grants certiorari before judgment here, it has an important purpose. It is assuring that the lower courts enforce its mandates correctly. When a lower court refuses to follow Supreme Court decisions or delays in doing so, the authority of the Supreme Court itself is tested.[241] The appellate system is not designed merely to channel errors upward on appeal.[242] It also allows the central control of lower courts from the top down and the authoritative pronouncement of legal rules. Certiorari before judgment to implement the Court's earlier decisions promotes these last functions in a hierarchical system.

It may appear that this argument goes too far. The Court's authority is in question every time lower courts do not properly apply *stare decisis*. But the obligation to follow precedent is less clear. Courts can distinguish earlier cases.[243] When the Court has spoken in a particular case, however, its interest in having its decision properly carried out is particularly strong—far more so than when the effect of its decision is limited simply to *stare decisis*.

---

was the scope of judicial inquiry in a removal proceeding, probably does not meet the standard of public importance discussed earlier.

[240]The only other case where the Court apparently granted early certiorari under this theory is Piedmont & Northern Ry. v. ICC, 286 U.S. 299 (1932). At issue in that case was the authority of the ICC to require a certificate for an extension of two railway lines by the railroad. On first appearance before the Court, it held that the district court had no jurisdiction, because of the technical manner in which the ICC order was framed. 280 U.S. 469 (1930). After this defect was cured, the case was brought before the Court on certiorari before judgment, and the Court then reached the merits.

[241]The supervisory aspects of Supreme Court review are noted directly in Sup. Ct. Rule 17, "Considerations governing review of Certiorari."

[242]See Block, Stump v. Sparkman and the History of Judicial Immunity, 1980 Duke L.J. 879, 882, 884–85; Hellman, Error Correction, Lawmaking, and the Supreme Court's Exercise of Discretionary Review, 44 U. Pitt. L. Rev. 795 (1983).

[243]Levi, An Introduction to Legal Reasoning (1949).

Since delay in implementing the Court's mandate may as successfully undercut it as error or defiance, unusual delay may also justify the grant of certiorari before judgment. An example is *Insurance Group v. Denver & Rio Grande Western Railroad.*[244] Here, the Interstate Commerce Commission began hearings on a plan of railroad reorganization in 1941. Over two years later a plan was approved by the district court. After another three years of litigation the Supreme Court affirmed the district court decision and reversed the Court of Appeals decision.[245] The debtor then began a new round of litigation, boldly arguing that the original circumstances had so changed that the original plan was obsolete. After the Court of Appeals stayed the district court's proceedings to consummate the plan, the Supreme Court granted certiorari before judgment in the Court of Appeals.[246] The Court gave the following reason for granting certiorari: "the importance of the questions raised to the efficient administration of railroad reorganizations under the Bankruptcy Act."[247]

Shortening litigation is not by itself enough to justify the writ. The policy here is the implementation of Supreme Court decisions, not time concerns alone. Thus, in *Peters v. Clark*,[248] for example, the Supreme Court denied early certiorari despite lower court delay.[249] There the Fifth Circuit had heard arguments over the validity

---

[244]329 U.S. 607 (1947). See also St. Louis, Kansas City & Colo. R.R. v. Wabash R.R., 217 U.S. 247 (1910), discussed at notes 75–79 *supra* and accompanying text.

[245]328 U.S. 495 (1946).

[246]329 U.S. 708 (1946).

[247]329 U.S. at 611. In Smith v. Baker, cert. denied, 409 U.S. 1012 (1972), a case whose facts were somewhat similar to the *Denver Railroad* case, the Court denied certiorari before judgment. Yet the railroad reorganization of the Penn Central Transportation Company and the New York, New Haven and Hartford Railroad Company had begun eleven years earlier and had already been before the Supreme Court in the New Haven Inclusion Cases, 396 U.S. 1056 (1970). While the petitioners asserted that the case should be heard along with another case raising similar issues concerning the railroad reorganization, they also argued that the Supreme Court could "lay finally to rest the controversies which have arisen as to the intention of this Court in the New Haven Inclusion Cases. This alone would permit acceleration of the reorganization process for the New Haven under Section 77 which has now taken more than eleven years." Petition for Certiorari at 10–13, cert. denied, Smith v. Baker, 409 U.S. 1012 (1972). Thus, the petitioners in Smith v. Baker looked to certiorari before judgment to shorten litigation that had already continued for an excessive time.

[248]419 U.S. 1110 (1975).

[249]Although the petitioners dids not explicitly base their unsuccessful petition on the two-and-a-half-year delay, the issue was clearly presented in the petition's recital of the facts.

of a county apportionment scheme on March 20, 1972, but had not rendered a decision by the date of the petition for certiorari, November 19, 1974.

Similarly, in *American Telephone and Telegraph Company v. United States*,[250] a case involving charges that the Bell System had monopolized telecommunications service and equipment markets, AT & T petitioned for certiorari before judgment as an alternative remedy to its motion for certiorari issued by the Supreme Court directly to the district court under the All Writs Act.[251] The petitioners sought a Supreme Court ruling on a jurisdictional question decided by the district court, which if resolved in their favor would eliminate years of complex litigation on the merits. They argued that, because of the size, importance, and slowness of the litigation, the question should be decided immediately. The Supreme Court denied certiorari before judgment.[252]

In sum, the grant of certiorari before judgment is justified for cases that have previously been before the court in two limited circumstances. One, as in *Fetters*, is when there would be little or nothing to gain by a return to the court of appeals. Few, if any, other cases should meet this description. Second, the grant may be appropriate when it is necessary to assist the court in effectively implementing its own decisions. Indeed, this latter circumstance is among the Court's most important uses of the writ.

D. CERTIORARI BEFORE JUDGMENT IN CASES WHERE A DIRECT
   APPEAL IS DISMISSED

In the final category of certiorari before judgment are those cases where a direct appeal to the Supreme Court is dismissed for want of jurisdiction. Typically, the litigant has filed a direct appeal to the Court and requested that, if the appeal is dismissed, certiorari before judgment be granted.[253] This form of alternative filing is

---

Petition for Certiorari, cert. denied, Peters v. Clark, 419 U.S. 1110 (1975). Mandamus to the court of appeals would have also been possible.

[250]429 U.S. 1071 (1977).

[251]See Motion for Leave to File Petition for Certiorari and Petition for Certiorari at 32, cert. denied, American Tel. & Tel. Co. v. United States, 429 U.S. 1071 (1977).

[252]429 U.S. 1071 (1977). The Court also denied a motion for certiorari under the All Writs Act. *Ibid.*

[253]Turner v. Memphis, 369 U.S. 350 (1962).

permissible. A litigant may appeal both to a circuit court of appeals and to the Supreme Court if there is a question whether the Supreme Court has the jurisdiction to hear the case on direct appeal. In such circumstances, the litigant's jurisdictional statement should contain a request that, if the Supreme Court does not have jurisdiction on appeal, it treat the jurisdictional statement as a petition for certiorari before judgment.[254] Alternatively, a jurisdictional statement and a separate petition for certiorari before judgment may be filed.[255] The Supreme Court will then review the jurisdictional statement and do one of four things: (1) note probable jurisdiction and place the case on its docket, (2) postpone decision on the jurisdictional issue until argument on the merits, (3) dismiss the appeal and deny certiorari, or (4) dismiss the appeal, grant certiorari before judgment, and place the case on its docket.

Even without any request by the litigants, the Court may treat a jurisdictional statement or other filing as a petition for certiorari before judgment, so long as an appeal has also been taken to the court of appeals. In several cases the Supreme Court has noted or postponed a decision on probable jurisdiction over a case appealed from a district court, later determining that the district court decision should not be appealed to the Supreme Court. Three times after holding the appeal jurisdictionally deficient, the Court has granted certiorari before judgment.[256] In another case, *New Orleans v. Barthe*,[257] the Court dismissed an appeal, granted certiorari before judgment, and affirmed the lower court's decision per curiam—all without argument in the Supreme Court. In yet another case, *Roe v. Wade*,[258] the Supreme Court noted that certain issues should have been raised by certiorari before judgment instead of direct appeal. But then the Court asserted that it could decide those issues on

---

[254]*E.g.*, Jurisdictional Statement at 4, appeal dismissed and cert. denied, Mason v. Francis, 419 U.S. 1042 (1974).

[255]*E.g.*, Stainback v. Mo Hock Ke Lok Po, 336 U.S. 368 (1949).

[256]St. Louis, Kansas City & Colorado R.R. v. Wabash R.R., 217 U.S. 247 (1910) (on appeal from the now-abolished lower circuit court, not a district court); Turner v. Memphis, 369 U.S. 350; Stainback v. Mo Hock Ke Lok Po, 336 U.S. 368.

[257]376 U.S. 189 (1964). Such a summary affirmance of a lower court's decision has been criticized as unfair and unnecessary when the decision affirmed is that of a court of appeals. Note, Supreme Court Per Curiam Practice: A Critique, 69 Harv. L. Rev. 707, 724 (1956). But here, where it obviates a full appeal in the court of appeals, it is truly suspect.

[258]410 U.S. 113 (1973).

appeal, despite its failure to grant certiorari before judgment.[259] In *NOW v. Idaho*,[260] the Court granted certiorari before judgment while postponing a decison on the jurisdictional issues posed by the appeal—only later to dismiss the case as moot.

The rationale for granting certiorari before judgment in cases of an erroneously taken appeal is again judicial efficiency. Because the case may already be fully briefed and argued, the Supreme Court elects to decide the case rather than send it back to the court of appeals.

In his dissent to the grant of certiorari before judgment in *Stainback v. Mo Hock Ke Lok Po*,[261] Justice Frankfurter attacked the judicial efficiency rationale in wrongly taken appeals:[262]

> I would leave the appeal now pending in the Court of Appeals for the Ninth Circuit to its adjudication there and not grant the petition for certiorari. The power which Congress has given to this Court to short-circuit the Courts of Appeals should not be exercised except for some compelling reason of wise judicial administration. No reason is here present that would not be equally available in almost every case which, even though a constitutional issue may be involved, cannot come here directly, but must first go to a Court of Appeals. Congress decided not to provide for such direct appeals here and we should not exercise our discretionary power to grant what Congress has withheld. This discretionary power should come into play only for those exceptional circumstances for which Congress designed it. . . . By lifting the case out of the Court of Appeals the Court is assuming the burden of canvassing issues not dealt with below. This entails the study of new questions and the task of opinion writing. These are precisely the burdens from which

---

[259]410 U.S. at 123. The clearly better course would have been to grant certiorari before judgment, rather than merely mention the Court's power to grant it. This could have been done on the Court's own motion.

[260]455 U.S. 918, 459 U.S. 809 (1982).

[261]336 U.S. 368 (1949).

[262]*Id.* at 384–86. Frankfurter also cited Justice Hughes's opinion in Layne & Bowler Corp. v. Western Well Works, 261 U.S. 387, 393 (1923), where the Supreme Court dismissed certiorari as improvidently granted after a full hearing and briefing in the Supreme Court because "the existence of a conflict [between circuits] did not survive argument. . . . If it be suggested that as much effort and time as we have given to the consideration of the alleged conflict would have enabled us to dispose of the case before us on the merits, the answer is that it is very important that we be consistent in not granting the writ of certiorari except in cases involving principles the settlement of which is of importance to the public as distinguished from that of the parties, and in cases where there is a real and embarrassing conflict of opinion and authority between the circuit courts of appeal. The present case certainly comes under neither head."

the Court asked to be saved and from which Congress saved
the court by the Judiciary Act of 1925. If the regular course of
proceeding were followed and the matter were to be disposed
of by the Court of Appeals, as it is now being disposed of here,
the necessity for future considerations here might never arise
beyond that involved in finding no reason for granting a petition
for certiorari were one to be applied for. Drains on the Court's
time through jurisdictional misconceptions should be strongly
discouraged. We should follow the honored practice of the Court
in dismissing a proceeding that should not be here ab initio,
even though this Court's time and effort have been expended
after full argument in concluding that a case should never have
been brought here.

Frankfurter's argument is appealing. But there is a subtle difference
here from the efficiency arguments noted earlier. In the other categories of cases, taking the case early would only save resources of
the court of appeals. If the Court grants certiorari after a wrongly
taken appeal, however, the savings goes beyond just the courts of
appeals. Rather, by accepting jurisdiction, the Court is simply assuring that its own work on the case has been productive. Dismissing a case after the Court has expended its own resources may
amount to a waste of the Supreme Court's own time. Any saving
of time in the courts of appeals is purely incidental. Frankfurter is
correct when he says that granting certiorari will mean additional
work for the Court, but not to grant it would mean that the Court
wasted its time in reading the briefs, hearing the arguments, and
deliberating.

Moreover, there is an important consideration besides judicial
efficiency. In cases where there are colorable grounds for appeal,
the policies behind the appeal statute may come into play even if
the case does not technically come within the Court's appellate
jurisdiction. An example of this is *NOW v. Idaho*. That case challenged the constitutionality of a House Joint Resolution extending
the time for ratifying the Equal Rights Amendment. A federal
district court struck down the extension as unconstitutional.[263] Both
NOW and the United States appealed, arguing that the House
resolution was an Act of Congress and therefore that direct appeal
was appropriate under 28 U.S.C.§1252. Both also petitioned for
certiorari before judgment.[264]

---

[263]529 F. Supp. 1107 (D.C. Id.), dismissed as moot, 459 U.S. 809 (1982).
[264]455 U.S. 918 (1982).

Whether a joint resolution, such as the ERA extension, technically falls under §1252 is not clear. But if direct appeal is allowed in cases in which federal statutes are found invalid, it is consistent with that policy to allow direct review in cases like *NOW v. Idaho*. A joint resolution may not be an "Act of Congress," but it is a congressional act. Thus, granting certiorari after wrongly taken appeals may effectuate congressional intent by supplementing a narrowly worded jurisdictional statute.

Certiorari on this basis should not be open-ended. A litigant should not be able to obtain early Supreme Court review by filing a frivolous direct appeal and then asking for certiorari before judgment.[265] A case where there is no colorable claim for appeal need not lead the Court to spend much time on it, nor should a petitioner be able to circumvent jurisdictional requirements so easily. Moreover, the case should generally further the policies of the appeal statute, even if it does not quite fit within the Court's direct appellate jurisdiction.

IV. CONCLUSION

The Supreme Court Rules, like most court rules, are designed to inform litigants about Court procedures and standards and to guide the Court itself in its discretion. Rule 18 does neither. It is obsolete and in fact was grossly inaccurate even when it was first promulgated in 1954. It should be rewritten to reflect the four situations in which the writ is available and the major criteria under each situation along the lines delineated in this article. Certainly, Rule 18 should at least be revised to reflect the Court's actual use of the writ.

---

[265]In this respect, although the *St. Louis Railroad* case foreshadowed this class of early certiorari, it does not fit within the category as delineated. In *St. Louis, Kansas City & Colorado Railroad*, 217 U.S. 247, the claim for direct appeal was frivolous. The case fits much more comfortably in the class of cases that have been before the Court once before.

BERNARD SCHWARTZ

MORE UNPUBLISHED WARREN COURT OPINIONS

After he had read my recent *The Unpublished Opinions of the Warren Court*,[1] former Justice Arthur J. Goldberg told me that I had left out what he considered the most important case in which the original opinion of the Court had been drastically changed by the circulation of a draft dissent. The case, he said, was *Harper v. Virginia Board of Elections*,[2] where his draft dissent had led the Justices to change their original decision to uphold the poll tax.

Justice Goldberg's comment led directly to this article. It contains the draft opinions in three further Warren Court cases, led by *Harper* itself. In all but one of them, the original draft opinion of the Court was replaced by opinions that reached the opposite result. In the *Gunn* case[3] the Court ultimately avoided the constitutional issue—leaving *Gunn* a constitutional landmark *manque* which might have removed the volume of natural speech with political content from all governmental control.

In presenting the draft opinions in this article, I have followed the format of my *Unpublished Opinions* book. The opinions are prefaced by a statement containing a short history of the case, as well as the setting in which the drafts were circulated. After the opinions there is an analysis of what took place after the drafts were sent round to the Justices. As in the book, I try to explain why the drafts were not issued as the final opinions and dissents in the

---

Bernard Schwartz is Webb Professor of Law, New York University School of Law.

[1] Oxford University Press (1985).

[2] 383 U.S. 663 (1963).

[3] Gunn v. University Committee, infra.

different cases. In particular, I try to show what would have happened if the draft opinions had come down as reprinted here. The differences between the draft and final opinions made for a substantial difference in the law in the different fields involved.

The opinions reproduced are all contained in the papers of Justice John Marshall Harlan in the Mudd Manuscript Library, Princeton University.[4] Reference is also made to conference discussions and communications among the Justices. The former are based upon conference notes made available to me upon a confidential basis. Sources for the latter are stated except where they were given to me in confidence. In such cases, I have tried to identify the documents, usually by title and date. I have personally examined every document to which reference is made.

I have not reproduced the unpublished draft opinions and told what happened in the Court in the cases covered in effort to produce a mini-*Brethren*.[5] The purpose is to give students of the Supreme Court further insight into the Court's largely unrevealed decision process. Even Court specialists, who have never been privy to the Court's internal workings, do not fully realize that Court decisions are basically collaborative efforts in which nine individualists must cooperate to achieve the desired result. Before the final opinions are issued, there may be politicking, vote switches and horsetrading to secure them, and ultimately compromises to obtain the necessary working majority. In the process, the quondam opinion of the Court may become the ultimate dissent and vice versa, or the potential constitutional landmark may become a minor footnote in Supreme Court history. It is my hope here, as in my *Unpublished Opinions* book, that the actual operation of the Court's decision process will be made clearer by this account of three cases and their opinions that never came down.[6]

I. Harper v. Virginia Board of Elections: The Poll Tax and Equal Protection

Harper v. Virginia Board of Elections[7] was the case to which Justice Goldberg referred as the most important case in which a

---

[4]I am grateful to the Library for their permission to reproduce these documents.

[5]Woodward and Armstrong, The Brethren: Inside the Supreme Court (1979).

[6]Paraphrasing Hutchinson, note 1 *supra*, jacket.

[7]383 U.S. 663 (1966).

draft dissent had led to a change in the original decision and opinion of the Court. In *Harper* the Warren Court almost handed down a decision upholding the poll tax—a device that made it more difficult for blacks to vote. Indeed, as Justice Goldberg noted in an unpublished draft *Harper* dissent, "the purpose of adoption of the poll tax as a prerequisite to voting was solely and exclusively to restrict voting. The Debates of the Virginia Constitutional Convention . . . make it clear that the principal aim of this limitation was disenfranchisement of the Negroes."[8]

Despite this, the poll tax, as a condition to exercise of the franchise, had been consistently upheld by the courts. The leading case was *Breedlove v. Suttles,*[9] where a poll tax that state law made a condition for voting for federal and state officers was ruled not violative of the Fourteenth Amendment. The Supreme Court reaffirmed its holding in 1951, just two years before Chief Justice Warren was appointed.[10]

The picture was partially changed with the adoption of the Twenty-Fourth Amendment in 1964, which outlawed the poll tax in all federal elections—that is, those in which federal officers are elected. "Upon adoption of the Amendment, of course, no state could condition the federal franchise upon payment of a poll tax."[11]

The Amendment did not specifically affect poll taxes imposed in state elections. Nor was the matter rendered academic by the fact that fewer states had poll tax requirements than had been the case half a century earlier, when eleven Southern states had poll taxes. In 1962, when Congress submitted the Twenty-Fourth Amendment for ratification, payment of a poll tax was still required in five states. By 1965, when *Harper* came before the Court, the number had declined to four—including Virginia, where the *Harper* case arose. Harper had brought an action challenging the $1.50 poll tax that had to be paid as a precondition for voting in Virginia elections. The lower court had dismissed the complaint, deeming itself bound by *Breedlove v. Suttles.*

By 1965, however, when *Harper* was considered by the Supreme Court, the legal justifications for the poll tax had become as outmoded as those used to support property qualifications upon suf-

---

[8]Goldberg draft dissent at 3.

[9]302 U.S. 277 (1937).

[10]Butler v. Thompson, 341 U.S. 937 (1951).

[11]Harman v. Forssenius, 380 U.S. 528, 540 (1965).

frage. According to the Court in *Breedlove v. Suttles*, the validity of
the poll tax is not affected by the fact that "always there are many
too poor to pay."[12] A state court had gone even further asserting
that failure to pay the poll tax was a moral failing, which had no
relation to the poverty of the would-be voter: "There are none so
poor that they cannot pay their poll-taxes, which for them is 'scot
and lot;' less than two days' hire out of the wages of the common
laborer being sufficient for that purpose. . . . It is not poverty that
creates delinquency, but a want of appreciation of the moral and
political nature of the franchise, which privilege is prized by many
white men, and the mass of the colored, simply because it enables
them to get money by the sale of it."[13]

Such a judicial attitude—reminiscent of the judges' approach not
too long ago to freedom of contract in the relations between employers and employees—now appears wholly anachronistic when
the law is dominated by an all-pervasive notion of equality between
voters. In the Supreme Court's words in a 1964 case on the right
to vote, "Our Constitution leaves no room for classification of people
in a way that unnecessarily abridges this right."[14] A state law that
places a burden upon the person of limited resources that bars him,
in practice, from exercising his right to vote seems to work just
such an abridgement. Nor should the fact that the particular poll
tax is small in amount make a difference. A state that may not
condition the right of appeal by requiring a $3 filing fee[15] should
not be able to impose a comparable condition on the most precious
right of the citizen—that to have a voice in the election of those
who operate the government under which he must live.[16]

But this reasoning did not sway a majority of the Justices when
they gathered in conference in February 1965 to consider the *Harper*
appeal. Although the Chief Justice and Justices Douglas and Goldberg spoke in favor of reversal, the others disagreed. They concluded that, in view of *Breedlove v. Suttles*, the constitutional claim
was so insubstantial that the case should be affirmed without argument by the one-sentence per curiam reprinted below. Several

---

[12]302 U.S. at 281.

[13]Frieszleben v. Shallcross, 19 Atl. 576, 586 (Del. 1890).

[14]Wesberry v. Sanders, 376 U.S. 1, 17–18 (1964).

[15]Smith v. Bennett, 365 U.S. 708 (1961).

[16]Compare Wesberry v. Sanders, 376 U.S. at 17.

of the Justices said that the poll tax issue had lost its importance, since the declining number of poll tax states demonstrated that the poll tax was dying out—especially with its elimination from federal elections by the Twenty-Fourth Amendment.

Soon thereafter, on March 4, 1965, Justice Goldberg, joined by Chief Justice Warren and Justice Douglas, circulated the draft dissent reprinted below. The draft states that, if the case had come up on a petition for certiorari, it might be appropriate to dispose of the matter summarily as described. Since this was an appeal, however, the majority decision was necessarily a determination on the merits that poll taxes were constitutional, even when "imposed upon citizens too poor to pay them."

The Goldberg draft stresses the cases since *Breedlove v. Suttles*, particularly those decided by the Warren Court, in which the Constitution was used to ensure both racial equality and equality between rich and poor. Justice Goldberg notes particularly those cases involving voting rights. He asserts that no reasonable state interest can be served by barring from voting citizens "who lack the requisite funds. . . . there can be no equal protection of the laws where a man's vote depends on the amount of money he has." If the Constitution means anything, "it means that with respect to the fundamental right to vote, a reverse means test cannot be applied."

The draft dissent concludes with a ringing affirmation: "A government is far less likely to mistreat any group of citizens and far more likely to respond to their needs when it is ultimately responsible to them through the ballot box. A government 'of the people' and 'by the people' is likely to be 'for the people' . . . If the poor man is to be accorded his equal right to vote, which the Constitution guarantees, Virginia's poll tax cannot stand."

SUPREME COURT OF THE UNITED STATES

HARPER et al. *v.* VIRGINIA STATE BOARD OF ELECTIONS et al.

APPEAL FROM THE UNITED STATES DISTRICT COURT FOR THE EASTERN DISTRICT OF VIRGINIA.

No. 835. Decided March —, 1965.

PER CURIAM.

The motion to affirm is granted and the judgment is affirmed.

MR. JUSTICE GOLDBERG, with whom THE CHIEF JUSTICE and MR. JUSTICE DOUGLAS join, dissenting.

The Court today affirms the judgment of a three-judge District Court. —— F. Supp. ——, holding constitutional the provisions of Virginia law (Va. Const., § 18; Va. Code, 1952, §§ 24–17, 24–22, 24–67, 24–120), which require the payment of poll taxes as a prerequisite to voting in state and local elections. This affirmance, although summary, constitutes a holding by this Court that such poll taxes imposed upon citizens too poor to pay them are constitutional.[1] With all deference, I dissent from this holding.

---

[1] If this were a petition for certiorari, the granting of which "is not a matter of right, but of sound judicial discretion, and will be granted only where there are special and important reasons therefor," Supreme Court Rules, 38, and the denial of which would "not remotely imply approval or disapproval" of the decision below, *Maryland v. Baltimore Radio Show*, 338 U. S. 912, 919 (opinion of Mr. Justice Frankfurter), the facts that there are now only four states which employ a poll tax as a prerequisite for voting, that, it might appear that the use of a poll tax in this fashion is dying out, and that the Twenty-Fourth Amendment has eliminated the use of the poll tax as a requirement for federal elections, would be appropriately considered in determining whether or not certiorari should be granted. However, this is an appeal, which by statute (28 U. S. C. §§ 1253, 2101 (b), we must and do determine on the merits. Whatever, may

It is undisputed that appellants, and other persons similarly impecunious, possess all of the other state qualifications for voting including residence requirements and that they desire to vote. They are precluded from voting solely because they do not have the means to pay the poll tax.

In *Reynolds* v. *Sims*, 377 U. S. 533, 554–555, we stated, "Undeniably the Constitution of the United States protects the right of all qualified citizens to vote, in state as well as federal elections. . . . The right to vote freely for the candidate of one's choice is the essence of a democratic society, and any restrictions on that right strike at the heart of representative government."

In *Baker* v. *Carr*, 369 U. S. 186; *Gray* v. *Sanders*, 372 U. S. 368; *Reynolds* v. *Sims, supra,* and our recent decision of *Carrington* v. *Rash,* —— U. S. ——, we held that the Equal Protection Clause of the Fourteenth Amendment prohibits a State from invidiously discriminating against a class of citizens in denying or diluting this constitutional right.

Gray v. *Sanders, supra,* at 379, plainly stated that discrimination between otherwise eligible voters based upon income is invidious. "Once the geographical unit for which a representative is to be chosen is designated, all who participate in the election are to have an equal vote— whatever their race, whatever their sex, whatever their occupation, whatever their *income* and wherever their home may be in that geographical unit. This is required by the Equal Protection Clause of the Fourteenth Amendment." (Emphasis added.)

In *Carrington* v. *Rash, supra,* decided this Term, we held unconstitutional a provision of the Texas Constitution which prohibited from voting in state and federal elections servicemen who had acquired bona fide residences. Such a provision, we declared imposed "an in-

have been my decision as to whether or not certiorari should be granted on this issue, since this case is an appeal, I am compelled to face up to the substantial constitutional issue presented.

vidious discrimination in violation of the Fourteenth Amendment," *id.*, at ——, because the provision was not reasonably related to a legitimate state purpose.

The State does not seek to justify the poll tax in this case on the ground that it is a revenue-producing measure. Indeed, the Virginia Supreme Court of Appeals has recognized that "the imposition [of the poll tax] was not intended primarily for the production of revenue." *Campbell v. Goode*, 172 Va. 463, 466, 25 S. E. 456, 457. The Attorney General of Virginia has stated in testimony before a Committee of Congress that, although in form a head tax on all citizens, it has never been enforced that way, no attempt is made to collect the tax from those who do not vote, and it is used solely as a requirement for voting.[*] Hearings before the Subcommittee No. 5 of the House Committee on the Judiciary on Amendments to Abolish Tax and Property Qualifications for Electors in Federal Elections, 87th Cong., 2d Sess., 98 (hereinafter cited as Hearings). Moreover, as the House Committee on the Judiciary recognized, there are available to the State alternative methods of producing revenue which do not operate to deprive poor people of their basic and fundamental right to vote.

Nor does the State seek to dispute the unassailable fact that the purpose of adoption of the poll tax as a prerequisite for voting was solely and exclusively to restrict voting. The Debates of the Virginia Constitutionl Convention of 1902, 2947–3080, make this absolutely clear and do not contain even a hint of any other State purpose. The Debates also make it clear that the principle aim of this limitation was the disenfranchisement of the Negroes. See Debates, *supra*, at 2978–2981, 2989–2998, 2999–3011.

---

[*] By law assessments cannot even be made until the annual tax is three years in arrears. See *Campbell v. Goode, supra.* The non-enforcement of the poll tax except as a means of restricting voting is apparently the general practice in the poll tax states. See Ogden, The Poll Tax in the South, 59–76 (1958).

3047, 3070–3080.[3] This was clearly and frankly expressed in the Debates by the sponsor of the suffrage provisions, the Honorable Carter Glass:

> "Discrimination! Why that is exactly what we propose; that, exactly, was what this Convention was elected for—to discriminate to the very extremity of permissible action under the limitations of the Federal Constitution." Debates, *supra,* at 3076.

In addition to the primary desire to disenfranchise the Negro, the debates indicate that a motivating force in the adoption of the poll tax was the desire to disenfranchise poor white persons as well as Negroes.[4] An exhaustive study by one commentator has explained this desire in Virginia, as well as the other States which adopted the poll tax in the period from 1890 to 1910, as a reaction to the rise of the Populist movement. See Ogden, *supra,* at 20–29.

In practice the poll tax in Virginia and other States has resulted in making it burdensome and difficult for poor white people, as well as Negroes, to vote. See Hearings, *supra,* at 14–22, 49–53; Ogden, *supra,* at 111–177.

---

[3] The only real debate on this point was whether the provisions adopted were sufficient to accomplish the disenfranchisement of the Negro or whether an additional provision requiring the interpretation of the Constitution was necessary. See Debates, *supra,* at 2978–2981, 2989–2998, 2999–3011, 3070–3080. Cf. *Louisiana v. United States.* — U. S. —; *United States v. Mississippi.* — U. S. —.

[4] As one delegate to the Virginia Convention stated:

"The need [to restrict suffrage through a poll tax] is universal, not only in the country, but in the cities and towns; not only among the blacks but among the whites, in order to deliver the State from the burden of illiteracy and poverty and crime, which rests on it as a deadening pall. . . . It is not the negro vote which works the harm, for the negroes are generally Republicans, but it is the depraved and incompetent men of our own race, who have nothing at stake in government, and who are used by designing politicians to accomplish their purpose, irrespective of the welfare of the community." Debates, *supra,* at 2998.

The legitimate State purpose served by the poll tax, Virginia argues, is "to limit the right of suffrage to those who took sufficient interest in the affairs of the State to qualify themselves to vote," *Campbell* v. *Goode, supra,* at 466, 25 S. E., at 457, by paying what the State considers to be the small amount required.[5] See Hearings, at 76. With respect to the identical contention, the Committee on the Judiciary of the House of Representatives, in reporting out the Twenty-Fourth Amendment, said, "While the amount of poll tax now required to be paid in the several State is small and imposes only a slight economical obstacle for any citizen who desires to qualify in order to vote, nevertheless, it is significant that the voting in poll tax states is relatively low as compared to the overall population which would be eligible. . . . [T]he historical analysis . . . indicates that where the poll tax

---

[5] While the State argues that the amount of the tax is small, neither the lower court in this case, nor the decision of this Court in *Breedlove* v. *Suttles*, 302 U. S. 277, on which the lower court relied, rested on this ground. The principle asserted by the lower court would seem to apply even if the amount were greater. Moreover, it is undisputed that appellants here were financially incapable of paying the tax. Finally, I cannot agree that the amount is small. The $1.50 annual poll tax is cumulative with the right to register and vote expressly conditioned upon payment of all poll taxes for the past three years, with a 5% penalty for late payment. As with one appellant here, where there are two otherwise qualified voters in the household, the poll tax payments would amount to $9.48. This Virginia pattern would appear to be typical of the States that have poll taxes. Alabama's poll tax is $1.50 annually, Ala. Code, Tit. 15, § 237 (1958), cumulative for two years, Ala. Const., Amend. 96; Mississippi's varies from $2 to $3 annually, Miss. Code Ann. § 9751 (1943), and is cumulative for two years, *id.*, at § 3235; and Texas' poll tax is $1.50 annually, Vernon's Tex. Rev. Civ. Stat. Art. 2.01 (1964 Cum. Supp.), and is apparently not cumulative, *id.*, at Art. 5102. Moreover, Virginia law provides that it is unlawful for one to pay the poll tax of another unless the beneficiary is a member of the payor's household or closely related to him. Va. Code § 24–129.

has been abandoned . . . voter participation increased."
H. R. Rep. No. 182, 87th Cong., 2d Sess., p. 3.[6]

Testimony before a Committee of Congress by Virginia's own witnesses tends to show that there is no substantial connection between payment of the poll tax and interest in the affairs of the State. Lieutenant Governor Mills E. Godwin, Jr., of Virginia, testified that of those who had paid their poll tax and were otherwise qualified to vote approximately 500,000 or 40% did not vote in the 1960 election. Hearings, at 77.

Conversely, as this very case demonstrates, appellants and others similarly situated ardently desire to vote but are precluded by their economic circumstances from paying the poll tax. The sole income of one of appellants is derived from federal social security benefits. Another appellant has not regular income, is not gainfully employed, and is dependent upon her children for support. A third appellant has a wife and nine children and his entire income is consumed in providing for their necessities of life. The District Court gave express recognition to "[t]he plaintiffs' impoverishment and eligibility to vote" except for their poverty. —— F. Supp. ——.

It was established in the various hearings on this subject before Committees of Congress that in Virginia and other States which impose poll taxes as a prerequisite for voting there are many persons like appellants who are otherwise qualified to vote, but like them are ineligible solely because they are poor. See Hearings, at 14–22, 49–53; Christensen, the Constitutionality of Anti-Poll Tax Bills, 33 Minn. L. Rev. 212, 228, and n. 60 (1949). This class of persons includes those without any economic

---

[6] The Committee also expressly noted that the then "five States which still require payment of a poll tax were among the seven States with the lowest voter participation in the 1960 Presidential election." *Ibid.* At the time of this report Alabama, Arkansas, Mississippi, Texas and Virginia had poll taxes. Since that date Arkansas has repealed the poll tax as a prerequisite for voting. See Ark. Const., Amend. 51; note 2, *infra.*

means whatsoever and who are dependent for subsistence
on relatives, friends, and in many instances public welfare or private charity. It likewise includes many employed in low-paying jobs, others who may be unem-
ployed, and still others who have minimal incomes in
the form of social security benefits, retirement pensions,
unemployment compensation, medical disability payments, and the like.[7] Yet it cannot be assumed that all
these people who cannot afford to pay the poll tax lack
political capacity nor are they exempt from the obligations and burdens of citizenship such as military service.[8]
The evidence before Congress as well as other statistical
and polling studies (see Ogden, *supra,* at 111–177) points
to the conclusion that precisely this class of persons substantially accounts for the increase in voting, noted by
the House Committee, when poll tax barriers are removed
and that the poll tax requirements prevent large groups
of such persons—white and Negro—from voting. In
view of the facts that substantial numbers of those who
pay the poll tax do not vote and that substantial numbers
of those who cannot afford to pay the poll tax qualify and

---

[7] The Federal Census for 1960 revealed that 27.9% of all families
in Virginia have annual incomes below $3,000, the amount which is
generally recognized as the boundary of poverty for a family of four.
Annual Report of the Council of Economic Advisors to the President
58 (1964). Furthermore 17.4% of all Virginia families have an
income even below $2,000. United States Department of Commerce,
Bureau of the Census, 1960 Census of Population, Supplementary
Report, P. C. (S 1)–43.

It can easily be seen that as to a family of four with an income
of $2,000 or less, the $3 annual poll tax for two voters is at least one-
half the family's entire daily allowance for subsistence, and the accum-
ulated tax and penalties which for the three years amounts to almost
$10 is at least almost twice the family's daily allowance. See also
Hearings, *supra,* at 49–50.

[8] Although it is not so argued, if the theory of the poll tax is that
only taxpayers should vote, there is little reason to limit the vote to
those who pay the poll tax, for every consumer today pays at least
hiddent taxes when he buys goods.

vote when poll tax barriers are removed. this justification advanced by Virginia cannot be accepted.[9]

The only other contention advanced is that administrative convenience is served by the poll tax in that the tax constitutes a method of identification and proof of residence.   However. the 46 States which do not have poll taxes find no administrative difficulty in administering their electoral processes and enforcing valid residence, identification and similar requirements by other legally nondiscriminatory means.   In dealing with an analogous contention concerning administrative convenience to the State as a justification for discrimination against a class of voters, we said in *Carrington*, "States may not casually deprive a class of citizens of the vote because of some remote administrative benefit to the State." *supra*, at ——. As we held in *Carrington*, even purported residence qualifications must be reasonable and must be finely tailored so as to test residence and not exclude persons who are legitimate residents.

Furthermore it is clear that the poll tax does not purport to nor does it serve as a trustworthy test of continuing residence.   The tax is accompanied by no declaration of prior residence or intent to remain.   The Virginia Constitution (§§ 18. 20. 21) and statutes (Va. Code § 24–17) provide for residence and the payment of poll tax as separate and distinct qualifications for voting. Virginia. like the 46 States that do not employ poll taxes to restrict voting. provides that election officials may challenge electors as to their residency and require an oath as well as proof of residency.   See Va. Code §§ 24–253, 24–254 (1950).   Payment of the tax must be made six months before an election; yet the date of the election

---

[9] It is obvious that the modern trend, by eliminating cumbersome paper ballots, increasing the number of polling places and extending the hours they are open, adopting permanent registration, etc., as well as by the elimination of the poll tax, is designed to encourage interest in public affairs precisely by removing barriers and impediments to voting.

is the determinative date for residence under Virginia law. Va. Code § 24–17 (1950). Obviously paying a poll tax, which can even be mailed in, see Hearings, *supra*, at 81, six months before the date in question does not show residence on the date in question. For these reasons it must be concluded that no reasonable state interest is served by barring from voting those citizens who desire to vote but who lack the requisite funds.

In applying the Equal Protection Clause to the administration of criminal justice, this Court said, "Providing equal justice for poor and rich, weak and powerful alike . . . is the central aim of our entire judicial system." *Griffin* v. *Illinois*, 351 U. S. 12, 16–17. Providing an equal vote for poor and rich, weak and powerful alike, should be the "central aim" of our voting system. Cf. *Carrington* v. *Rash*, *supra*, at ——, where we stated that the right to vote is a matter "close to the core of our constitutional system." Just as "there can be no equal justice where the kind of trial a man gets depends on the amount of money he has," *Griffin* v. *Illinois*, *supra*, at 16–17, so in voting cases, there can be no equal protection of the laws where a man's vote "depends on the amount of money he has."

The application of these principles obviously does not mean that Government—State or Federal—must equalize all economic inequalities among citizens. Nor does it mean that the Government cannot impose burdens or exactions which by reason of economic circumstances fall more heavily upon some than others. Nor however desirable it may be as a matter of social and legislative policy, does it require the State affirmatively to provide relief for all the incidents of poverty. The Constitution does not command absolute equality in all areas. It does mean, however, that a State may not frustrate or burden the exercise of the basic and precious right to vote by imposing substantial obstacles upon that exercise by a class of citizens not justified by any legitimate state interest. In particular it means that with respect to the fundamen-

tal right to vote, a reverse means test cannot be applied.
A classification based upon financial means embodied in a
voting statute is inherently not "reasonable in light
of . . . [the statute's] purpose." *McLaughlin* v. *Florida,*
— U. S. —.

Nor does my view of this case mean that the States do
not have "unquestioned power to impose reasonable residence restrictions" and "to establish, on a nondiscriminatory basis, and in accordance with the Constitution, other
qualifications for the exercise of the franchise. *Carrington* v. *Rash, supra,* at —. It does mean, however, that
qualifications for voting, which the State establishes, and
which they are authorized to establish under Art. I, § 2
of the United States Constitution are, as our cases hold,
limited by other provisions of the Constitution, such as
the Equal Protection Clause. *Carrington* v. *Rash, supra.*

The fact that historically property qualifications and
poll taxes were imposed in some of the States does not
immunize these statutes from constitutional condemnation. Much of this history is before the Fourteenth
Amendment, and in any event we must consider voting
rights in light of their full development, their "present
place in American life throughout the nation," cf.
Brown v. *Board of Education,* 347 U. S. 483, 492–493, and
our present conception of the meaning and application of
the Equal Protection Clause. See *Baker* v. *Carr, supra;
Reynolds* v. *Sims, supra; Gray* v. *Sanders, supra;
Carrington* v. *Rash, supra.* See also Christensen, *op. cit.
supra,* at 232.

Breedlove v. *Suttles,* 302 U. S. 277, relied upon by the
District Court, is in my view not controlling. The *Breedlove* case did not deal with the question of whether persons may be discriminated against on economic grounds
in their voting rights; in fact they did not claim that they
could not afford to pay the tax. The challenge to the poll
tax statute in *Breedlove* under the Equal Protection
Clause was solely on the ground that its exemptions in

favor of women, older persons, and minors resulted in an unreasonable classification to the disadvantage of those persons not exempt. The Court in *Breedlove* therefore did not rule directly on the question facing us.[10] Moreover, *Breedlove* was decided long before our recent decisions applying the Equal Protection Clause of the Fourteenth Amendment in the voting area so as to make it clear that the effect of the Fourteenth Amendment is to nullify invidious discrimination in the polling booth.

Finally, nothing in the language or history of the Twenty-Fourth Amendment, which was an affirmative effort to eliminate the poll tax in federal elections, even suggests that in so doing, Congress and the state legislatures attempted impliedly to repeal the operation of the Fourteenth Amendment in this fundamental area. In fact the long history of the Twenty-Fourth Amendment leads to just the opposite conclusion. The Hearings before a Committee of Congress. Hearings. *supra*. at 29–43, contain a long history of bills that had been introduced to abolish the poll tax in both state and federal elections by legislation based upon effectuation of the Fourteenth and Fifteenth Amendments. The fact that the measure was finally passed as a constitutional amendment applicable to federal elections shows, at best, that the passage of this Amendment in this manner was a compromise necessary at this time to get some progress in this area. Finally, the history of the inter-relationship of the Fourteenth and Fifteenth Amendments in the area of voting rights, shows that these constitutional Amendments are to be read together and not as implied repudiations of each other. See *Nixon v. Herndon*, 273 U. S. 536; *Louisiana v. United States*, — U. S. —; *United States v. Mississippi*, — U. S. —; *Davis v. Schnell*, 336 U. S. 933, affirming. 51 F. Supp. 872 (D. C. S. D. Ala.).

---

[10] *Butler v. Thompson*, 341 U. S. 937, was a summary affirmance without argument, presumably on the supposed authority of *Breedlove v. Suttles*, *supra*.

In *Wesberry* v. *Sanders*, 376 U. S. 1, 17–18, the Court said, "No right is more precious in a free country than that of having a voice in the election of those who make the laws under which, as good citizens, we must live. Other rights even the most basic, are illusory if the right to vote is undermined. Our Constitution leaves no room for classification of people in a way that unnecessarily abridges this right."

Our cases have recognized that the fundamental right of voting is the cornerstone of a citizen's rights. It is through the ballot box that the citizen can exert his power to make his representatives responsive to his needs and desires. A government is far less likely to mistreat any group of citizens and far more likely to respond to their needs when it is ultimately responsible to them through the ballot box. A government "of the people" and "by the people" is likely to be "for the people."

Benjamin Franklin deemed it necessary that the Government should fairly and equally represent the entire electorate, since "the *all* of one man is as dear to him as the *all* of another . . . the poor man has an *equal* right but the *more* need to have representatives in the legislature than the rich one." [11]

If the poor man is to be accorded his equal right to vote, which the Constitution guarantees, Virginia's poll tax cannot stand.

---

[11] Harris, The Quest For Equality, 14 (1960), quoting 10 The Writings of Benjamin Franklin 59–60, 130–131 (Smythe ed. 1910).

The Goldberg draft dissent in *Harper* was never published, but it had a crucial effect. Had it not been written, *Harper* would have been decided in favor of the poll tax under the one-sentence per curiam opinion. That would have meant a break in the equal protection jurisprudence of the Warren Court that might have had a baneful effect. True, the import of the decision would have been more moral than material, in view of the indications that the poll tax was gradually dying out. Still, as the first anti-civil rights decision in the field of voting rights since the accession of Chief Justice Warren, it would, at the least, have signaled a retreat from the "egalitarian revolution" instituted by the *Brown* school segregation case.[17]

The summary affirmance under the one-sentence per curiam did not occur because the Goldberg draft dissent led the Justices to reconsider their vote in *Harper*. After he read the Goldberg draft, Justice Black circulated a March 4, 1965 *Memorandum for the Conference*: "Brother Goldberg's circulation persuades me that our line of decisions since *Breedlove v. Suttles* presents new arguments against the *Breedlove* poll tax holding that call for consideration by the Court after full hearings. For that reason I shall vote against summary decision by a *per curiam* opinion."

At a March 8 conference, the Justices decided against the summary affirmance. With the Chief Justice and Justices Black, Douglas, Brennan, White, and Goldberg voting in favor, the Court voted to hear the *Harper* appeal and set the case for argument during the 1965 Term.

At the January 28, 1966, postargument conference, six voted for the view expressed by Chief Justice Warren: "This was a discrimination against the poor and Negroes as a matter of fact." Justice Black, whose memo had urged reconsideration of the summary affirmance the previous term, and Justices Harlan and Stewart voted the other way.

Justice Goldberg could not recast his draft dissent as the new *Harper* opinion of the Court, for he had resigned from the the Court just after the 1964 Term. The opinion was assigned to Justice Douglas, who announced it on March 24, 1966. The *Harper* opinion as issued followed the approach of Justice Goldberg's draft dissent and categorically struck down the poll tax as violative of equal

---

[17]Brown v. Board of Education, 347 U.S. 483 (1954).

protection. The right to vote, said the Douglas opinion, may no longer have anything to do with "whether the citizen, otherwise qualified to vote, has $1.50 in his pocket"[18]—close to the Goldberg draft statement that "there can be no equal protection of the law when a man's vote 'depends on the amount of money he has.' " Justice Fortas, who had taken the Goldberg seat, had circulated a short concurrence on March 21 that said, "I would emphasize that the Virginia poll tax is an impermissible attempt to impose a charge or penalty on the exercise of a fundamental right." The Goldberg draft had stressed that the right to vote was a "fundamental right." The final *Harper* opinion also characterized the right to vote as "fundamental" and Justice Fortas withdrew his concurrence.

As finally decided, *Harper* was a reaffirmation of the Warren Court's commitment to racial and political equality. It also was one of the first Warren Court decisions articulating the principal that cases involving "fundamental rights" should be scrutinized more strictly than other cases—a principle that was to become of basic importance in the 1969 case of *Shapiro v. Thompson*.[19] None of this would have happened had the Goldberg draft dissent not persuaded the majority of the Court to reconsider their decision to affirm summarily. Had the proposed per curiam opinion been issued as the *Harper* opinion, it would have meant a decision that seemed like a voice from an earlier day. Students of the Court might even today be hard pressed to explain the aberrational return to the pre-Warren Court equal protection jurisprudence.

II. POWELL V. TEXAS: ALCOHOLISM AND ILLNESS

Does the conviction of a chronic alcoholic for a public drunkeness violate the Eighth Amendment's prohibition against cruel and unusual punishment? This question—posed to the Court by *Powell v. Texas*[20]—was answered with a resounding affirmation in Justice Fortas' draft opinion of the Court, reprinted below. That opinion was, however, never delivered for a majority of the Court. Instead, it was ultimately recast as the dissent that Justice Fortas issued for four Justices in the *Powell* case.

---

[18]383 U.S. at 668.

[19]394 U.S. 618 (1969).

[20]392 U.S. 514 (1968).

Powell had been found guilty of violating a law that made appearance in public while drunk an offense. His counsel contended that he was "afflicted with the disease of chronic alcoholism" and his appearance in public while intoxicated was consequently not of his own volition: To penalize him for behavior that he could not control would be to inflict upon him cruel and unusual punishment. The Texas court rejected the defense and Powell appealed to the Supreme Court.

Powell's principal claim in the Supreme Court was that his case came within the protection of the Cruel and Unusual Punishment Clause announced in the 1962 case of *Robinson v. California.*[21] At issue there had been a state statute making it a criminal offense for a person to "be addicted to the use of narcotics." The Court held the statute invalid because it imposed a penalty for "addiction"— a condition that the addict could not control. In the Court's view, addiction must be considered an illness and a state law that punishes a person for being ill inflicts cruel and unusual punishment: "Even one day in prison would be a cruel and unusual punishment for the 'crime' of having a common cold.' "[22]

One may have at least a modest doubt about the cogency of constitutional construction that equates narcotics addiction with the common cold. Even if one agrees that it is beyond governmental power to punish illness as a crime, he may question whether it is proper for a court to strike down a law on the ground that it is conclusively established that narcotics addiction is only an illness that may be contracted irrespective of the will of the individual.

At the original *Robinson* conference on April 20, 1962,[23] Justice Black had led the argument against striking down the statute. Chief Justice Warren had also been doubtful about the Eighth Amendment approach adopted by the majority. Both had, nevertheless, ultimately joined the *Robinson* opinion of the Court. Now, at the March 8, 1968, *Powell* conference, the Chief Justice and Justice Black refused to extend *Robinson* to the public drunkeness law. Both had originally voted against taking the *Powell* appeal (the only members of the Court to vote against noting probable jurisdiction) and now urged affirmance at the *Powell* conference.[24] They argued that

---

[21]370 U.S. 660 (1962).

[22]*Id.* at 667.

[23]See Schwartz, Super Chief: Earl Warren and His Supreme Court 439 (1983).

[24]*Id.* at 693.

the case was different from *Robinson*, because it was not chronic alcoholism, but being drunk in public that was criminal.

The vote at the *Powell* conference went the other way—to reverse Powell's conviction—by a bare majority (composed of Justices Douglas, Brennan, Stewart, White, and Fortas). Justice Douglas, the senior majority Justice, assigned the opinion to Justice Fortas. He circulated the draft opinion of the Court reprinted below on April 23, 1968. The Fortas draft is substantially similar to the dissent that he ultimately issued in the case.[25] The only change of substance was that, in the last sentence, from the draft's "Accordingly, the judgment below is *Reversed*," to the dissent's, "I would reverse the judgment below."[26]

The Fortas draft opinion of the Court was countered by the draft dissent of Justice Black, circulated on April 30, which is also reprinted below. The draft contains stronger language than the *Powell* concurrence that Justice Black ultimately issued,[27] though most of the draft dissent was used in the Black concurrence.

In particular, Justice Black charged in the draft that the then majority had relied upon findings of fact that bore no relation to reality: "The findings of fact so mechanically employed by the Court have no concrete meaning in terms of actual human behavior." The discussion in the Black draft is fuller on this point than that in the final Black concurrence.

The then-decision of the Court, the Black draft urged, was going beyond the proper limits of judicial power—a theme that Justice Black constantly expressed during his last years on the Warren Court. In the very first paragraph of his draft, Justice Black asserts, "The Court thus significantly limits the States in their efforts to deal with a widespread and important social problem, and it does so by announcing a revolutionary doctrine of constitutional law that tightly restricts state power to deal with a wide variety of other harmful conduct."

To Justice Black, the Fortas opinion of the Court was a prime example of the type of judicial approach that Black had criticized since his appointment to the Court: "I will point out in this opinion," the Black draft dissent declares, "that the Court relies on its own notions of the wisdom of this Texas law to erect a constitutional

---

[25]392 U.S. at 554.

[26]*Id.* at 570.

[27]*Id.* at 537.

barrier the desirability of which is far from clear, and that the findings of fact so mechanically employed by the Court have no concrete meaning in terms of actual human behavior and therefore cannot be considered controlling on the constitutional question before us."

SUPREME COURT OF THE UNITED STATES

No. 405.—October Term, 1967.

Leroy Powell, Appellant,	On Appeal From the County
v.	Court at Law No. 1 of
State of Texas.	Travis County, Texas.

[April —, 1968.]

Mr. Justice Fortas delivered the opinion of the Court.

In late December 1966, appellant was arrested and charged with being found in a state of intoxication in a public place. This is a violation of Article 477 of the Texas Penal Code which reads as follows:

"Whoever shall get drunk or be found in a state of intoxication in any public place, or at any private house except his own, shall be fined not exceeding one hundred dollars."

Appellant was tried in the Corporation Court of Austin, Texas. He was found guilty and fined $20. He appealed to the County Court at Law No. 1 of Travis County, Texas, where a trial *de novo* was held. Appellant was defended by counsel who urged that appellant was "afflicted with the disease of chronic alcoholism which has destroyed the power of his will to resist the constant, excessive consumption of alcohol; his appearance in public in that condition is not of his own volition, but a compulsion symptomatic of the disease of chronic alcoholism." Counsel contended that to penalize appellant for public intoxication would be to inflict upon him cruel and unusual punishment, in violation of the Eighth and Fourteenth Amendments to the United States Constitution.

At the trial in the county court, the arresting officer testified that he had observed appellant in the 2000 block

2   POWELL *v.* TEXAS.

of Hamilton Street in Austin; that appellant staggered
when he walked; that his speech was slurred; and that he
smelled strongly of alcohol. He was not loud or boist-
erous; he did not resist arrest; he was cooperative with
the officer.

The defense established that appellant had been convicted of public intoxication approximately 100 times
since 1949, primarily in Travis County, Texas. The circumstances were always the same: the "subject smelled
strongly of alcoholic beverages, staggered when walking,
speech incoherent." At the end of the proceedings, he
would be fined: "down in Bastrop County, it's $25.00
down there and it's $20.00 up here [in Travis County]."
Appellant was usually unable to pay the fines imposed
for these offenses, and therefore usually has been obliged
to work the fines off in jail. The statutory rate for working off such fines in Texas is one day in jail for each $5
of fine unpaid. Texas Code Crim. Proc. Art. 43.09.

Appellant took the stand. He testified that he works
at a tavern shining shoes. He makes about $12 a week
which he uses to buy wine. He has a family, but he
does not contribute to its support. He drinks wine every
day. He gets drunk once a week. When he gets drunk,
he "mostly" goes to sleep, in public places or on the
sidewalk. He does not disturb the peace or interfere
with others.

The defense called as a witness Dr. David Wade, a
Fellow of the American Medical Association and a former
President of the Texas Medical Association. Dr. Wade
is a qualified doctor of medicine, duly certificated in psychiatry. He has been engaged in the practice of psychiatry for more than 20 years. During all of that time
he has been especially interested in the problem of alcoholism. He has treated alcoholics; lectured and written
on the subject; and has observed the work of various
institutions in treating alcoholism. Dr. Wade testified

that he had observed and interviewed the appellant. He said that appellant has a history of excessive drinking dating back to his early years; that appellant drinks only wine and beer; that "he rarely passes a week without going on an alcoholic binge"; that he buys a "fifty cent bottle" of wine, always with the thought that this is all he will drink; but that he ends by drinking all he can buy until he "is passed out in some joint or on the sidewalk." According to Dr. Wade, appellant "has never engaged in any activity that is destructive to society or to anyone except himself." He has never received medical or psychiatric treatment for his drinking problem. He has never been referred to Alcoholics Anonymous, a voluntary association for helping alcoholics, nor has he ever been sent to the State Hospital.

Dr. Wade's conclusion was that "Leroy Powell is an alcoholic and that his alcoholism is in a chronic stage." Although the doctor agreed that the appellant's taking the first drink on any given occasion is "a voluntary exercise of will," he said that "we must take into account" the fact that chronic alcoholics have a "compulsion" to drink which "while not completely overpowering, is . . . an exceedingly strong influence," and that this compulsion is coupled with the "firm belief in their mind that they are going to be able to handle it from now on." In summary, it was Dr. Wade's opinion that appellant "does not have the will power [to resist the constant excessive consumption of alcohol or to avoid appearing in public when intoxicated] nor has he been given medical treatment to enable him to develop this will power."

The trial judge in the county court, sitting without a jury, made the following findings of fact:

"(1) That chronic alcoholism is a disease which destroys the afflicted person's will power to resist the constant, excessive consumption of alcohol.

4   POWELL *v.* TEXAS.

"(2) That a chronic alcoholic does not appear in public by his own volition but under a compulsion symptomatic of the disease of chronic alcoholism.

"(3) That Leroy Powell, defendant herein, is a chronic alcoholic who is afflicted with the disease of chronic alcoholism."

The court then rejected appellant's constitutional defense, entering the following conclusion of law:

"(1) The fact that a person is a chronic alcoholic afflicted with the disease of chronic alcoholism, is not a defense to being charged with the offense of getting drunk or being found in a state of intoxication in any public place under Art. 477 of the Texas Penal Code."

The court found appellant guilty as charged and increased his fine to $50. Appellant did not have the right to appeal further within the Texas judicial system.[1] He filed a jurisdictional statement in this Court. We noted probable jurisdiction. 389 U. S. 810 (1967).

I.

The issue posed in this case is a narrow one. There is no challenge here to the validity of public intoxication statutes in general or to the Texas public intoxication statute in particular. This case does not concern the infliction of punishment upon the "social" drinker—or upon anyone other than a "chronic alcoholic" who as the trier of fact here found cannot "resist the constant, excessive consumption of alcohol." Nor does it relate to any offense other than the crime of public intoxication.

The sole question presented is whether a criminal penalty may be imposed upon a person suffering the disease of "chronic alcoholism" for an action (appearing in public while intoxicated) which is a characteristic part of the

---

[1] See Texas Code Crim. Proc. Art. 4.03.

POWELL v. TEXAS.   5

behavior pattern of the disease and which, the trial court found, was not the consequence of appellant's volition. We must consider whether the Eighth Amendment, made applicable to the States through the Fourteenth Amendment, prohibits the imposition of this penalty in these rather special circumstances as "cruel and unusual punishment." This case does not raise any question as to the right of the police to stop and detain those who are intoxicated in public, whether as a result of the disease or otherwise; or as to the State's power to commit chronic alcoholics for treatment. Nor does it concern the criminal responsibility of an alcoholic for acts other than the mere condition of being intoxicated and appearing in public while in that condition.[2]

II.

As we shall discuss, the Eighth Amendment issue in this case turns upon an understanding of "the disease of chronic alcoholism" with which, as the trial court found, appellant is afflicted, which has destroyed his "will power to resist the constant excessive consumption of alcohol, and which leads him to "appear in public [not] by his own volition but under a compulsion symptomatic of the disease of chronic alcoholism."

Alcoholism is a major problem in the United States.[3] The term has been variously defined. It is used in this opinion in the medical or psychiatric sense of the term to refer to the medical problems recognized by competent authorities. The National Council on Alcoholism has defined the term "alcoholic" as "a person who is power-

---

[2] If an alcoholic should be convicted for other criminal conduct such as driving while intoxicated or assault, which is not a characteristic and involuntary part of the pattern of the disease as it afflicts him, nothing herein would apply to him.

[3] It ranks among the top four public health problems of the country. Block, Alcoholism—Its Facets and Phases (1962).

6   POWELL v. TEXAS.

less to stop drinking and whose drinking seriously alters his normal living pattern." The American Medical Association has defined alcoholics as "those excessive drinkers whose dependence on alcohol has attained such a degree that it shows a noticeable disturbance or interference with their bodily or mental health, their interpersonal relations, and their satisfactory social and economic functioning." [4]

In 1956 the American Medical Association for the first time designated alcoholism as a medical problem and urged that alcoholics be admitted to general hospitals for care.[5] This significant development marked the acceptance among the medical profession of the "disease concept of alcoholism." [6] Today most alcohologists and qualified members of the medical profession recognize the validity of this concept. Recent years have seen an intensification of medical interest in the subject.[7] Medical groups have become active in educating the public, medi-

---

[4] For other common medical definitions of alcoholism, see Keller, Alcoholism: Nature and Extent of the Problem, in Understanding Alcoholism, 315 Ann. Am. Acad. Polit. & Soc. Sc. 1, 2 (1958); Diethelm, Etiology of Chronic Alcoholism 4 (1955); Plaut, Alcohol Problems—A Report to the Nation by the Cooperative Commission on the Study of Alcoholism 39 (1967) (hereafter cited as Plaut); Aspects of Alcoholism 9 (1963) (published by Roche Laboratories); The Treatment of Alcoholism—A Study of Programs and Problems 8 (1967) (published by the Joint Information Service of the American Psychiatric Association and the National Association for Mental Health) (hereafter cited as The Treatment of Alcoholism); 2 Cecil & Loeb, A Textbook of Medicine 1620, 1625 (1959).

[5] American Medical Association: Report of Reference Committee on Medical Education and Hospitals, 162 J. A. M. A. 82 (1956).

[6] See generally Jellinek, The Disease Concept of Alcoholism (1960).

[7] See, e. g., Harrard & Jellinek, Alcoholism Explored (1942); Diethelm, Etiology of Chronic Alcoholism (1955); Ullman, To Know the Difference (1960); Pittman & Snyder, Society, Culture, and Drinking Patterns (1962).

POWELL v. TEXAS.   7

cal schools, and physicians in the etiology, diagnosis, and treatment of alcoholism.[8]

Authorities have recognized that a number of factors may contribute to alcoholism. Some studies have pointed to physiological influences, such as vitamin deficiency, hormone imbalance, abnormal metabolism, and hereditary proclivity. Other researchers have found more convincing a psychological approach, emphasizing early environment and underlying conflicts and tensions. Numerous studies have indicated the influence of sociocultural factors. It has been shown, for example, that the incidence of alcoholism among certain ethnic groups is far higher than among others.[9]

The manifestations of alcoholism are reasonably well identified. The late E. M. Jellinek, an eminent alcohologist, has described five discrete types commonly found among American alcoholics.[10] It is well-established that alcohol may be habituating and "can be physically addicting."[11] It has been said that "The main point for the nonprofessional is that alcoholism is not within the control of the person involved. He is not willfully drinking."[12]

---

[8] See Alcoholism, Public Intoxication and the Law, 2 Col. J. of Law & Soc. Prob. 109, 113 (1966). There is, however, no unanimity of medical opinion on such fundamental questions as the causes of alcoholism, its effects, and the best methods of treatment.

[9] See Alcohol and Alcoholism 24–28. "Although many interesting pieces of evidence have been assembled, it is not yet known why a small percentage of those who use alcohol develop a destructive affinity for it." The Treatment of Alcoholism 9.

[10] See Jellinek, The Disease Concept of Alcoholism 35–41 (1960).

[11] Alcoholism 3 (1963) (published by the Public Health Service of the U. S. Department of Health, Education, and Welfare) (hereafter cited as Alcoholism). See also Bacon, Alcoholics Do Not Drink, in Understanding Alcoholism, 315 Ann. Am. Acad. Polit. & Soc. Sc. 55–64 (1958).

[12] Ullman, To Know the Difference 22 (1960).

8   POWELL *v.* TEXAS.

Although the treatment of alcoholics has been succesful in many cases,[13] physicians have been unable to discover any single treatment method that will invariably produce satisfactory results. A recent study of available treatment facilities concludes as follows:[14]

> "Although numerous kinds of therapy and intervention appear to have been effective with various kinds of problem drinkers, the process of matching patient and treatment method is not yet highly developed. There is an urgent need for continued experimentation, for modifying and improving existing treatment methods, for developing new ones, and for careful well-designed evaluative studies. Most of the facilities that provide services for alcoholics have made little, if any, attempt to determine the effectiveness of the total program or of its components."

Present services for alcoholics include state and general hospitals, separate state alcoholism programs, outpatient clinics, community health centers, general practitioners, and private psychiatric facilities.[15] Self-help organizations, such as Alcoholics Anonymous, also aid in treatment and rehabilitation.[16]

---

[13] In response to the question "can a chronic alcoholic be medically treated and returned to society as a useful citizen?" Dr. Wade testified below as follows:

"We believe that it is possible to treat alcoholics, and we have large numbers of individuals who are now former alcoholics. They themselves would rather say that their condition has been arrested and that they remain alcoholics, that they are simply living a pattern of life, through the help of medicine or whatever source, that enables them to refrain from drinking and enables them to combat the compulsion to drink."

[14] The Treatment of Alcoholism 13.

[15] *Id.*, at 13–26. See also Alcohol and Alcoholism 31–40; Plaut 53–85.

[16] See Ullman, To Know the Difference 173–191 (1960).

POWELL v. TEXAS. 9

Behavior such as public drunkenness is punished as a crime, under a variety of laws and ordinances, in every State of the Union.[17]   The Task Force on Drunkenness of the President's Commission on Law Enforcement and Administration of Justice has reported that "two million arrests in 1965—one of every three arrests in America—were for the offense of public drunkenness." [18]   Drunkenness offenders make up a large percentage of the population in short-term penal institutions.[19]   Their arrest and processing place a tremendous burden upon the police, who are called upon to spend an inordinate amount of time in arresting for public intoxication and in appearing at trials for public intoxication, and upon the entire criminal process.[20]

It is not known how many offenders are chronic alcoholics, but "there is strong evidence that a large number of those who are arrested have a lengthy history of prior drunkenness arrests." [21]   "There are instances of the same person being arrested as many as 40 times in a single year on charges of drunkenness, and every large urban center can point to cases of individuals appearing before the courts on such charges 125, 150, or even 200 times in the course of a somewhat longer period." [22]

---

[17] For the most part these laws and ordinances, like Article 477 of the Texas Penal Code, cover the offense of being "drunk in a public place." Other laws, with which we do not here deal, include the condition that the offender cause a breach of the peace or be guilty of disorderly conduct. See Task Force Report: Drunkenness 1 (1967) (published by The President's Commission on Law Enforcement and Administration of Justice) (hereafter cited as Task Force Report).

[18] Ibid.

[19] See Alcoholism, Public Intoxication and the Law, 2 Col. J. Law. & Soc. Prob. 109, 110 (1966).

[20] See Task Force Report 3–4.

[21] Id., at 1.

[22] Allen, The Borderland of Criminal Justice 8 (1964). It does not, of course, necessarily follow from the frequency of his arrests that a person is a chronic alcoholic.

It is entirely clear that the jailing of chronic alcoholics is punishment. It is not defended as therapeutic, nor is there any basis for claiming that it is therapeutic (or indeed a deterrent). The alcoholic offender is caught in a "revolving door"—leading from arrest on the street through a brief, unprofitable sojourn in jail back to the street and, eventually, another arrest.[23] The jails, overcrowded and put to a use for which they were never intended, have a destructive effect upon alcoholic inmates.[24]

Most commentators, as well as experienced judges,[25] are in agreement that "there is probably no drearier example of the futility of using penal sanctions to solve a psychiatric problem than the enforcement of the laws against drunkenness." [26]

> "If all of this effort, all of this investment of time and money, were producing constructive results, then we might find satisfaction in the situation despite its costs. But the fact is that this activity accomplishes little that is fundamental. No one can seriously suggest that the threat of fines and jail sentences actually deters habitual drunkenness or alcoholic addiction. . . . Nor, despite the heroic efforts being made in a few localities, is there much reason to suppose that any very effective measures of cure and therapy can or will be administered in

---

[23] See Pittman & Gordon, Revolving Door: A Study of the Chronic Police Case Inebriate (1958). See also Pittman, Public Intoxication and the Alcoholic Offender in American Society, Appendix A to Task Force Report.

[24] See, e. g., MacCormick, Correctional Views on Alcohol, Alcoholism, and Crime, 9 Crime and Delinquency 15 (1963).

[25] See, e. g., Murtagh, Arrests for Public Intoxication, 35 Fordham L. Rev. 1 (1966).

[26] Guttmacher & Weirhofen, Psychiatry and the Law 319 (1952).

POWELL *v.* TEXAS. 11

the jails. But the weary process continues to the detriment of the total performance of the law enforcement functions." [27]

III.

These data provide a context for our consideration of the instant case. They do not dictate our conclusion. The questions for us are not settled by reference to medicine or penology. Our task is to determine whether the principles embodied in the Constitution of the United States place any limitations upon the type of conduct for which punishment may be inflicted, and, if so, whether, in the case now before us, those principles preclude the imposition of the penalty.

It is settled that the Federal Constitution places some substantive limitation upon the power of state legislatures to define crimes for which the imposition of punishment is ordered. In *Robinson* v. *California*, 370 U. S. 660 (1962), the Court considered a conviction under a California statute making it a criminal offense for a person to "be addicted to the use of narcotics." At Robinson's trial, it was developed that the defendant had been a user of narcotics. The trial court instructed the jury that "to be addicted to the use of narcotics is said to be a status or condition and not an act. It is a continuing offense and differs from most other offenses in the fact that [it] is chronic rather than acute; that it continues after it is complete and subjects the offender to arrest at any time before he reforms." 370 U. S., at 662–663.

This Court reversed Robinson's conviction on the ground that punishment under the law in question was cruel and unusual, in violation of the Eighth Amendment of the Constitution as applied to the States through

---

[27] Allen, The Borderland of Criminal Justice 8 (1964).

the Fourteenth Amendment. The Court noted that nar-
cotic addiction is considered to be an illness and that
California had recognized it as such. It held that the
State could not make it a crime for a person to be ill.[28]
Although Robinson had been sentenced to only 90 days
in prison for his offense, it was beyond the power of the
State to prescribe such punishment. As MR. JUSTICE
STEWART, speaking for the Court, said: "even one day
in prison would be a cruel and unusual punishment for
the 'crime' of having a common cold." 370 U. S., at 667.

Robinson stands upon a principle which, despite its
subtlety, must be simply stated and respectfully applied
because it is the foundation of individual liberty and the
cornerstone of the relations between a civilized state and
its citizens: Criminal penalties may be inflicted only if
the accused has in fact elected to engage in the activities
defined as an offense. In all probability, Robinson at
some time before his conviction "elected" to take narcotics. But the crime as defined did not punish this
conduct.[29] The statute imposed a penalty for the offense
of "addiction"—a condition which Robinson could not
control. Once Robinson had become an addict, he was
utterly powerless to avoid criminal guilt. He was powerless to choose not to violate the law.

---

[28] "We would forget the teachings of the Eighth Amendment if
we allowed sickness to be made a crime and permitted sick people
to be punished for being sick. This age of enlightenment cannot
tolerate such barbarous action." 370 U. S., at 678 (DOUGLAS, J.,
concurring).

[29] The Court noted in *Robinson* that narcotic addiction "is apparently an illness which may be contracted innocently or involuntarily." 370 U. S., at 667 In the case of alcoholism it is even more
likely that the disease may be innocently contracted, since the drinking of alcoholic beverages is a common activity, generally accepted
in our society, while the purchasing and taking of drugs are crimes.
As in *Robinson*, the State has not argued here that Powell's conviction may be supported by his "voluntary" action in becoming
afflicted.

In the present case, appellant is charged with a crime comprised of two elements—being intoxicated and being found in a public place while drunk. The crime, so defined, differs from that in *Robinson*. The statute covers more than a mere status.[30] But the essential constitutional defect here is the same as in *Robinson*, for in both cases the particular defendant was accused of conduct which he had no capacity to resist. The trial judge sitting as trier of fact found, upon the medical and other relevant testimony, that Powell is a "chronic alcoholic." He defined appellant's "chronic alcoholism" as "a disease which destroys the afflicted person's will power to resist the constant, excessive consumption of alcohol." He also found that "a chronic alcoholic does not appear in public by his own volition but under a compulsion symptomatic of the disease of chronic alcoholism." We read these findings in light of the record to the effect that appellant was under "compulsion," which was "a very strong influence" to take the first drink; that having taken his first drink, he had "an uncontrollable compulsion to drink"; and that, once intoxicated, he could not prevent himself from appearing in public places.

Article 477 of the Texas Penal Code is specifically directed to the accused's presence while in a state of

---

[30] In *Robinson*, we distinguished between punishment for the "status" of addiction and punishment of an "act":

"The statute . . . is not one which punishes a person for the use of narcotics, for their purchase, sale or possession, or for antisocial or disorderly behavior resulting from their administration. It is not a law which even purports to provide or require medical treatment. Rather, we deal with a statute which makes the 'status' of narcotic addiction a criminal offense, for which the offender may be prosecuted 'at any time before he reforms.' California has said that a person can be continuously guilty of this offense, whether or not he has ever used or possessed any narcotics within the state, and whether or not he has been guilty of any antisocial behavior there." 370 U. S., at 666.

14 POWELL *v.* TEXAS.

intoxication, "in any public place, or at any private house except his own." This is the essence of the crime. Ordinarily when the State proves such presence in a state of intoxication, this will be sufficient for conviction, and the punishment prescribed by the State may, of course, be validly imposed. But here the findings of the trial judge call into play the ancient principle of our law that a person may not be punished if the acts essential to constitute the defined crime are not voluntary but are part of the pattern of a disease. This principle, narrow in scope and applicability, is implemented by the Eighth Amendment's prohibition of "cruel and unusual punishment." It is true that the command of the Eighth Amendment and its antecedent provision in the Bill of Rights of 1688 were initially directed to the type and degree of punishment inflicted.[31] But in *Robinson* we recognized that "the principle that would deny power to exact capital punishment for a petty crime would also deny power to punish a person by fine or imprisonment for being sick." 370 U. S., at 676 (MR. JUSTICE DOUGLAS, concurring.[32]

The record in this case, read against the background of the medical and sociological data to which we have referred, compels the conclusion that the infliction upon appellant of a criminal penalty for being intoxicated in a public place would be "cruel and inhuman punishment" within the prohibition of the Eighth Amendment. This

[31] See, *e. g., Trop* v. *Dulles,* 356 U. S. 86 (1958); *Weems* v. *United States,* 217 U. S. 349 (1910). See generally, The Cruel and Unusual Punishment Clause and the Substantive Criminal Law, 79 Harv. L. Rev. 635, 636–645 (1966).

[32] Convictions of chronic alcoholics for violations of public intoxication statutes have been invalidated on Eighth Amendment grounds in two circuits. See *Easter* v. *District of Columbia,* 361 F. 2d 50 (C. A. D. C. Cir. 1966); *Driver* v. *Hinnant,* 356 F. 2d 761 (C. A. 4th Cir. 1966).

POWELL *v.* TEXAS. 15

holding follows because appellant is a "chronic alcoholic" who, according to the trier of fact, cannot resist the "constant excessive consumption of alcohol" and "does not appear in public by his own volition but under a compulsion" which is part of the behavior pattern of his condition.

Accordingly, the judgment below is

Reversed.

SUPREME COURT OF THE UNITED STATES

No. 405.—October Term, 1967.

Leroy Powell, Appellant, *v.* State of Texas.	On Appeal From the County Court at Law No. 1 of Travis County, Texas.

[May —, 1968.]

Mr. Justice Black, dissenting.

The Court today holds that the State of Texas may not impose criminal penalties on persons who appear drunk on the public streets of that State, whenever the trier of fact may find that "the acts essential to constitute the defined crime are not voluntary but are part of the pattern of a disease." *Ante,* p. 14. The Court thus significantly limits the States in their efforts to deal with a widespread and important social problem, and it does so by announcing a revolutionary doctrine of constitutional law that tightly restricts state power to deal with a wide variety of other harmful conduct. I will point out in this opinion that the Court relies on its own notions of the wisdom of this Texas law to erect a constitutional barrier the desirability of which is far from clear, and that the findings of fact so mechanically employed by the Court have no concrete meaning in terms of actual human behavior and therefore cannot be considered controlling on the constitutional question before us. I will also point out why this new rule of constitutional law is not required by *Robinson* v. *California,* 370 U. S. 660 (1962), which held that the status of being a narcotics addict is not punishable. Finally, I will suggest that the "narrow" limits promised by the Court are illusory and that even as limited, the Court's decision will have a sweeping and revolutionary impact on the criminal law.

2   POWELL *v.* TEXAS.

I.

The Court relies on its own notions of the wisdom of this Texas law to erect a constitutional barrier the desirability of which is far from clear. Although the Court disclaims reliance on Part II of its own opinion, *ante,* p. 11, it is clear that the medical and sociological data which fill almost half the Court's opinion do reflect its real concern. The Court stresses that medical authorities consider alcoholism a disease and have urged a variety of medical approaches to treating it. The Court notes that a high percentage of all arrests in America are for the crime of public drunkenness and offers its opinion that the enforcement effort required constitutes a "tremendous burden" and that the amount of time spent on the problem by local law enforcement authorities is "inordinate." *Ante,* p. 9. Next, the Court informs us that there is no basis whatever for claiming that the jailing of chronic alcoholics can be a deterrent or a means of treatment; on the contrary, jail has, in the expert judgment of the Court, a "destructive effect." *Ante,* p. 10.

Of course, the desirability of this Texas legislation should be irrelevant in a court charged with the duty of interpretation rather than legislation, and that should be the end of the matter. But since the Court insists on offering its pronouncements on these questions of medical diagnosis and social policy, I am compelled to add that with all deference I think the Court has ventured far beyond the realm of problems for which we are in a position to know what we are talking about.

Public drunkenness has been a crime throughout our history, and even before our history it was explicitly proscribed by a 1606 English statute, 4 Jac. 1, c. 5. It

is today made an offense in every State in the Union.
The number of police to be assigned to enforcing these
laws and the amount of time they should spend in the
effort would seem to me a question for each local community. Never, even by the wildest stretch of this
Court's natural-law-due-process formula could it be
thought that a State's criminal law could be struck down
because the amount of time spent in enforcing it was,
in this Court's opinion, "inordinate."

Jailing of chronic alcoholics is definitely defended as
therapeutic, and the claims of therapeutic value are not
insubstantial. As appellees note, the alcoholics are removed from the streets, where in their intoxicated state
they may be in physical danger, and are given food,
clothing, and shelter until they "sober up" and thus at
least regain their ability to keep from being run over by
automobiles in the street. Of course, this treatment may
not be "therapeutic" in the sense of curing the underlying causes of their behavior, but it seems probable that
the effect of jail on any criminal is seldom "therapeutic"
in this sense, and in any case the medical authorities
relied on so heavily by the Court themselves stress that
no generally effective method of curing alcoholics has
yet been discovered.

Apart from the value of jail as a form of treatment,
jail serves other traditional functions of the criminal law.
For one thing, its gets the alcoholics off the street, where
they may cause harm in a number of ways to a number
of people, and isolation of the dangerous has always
been considered an important function of the criminal
law. In addition, punishment of chronic alcoholics can
serve several deterrent functions—it can give potential
alcoholics an additional incentive to control their drinking, and it may, even in the case of the chronic alcoholic,

POWELL *v.* TEXAS.

strengthen his incentive to control the frequency and location of his drinking experiences.[1]

These values served by criminal punishment assume even greater significance in light of the available alternatives for dealing with the problem of alcoholism. Civil commitment facilities may not be any better than the jails they would replace. In addition, compulsory commitment can hardly be considered a less severe penalty from the alcoholic's point of view. The commitment period will presumably be at least as long, and it might in fact be longer since commitment often lasts until the "sick" person is cured. And compulsory commitment would of course carry with it a social stigma little different in practice from that associated with drunkenness when it is labeled a "crime."

The situation is, I think, best summed up by the Court's own quotation from one alcoholism report, in which the need for continued experimentation with a variety of approaches is stressed. I cannot say that the States should be totally barred from one avenue of experimentation, the criminal process, in attempting to find a means to cope with this difficult social problem. From what I have been able to learn about the subject, it seems to me that the present use of criminal sanctions might possibly be unwise, but I am by no means convinced

---

[1] The Court does not claim that the findings in this case establish that legal sanctions can have absolutely no influence over the precautions that people like appellant might take to insure that their drunkenness occurs in private or even that legal sanctions can have no influence over the frequency of the periods of drunkennesss; nor does any evidence in the record provide a basis for any such conclusions. In fact, appellant himself actually testified that he took one drink on the day of trial but overcame his desire to take another drink because he knew he had to appear in court. The apparent ineffectiveness of jail as a deterrent in some cases may therefore suggest only that deterrence could be achieved by imposing more severe sentences.

that *any* use of criminal sanctions would inevitably be unwise or, above all, that I am qualified in this area to know what is legislatively wise and what is legislatively unwise.

II.

The findings of fact so mechanically employed by the Court have no concrete meaning in terms of actual human behavior. After presenting medical testimony, appellant asked the trial judge to make findings, and the judge complied by entering findings of fact in language virtually identical to that requested by appellant. The trial judge "found" that appellant is afflicted with the "disease" of chronic alcoholism, and that this disease "destroys the afflicted person's will power to resist the constant, excessive consumption of alcohol." The judge also found that, as a chronic alcoholic, appellant "does not appear in public of his own volition but under a compulsion symptomatic of the disease . . . ."

The Court gives no thought to the question of exactly what the judge who convicted appellant and "found" these "facts" actually meant by them. First, it is clear that the judge did not mean that appellant had no "will to resist" taking the first drink that was the start of any given episode, for the undisputed testimony of appellant's own witness was that in taking the first drink from a sober condition, appellant's action was a "voluntary exercise of his will." In addition, in making the requested findings, the judge apparently indicated only that he accepted the medical testimony as accurate, and he thus used such terms as "disease," "volition," and "will to resist" in their medical senses. Whatever the merits of the Court's rule that punishment must be limited to those who act voluntarily, I assume it is indisputable that "voluntariness" in this sense is a legal concept, reflecting a moral judgment. Medical decisions as to when use of this term is appropriate, based as they

6   POWELL v. TEXAS.

are on the clinical problems of diagnosis and treatment, bear no necessary corrrespondence to the legal decision whether certain aspects of a person's personality so dominated his behavior that he should not be held responsible for his action as an ethical matter.[2]

Even if the trial judge was thinking of "volition" in some legal sense, however, I could not consider such a finding controlling on the question whether a specific instance of human behavior should be immune from punishment as a constitutional matter. When we say that appellant's appearance in public is caused not by "his own" volition but rather by some other force, we are clearly thinking of a force that is nevertheless "his" except in some special sense.[3] The accused undoubtedly commits the proscribed act and the only question is whether the act can be attributed to a part of "his" personality that should not be regarded as criminally responsible. Almost all of the traditional purposes of the criminal law can be significantly served by punishing the person who in fact committed the proscribed act, without regard to whether his action was "compelled" by some elusive "irresponsible" aspect of his personality. As I have already indicated, punishment of such a defendant can clearly be justified in terms of deterrence, isolation, and treatment. For these reasons, much as I think that criminal sanctions should in many situations be applied only to those whose conduct is morally blameworthy, see *Morissette* v. *United States*, 342 U. S. 246 (1951), I cannot think the States should be held constitutionally required to make the inquiry as to what part

----

[2] See *McDonald* v. *United States*, 312 F. 2d 847, 851 (C. A. D. C. Cir. 1962).

[3] If an intoxicated person is actually carried into the street by someone else, "he" does not do the act at all, and of course he is entitled to acquittal. *E. g.*, *Martin* v. *State*, 31 Ala. App. 334, 17 So. 2d 427 (1944).

of a defendant's personality is responsible for his actions
and to excuse anyone whose action was, in some complex,
psychological sense, "involuntary."

III.

The rule of constitutional law announced by the Court
today is not required by *Robinson* v. *California, supra.*
In that case we held that a person could not be punished
for the mere status of being a narcotics addict. We
explicitly limited our holding to the situation where no
conduct of any kind is involved, stating:

> "We hold that a state criminal law which im-
> prisons a person thus afflicted as a criminal, *even
> though he has never touched any narcotic drug
> within the State or been guilty of any irregular
> behavior there,* inflicts a cruel and unusual punish-
> ment in violation of the Fourteenth Amendment."
> 370 U. S., at 667. (Emphasis added.)

Yet the Court in effect holds, relying solely on *Robinson,*
that it is now cruel and unusual to punish a narcotics
addict for using narcotics.

A different question, I admit, is whether our attempt
in *Robinson* to limit our holding to pure status crimes,
involving no conduct whatever, was a sound one. I
believe it was. Although some of our objections to the
statute in *Robinson* are equally applicable to statutes
that punish conduct "symptomatic" of a disease, any
attempt to explain *Robinson* as based solely on the lack
of voluntariness encounters a number of logical difficulties.[4] Other problems raised by **status crimes** are in

---

[4] As Glanville Williams puts it, "that crime requires an act is
invariably true if the proposition be read as meaning that a private
thought is not sufficient to found responsibility." Williams, Criminal
Law—the General Part 1 (1961). (Emphasis added.) For the
requirement of some act as an element of conspiracy and attempt,
see id., at 631, 663, 668; Perkins, Criminal Law 482, 531–532 (1957).

A. 4 - see P. 8

8   POWELL *v.* TEXAS.

no way involved when the State attempts to punish for conduct, and these other problems were, in my view, the controlling aspects of our decision.

Punishment for a status is particularly obnoxious, and can reasonably be called cruel and unusual, because it involves punishment for a mere propensity, a desire to commit an offense; the mental element is not simply one part of the crime but constitutes all of it. This is a situation universally sought to be avoided in our criminal law; the fundamental requirement that some action be proved is solidly established even for offenses most heavily based on propensity, such as attempt, conspiracy, and recidivist crimes. In fact, one eminent authority has found only one isolated instance, in all of Anglo-American jurisprudence, in which criminal responsibility was imposed in the absence of any act at all.[6]

The reasons for this refusal to permit conviction without proof of an act are difficult to spell out, but they are nonetheless perceived and universally expressed in our criminal law. Evidence of propensity can be considered relatively unreliable and more difficult for a defendant to rebut; the requirement of a specific act thus provides some protection against false charges. See 4 Blackstone, Commentaries 21. Perhaps more fundamental is the difficulty of distinguishing, in the absence of any conduct, between desires of the day-dream variety and fixed intentions that may pose a real threat to society; extending the criminal law to cover both types of desire would be unthinkable, since "[t]here can hardly be anyone

---

[6] Williams, *supra,* n. 4, at 11.

[7] Although we noted that narcotics addiction apparently is an illness that can be contracted innocently or involuntarily, we barred punishment for addiction even when it could be proved that the defendant had voluntarily become addicted. And we compared addiction to the status of having a common cold, a condition that most people can either avoid or quickly cure when it is important enough for them to do so.

h.S. see p.7.

POWELL v. TEXAS. 9

who has never thought evil. When a desire is inhibited it may find expression in fantasy; but it would be absurd to condemn this natural psychological mechanism as illegal."[7]

In contrast, crimes that require the State to prove that the defendant actually committed some proscribed act involve none of these special problems. In addition, the question whether an act is "involuntary" is, as I have already indicated, an inherently elusive question, and one which the State may, for good reasons, wish to regard as irrelevant. In light of all these considerations, our limitation of our *Robinson* holding to pure status crimes seems to me entirely proper.

IV.

The limits promised by the Court in its supposedly "narrow" holding are wholly illusory. Although the Court purports to deal only with defendants who are afflicted with "disease" and whose conduct is "symptomatic" of that disease, nothing in the Court's reasoning suggests that these factors are of any relevance. It is beyond dispute, I think, now that the Court has discarded the original boundaries of *Robinson,* that these new limits too will soon fall by the wayside and that the Court will be compelled to hold the States powerless to punish any conduct that can be shown "involuntary" in the complex, internal sense in which the Court uses that term.[8] The result, to choose just one illustration,

---

[7] *Id.,* at 2.

[8] The Court concedes that under its holding even conduct resulting in extremely serious harm must be excused if the conduct is a "characteristic and involuntary part of the disease." *Ante,* p. 5, n. 2. And even factors such as "disease" and "symptoms" are irrelevant under the Court's reasoning, which stresses that "[c]riminal penalties may be inflicted only if the accused has in fact elected to engage in the activities defined as an offense." *Id.,* at 12. The accused must not be "powerless to choose not to violate the law," *ibid.,* or without "capacity to resist," *id.,* at 13.

10   POWELL v. TEXAS.

would be that any crime committed in a state of intoxication serious enough to destroy "will power" would be
immunized from punishment, and this would presumably be true even if the defendant had voluntarily taken
the first drink, because in the present case itself appellant's act in taking the first drink on any given occasion
was, according to the undisputed evidence, "a voluntary
exercise of his will." This new rule, making serious,
will-destroying intoxication a complete defense to any
crime, is probably contrary to present law in most if not
all American jurisdictions.[9]

The real reach of the Court's decision, however, is
broader still, for the basic premise underlying the opinion
is that it is cruel and unusual to punish a person who is
not morally blameworthy. I state the proposition in this
sympathetic way because I feel there is much to be said
for avoiding the use of criminal sanctions in many such
situations. See *Morissette* v. *United States, supra*. But
the question here is one of constitutional law. The
legislatures have always been allowed wide freedom to
determine the extent to which moral culpability should
be a prerequisite to conviction of a crime. *E. g., United
States* v. *Dotterweich*, 320 U. S. 277 (1943). The criminal law is a social tool that is employed in seeking a wide
variety of goals, and I cannot say the Eighth Amendment's limits on the use of criminal sanctions extend as
far as the Court's viewpoint would inevitably carry it.

But even if we accept the artificial limits the Court
has proposed for its holding, the sweep of today's decision
is still startling. The Court holds that acquittal is now
required for any defendant who can show that "the acts
essential to constitute the defined crime are not voluntary but are part of the pattern of a disease." *Ante,*
p. 14. This ruling makes it clear beyond any doubt that

---

[9] Perkins, *supra*, n. 4, at 787–791.

POWELL v. TEXAS.

a narcotics addict cannot be punished for taking drugs. A wide variety of sex offenders are now immune from punishment if they can show that their conduct is not voluntary but part of the pattern of a disease. More generally speaking, a form of the insanity defense is now made a constitutional requirement throughout the Nation, for the Court holds it cruel and unusual to punish a person afflicted with any mental disease, if his conduct was "not voluntary but . . . part of the pattern of [the] disease." The Court thus undeniably overrules *Leland v. Oregon*, 343 U. S. 79 (1952), where the majority opinion and the dissenting opinion in which I joined both stressed the indefensibility of imposing on the States any particular test of criminal responsibility. *Id.*, at 800–801; *id.*, at 803 (Frankfurter, J., dissenting).

The impact of today's decision will, of course, be greatest in those States which have until now refused to accept any qualifications to the "right from wrong" test of insanity; apparently at least 30 States fall into this category.[10] But even in States which had recognized insanity defenses similar to the Court's new constitutional rule, or where comparable defenses could be presented in terms of the requirement of a guilty mind (*mens rea*) the Court's decision will be devastating, for constitutional questions will now be raised by every state effort to regulate the admissibility of evidence relating to "disease" and "volition," and by every state attempt to explain these concepts in instructions to the jury. The Court's test, formulated in terms of the question whether conduct is "not voluntary but . . . part of the pattern of a disease," will make it necessary to determine not only what constitutes a "disease," but what is the "pattern" of the disease, what conduct is "part" of the pattern, and finally what parts of this pattern are "not voluntary."

---

[10] See Model Penal Code § 4.01, at 160 (Tent. Draft No. 4, 1955).

12   POWELL *v.* TEXAS.

The resulting confusion and uncertainty will make us envy the experience of the District of Columbia Circuit in attempting to give content to its similar, though somewhat less complicated test of insanity.[11] The range of problems created would seem totally beyond our capacity to settle at all, much less to settle wisely, and even the attempt to define these terms and thus to impose constitutional and doctrinal rigidity seems absurd in an area where our understanding is even today so incomplete.

V.

Perceptive students of history at an early date learned that one country controlling another could do a more successful job if it permitted the latter to keep in force the laws and rules of conduct which it had adopted for itself. When our Nation was created by the Constitution of 1789, many people feared that the 13 straggling, struggling States along the Atlantic comprised too great an area ever to be controlled from one central point. As the years went on, however, the Nation crept cautiously westward until it reached the Pacific Ocean and finally the Nation planted its flag on the far-distant Islands of Hawaii and on the frozen peaks of Alaska. During all this period the Nation remembered that it could be more tranquil and orderly if it functioned on the principle that the local communities should control their own peculiarly local affairs under their own local rules.

This Court is forgetting that lesson today. It is now telling the most-distant Islands of Hawaii that they cannot apply their local rules so as to protect a drunken man on their beaches and the local communities of Alaska that they are without power to follow their own

---

[11] *Durham* v. *United States,* 214 F. 2d 862 (C. A. D. C. Cir. 1954). Some of the enormous difficulties encountered by the District of Columbia Circuit in attempting to apply its *Durham* rule are related in H. R. Rep. No. 563, 87th Cong., 1st Sess. (1961).

POWELL v. TEXAS. 13

course in deciding what is the best way to take care
of a drunken man on their frozen soil. This Court,
instead of recognizing that the experience of human
beings is the best way to make laws, sets itself up as
a board of Platonic Guardians to establish rigid, binding
rules upon every small community in this large Nation
for the control of the unfortunate people who fall victim
to drunkenness. It is always time to say that this
Nation is too large, too complex and composed of too
great a diversity of peoples for any one of us to have
the wisdom to establish the rules by which local Americans must govern their local affairs. This opinion of
the Court today is not merely revolutionary—it departs
from the ancient faith based on the premise that experience in making local laws by local people themselves
is by far the safest guide for a nation to follow. I suspect today's decision will be greeted by a great many,
throughout our land, who will echo the words of the late
Judge Learned Hand, who so wisely said:

> "For myself it would be most irksome to be ruled
> by a bevy of Platonic Guardians, even if I knew
> how to choose them, which I assuredly do not."
> Hand, The Bill of Rights 73 (1958).

I would confess the limits of my own ability to answer
the age-old questions of the criminal law's ethical founda-
tions and practical effectiveness. I would hold that
Robinson v. *California* establishes a firm and impene-
trable barrier to the punishment of persons who, whatever their bare desires and propensities, have committed
no proscribed act. But I would refuse to plunge from
the concete and almost universally recognized premises of
Robinson into the murky problems raised by today's
decision, problems that no person, whether layman or
expert, can claim to understand, and with consequences
that none of them can safely predict. I would affirm this
conviction.

Had the Fortas draft come down as the opinion of the Court in *Powell v. Texas*, it might have had important criminal law consequences. *Powell* then might have made *Robinson v. California* the starting point for a series of cases immunizing behavior from punishment because "compelled" by "conduct that can be shown 'involuntary' in the complex, internal sense in which the Court uses that term."[28]

The Fortas draft opinion of the Court would have extended the *Robinson* ruling on drug addiction to chronic alcoholism. If the Court went that far, it is unlikely that it would have stopped there. If what the Court said in *Robinson* is true of alcoholic addiction, why would it not also be true of addiction to sexual offenses? Relying on the *Robinson* decision, one court has gone so far as to assert, "Imprisoning [defendant] for his homosexual conduct is not unlike putting a person in jail for being addicted to the use of narcotics, as was done in *Robinson v. California*."[29]

If such an approach prevailed, why stop at the addict and sex offender? What about the defendant who commits a criminal act as the result of an uncontrollable impulse, even though he is not insane within the legal test of knowing the difference between right and wrong?

As Justice Black points out, the *Robinson-Powell* approach, under the Fortas *Powell* draft opinion of the Court, might have tremendous impact upon those states that follow the "right from wrong" test for insanity.[30] There are some who might go even further and argue that most criminals are victims of mental illness, and propensity to crime is comparable in this respect to propensity to narcotic addiction. Yet, even under the Fortas *Powell* draft, it would stretch constitutional doctrine beyond the breaking point for a judge to follow such a view to its logical extreme, and, using the *Robinson* reasoning, to strike down all punishment of such criminals as cruel and unusual punishment.

As it turned out, however, the Fortas draft, with its implications just noted, did not become the *Powell* opinion of the Court. The conference vote, as mentioned, was five-to-four in favor of applying the *Robinson* rule to Powell's conviction. Justice White had been a

---

[28]Black draft dissent at 9.

[29]Perkins v. North Carolina, 234 F.Supp. 333, 336–337 (W.D.N.C. 1964).

[30]Black draft dissent at 11–12; compare 392 U.S. at 546.

member of the conference majority, but he had increasing doubts about the reversal of Powell's conviction. On May 8, he wrote Justice Fortas that he had changed his vote. "I am with you part way but I am leaving you in other respects and in the result, the upshot being that I do not join your opinion or those on the other side either. I have been back and forth for weeks but it is more than likely that I am at rest, at least for now."[31] The result was that Justice White concurred in the decision to affirm but wrote his own opinion to explain why he reached that result.

There was now a majority for affirmance of Powell's conviction. The Chief Justice assigned the case to Justice Marshall, who delivered the *Powell* opinion refusing to extend the *Robinson* rule to Powell's offense. *Robinson* may show that the Eighth Amendment imposes substantive limits on what may be made criminal and punished as such.[32] But its limitation is one to be applied sparingly.[33] As *Powell* turned out, *Robinson* remains an exceptional, almost aberrational, case—rather than the foundation for a new doctrine of constitutional responsibility.[34]

III. Gunn v. University Committee: Volume of Speech and First Amendment

Gunn v. University Committee To End the War in Viet Nam[35] almost led to a decision on an important First Amendment issue that has never been addressed by the Supreme Court. The case arose out of a speech made by President Johnson near Fort Hood, Texas. Members of the University Committee arrived at the edge of the crowd listening to the President with placards protesting the war in Vietnam. Though they were quiet and orderly, they were set upon by members of the crowd and subjected to physical abuse. The committee members were arrested and charged with violating a Texas law making it a breach of the peace to use "loud and vociferous . . . language . . . in a manner calculated to disturb the person or persons present" in a public place. They brought an action

---

[31]See Schwartz, note 23 *supra*, at 694.

[32]Ingraham v. Wright, 430 U.S. 651, 667 (1977).

[33]*Ibid.*

[34]Compare 392 U.S. at 534.

[35]399 U.S. 383 (1970).

in a federal court for a declaratory judgment that the Texas statute was unconstitutional on its face and as applied to their conduct and an injunction against their prosecution.

A few days later the state charges were dismissed because the conduct involved had taken place on a military enclave over which Texas had no jurisdiction. The federal court refused to dismiss for mootness and held that the Texas statute was "impermissibly and unconstitutionally broad" and that plaintiffs were entitled to the declaratory judgment and injunction. However, the Court stayed its mandate and retained jurisdiction pending the next session of the Texas Legislature, "at which time the State of Texas may, if it so desires, enact such disturbing-the-peace statute as will meet constitutional requirements."[36] In this posture, defendants took a direct appeal to the Supreme Court. Justices Black, Harlan, Stewart, and White voted to hear the appeal.

As the case came to the Supreme Court it presented a more hypothetical than actual case. The district court had stated expressly, "This case does not involve in any way an appraisal of the constitutionality of the application of the statute to the plaintiffs." Instead, the court decided only whether the statute "on its face is, as plaintiffs argue, constitutionally defective as being overly broad."[37] Thus the fact that the demonstrators were quiet and orderly was irrelevant to the Supreme Court's consideration of the case. From the Court's point of view, the case had to be treated as one in which "loud and vociferous" language had been used "in a manner calculated to disturb the person or persons present."

In these circumstances, *Gunn* presented an issue that had never before been decided by the Supreme Court—that of the extent to which government could restrain the volume of natural speech unaided by amplification devices. The Court had dealt with regulation of speech aided by sound amplifiers in two cases decided in 1948 and 1949.[38] The Court held that, since the sound amplifier is an essential implement of present-day speech, it can no more either be prohibited absolutely or be made dependent upon the unfettered discretion of a designated official than can speech with the naked voice alone. On the other hand, the abuses to which speech by

---

[36]*Id.* at 386.

[37]Stewart draft dissent at 9.

[38] Saia v. New York, 334 U.S. 558 (1948); Kovacs v. Cooper, 336 U.S. 77 (1949).

loud-speaker is subject make such speech peculiarly appropriate for reasonable, nondiscriminatory regulation. Hence, it is clear that "Noise can be regulated by regulating decibels. The hours and place of [loud-speaker use] can be controlled."[39] *Kovacs v. Cooper*[40] upheld a municipal ordinance that forbade the use on the public streets of sound trucks or other amplifying devices that emitted "loud and raucous" noises. "We think," said the Court, "it is a permissible exercise of legislative discretion to bar sound trucks with broadcasts of public interest, amplified to a loud and raucous volume, from the public ways of municipalities."[41]

Thus, though loudspeakers may not be prohibited in public places, their volume may be regulated, as by ordinances limiting decibels (particularly in residential areas). In the same way, the more recent case of *Grayned v. Rockford*[42] upheld a city anti-noise ordinance prohibiting a person on grounds adjacent to a school in session from willfully making a noise or diversion that disturbs the peace or good order of the school session.

The Texas statute at issue in *Gunn* was aimed at "loud and vociferous" language. As such it was similar to the ordinance sustained in *Kovacs v. Cooper*. Unlike that ordinance, however, the *Gunn* statute restricted natural, not mechanically amplified, speech. Nor was it limited, as in the *Grayned* case, to grounds adjacent to a school in session. On the contrary, the Texas law applied to "any public place." Was its broadside restriction of "loud and vociferous" natural speech valid?

The *Gunn* conference answered the question in the negative, voting to strike down the Texas restriction as an invalid interference with First Amendment rights. The Chief Justice assigned the case to Justice Fortas, who circulated a March 14, 1969, draft opinion of the Court, reprinted below. The draft first rejects the argument that, since the state criminal charges had been dismissed, there was no case or controversy. On the constitutional merits, the draft concedes "that Texas could punish persons under this statutory language for engaging in types of activity other than those that the First Amendment embraces—for disturbing those present at a chess

---

[39]Saia v. New York, 334 U.S. at 562.

[40]336 U.S. 77 (1949).

[41]*Id.* at 87.

[42]408 U.S. 104 (1972).

tournament or a ladies sewing circle, for example, or a schoolroom or library, by 'loud and vociferous' shouting foreign to the surroundings and deliberately designed to disrupt the proceedings."

The case, however, involved "activities in the First Amendment area." With regard to them, Justice Fortas declares, the rule is different. "First Amendment rights cannot be delimited by a standard that is as broad as that of the Texas statute. Speech is not necessarily deprived for First Amendment protection solely because it is 'loud and vociferous' and because it is 'calculated to disturb the person or persons present.' Much conventional political debate falls within this vast category. Neither the decibels of the human voice nor the 'disturbance' of listeners at an otherwise appropriate rally in a public square set the limits of First Amendment rights."

On April 9, Justice Stewart sent around the draft dissent reprinted below. The first part of the draft asserts, "we have no business dealing with this case at all." According to Justice Stewart, there was no order by the lower federal court granting or denying an injunction. "In fact, there was no judgment of any kind—not even a declaratory judgment." A direct appeal to the Supreme Court was then authorized only from a three-judge district court order granting or denying an injunction. Consequently, "The failure of the District court to grant or deny an injunction clearly deprives this Court of any lawful power to act in this case." Much of the draft on this point was used by Justice Stewart in the *Gunn* opinion of the Court that he ultimately issued.

Justice Stewart also urges that there was no case or controversy to permit the ruling that the Texas statute was unconstitutional. To hold otherwise, he contends, "is wholly alien to the federal system as it has operated for almost 180 years under our Constitution."

On the constitutional issue, Justice Stewart uses strong language to support his contention that "the Court today has gone quite remarkably astray." The Stewart draft asserts, "I cannot agree that this provision, as so construed, is unconstitutional on its face. Surely if recent history has taught us anything, it has taught us that noise is not necessarily speech—that sound and fury can as often stifle free expression as promote it."

On April 16, Justice White also circulated a draft dissent. It notes that the Texas statute was "aimed at undue noise, not at the content of verbal utterances." This made the question of "whether the Con-

stitution guarantees the right go into a public place . . . and deliberately use loud language calculated by its loudness to disturb other
persons." Justice White had no doubt how this question should be
answered: "I am unaware of a constitutional right to disturb others
by loud noises, whether the noise is speech or otherwise. The
uninvited mouth is as obnoxious as the uninvited ear." Speech is
not insulated by the Constitution "when the level of loudness is
designed to bombard involuntary listeners."

SUPREME COURT OF THE UNITED STATES

No. 269.—October Term, 1968.

Lester Gunn et al., Appellants. *v.* University Committee To End the War in Viet Nam et al.	On Appeal From the United States District Court for the Western District of Texas.

[March —, 1969.]

Mr. Justice Fortas delivered the opinion of the Court.

I.

The University Committee To End the War in Viet Nam is an unincorporated association approved by the University of Texas to operate on its campus at Austin, Texas. The organization's purpose is to protest the United States' participation in the Vietnam conflict "by means of discussions, publications, demonstrations, and non-violent direct action." 289 F. Supp. 469, 470 (1968). The other appellees are two members of the Committee and one nonmember who is sympathetic to its goals and activities. The appellants are officials of Bell County, Texas.

On December 12, 1967, President Johnson spoke at a dedicatory program at Central Texas College, which is near Killeen, a city in Bell County, Texas. Killeen serves nearby Fort Hood, a large United States military installation. Members of the University Committee and their sympathizers had learned of the President's scheduled appearance, and a number of them had driven to Killeen to stage a protest.[1]

---

[1] The District Court made no finding as to the number of demonstrators. One of the appellees in his affidavit said that there were only seven. Another said that although there were only seven in his "immediate party," "several carloads" of demonstrators attended the speech.

2 GUNN v. COMMITTEE TO END WAR.

The demonstrators parked their cars and walked to the part of the college grounds where the President was speaking. They carried placards and signs protesting the Vietnam conflict.[2] They were quiet and orderly. By the time they arrived, the President had started speaking, and about 25,000 spectators had assembled. Many of the spectators were soldiers from Fort Hood. Some of the soldiers accosted the demonstrators as soon as they arrived. They snatched away the demonstrators' placards, and they struck several demonstrators. The military police removed from the crowd the three demonstrators who are appellees in this suit, and handed them over to deputies of the Bell County sheriff.[3]

The appellees were handcuffed and frisked and taken to the Bell County jail where they were charged with disturbing the peace. They were later taken before a justice of the peace, and they pleaded not guilty. In Texas, the maximum penalty for the misdemeanor of disturbing the peace is a fine of $200, but the justice of the peace set the bond for each of the appellees at $500.

The Texas disturbing the peace statute under which the appellees were charged provides:

> "Whoever shall go into or near any public place or into or near any private house, and shall use loud and vociferous, or obscene, vulgar or indecent language or swear or curse, or yell or shriek or expose

---

[2] The signs that the appellees carried contained quotations of General Ky, U Thant, and General Shoup. The signs read: " 'I have but One Idol—Hitler,' General Ky"; " 'The War in Vietnam May be the Initial Phase of World War III,' U Thant"; and " 'Wrong War, Wrong Time, Wrong Place,' General Shoup."

[3] The appellees deny that it was the military police who initially arrested them. They claim that they were carried out of the crowd by the Bell County Police. Brief for the Appellees, p. 4, n. 3. The District Court, however, said that the military police removed the appellees from the crowd. 289 F. Supp., at 471.

GUNN v. COMMITTEE TO END WAR.   3

his or her person to another person of the age of
sixteen (16) years or over, or rudely display any
pistol or deadly weapon, in a manner calculated to
disturb the person or persons present at such place
or house, shall be punished by a fine not exceeding
Two Hundred Dollars ($200)." Texas Penal Code,
Article 474.

The District Court viewed the case as arising under that
part of the statute prohibiting the use of "loud and
vociferous . . . language . . . in a manner calculated to
disturb the person or persons present . . . ."

The individual appellees were released on bail on
December 12, 1967. On December 21, 1967, before the
charges against them were brought to trial, the appellees
filed this action in the United States District Court,
seeking a declaration that the Texas disturbing the peace
statute is unconstitutional on its face and as applied
to their conduct and an injunction against prosecution
for violation of the statute. A three-judge court was
convened to hear the case. On February 13, 1968,
before the present case was argued to the three-judge
court, the justice of the peace before whom the criminal
proceedings were pending, on motion of the county
attorney, dismissed the criminal charges against the
appellees on the ground that the court did not have jurisdiction over the offense because it occurred on a federal
enclave.[4] The Bell County officials, the appellants in
this Court, then filed a motion to dismiss in this cause on
the ground that the present suit was moot.

The District Court denied the motion to dismiss, ruling
that the abandonment of the criminal proceedings did
not moot the controversy between the parties. It held

---

[4] Until that time, the State had claimed that the offense was
within their jurisdiction. The appellees do not concede that the
place where they demonstrated was within the federal enclave. See
Brief for the Appellees, p. 3, n. 2.

4   GUNN *v.* COMMITTEE TO END WAR.

that the statute is unconstitutionally broad and that, although appellees' prayer for an injunction against prosecution of the criminal charges was no longer before it because those charges had been dismissed, there was a continuing controversy which required adjudication. Accordingly, the court concluded that the appellees "are entitled to their declaratory judgment [as to the unconstitutionality of the statute], and to injunctive relief against the enforcement of Article 474 as now worded, insofar as it may affect rights guaranteed under the First Amendment." 289 F. Supp., at 475. The court stayed the issuance of its mandate, however, and retained jurisdiction pending the next session of the Texas Legislature so that the State could, if it so desired, enact a statute to replace the one held unconstitutional. In its next session the Texas Legislature did not legislate on the subject. The Bell County officials brought the case here on appeal from the judgment of the District Court.

II.

Appellants renew in this Court their argument that since the state criminal charges have been dismissed, there is no case or controversy between the parties. We agree with the District Court, however, that the appellees were entitled to adjudication of their complaint. It is clear that the appellees have a continuing interest in protesting the Vietnam conflict. If the appellees again determine to engage in peaceful demonstrations in Bell County, Texas, as they assert they desire to do, they would have reason to fear that they would be arrested and prosecuted under this statute.[5] The dismissal of

---

[5] According to the appellees' affidavits, they were roughly handled by the Bell County Police, who referred to them as "college peace creeps." The Chief of Police warned them as they left the Killeen jail, "Don't come back here. We don't like your kind. I want you to tell all your University friends. We got all the education we want right here at Killeen Junior College."

GUNN v. COMMITTEE TO END WAR.   5

the charges against them did not erase the controversy. It was based not on an admission that prosecution for their conduct under this statute was improper, but upon the assertion that the offense occurred on a federal enclave. The District Court credited the appellees' statements that their fear of prosecution under the statute had led them to cease their protest activities.

In these circumstances, there is "an existing unresolved dispute which continues," and the case is not moot. *Bus Employees* v. *Missouri*, 374 U. S. 74, 78 (1963). See *United States* v. *Trans-Missouri Freight Assn.*, 166 U. S. 290, 307–310 (1897); *Southern Pacific Terminal Co.* v. *ICC*, 219 U. S. 498 (1911); *United States* v. *W. T. Grant Co.*, 345 U. S. 629 (1953); *Epperson* v. *Arkansas*, 393 U. S. 97 (1968); *Carroll* v. *President and Commissioners of Princess Anne*, 393 U. S. 175 (1968). See also S. Rep. No. 1005, 73d Cong., 2d Sess., 2–3 (1934) (relating to the Declaratory Judgments Act, 28 U. S. C. § 2201). We agree with the District Court that the petition for a declaratory judgment and injunction against future enforcement of the statute calls for adjudication.

III.

The District Court expressly stated that it did not consider the constitutionality of the statute as it applied to the appellees' conduct. 289 F. Supp., at 473. Instead, it held that the statutory prohibition against using "loud and vociferous . . . language . . . in a manner calculated to disturb the person or persons present" is unconstitutional on its face "insofar as it may affect rights guaranteed under the First Amendment." 289 F. Supp., at 475. We agree.

First Amendment rights cannot be delimited by a standard that is as broad as that of the Texas statute. Speech is not necessarily deprived of First Amendment protection solely because it is "loud and vociferous" and

6   GUNN *v.* COMMITTEE TO END WAR.

because it is "calculated to disturb the person or persons present." Much conventional political debate falls within this vast category. Neither the decibels of the human voice nor the "disturbance" of listeners at an otherwise appropriate rally in a public square set the limits of First Amendment rights. *Edwards* v. *South Carolina*, 372 U. S. 229, 233 (1963), and *Cox* v. *Louisiana*, 379 U. S. 536, 546–548 (1965), for example, both involved noisy demonstrations, but, viewed in context, the demonstrations were held protected by the First Amendment.

It may be that Texas could punish persons under this statutory language for engaging in types of activity other than those that the First Amendment embraces—for disturbing those present at a chess tournament or a ladies' sewing circle, for example, or a schoolroom or library, by "loud and vociferous" shouting foreign to the surroundings and deliberately designed to disrupt the proceedings. But the present case is not in that category. We deal here with activities in the First Amendment area—with expression or communication of views and opinions. We are here concerned with a basic, fundamental right under our Constitution, and statutes that are cast in terms so broad that they forbid constitutionally protected speech cannot be sustained.

The determination of when language is "loud and vociferous" and the definition and appraisal of its "disturbing" effect are much too subjective to provide a tolerable basis for state regulatory or punitive action with respect to the activities of persons engaged in activity in the First Amendment area—that is, the expression of views, the communication of ideas, or the attempt to persuade others with respect to subjects of consequence to society or to the particular community. As Mr. Justice Douglas said for the Court in another context, "Annoyance at ideas can be cloaked in annoyance at

GUNN v. COMMITTEE TO END WAR.   7

sound." *Saia* v. *New York*, 334 U. S. 558, 562 (1948)." And this Court has already rejected "disturbance" of listeners as a limit upon First Amendment rights because of its subjectivity. See *Ashton* v. *Kentucky*, 384 U. S. 195, 200 (1966).

IV.

The State had threatened to prosecute the appellees under its disturbing-the-peace statute for conduct in the area of First Amendment liberties; the criminal charges had been dismissed only after institution of this suit and on a technical basis that did not relate to the underlying issues; the appellees discontinued their activities because they feared future harassment, and in the circumstances that fear was plausible. The provision of the disturbing-the-peace statute under which the appellees had been charged was unconstiutional. On these facts, there was clearly a basis for granting relief to the appellees. See *Dombrowski* v. *Pfister*, 380 U. S. 479 (1965); *Zwickler* v. *Koota*, 389 U. S. 241 (1967).

The judgment is affirmed and the case remanded to the District Court for such further proceedings as it may deem appropriate in the light of our opinion.

It is so ordered.

---

⁶ Appellants argue that the statutory provisions should be sustained because its prohibition does not turn on the content of the speech but only on its loudness, and they cite several Texas cases that support this construction of the statute. *Anderson* v. *State*, 20 S. W. 358 (1892); *Thomason* v. *State*, 265 S. W. 579 (1924); *West* v. *State*, 97 S. W. 2d 476 (1936). We accept the appellants statutory construction, but hold that the prohibition is nevertheless invalid because its standards are too subjective and because it is overbroad.

1

SUPREME COURT OF THE UNITED STATES

No. 269.—October Term, 1968.

Lester Gunn et al., Appellants.	On Appeal From the
v.	United States District
University Committee To End	Court for the Western
the War in Viet Nam et al.	District of Texas.

[April —. 1969.]

Mr. Justice Stewart, dissenting.

Article 474 of the Texas Penal Code provides:

"Whoever shall go into or near any public place, or into or near any private house, and shall use loud and vociferous, or obscene, vulgar or indecent language or swear or curse, or yell or shriek or expose his or her person to another person of the age of Sixteen (16) years or over, or rudely display any pistol or deadly weapon, in a manner calculated to disturb the person or persons present at such place or house, shall be punished by a fine not exceeding Two Hundred Dollars ($200)."

In the present case a three-judge Federal District Court rendered an opinion that this law is, on its face, "impermissibly and unconstitutionally broad." 289 F. Supp. 469, 475. Today the District Court's "judgment" is affirmed, on the ground that the Texas law is not only "overbroad," but "much too subjective." I respectfully dissent, because I am convinced the Court today has gone quite remarkably astray.

I.

In the first place, we have no business dealing with this case at all. The parties say we have jurisdiction of the appeal under 28 U. S. C. § 1253. But that section of the Code authorizes a direct appeal to this Court only

2   GUNN v. COMMITTEE TO END WAR.

from an order of a three-judge district court "granting
or denying . . . an interlocutory or permanent injunction." [1] In this case there was no order granting an
injunction, and no order denying an injunction—either
interlocutory or permanent. In fact, there was no
judgment of any kind—not even a declaratory judgment.
All the District Court did was to write a rather
discursive *per curiam* opinion,[2] ending with the following
paragraph:

> "We reach the conclusion that Article 474 is
> impermissibly and unconstitutionally broad. The
> Plaintiffs herein are entitled to their declaratory
> judgment to that effect, and to injunctive relief
> against the enforcement of Article 474 as now
> worded, insofar as it may affect rights guaranteed
> under the First Amendment. However, it is the
> Order of this Court that the mandate shall be stayed
> and this Court shall retain jurisdiction of the cause
> pending the next session, special or general, of the
> Texas legislature, at which time the State of Texas
> may, if it so desires, enact such disturbing-the-peace
> statute as will meet constitutional requirements."

The failure of the District Court to grant or deny
an injunction clearly deprives this Court of any lawful
power to act in this case.[3] This is no mere technicality.

---

[1] "Except as otherwise provided by law, any party may appeal
to the Supreme Court from an order granting or denying, after
notice and hearing, an interlocutory or permanent injunction in any
civil action, suit or proceeding required by any Act of Congress
to be heard and determined by a district court of three judges.
June 25, 1948, c. 646, 62 Stat. 928."

[2] The court also wrote an "addendum" in response to a motion
for a new trial. 289 F. Supp., at 475.

[3] And the total absence of *any* judgment would prevent direct
review even by the Court of Appeals.

GUNN *v.* COMMITTEE TO END WAR.   3

One of the common sense reasons for this basic jurisdictional rule is that until a district court issues an injunction, or enters an order denying one, it is simply not possible to know with any certainty what the court has decided—a state of affairs that is conspicuously evident here. Did the District Court intend to hold all the provisions of the statute unconstitutional? Or did the court intend to hold the statute unconstitutional only as applied to speech, including so-called symbolic speech? Or was the court confining its attention to that part of the statute that prohibits the use, in certain places and under certain conditions, of "loud and vociferous" language? One simply cannot tell with any degree of assurance.

The absence of an injunctive order or even of a declaratory judgment in this case has been fully recognized by the parties. In their motion for a new trial, the appellants pointed out to the District Court that it had "given not a declaratory judgment but an advisory opinion." And the appellees, in their brief in this Court, emphasized that "[n]o final relief—of any kind—has been ordered below." Accordingly, they said, "no question is now properly raised as to the precise form of federal remedy which may be granted." They asserted that "the issuance of declaratory and injunctive relief will be appropriate at an appropriate time, to-wit, on remand to the court below."

The Court today manages to skirt this impassable jurisdictional barrier by the simple expedient of pretending it does not exist. Though the District Court entered no judgment, this Court ends its opinion by *affirming* the "judgment," and *remanding* the case to the District Court for "further proceedings." Those "further proceedings" will presumably consist of the entry, for the first time, of an injunction or declaratory judgment.

4   GUNN *v.* COMMITTEE TO END WAR.

Clearly, the Court should dismiss this appeal for want of jurisdiction. But since the Court does not do so, I am impelled to state my opposing views with respect to the merits of this case.

II.

On December 12, 1967, President Johnson made a speech in Bell County, Texas, to a crowd of some 25,000 people, including many servicemen from nearby Fort Hood. The appellees arrived at the edge of the crowd with placards signaling their strong opposition to this country's military presence in Vietnam. They were quiet, and the messages on their placards were in no sense "obscene, vulgar, or indecent." Almost immediately after their arrival, they were set upon by members of the crowd, subjected to some physical abuse, promptly removed from the scene by military police, turned over to Bell County officers, and taken to jail. When they asked why they had been arrested, they were given uninformative answers.[4] Soon afterwards, they were brought before a justice of the peace on a complaint signed by a deputy sheriff, charging them with "Dist the Peace." They pleaded not guilty, were returned briefly to jail, and were soon released on $500 bond. According to affidavits later filed in the present case, they were subjected to verbal indignities by the sheriff, his deputies, and the justice of the peace.

Nine days later they brought this action in the Federal District Court against Bell County officials, asking that a three-judge court be convened, that the state prosecution be enjoined, and that the Texas disturbing-the-peace

---

[4] "[O]ne of us asked what we were being arrested for and what would happen next. One officer said we would be taken before the judge and charged in a while; another said were disturbing the peace; and still later another explained to me that under Texas law we could be held on 'suspicion.'"

GUNN v. COMMITTEE TO END WAR.   5

statute, Article 474, be declared unconstitutional on its face, "and/or as applied to the conduct of the plaintiffs herein."

A few weeks later the state charges were dismissed upon motion of the county attorney, on the ground that the appellees' conduct had taken place within a federal enclave over which Texas did not have jurisdiction. After dismissal of the state charges the defendants in the federal court action filed a motion to dismiss the complaint because "no useful purpose could now be served by the granting of an injunction to prevent the prosecution of these suits because same no longer exists." The appellees filed a memorandum in opposition to this motion, conceding that there was no remaining controversy with respect to the prosecution of the state charges, but asking the federal court nonetheless to retain jurisdiction and to hold Article 474 unconstitutional. It was with the case in that posture that the three-judge District Court rendered its *per curiam* opinion concluding that "Article 474 is impermissibly and unconstitutionally broad."

The court based its refusal to dismiss the complaint primarily upon its understanding of this Court's decisions in *Dombrowski* v. *Pfister*, 380 U. S. 479, and *Zwickler* v. *Koota*, 389 U. S. 241.[5] Those cases, the Court thought, stand for the proposition that "the statute's simple presence on the books (which is what the plaintiffs are attacking) may have the requisite 'chilling effect' on constitutionally protected behavior to warrant close judicial scrutiny." 289 F. Supp., at 473. The court found the "requisite 'chilling effect'" in certain statements in the affidavits that the appellees and their associates had stopped demonstrating in Bell County on behalf of their

---

[5] Reliance was also placed upon *Baldwin* v. *Morgan*, 251 F. 2d 780, and *Carmichael* v. *Allen*, 267 F. Supp. 985.

6   GUNN v. COMMITTEE TO END WAR.

Vietnam views because of the charges brought against the appellees.[6]

But neither *Dombrowski* nor *Koota* stands even remotely for the proposition that a person can go into a federal court, point to a state statute's "simple presence on the books," say that this "simple presence" may have a "chilling effect" upon the future activities of himself or others, and ask the court for that reason to hold the statute unconstitutional on its face. Whether considered in terms of "standing," or in the broader context of the whole relationship between state and national courts, any such proposition is wholly alien to the federal system as it has operated for almost 180 years under our Constitution. Cf. *Greenwood* v. *Peacock*, 384 U. S. 808; *Stefanelli* v. *Minard*, 342 U. S. 117; *Douglas* v. *City of Jeannette*, 319 U. S. 157.

The *Dombrowski* case, as this Court made clear in its opinion, involved a pattern of concerted and ongoing misuse of patently unconstitutional state laws in order to harass the appellants. The Court held that a federal injunction could properly issue in those exceptional circumstances. Compare *Cameron* v. *Johnson*, 390 U. S. 611. In the *Koota* case the appellant had been previously convicted under a state law for distributing hand

---

[6] Actually, three of the affiants stated only that they had decided to postpone further demonstrations until the charges against the appellees were disposed of:

The affidavit of John E. Morby stated, "Until the charges are disposed of I do not intend to engage in such demonstrations again."

The affidavit of Sandra Sue Granville stated, "I have stopped picketing, demonstrating and engaging in other nonviolent methods of protesting the war in Vietnam around Killeen until the status of James M. Damon, John E. Morby and Zigmunt W. Smigaj, Jr., has been resolved in court . . . ."

The affidavit of Phillip Jumonville stated, "I just do not demonstrate in Bell County and will not until their cases are finally decided."

GUNN *v.* COMMITTEE TO END WAR.   7

bills in connection with an election. The Court held that with another election imminent, the federal district court should not have abstained from considering the merits of the appellant's prayer for a declaratory judgment in view of the delay that would be incurred in starting anew in a state court. Compare *Zwickler* v. *Golden,* —— U. S. ——.

The present case bears not the slightest resemblance to either *Dombrowski* or *Koota.* Indeed, it is almost impossible here to perceive how any state statute is really implicated at all. The appellees clearly did not violate any provision of Article 474 on the day of President Johnson's speech, and none of the affidavits filed by the appellees indicate an intention or desire to engage in any future conduct that would be contrary to the provisions or Article 474. This was made clear by counsel for the Bell County officials themselves in the District Court.[7] It was again freely conceded by counsel for these appellants during oral argument here.[8]

---

[7] The motion for a new trial in the district court stated:

"Nowhere can the Court demonstrate that any charge was made that the Plaintiffs or any of them used loud and vociferous language in any manner. By the same token there is no showing that any of the Plaintiffs were charged with obscene, vulgar or indecent language or swearing or cursing. Nor were any of the Plaintiffs charged with exposing his or her person to another person of the age of sixteen (16) years or over. Nor were any of the Plaintiffs charged with rudely displaying any pistol or deadly weapon. Nor were any of the Plaintiffs charged with yelling and shrieking. Likewise, none of the Plaintiffs have manifested any desire to do any of the enumerated things prohibited by Article 474 nor have they claimed to have a constitutional right to expose themselves to persons over the age of sixteen (16) years or to rudely display a pistol or deadly weapon or any of the other prohibited things."

[8] "I don't see how it was possible to conceive that that statute would have any application to anything that these plaintiffs had been involved in.

[*Footnote 8 continued on page 8.*]

8   GUNN *v.* COMMITTEE TO END WAR.

If, therefore, the appellees were deprived of their constitutional right of free expression on the day of President
Johnson's speech in Bell County, it was certainly not
because of any of the provisions of Article 474. It was
because the appellees were removed from the area by
federal officers, turned over to state officers, lodged in
jail, subjected to indignities, and booked on a wholly
false and baseless charge. What redress may be available to the appellees under state law for false arrest or
malicious prosecution, and under federal law for depriva-
tion of their federal civil rights, is a question not before
us. Nor need we consider whether, if the state charges
had not been dismissed, federal injunctive relief might
have been permissible or appropriate.

The question here is simply whether, after the state
charges were dropped, the appellees should have been
allowed to maintain a broadside attack upon the constitutionality of Article 474. Suppose on the day of
President Johnson's speech the appellees had been removed from the area, carried off to jail, and falsely
charged with grand larceny. Could the appellees, after
the state charges were dropped, have maintained a suit
in a federal court attacking the state larceny statute
as unconstitutional on its face because its "simple
presence on the books" had a "chilling effect" on their
First Amendment rights? The logic of the present case
would say yes, but I cannot believe it. I think the
complaint should have been dismissed.

"It just had nothing to do, this particular statute, with any of the
facts that the record shows.

"I am saying that I cannot conceive how that complaint would
make a charge—that is, a sustainable charge—under 474."

GUNN v. COMMITTEE TO END WAR.   9

III.

Since, however, the District Court entertained this lawsuit and rendered an opinion that Article 474 is unconstitutional, and since this Court today approves that opinion, I add a final word in dissent.

The District Court, it is to be emphasized, did not concern itself with application of the statute to any concrete case. It held that the statute was unconstitutional on its face. The court's words on that score were very clear:

> "Before we discuss the issues presented as to the merits of this controversy, it may be wise to state what is not involved. This case does not involve in any way an appraisal of the constitutionality of the application of the statute to the plaintiffs; we do not evaluate whether Article 474 was constitutionally applied to these plaintiffs' activities. Our sole concern is the determination of whether Article 474 on its face is, as plaintiffs argue, constitutionally defective as being overly broad."

I shall assume, as does this Court, that in holding Article 474 unconstitutional, the District Court intended to confine its ruling to that portion of the statute that prohibits the use of "loud and vociferous . . . language . . . in a manner calculated to disturb," although the matter is far from clear. But even if the District Court opinion is understood to be so limited, I ~~cannot agree that this statutory provision is on its face unconstitutional~~. still think it is wrong.

The Texas decisions construing this provision have made clear that the gravamen of the offense lies not at all in the content of the language, but wholly in its decibel level. See *Anderson v. State*, 20 S. W. 358; *Thomason v. State*, 265 S. W. 579; *West v. State*, 97

10   GUNN v. COMMITTEE TO END WAR.

S. W. 2d 476 (all reversing convictions for insufficient evidence that the language was "loud and vociferous"). We must, of course, accept the construction of the statutory language that the Texas courts have put upon it. *Albertson v. Millard*, 345 U. S. 242; *United States v. Burnison*, 339 U. S. 87; *Aero Mayflower Transit Co. v. Board of R. R. Comm'rs*, 332 U. S. 495.

I cannot agree that this provision, as so construed, is unconstitutional on its face. Surely if recent history has taught us anything, it has taught us that noise is not necessarily speech—that sound and fury can as often stifle free expression as promote it.

For all the reasons indicated, I ~~respectively~~ *respectfully* dissent.

SUPREME COURT OF THE UNITED STATES

No. 269.—October Term, 1968.

Lester Gunn et al., Appellants,	On Appeal From the
v.	United States District
University Committee To End	Court for the Western
the War in Viet Nam et al.	District of Texas.

[April —, 1969.]

Mr. Justice White, dissenting.

Only a narrow category of speech can be made criminal. Fighting words, for example, are not protected by the First Amendment. But a statute which in general terms and regardless of the circumstances punishes a person for what he says simply because it is disturbing to others cannot survive scrutiny under the Amendment. Apparently, this is the way the District Court construed the Texas statute forbidding the use of loud and vociferous language calculated to disturb other persons. So construed and given a case or controversy, declaratory relief was unexceptionable.

But the loud and vociferous portion of the statute, which alone was dealt with by the District Court, seems by its very terms aimed at undue noise, not at the content of the verbal utterances; and Mr. Justice Stewart points to Texas cases interpreting its law as proscribing loud speech, wholly apart from what is said. The issue which emerges is whether the Constitution guarantees the right to go into a public place or near private dwellings and deliberately use loud language calculated by its loudness to disturb other persons.

It is this issue which is tendered and which the Court accepts and answers: Speech otherwise protected by the First Amendment "is not necessarily deprived of First Amendment protection solely because it is 'loud and

2   GUNN *v.* COMMITTEE TO END WAR.

vociferous' and because it is 'calculated to disturb the
person or persons present,'" *ante,* at 6; "Neither the
decibels of the human voice nor the 'disturbance' of
listeners at an otherwise appropriate rally in a public
square sets the limits of First Amendment rights," *ante,*
at 6; "The determination of when language is 'loud and
vociferous' and the definition and appraisal of its 'disturbing' effect are much too subjective to provide a
tolerable basis" for regulatory measures permitted by the
First Amendment, *ante,* at 7.

I am not so sure, for I am unaware of a constitutional
right to disturb others by loud noises, whether the noise
is speech or otherwise. The uninvited mouth is as
obnoxious as the uninvited ear. Undue loudness seems
a suitable subject for state police power, and "loud and
vociferous" language "calculated to disturb" others is
an acceptable measure of the proscribed speech. When
one speaks in this manner, he intends his loudness to
disturb. But common experience would indicate that
those who want to listen will not be disturbed at all;
a voice no louder than necessary to reach the speaker's
voluntary audience would not violate the statute even
if others are within range. The Texas law is triggered
only when the level of loudness is designed to bombard
involuntary listeners.

Surely a State may prevent one person or group from
standing in a public street and, with or without mechanical aids, yelling a message to the occupants of adjacent
homes or offices who do not care to listen, prefer to
converse among themselves, have a job to do or would
rather sleep. Neither should the Constitution insulate
those who move to the edge of a meeting in progress and
~~disrupt~~ *disrupt* it by loud language designed to pre-empt the
audience assembled to hear someone else.

Perhaps the Court leaves room for proscribing these
gross intrusions on the rights of other persons. Perhaps

GUNN v. COMMITTEE TO END WAR.   3

its rationale is that, even so, the Texas law possibly reaches other situations protected by the First Amendment and is therefore wholly unenforceable because unconstitutionally overbroad. But I do not so construe the statute and would not strain to invalidate it. Preferably, it should be construed by federal courts with the First Amendment in mind.

Even if the declaratory judgment was proper, however, the Court should have withheld injunctive relief. *Douglas v. City of Jeannette*, 319 U. S. 157, 162 (1943); see *Zwickler v. Koota*, 389 U. S. 241, 254–255 (1967).

For these reasons I respectfully dissent.

The unrestrained language of the Fortas draft would inevitably have been construed broadly by the lower courts had it come down as the *Gunn* opinion of the Court. The result might have been to immunize the level of natural speech (at least that with a political content) from all governmental restraint—even where, in the phrase of Justice White's draft dissent, it involved "loud language designed to pre-empt the audience assembled to hear someone else." Even such "gross intrusions on the rights of other persons" might have been placed beyond the regulatory pale by the Fortas opinion.

But the Fortas draft was never delivered—either as the opinion of the Court or even in dissent. Justice Fortas recirculated the final draft of his *Gunn* opinion on May 6. By then, however, he was enveloped in the controversy that led to his forced resignation on May 14. His *Gunn* opinion of the Court was never delivered. Instead, on June 16, the case was set for reargument the following term. Ultimately, on June 29, 1970, a year after Chief Justice Warren had retired, *Gunn* was decided, with an opinion by Justice Stewart avoiding the constitutional issue along the lines stated by him in Part I of his draft dissent.[43] The question whether the volume of natural speech can be controlled, which the Fortas *Gunn* opinion had answered with a resounding negative, remained unanswered by the Supreme Court.

---

[43]399 U.S. 383.